# MegaSkills® — practical, creative, a lifesaver!

"Dorothy Rich continues to do the impossible.... This new edition of *MegaSkills* is outstanding in every way. The advice in this book when put into practice by teachers and parents will have a profound influence on future generations."

> — **Phillip Harris**
> **Director, Center for Professional**
> **Development and Services,**
> **Phi Delta Kappa**

"As a researcher, I know the value of this program. There is evidence in educational research that a program like this really works."

> — **Herbert J. Walberg**
> **Educational Psychologist and**
> **Research Professor of Education,**
> **University of Illinois at Chicago**

"Dorothy Rich knows what parents want and need, and in this book, she provides it. She puts this knowledge into action by providing programs every parent can use and every child can benefit from. We salute her and *MegaSkills*."

> — **Arnold Fege**
> **Director, Government Relations,**
> **National PTA**

"School principals urge all parents to become partners in their children's education.... *MegaSkills* provides very doable methods for schools and families to help their children succeed."

> — **Samuel G. Sava**
> **Executive Director,**
> **National Association of Elementary**
> **School Principals**

"We taught our three daughters early that hard work won't kill you. Our daughter Cathy, who does the Cathy comic strip, makes people laugh—but she knows, as do her sisters, that our message has been very serious about what it takes to succeed in life. That's what *MegaSkills* is about and that's why we admire the work of Dorothy Rich."

> — **Anne and Bill Guisewite**

"This revised and expanded edition of *MegaSkills* with its new emphasis on readiness is especially important to the national education goals and to literacy so that children will enter school ready to learn and eager to read."

> — **Susan Roman, Ph.D.**
> **Executive Director, Association**
> **for Library Service to Children,**
> **American Library Association**

"Let's salute *MegaSkills*. It's bigger and better and more helpful than ever."

> — **Marguerite Kelly**
> **Author, *The Mother's Almanac***
> ***Series***

# MegaSkills® — a lifeline for today's family

"Dorothy Rich really *gets* it. She understands that parents don't need a lot of psychobabble or theory or 'defensive' what-to-do-when-you-have-this-problem stuff. We've preached for years that parents need an *offense*—what to do to reach certain goals with kids. The goals are MegaSkills, and Dorothy Rich gives us the plans."

> — **Richard and Linda Eyre**
> **Authors of *Teaching Your Children Values* and *Three Steps to the Strong Family***

"The business community understands and respects the central role of parents and other adults in ensuring the maximum development of all our children. The MegaSkills Program has demonstrated its effectiveness, and a number of business leaders have successfully sponsored the program for their employees and their communities."

> — **Milton Goldberg**
> **Executive Vice President, National Alliance of Business**

"*MegaSkills* offers every child the chance to be educationally advantaged. If our country wants students and citizens who can lead us successfully into the next century, we should all listen to Dorothy Rich."

> — **Jane Healy**
> **Author of *Endangered Minds***

"As a psychiatrist, I am deeply concerned about what is happening to children today. Many parents simply don't know how to relate to their kids. In my view, *MegaSkills* and the programs of the Home and School Institute are essential elements in helping parents and children grow together, living and learning."

> — **Foster Cline, M.D.**
> **Author of *Parenting with Love and Logic***

"Our children need thinking skills, they need to know how to solve problems, they need the will and the drive to learn. *MegaSkills* shows parents how to help their children prepare for life in the twenty-first century."

> — **Douglas J. Besharov**
> **Resident Scholar, American Enterprise Institute**

# In School and in Life—
# The Best Gift You Can Give Your Child

## MegaSkills®

- **Confidence:** *feeling able to do it*
- **Motivation:** *wanting to do it*
- **Effort:** *being willing to work hard*
- **Responsibility:** *doing what's right*
- **Initiative:** *moving into action*
- **Perseverance:** *completing what you start*
- **Caring:** *showing concern for others*
- **Teamwork:** *working with others*
- **Common Sense:** *using good judgment*
- **Problem Solving:** *putting what you know and what you can do into action*
- **Focus:** *concentrating with a goal in mind*

*These are MegaSkills*—the values, the abilities, the inner engines of learning that determine success in school and beyond. We know they are important. We now know they can be taught and learned, using the activities in this book. MegaSkills is not about getting an A on tomorrow's test. It's about getting an A for life.

**Also by Dorothy Rich**

**MegaSkills®**
*How Families Can Help Children Succeed in School and Beyond*

**MegaSkills®**
*The Best Gift You Can Give Your Child*

**What Do We Say? What Do We Do?®**
*Vital Solutions for Children's Educational Success*

*Joe DiDio, courtesy of the National Education Association*

# MegaSkills®

## Building Children's Achievement for the Information Age

EXPANDED EDITION

## Dorothy Rich

A Message from Bob Chase

*President, The National Education Association*

A Message from Bill Bradley

*Former Senator and Current Chair, The Advertising Council's Campaign to Improve the Lives of Youth*

HOUGHTON MIFFLIN COMPANY
Boston  New York

*To my parents, who taught me the most important things
I know about MegaSkills*

*To the leaders and parents in the MegaSkills Workshop Program
in almost three thousand schools in forty-eight states who taught
me how MegaSkills works for them*

---

*Library of Congress Cataloging-in-Publication Data*
Rich, Dorothy
   MegaSkills: building children's achievement for the information age / Dorothy
Rich ; a message from Bob Chase, a message from Bill Bradley. — Rev. and
expanded ed.
       p.        cm.
   Includes index.
   ISBN 0-395-87757-1
   1. Children — United States — Life skills guides. 2. Education — Parent participation
— United States. 3. Success — United States.   I. Title.
HQ792.U5R533    1988
649'.1 — dc21                                                    97-44833    CIP

Printed in the United States of America

Book design: Joyce C. Weston

MegaSkills curriculum is a registered trademark of Dorothy Rich

The author gratefully acknowledges permission to reproduce photographs from the
following sources: National Education Association (pages 277, 290; photographs by Joe
DiDio, pages 3, 18, 25, 29, 42, 140, 155, 175, 211, 234, 247, 254, 267, 279; Elvira Crocker,
page 126; Michael Lydick, page 185; Carolyn Salisbury, page 304), National Association
of Elementary School Principals (pages 12, 68, 183, 231), National School Boards
Association (page 55), Association for Supervision and Curriculum Development
(photographs by Debra S. McKay, page 80; Susan M. Vandertie, pages 93, 221; Gary
Kubat, page 103; Reta S. King, page 114; Helen S. Craymer, page 197; Betty Buchignani,
page 299), John C. Lei Studios, Inc. (pages 167, 262), and Olmsted Studios (page 241).

# Contents

MegaSkills: Information-Age Basics ............ *ix*

More Than Ever, Our Children Need
    MegaSkills ............ *x*

A Message from Bob Chase ............ *xiii*

A Message from Bill Bradley ............ *xv*

Introducing This Expanded Edition ............ *xvi*

Opening New Doors ............ *xvii*

## SECTION A

### MegaSkills: The Stuff Achievement Is Made Of

1. MegaSkills and Our Children ............ *3*
2. First Steps: The MegaSkills
   Program and How It Works ............ *12*
3. Knowing What We're Teaching:
   MegaSkills and Academics ............ *18*

## SECTION B

### Teaching MegaSkills at Home: What to Do and How to Do It

(For a chapter-by-chapter listing of the MegaSkills "home learning" activities, with academic objectives and children's ages indicated, see Appendix E, beginning on page 336.)

4. MegaSkills and the Technology
   Connection ............ *25*
5. MegaSkill One: Confidence ............ *29*
6. MegaSkill Two: Motivation ............ *42*
7. MegaSkill Three: Effort ............ *55*
8. MegaSkill Four: Responsibility ............ *68*
9. MegaSkill Five: Initiative ............ *80*
10. MegaSkill Six: Perseverance ............ *93*
11. MegaSkill Seven: Caring ............ *103*
12. MegaSkill Eight: Teamwork ............ *114*
13. MegaSkill Nine: Common Sense ............ *126*
14. MegaSkill Ten: Problem Solving ............ *140*
15. MegaSkill Eleven: Focus ............ *155*

## SECTION C

### Readiness to Learn: Translating "Educational Goals" into Practical Action at Home

16. Getting Ready for School:
    We Have a Little List ............ *167*
17. The Three R's: Before School ............ *175*

## SECTION D

### Strengthening the Three R's at Home

Introduction: MegaSkills and the Three
    R's: The Chicken and the Egg ............ *183*

18. Reading: Moving Along with
    Books ............ *185*
19. Writing: Everyone Can Do It ............ *197*

20. Math: No More Excuses    *211*
21. Transitions: To the Teen Years    *221*

## SECTION E

### The MegaSkills Support Network: People Helping People

Introduction: Beacons in the Fog    *231*
22. Parent to Parent: Looking to Each Other for Help    *234*
23. Grandparents: MegaSkills Across the Generations    *241*
24. Parents and At-Home Child Care: Making Sure Sitters Do More Than Sit    *247*
25. Parents and Teachers: Super-powers, Not Superhuman    *254*
26. Single Parents and the Schools: Making the Connection    *262*
27. Parents and Students: Helping Children Feel More at Home in School    *267*

## SECTION F

### Creativity: The Spark and the Satisfaction

Introduction: A Sense of Balance    *277*
28. The "Right Brain" at Home    *279*
29. Inspiration and Perspiration    *290*

## SECTION G

### MegaSkills: Powerful and Surprising

30. Secrets of MegaSkills    *299*
31. Critical Resources for the Twenty-first Century — School-abilities and Employabilities    *304*

## Appendixes

A: Seeing Children's MegaSkills in Action    *312*
B: MegaSkills Measure: A Quiz for Parents    *314*
C: The MegaSkills Library for Children Plus Resources and More for Adults    *319*
D: The Handwriting on the School Wall    *329*
E. MegaSkills "Recipes," Chapter by Chapter, by Age Range and Academic Objective    *336*

Acknowledgments    *344*
Index    *347*

# MegaSkills: Information-Age Basics

It's been said that finding information in today's information age can be like trying to take a sip of water from a gushing fire hydrant. Actually, it may be more like trying to get a sip from Niagara Falls.

There is so much information and so many ways to acquire it that it can be easier to get inundated than informed. This means that there are many more ways today to get misinformed and confused.

To be able to drink heartily from the information spigot, our children need support structures. They need buckets and hoses to get real water. MegaSkills are now more important than ever to thrive in our information age.

Our children need not only to be able to drink from the information hydrant but also to be able to judge the information they are getting . . . to judge whether it's on target or off base. This requires the ability to organize and to make critical judgments. It means that our children need to know *how* to find what they need to know and *how* to use multiplying resources.

Think of the MegaSkills this requires: confidence to be able to tackle the situation, motivation to want to keep on going . . . all the way through to problem solving.

As technology makes information more accessible, our children need to be able to focus, concentrate, assimilate, integrate, and synthesize as never before. These are higher-order thinking skills: they demand MegaSkills.

Machines are nice but they do not replace the brain and habits of mind and heart that make all else possible. Machines wear out and grow obsolete. MegaSkills don't. MegaSkills enable us and our children to move forward to realize the benefits of this golden age of knowledge.

# More Than Ever, Our Children Need MegaSkills

It makes no difference whether we use pencils or computers, whether the subject is how to learn to read or how to send a rocket into space—our children need MegaSkills.

I am more convinced of this today than when I first began the programs that set the base for MegaSkills over thirty years ago.

We all want the best for our children, and MegaSkills help us teach the values we hold dear.

I feel confident in urging you to read this book because children across the country have been telling me that having their parents involved in MegaSkills learning activities with them at home has made a big difference in their lives.

I originally identified ten MegaSkills (these are superbasics, the inner engines of learning) from school report cards and job performance evaluations: confidence, motivation, effort, responsibility, initiative, perseverance, caring, teamwork, problem solving, and yes, even common sense. MegaSkills are the values, the attitudes, the behaviors, that determine our success in school and on the job. In this edition I have identified a new MegaSkill—Focus: concentrating with a goal in mind. These MegaSkills form what I call the Never-Ending Report Card.

## WHAT WE'VE LEARNED ABOUT MEGASKILLS

It was clear from the strong reception to the first editions that parents across geographic and socioeconomic lines recognize the importance of MegaSkills in their children's lives and that they want specific, practical activities to help their children learn.

There has been a lot of learning about MegaSkills since the very first edition in 1988. What we have learned specifically is how parents and children use MegaSkills activities at home and what they gain from this program.

Wanting to reach as many parents as possible well beyond the bookstore, I set about designing a series of programs to train MegaSkills workshop leaders to conduct programs for parents on how to teach MegaSkills at home. MegaSkills Programs have had phenomenal growth and are now in almost three thousand schools in forty-eight states. The voices and experiences of these parents, teachers, and children speak to us in the margins of this edition. These words from workshop leaders and parents show how ready we are to help one another at a time when help is so greatly needed.

It does take a healthy dose of help and hope to be a good parent today. Disintegrating family life, increasing crime in the community, and low test scores at school give us more than enough to worry about.

Teachers tell us that children aren't paying attention, that they don't seem to be able to buckle down. They say that students have more problems getting organized. And, employers report that new employees don't seem to have what it takes to do well on the job.

## IF ONLY WORRY COULD DO THE JOB

If worry alone could solve these problems, I'd say, "Let's worry our heads off." Instead, we need to take action and we need to know what action to take. Most of us know the basics about parenting (be a good role model, be involved in our child's schooling, and so on), but we long for and need *specifics*. We used to think these came naturally. Maybe they did, but they don't come naturally anymore.

We seem to have heightened sophistication about parenting and schooling but diminished common sense. I used to think that everyone knew about home learning activities—about teaching math at the grocery store or in the kitchen and teaching reading with napkins, dishes, spoons, and forks. I have learned better now, and I've learned this lesson from parents.

## A WORKABLE PARENT PLAN

Thirty years ago, as a teacher and a parent, when I began to receive mixed messages about both my roles, I decided I had to find a way to help parents know what they could do and what they should do to help children learn. I analyzed the research studies; I did my own research; I developed parenting and teacher training programs.

I got to the point where I was talking to myself, and I was saying, "Figure out what every family can do. Come up with a system that works and share it. Don't make it too hard or too long. Make it look so simple, so easy, that everyone can do it. Make it practical. Make it enjoyable. Remember, it doesn't take a lot of time to do a lot of good."

I knew I had to come up with a system that was active yet small enough to handle—a system that got people doing things together, experiencing success together.

I also knew that my system had to remind parents that they didn't need to be perfect to be good, and that went for their children too.

My system had to provide children with alternate routes to success so that what they did at home was different from what they did in school. Home and school are different places. They need to reinforce, not duplicate, one another.

I knew I had to tell parents that there was a new kind of involvement in education today, different from being involved in children's schooling alone, which had usually meant meetings and time spent at the school. That's because fewer and fewer parents, especially employed mothers, could participate that way anymore.

I wanted to tell parents not to feel guilty. What they needed to care about was their involvement in their children's education well beyond the school setting.

I knew I wanted to help parents convey to their children that learning matters, and that they matter. And I had to find ways to help parents and teachers look at what's right instead of what's wrong.

Through all of these years, I have heard the very real concerns of both parents and teachers, while I lived in both worlds. Through it all, I heard my own inner voice, and I determined to share what I had learned with every parent and teacher who would listen. The Institute programs I founded and this book are the result.

The good part of bringing you a program after it's been tested for so many years is that much has been learned along the way. But some readers may say, "Why didn't I do this sooner?" My answer is, "Don't worry about what you did or didn't do before. Start now."

# A Message from Bob Chase

## President, The National Education Association

Books on education and parenting are usually written for teachers or for parents. This very special book, *MegaSkills*, is for all of us.

It's been said, and I have been among the leaders in saying it, that education is a shared responsibility . . . teachers can't do it alone, parents can't do it alone. We need each other.

What makes our times so extraordinary is that there are remarkable opportunities for learning that never existed before. All of our children need to be able to take advantage of these opportunities.

That's what this book is all about. It spells out our responsibilities to each other and to our children—not in vague theoretical terms but in specific, practical ways that we can all use to ensure that our children achieve.

Partnerships in education have never been more important and more critical for our own and our nation's success now and for the future.

Until the middle of this century, schools were a part of a set of intimately connected social and educational institutions—the family, the neighborhood, the church, and community clubs and groups. Raising children held a sense of community responsibility, community pride. The boundaries between the institutions overlapped. A variety of players was involved in the educational team, strengthening the message, keeping the focus firm.

Today the network—the vital web of community social and educational institutions, literally the safety net—is punctured with gaping holes.

A big question that this book and the MegaSkills training programs help to answer is this: what can be done to reweave the educational web, albeit in somewhat different patterns from the earlier designs, to reweave a strong and secure safety net for the larger vision of education that we must have for today and the twenty-first century?

Many of our children, who need to hear a strong message about the importance of education, are being buffeted by forces often beyond the control of the family and beyond the control of the school. All this is happening at the very time when other nations are moving quickly into competition with us. We face tremendous growth in high technology and rising numbers of poorly educated students. Today we must educate students in the basics plus take on the new technology and our competitors at the same time.

One of the major differences in education now is that we have learned more about when and how children learn. When many of us began school, our parents said, "Now you will start learning." And that is what was commonly believed. Today we know that children learn a great deal before they begin school and well beyond school hours.

We now know that education is a life-long process, and we need the skills and abilities to enable us to learn throughout our lives. That's what *MegaSkills* provides.

Schools are no longer the only source of information. Information is everywhere, arriving at the school at the same time that it comes into homes and the community. In fact, today we may get more information than we can handle. A major new role for the school is to help children sort information, think it through, figure out what it means, and use it in a meaningful way.

This is a new, exciting dimension in education. It calls for the kind of school, home, and community partnership that has not existed before. We need training to know how to make it work effectively. Yet one of the first items cut from school budgets is in-service training for teachers. In the regular worksite, employers know the value of training and spend a lot of time and money on it. Being informed and up-to-date is *vital* to good teaching.

There has been a dream, a fond hope, that somehow there is a quick fix in educa-tion. If only we could find it. There is a tendency to retool the system rather than retooling the people. A new emphasis on staff development, so sorely needed, can help to remedy the situation. However, there is no quick fix. The best investment, if we're aiming to help our students be as successful as they can be, is not in the machines but in the people who can make the real difference. Dorothy Rich knows this, and she's been practicing what she preaches for more than thirty years.

National Education Association members have been among the first backers and participants in the MegaSkills training programs. At NEA sites nationally, teachers are using MegaSkills to build sustaining partnerships with families. They are doing this voluntarily and on their own because they know that no matter how good they are as teachers, they need the support and reinforcement of the home.

We are building school communities— places where people know one another and look out for one another. *MegaSkills* has proven to have extraordinary power in helping us come together with shared language and shared commitment.

Today's schools need parents, and today's parents need the school. And children need them both more than ever. In many ways, this is our greatest hope for improving education.

# A Message from Bill Bradley

Former Senator and Current Chair, The Advertising Council's Campaign to Improve the Lives of Youth

It's no secret that education is our nation's number-one priority. More than ever we understand that our children need a strong education, not only for today's fast-paced information age but for what we don't know about in the future.

It's also no secret that it's probably never been more difficult to be a parent and a teacher. At every turn something seems to threaten our children and our sense of well-being—drugs, guns, troubled schools, and yes, troubled families.

We have in our nation, however, a special group of Americans who are working to help children even as times have become more difficult. I call these Uncommon Americans—they are changing the lives of America's children.

Dr. Dorothy Rich has focused her work, over three decades, on the educational role of all families. To extend the impact of her book *MegaSkills*, she created training programs for teaching MegaSkills. She knows that children bring learning potential and abilities from home that help determine success in school and beyond. She has figured out how to help families and teachers build the capabilities of all children to succeed in this rich and rigorous information age.

Today, MegaSkills programs are in almost three thousand schools serving many more thousands of children and parents. This growth provides strong evidence that parents and teachers recognize the program's value and are ready to do what it takes to help children achieve.

In this new edition of her book (I wrote the preface for the original edition in 1988), Dr. Rich has expanded the dimensions of MegaSkills to help children and families learn to manage the new demands of education in a technological age saturated with information.

There is no doubt that the great majority of parents are trying to teach children the values of hard work, responsibility, honesty, and yes, all the MegaSkills. This is made doubly difficult when "anti-learning" messages from outside the home and school compete all too successfully with the message of parents and teachers. This is why I believe in the importance of MegaSkills and the work of Dr. Rich and her colleagues. Throughout the nation, they are working to help parents and teachers put across the vital message about the importance of education with practical information on how every child can become a learner for now and for life.

# Introducing This Expanded New Edition

At the time of the first edition of *MegaSkills*, the word "Internet" was not even mentioned. In the second edition in 1992, a few paragraphs on "The New Machines in Our Lives" addressed parent concerns about Nintendo and computer games.

Clearly, great advances have been made in the world, about and beyond machines, in the last five years. The number of TV channels grows. The concern about education has become stronger. There are ongoing controversies about academic standards and our nation's ability to compete globally. Will our children be able to keep themselves focused and directed, when there is so much information bombarding them? There is growing worry about whether they will have what it takes to learn when there is so much to learn.

This edition reflects these concerns with new and expanded features.

- *Focus, a new MegaSkill,* has been added and explained, and twenty new learning activities are provided.

- *Academic Objectives* have been identified for each MegaSkills activity or learning "recipe."

- *Knowing What We're Teaching* explains how MegaSkills combines academics, multiple intelligences, and character development.

- *MegaSkills and the Technology Connection* presents a brief guide to how MegaSkills connect with technology: what computers would say to us if they could give advice.

- *Schoolabilities and Employabilities* focuses on looking ahead to help us be more aware of what our children will need for the new world of work.

## And in the Appendix ...

- *MegaSkills Report Card* is designed to help chart children's progress in Mega-Skills at home and in school.

- *Research Notes* present updated references on children's learning and parent involvement.

- *MegaSkills Library for Children* has been expanded, providing related children's books and parent/teacher resources for each MegaSkill.

# Opening New Doors

Education never ends. A good education opens doors and raises lots of questions. *MegaSkills* enables us to seek answers and to keep us questioning and wanting to know and to understand more.

This book is essentially about building our children's love of learning, not in the abstract, but in the specific, the real, the practical. This love of learning is what makes it possible for teachers to teach successfully. Without exaggeration, it is also what America's future depends on.

This book helps us put across the essential values of education, the pleasure of hard work, the delight in accomplishment, the joy of working together. How these expand our children's potential for learning in our age of technology and change is a consistent theme throughout this new edition. Truly, *MegaSkills* continues to be the best gift we can give to our children.

*Dorothy Rich*
*Washington, D.C., 1998*

SECTION

A

# MegaSkills: The Stuff Achievement Is Made Of

**M**egaSkills are more than ever "our inner engines of learning." When everything around us changes or looks as if it's changing, our children need MegaSkills. In the midst of change, MegaSkills grow in power. They are the power that drives our learning for today and tomorrow.

*Joe DiDio, courtesy of the National Education Association*

**CHAPTER 1**

# MegaSkills and Our Children

## Raising and Educating Children Today

Being a parent has never been easy, but it wasn't always this hard either. No longer can most of us command, "Do this or do that" and expect our kids to just obey, no questions asked.

The twenty-first century will be time for thinking learners, and that's what our children will have to be. While children may not be listening (as we're told they once did) to their elders, they're listening to advertisers, to peers, and to others who may not have their best interests at heart and who may not be offering the best advice. That's why it's especially important for children to have what it takes to build their self-discipline.

At the same time, as parents, we have to put across the sense of standards and limits that children need for stability, for reassurance, and for the real freedom that comes with self-direction. This is no easy assignment, and that's why MegaSkills are so important.

In the midst of the headlines about the Information Age and the Computer Revolution, it can get very confusing to figure out what is really important in our children's education. How we wish we knew all the answers right now.

It's an exciting time and an anxious one. In many ways, we're caught in the middle—we don't know all the answers and we don't even know all the questions.

There's long been a saying that the only two things we can count on are death and taxes. Today I add a third: **change.** Around us and to us.

Coping with change takes a new and higher level of competence and understanding. We have to deal with the expected and the unexpected. Knowing the level of change we face today, we can only imagine how much more our children will face in the years ahead.

Some experts tell us to get computers and all will be well. I wish I could believe that we can solve our education problems that easily. There's no doubt that computers open up brave new worlds for many students. But they are still machines. While machines can get us to places faster, we still have to know where we are going.

## MegaSkills: The Inner Engines of Learning

In school, test scores tell us that students today are scoring about as well as they did in the 1970s. With increased technology demanding more know-how and increased global competition demanding more effort, what was good enough for the seventies just isn't good enough anymore.

> In the midst of change and uncertainty, MegaSkills are constants: they do not change. They are our passport to the present and the future. They are our North Stars, the true bridge to the next century and to all that we don't know and need to know.

In the workplace, employers are alarmed. Today's graduates, they say, are only marginally prepared for job success. The problem is not just literacy. Students have trouble giving their best to their work and in having disciplined work habits.

At home, parents see children struggling to deal with the growing complexity and often overwhelming choices in their daily lives. Younger and younger children face emotional and dangerous problems such as sex, drugs, and AIDS. They are asked to be grown up when they are still children.

It is generally agreed that children need certain basic skills (usually called the three R's) in order to succeed. But for children to keep learning basic skills at school, they need to learn another important set of basics at home.

"MegaSkills" are our children's inner engines of learning. Though reinforced in the classroom, they get their power from the home.

I know it's fashionable to talk about mega-this and mega-that, and because of

this, in some ways, I hesitate to use the word "MegaSkills." But when I think about what it really takes for children to learn and use the skills they learn, when I think about what it takes to resist the temptations of taking drugs or dropping out of school, I think about attitudes and abilities that are bigger than ordinary skills. I think about confidence and motivation, perseverance and problem solving. And the word "MegaSkill" to define these seems appropriate and right. A MegaSkill, like confidence, is a long-lasting, achievement-enhancing skill. It's what makes possible the use of the other skills that we learn. MegaSkills keep children reading long after they learn to decode the alphabet. A MegaSkill is like gas to make the car go.

This book explains how to help children develop these MegaSkills:

**Confidence:** feeling able to do it
**Motivation:** wanting to do it
**Effort:** being willing to work hard
**Responsibility:** doing what's right
**Initiative:** moving into action
**Perseverance:** completing what you start
**Caring:** showing concern for others
**Teamwork:** working with others
**Common Sense:** using good judgment
**Problem Solving:** putting what you know and what you can do into action
**Focus:** concentrating with a goal in mind

These aren't the only MegaSkills, but they play a strong role in determining success in school and beyond. They don't drop from the sky and land on a lucky few. They

A MegaSkill is a catalyst. It's like yeast making bread rise. It's like a megaphone—designed to send the voice farther than it can ordinarily reach. That's what MegaSkills do for the bits and pieces of learning that children acquire in school and out. MegaSkills make it possible for children not only to learn but to use that learning as part and parcel of everyday life.

> Sometimes MegaSkills, like character- and value-building, are considered "soft" stuff when compared to "hard" stuff like scores on multiple-choice tests. Nonsense! This so-called soft stuff is the bone and muscle of learning, the educational structure that carries us all through our lives.

can be taught at home by parents, even today. They are the values that undergird our work ethic, our national character, and our personal behavior.

Much as I admire academic prowess, and I do, research has shown that adult productivity and happiness are the results of more than academic competency. The happiest and most successful adults are those who possess MegaSkills qualities and, of course, a sense of humor. I can teach MegaSkills, but as to the sense of humor, now that's really hard!

## TOMORROW IS NOT FAR AWAY

We don't know for sure whether our children are learning today what they will need tomorrow, but we do know that children will need the skill and ability to take what they know and put it together in new ways to solve new problems. The academic term for this is "transfer."

To be useful for the 1990s and beyond,

education has got to transfer. Little is really known now about what technical skills will be needed for the twenty-first century. We don't know the specific situations our children will face or even the machines they will use. What we do know is that our children will have to be able to use and adapt what they learn today. They need knowledge-enhancing skills, good any year and any place. They need MegaSkills.

## THE IMPORTANCE OF MEGASKILLS TODAY

There is justifiable concern about American education today and about whether our children are learning enough and working hard enough. The remarkable school success of recently arrived immigrant children has prompted questions about what these children have that American youngsters don't have.

The problem is not that our children don't learn how to read. They do. Educational research has indicated that most of our children do learn the basics of reading and math in the early grades. Many chil-

> What American children must have are abilities that include reading, writing, and math—but that also go beyond them. We know that while it is an essential to be able to read, it is not enough.

dren, however, do not keep on reading and wanting to learn more.

There are books on how parents can help children learn to read and perform better on tests. *MegaSkills* is about how families can help children not only acquire basics but go beyond them and become learners for *life*. No school is an island. The job of the home is to help students use what they have been taught so that the school is surrounded by a community of learning, enthusiasm, and support.

Every parent and teacher wants children who are smart, motivated, responsible, cooperative, good listeners, and contributors with self-confidence, self-discipline, and good judgment. This is no small order.

Coincidentally, these are the very qualities this nation needs in its citizens now and for the next century—learners who can and who want to keep on learning.

### The New Never-Ending Report Card

MegaSkills show up on every school report card and on every job performance evaluation. These are the key sources from which I identified the MegaSkills. We are graded on our MegaSkills all through our lives, and that's why I call this the Never-Ending Report Card.

To illustrate how we are graded on our MegaSkills, the first page of each MegaSkills chapter in Section B illustrates the connection between the in-school and the on-the-job report card. Here are some examples:

What's new about the Never-Ending Report Card is that today it's more never-ending than ever. Chances are, we'll live longer than our parents and our children will live longer than we do. They can expect more frustrations and more opportunities, and they may confront them all at once.

The MegaSkills we help to build within our children must last longer and work under more demanding and unpredictable conditions. MegaSkills, now more than ever, provide the railing to hold on to when the stairway is dark.

## LUCK AND EFFORT

When I talk about MegaSkills, especially with young professionals, I am sometimes greeted with disbelief. They ask, "How can you believe in such old-fashioned ideas as effort, initiative, and perseverance when what really matters is luck, being in the right place at the right time, plus the all-important who you know?"

Of course I believe in luck—in the luck of not being hit by a speeding car, of being born basically healthy, of living in a caring

---

Children aren't born with MegaSkills; they learn them. Parents and educators teach MegaSkills, not all at once and not perfectly, but little by little, day by day.

| In-School Report Card | On-the-Job Report Card |
|---|---|
| Displays self-confidence. Is willing to take risks. | Shows ability and willingness to make decisions. |
| Completes work independently. Understands and applies new concepts. | Demonstrates ability and willingness to solve problems. |
| Is responsive. Demonstrates self-control. | Delegates responsibility or authority as applicable. |
| Concentrates on work. Masters new materials and techniques. | Has integrity. Is results-oriented and employs innovative approaches. |
| Values quality of work. | Has knowledge and technical skills. Completes assignments. |
| Shows courtesy and consideration. Maintains a sense of fair play. | Shows ability to work with people. Maintains positive personal relationships. |

home and in going to a good school. I even occasionally knock wood.

It takes luck, but it takes more. I believe that for most of us to be lucky, we first have to put in the effort, for example, to be in the right place at the right time. In the inimitable words of former baseball great Branch Rickey, the general manager of the Brooklyn Dodgers who brought the first black player, Jackie Robinson, to the major leagues, "Luck is the residue of effort."

I don't define success as having a lot of money or ready-made good luck. These things aren't bad, but most of us won't have them. What we *do* have is the capacity to try. I believe that success is in the trying, in our power to deal constructively with the breaks in life, good and bad, and to keep on going. Success is the ability to make some of our own good breaks and not wait for luck to strike. That's what MegaSkills enable us to do.

## I CARE ABOUT YOU

Most parents are making all-out, caring efforts with children. Anyone picking up this book is a person who cares. But as busy adults, we can forget how much our children need us.

I've heard the excuses, and there aren't any good ones. "I'm just too busy" and "My kid doesn't want to do anything with me anyway" are not acceptable, not now when our children need parents as much as they do.

What does this time together do? It says to a child, "I care about you. I want to spend special time with you. I want to hear what is on your mind and what you are feeling. You are important. You are needed."

When I talk about parent-child time together, I am not talking about trying to use absolutely every minute in the most productive way possible. We'd feel enormous pressure, and it wouldn't work. Children need time to relax and to think and to be on their own, and so do parents.

I am talking about special moments that adults who care for children can help to create. It doesn't take a lot of time to do a lot of good. Activities in this book usually take ten, fifteen, or twenty minutes. They focus on the critical make-or-break elementary school years. This is the time when lifelong learning patterns are set into place. The goal is to help children become learners over the long haul, for a lifetime, not to focus on the short term.

*MegaSkills* is for all adults who care for

> Many children today feel they are not getting the time they need. And it's not because Mother is employed outside the home or because there are more single parents. The cry for time comes both from children of unemployed mothers and from children with two parents in the home.

children—parents, aunts, uncles, grandparents, baby sitters, foster parents. Fathers today are playing an increasingly important role in the care and education of their children. This is good for kids, but it's even better for dads. Every activity in this book works as well for fathers as for mothers.

## OUR CHILDREN'S WORLD: A SCARY PLACE

The world is an increasingly frightening place, with temptations and pitfalls for children that didn't seem to exist before. There are more reasons for us all to be worried.

When I went to school, no one offered me drugs. AIDS was unheard of. The music I listened to had sweet lyrics and melodies compared to today's torrid words and music. The movies (I went to almost all of them) showed waves crashing against the shore instead of explicit sex scenes. There was violence in films, but it seemed as if we knew what was real and what wasn't. I never thought dropping out was even a choice, and while I was told over and over to be "a good girl," my family really didn't have to worry about my getting pregnant because I automatically said *no*. There just wasn't any other answer. There seemed to be a communally shared sense of right and wrong and a greater sense of safety.

As a youngster, I didn't know a lot about adult things. Looking back, I don't think I needed to know everything at once, all so soon.

Looking around now, it seems that children are being told and shown more than they want or need to know. It's as if anything goes, and it makes growing up harder. Parental guidance is more than suggested. It's essential. Today many children, including those with advantages, are full of stress. Some feel suicidal. I hear many reasons, from the threat of crime to the threat of their parents' divorce to fears about getting bad grades. I can't say with absolute certainty that spending time on MegaSkills activities will keep children in school, off drugs, not pregnant, and free of AIDS. But if we believe—and there is evidence to believe—that a sense of self along with increased academic skills will help keep kids out of trouble, then we must understand

> All this isn't meant to be a song of praise for the good old days, which by no means were all that good. It's to emphasize that children now face new and different pressures for which they need to be prepared.

> Children need to be able to believe in themselves and in the people around them. Children need to feel that they matter. That's why these activities, which seem so easy, yet which help children gain a sense of competence and confidence, have results that are surprisingly complex.

that time spent with children developing these is the best possible vaccine that families can use.

## HOPE: A VITAL INGREDIENT

There's a well-known story of two children put in a room that contains a big pile of manure. One child looks at the pile and falls into despair. The other starts searching the room, saying, "With all this manure, there must be a pony somewhere."

The child who hopes for the pony and starts searching for it has a better chance of finding good things all through life.

I believe that in everyday ways we can help children feel more hopeful and optimistic. Children need to be able to expect and to predict. They need a sense of schedule and of routine. That's why activities in this book for family calendars and homework systems are important.

What is in these modest activities that makes them so potent? What it boils down to, I think, is that the experience of doing the activities helps to change parents' ways of seeing themselves as teachers of their children and of seeing their children as learners. They help families work together.

That is the wonder and power of Mega-Skills.

## OUR GOLDEN AGE FOR LEARNING

I really do believe that this is a remarkable and wonderful time to be a parent. No, I am not crazy, and I am not a Pollyanna. This is a golden age of learning, but families have to know how to take advantage of it.

As an elementary grader, I went to a little library in that small Michigan town where I grew up. Most of the information I got for my reports came from ten-year-old encyclopedias. Today on television and through computers is a world of information I never knew. If anyone had told me as a kid that I would fly across the country in a few hours or use a word processor or sleep under an electric blanket, I would have had a hard time believing it.

Yet all this is so accepted today that it makes me wonder—hopeful and a little scared—about what we can't envision about tomorrow. All we can count on

for sure is that we will have to keep on learning.

## EDUCATIONAL CHANGE IN EVERY HOME

Institutional education change, as in the education reform movement, is always long in coming, even when change is wanted as much as it is by parents and teachers today. Experts say school change can take thirty years. That is why we can't wait for changes to happen "out there." Our children aren't waiting.

What is encouraging beyond measure is that there is so much agreement about the value of teaching MegaSkills. We know their importance without having to be persuaded. We know that our children will need MegaSkills no matter what kinds of machines they will be using by the time they're adults.

Educational change can start in every home today. I know this from experience with thousands of teachers and parents across the country. I don't pretend it's easy. There is so much pressure on families and teachers, so much going on outside the home and outside the classroom. But the education this book talks about is doable by everyone.

*Courtesy of the National Association of Elementary School Principals*

# CHAPTER 2

---

# First Steps

The MegaSkills Program
and How It Works

It happens in every home. Children forget, they demand, they are uncaring, they are irresponsible—you love them and you hate them and you wish they would stop just growing and just grow up.

And as a parent who has just lost your temper for the fifteenth time that day, you say, *There has got to be a better way.*

That's what I said to myself almost thirty years ago. I set to the task of trying to figure out not just what to *say* but what to *do*, without hurting my child or myself when for the tenth time that day my darling child said:

> *"I forgot."*
> Or
> *"I can't find them anywhere."*
> Or
> *"I want to watch more TV."*
> Or
> *"I need some money."*

Every parent has at least a dozen more to fill in.

We all want our children to remember, to be responsible, to be concerned. As a teacher I thought, "If I can figure out how to teach the parts of speech, I ought to be able to come up with some ways to help teach these important basics."

I think that's when I started the Mega-Skills program.

Believe me, it didn't start out with headlines. It started in my kitchen when my older daughter, then five and now thirty-eight, said on the phone, calling from school, "I forgot my lunch." And I screamed back, "Well, you are supposed to remember."

I am not absolutely sure that was the exact moment of the inception of the program, but it's close, and I said to myself, "You're such a terrific teacher—OK, teach something really hard, like *personal responsibility.*"

Using what I knew from the classroom, I decided that my method would focus on what is to be taught and then break it into teachable bits—like the directions of a recipe.

That was the beginning of the *home learning recipe.* It is the heart of the program.

## IT STARTS AT HOME

Over this quarter century, I have designed and tested hundreds, actually thousands, of "recipes" to enable parents to help their children learn. The goal then and now is to help parents set the framework for their children's learning, not just for tomorrow's test, but for the whole school year and the next and the next.

---

This program uses everyday things, like doing laundry or paying bills, and places, like supermarkets or gas stations, for teaching. It is easy. It is fun. It takes little time. Everyone can do it. It costs no money. The idea is to enable children to apply outside of school what they learn in school. It does not duplicate what children achieve in school, and it builds positive attitudes toward school and learning.

Even today the home can do a lot of things the school can't. A parent is with children at times and in places available only at home and in the neighborhood—at breakfast, while watching TV, during a bus ride. These are the moments that prepare children for school, reinforce the school, and extend its impact.

## COMMON SENSE IS STILL IN FASHION

The MegaSkills in this book are old-fashioned. They are full of common sense and experience. And they're modern, too, because many parents today have forgotten or never learned what to do at home to pave the way for their children's school success. In recent years, education became

There is a coming together of ideas and understandings that were not around before. Today there is research showing that families are important educators of their children, teaching even when they don't know they are teaching. Today more and more teachers realize that to educate children they have to work with parents. Before, teachers told parents, "Hands off, you don't know how to do it." Today, thanks to this research and to common sense, we know better. No matter how good they are, teachers cannot do the job alone.

the job for the school and usually for the school alone. We now know education has to be a home-school team effort.

Today, in this country, we are thinking and doing more about self-help rather than waiting for big institutions or even government to do the job. We know from nationwide polls that parents are ready to help their children. The signs are good.

This book uses a straightforward formula as the basis for all of the "recipes": Why Do You Do It? What Do You Need? What Do You Do? and More Ideas. The formula provides a habit-forming, continuing way to think about and use everyday moments for teaching and learning.

Children do not have to sit with paper and pencil quietly at desks in order to learn. For a lot of learning, this can be the wrong way to teach. Children, young ones especially, need physical activity and the opportunity to ask questions, to explore, and to experiment without competitive pressures. That's what these activities provide.

## WHAT'S IN A HOME LEARNING RECIPE?

A home learning recipe has to meet certain standards to qualify for the program. I explain these ingredients for two reasons: (1) so that you can see how the "recipes" in this book were prepared, and (2) so that you can create home learning recipes on your own, long after you complete those in this book.

A home learning recipe has to:

▪ **Tie to Schoolwork but Not Be School-work:** Children need ways to succeed at home that are different from school but at the same time help them succeed in school. Parents need ways to help their children learn other than by nagging, "Did you do your homework?"

▪ **Be Serious and Be Fun at the Same Time:** Every "recipe" in this book has a serious academic purpose. Not one says it will teach you how to have fun with your children. You know how to do that. The trick of these "recipes" is that you will be teaching an awesome subject such as responsibility and having fun at the same time.

▪ **Have a Teachable Focus:** When you teach responsibility, for example, you start by teaching one part of it, like "following directions." And you look for a practical, concrete way to teach it. You don't send a very young child upstairs to "clean a room." You send a young child to do one thing: to make the bed or to vacuum the rug or to open the shades. It's even helpful to resist sending an older youngster to *clean up that whole mess at once.* Good teaching is a step-by-step operation.

▪ **Be Easy to Do, Take Little Time, and Cost Little or No Money:** Parents can teach and learn with their children joyously, without worry, without hassle. That won't happen with "recipes" that only a martyr parent could or would do.

A good home learning recipe gives everyone a chance to succeed. There is no one right way to do it. A recipe is a road map, not a set of rigid rules. The activity itself is designed to provide a feeling of accomplishment. It gives parents a chance to step back and children a chance to step forward. The idea is to help both parent and child feel good and get to know each other better in the bargain.

You won't find activities in this book on how to weave baskets or design chessboards with children. I was never able to rush out for Popsicle sticks or other special arts and crafts items after a day at work. I needed activities that could be done alongside my household routines, using whatever I had at home. Today's busy parents need these easy-to-do "recipes" more than ever.

Not every parent is a born teacher. I try to provide a "handle" or a strategy for teaching so that you can jump right in with "recipes" that, for example, help children organize their belongings or know what to do when the TV is turned off. I want you to use these ideas to take off on your own, using your and your child's creativity to come up with additional "recipes."

## DIFFERENT "RECIPES" FOR DIFFERENT AGES

It makes sense that what works for pre-schoolers won't work for fifth graders. Parents have to be ready to change gears as children grow. The "recipes" in each chapter give activities for children of different ages.

You'll notice that the activities aim at increasingly more grown-up interests and understandings.

Around ages four through six, many of the "recipes" have to do with getting ready for school and using primary school subjects like counting, sorting, and early reading at home.

Around ages seven through nine, many of the "recipes" focus on helping children get organized, build study skills, and develop solid work habits.

Around ages ten through twelve, "recipes" work toward helping children understand themselves, their friends, and their family. Activities aim at developing greater self-reliance, building career awareness, and establishing healthy habits and self-esteem that can help prevent destructive habits, such as drug abuse.

These are not hard and fast age and grade distinctions. Many four-year-olds will enjoy a "seven-year-old" activity, and vice versa. Use all and any of the activities that appeal to you and your child. I indicate ages only to provide some guidance for selecting activities. I hope that all of the activities in whole or in part will be useful to everyone.

Providing activities that span the age ranges is a challenge. Some activities for the ages-four-to-six group may call for some reading skills that are more appropriate for six-year-olds than for four-year-olds. For children who do not yet read, I recommend that parents read all directions aloud, that children dictate their ideas for parents to write, and that symbols be used alongside words as needed. In labeling a dresser drawer, draw a sock next to the word "socks." In marking off danger points at home, use a sign next to the word "danger." In making lists of what to do in the morning, draw pictures to show toothbrushing and so forth. Don't worry if your children are not reading early, but provide the clues that will gradually ease them into reading.

The "recipes" are designed to be used at any time, summer and vacation days as well as school days. What parents do with children over the summer can make a great deal of difference in their school success.

## THE MAKING OF A LEARNER

One "recipe" will not result in overnight, cataclysmically positive change. If it does, I want you to be sure to get in touch with me immediately.

In our school-to-home programs, we use a series of ten "recipes" over a period of ten weeks, one a week. This is designed to get parents and youngsters tuned in to the idea of using "recipes."

If you ask my advice, I'd suggest reading through this entire book and its collection of "recipes" first, starring or checking the ones that appeal to you. Then ask your child to help you select the ones you both like.

Work out your own schedule—but guard against overkill. Once a week is really fine. You can build a whole year of activities as you go along. Remember that abilities in academics are not so different from abilities in sports. Just as in sports, it takes practice to gain confidence, to acquire motivation, and to achieve.

## STAYING WITH THE PROGRAM

Sometimes a book like this will get you and the children going. But it can be tough to keep on going after the novelty and first

You might ask, "How am I going to know when my kids are learning?"

My answer: You will. You will hear your children say, "Let me try it." You will almost hear a click that says, "Now I understand." You will hear, "Let me show you! Let me! Let me!" And you had better get out of the way, and let them.

flush of enthusiasm wear off. Like a good diet, one of the secrets of this program is that it has to become a habit. In a diet you eat good foods most of the time, not just once a month. That's true with these MegaSkill-building activities. Use them on a regular basis. If you've used one part of an activity, go back to it to find the extra idea you haven't tried. Think of ways you can build on what you have done. Improvise, be creative; you can't do anything wrong.

## CHAPTER 3

# Knowing What We're Teaching

## MegaSkills and Academics

MegaSkills activities are so enjoyable that I am often asked, "What do these have to do with school? These are fun. Are they really connected with academics and with school?"

The answer, which I am always delighted to provide, is *yes*. All of the MegaSkills activities are school-related. These questions, however, told me that the MegaSkills academic connection needed to be made clearer. So, for the first time in this edition, specific academic objectives for each activity are noted next to the activity. They provide a framework that recognizes the importance of these informal activities and what they truly teach.

The MegaSkills activities are designed to support academics. They also meet the needs of children who learn in different ways. There are MegaSkills activities for the interpersonal and intrapersonal learners; the logical/mathematical/problem-solving learners; the linguistic learners, who use language creatively; the spatial learners, organizing space and manipulating objects; and kinesthetic and musical learners, using movement and body control. The goal is to enable every child to find success through a variety of MegaSkills activities.

## Teaching a Lot . . .

When we teach MegaSkills, we are teaching a lot at once. We are teaching academics. We are teaching the work ethic. We are helping to develop our children's character. And we are doing all this through a variety of enjoyable activities that motivate children to learn. Can all this be done all at once? Evidence from MegaSkills programs around the nation suggests very strongly that it can and that it is.

For example, take the early grades activity, The Importance of Me in Chapter 5, Mega-Skill One: Confidence. It calls for children to create a "me" poster, and it may seem like just more cutting and pasting. In reality, this activity develops many abilities, including:

- building literacy by having to communicate clearly, compare information, think abstractly, and use new vocabulary
- describing personal interests, abilities, and strengths
- identifying supporting details and facts, making connections between symbols and words
- relating physical materials, pictures, and symbols

This activity may look like play. And it may even feel like play, but it is a powerful teaching activity.

> "MegaSkills is filled to the brim with hundreds of practical ideas for parents that can help kids become real winners in life. I'm especially struck with how useful it can be in working with children who've experienced learning or behavior problems at home and school. With these sure-fire recipes, these difficult kids can be helped to overcome their limitations and realize their true inner gifts."
>
> —Thomas Armstrong, Ph.D.,
> Author of *In Their Own Way* and *Awakening Your Child's Natural Genius*

Some MegaSkills activities have obvious school connections. For example, Practice Makes Almost Perfect, in Chapter 10, Mega-Skill Six: Perseverance, is designed to help students:

- develop an awareness of the benefits of learning something new and the relationship between work and learning
- build a greater awareness of personal responsibility, effort, and good work habits

For older children, see the activity *Today in the News* from Chapter 21, Transitions: To the Teen Years. This may look like exchanging headlines. Actually, it teaches a lot including:

- using persuasive language to express opinions
- increasing reading comprehension by drawing inferences, developing discussion skills, retelling the story, and identifying settings and main ideas
- evaluating author's purpose, point of view, and changing perspectives
- identifying visual media strategies, text, and narrative

## Academics in MegaSkills

In identifying an academic objective for each MegaSkill activity, I have used generally accepted report card categories. Primarily these are subject matter areas: Reading, Writing, Mathematics, Social Studies, Science, Communication, and Study Skills. I include Thinking as a category. Even though thinking is still not listed on many report cards, we know now that it can be and should be taught. I have also identified competencies taught by the MegaSkill activity, such as Reading Comprehension, Vocabulary Building, Organization, and Information Building.

Many lists of academic objectives are so detailed that it's possible to get lost in them and forget the subject being taught. For example, in Reading there's traditionally an objective called "identifying blends and digraphs." The idea behind this probably once seemed very reasonable: the more we break up the big subject, the easier it will be to teach and to learn.

However, it can work the other way and it often does. Long lists of objectives get very discouraging for teachers as well as parents and students. Like Humpty Dumpty, sometimes the itty, bitty pieces break apart and don't get put back together again.

I have tried to be detailed but not overly so. Think of my labeling of the MegaSkills academics as stepping stones rather than set in stone. Use them as clues to the important concepts and skills being taught by the learning "recipes."

## The Language of Academics

The way academic objectives are worded depends on which school district's report card you're looking at. The very same academic areas in one report card can be labeled "communication skills." In another district, it might be called "language arts" or simply "reading and writing."

It would be easier if we all spoke the same language. But it really doesn't matter as long as we all reach the same goal—a well-educated student who has had the opportunity to master these skills. However, it can be confusing, particularly these days, when there is a greater focus on goals, on standards, and on identifying and achieving academic objectives.

In our nation, unlike other industrialized countries, there is no national curriculum. In the same district, schools may offer different kinds of instruction in the same grades. This is more than confusing—it is a major concern. Today we live in a smaller world and a highly mobile one. Children who go to school in California may live their adult lives in New York. And they may be competing for jobs with students from other nations across the globe.

While a growing number of school districts work to adhere to high standards for students by providing a solid curriculum, teacher training, and parental involvement, some districts may not be doing so. That's why, whatever schools our children attend, it is increasingly up to all of us, inside and outside the school walls, to ask questions and to try to learn as much as possible about what our children are learning and need to learn.

It's not important that we know all the technical language in order to use the MegaSkills Program. What is important is that we realize how important these easy and enjoyable activities are for children's success. The work of the home in insuring children's success deserves enormous

respect. Identifying the academic objectives of these activities is one more way to help build the respect that parents, working with their children in this program, deserve.

MegaSkills are the keys to achieving great education goals. They are the vital habits for learning, regardless of the city or state we live in. While we may not agree on exactly the same language to identify the academic objectives, there is a growing agreement throughout our nation of the importance of education. We must make sure that students, no matter where they go to school, will be ready to pursue advanced education, perform well on jobs, and have the basic abilities to do well now and in the twenty-first century with its growing technology, complexity, and change.

---

## FIND MORE ANSWERS IN THIS BOOK

- For specific teaching tips on introducing the activities to children, see Chapter 29, Inspiration and Perspiration. The section entitled The Art of Teaching provides tested, practical tips.

- For ideas on expanding the activities for further discussion with children, use the page entitled "Teaching Tips . . ." at the end of each MegaSkill chapter (Chapters Five through Fifteen).

# Teaching MegaSkills at Home: What to Do and How to Do It

**E**very child is entitled to know what it takes to succeed. This is virtually a birthright, and yet, many children today do not understand what it takes to achieve—what it means to be responsible and persevering, to use common sense.

We assume they know. We assume that we are all talking the same language. But a growing number of our children are not acquiring these vital basics. The good news is that these basics, these MegaSkills, can be taught!

## CHAPTER 4

# MegaSkills and the Technology Connection

## MEGASKILLS AND THE TECHNOLOGY CONNECTION

Machines may get us there faster, but we still have to know where we are going.

There are books and magazines galore to provide advice on what computer to buy and which new Web sites to explore. Their numbers grow daily, and the content changes just as quickly. It's coming at us fast and heavy, and while it's truly exciting and in many ways miraculous, there is a danger in getting lost in it all.

Usually, when people talk or write about the information explosion, the message is very upbeat—it's great, it will change our lives for the better. We're urged to get with the program and not to be old-fashioned.

But wait a minute. Is it all so wonderful? The possibilities for excellence are remarkable, but so is the potential for trash. What about the down side—the misleading and false information, the silly games and time-wasters, the information that isn't really information—just a new way to advertise.

How can we protect ourselves and our children? How can we get the best and not the worst from this new information medium?

I will admit that I know as much about how a computer works as I know about how a car works. I just want it to work. But I *am* very interested in what the computer can offer. I am open to it, I accept it, and I want to learn. Sometimes, though, I come to my machine and feel overwhelmed even before I start. There is so much to wade through. What new torrents of information will I have to deal with today? If I feel this way, others must also.

In a period of discouragement, as I was ready to turn off the machine, I suddenly sensed that my computer was trying to tell me something. It was as if the computer was tapping me on the shoulder and giving me advice: "Use me well. Be careful. Don't be afraid, but don't be a fool either. When it comes to getting the best out of me, remember your MegaSkills."

It makes sense that MegaSkills are especially important when we feel overwhelmed by what's going on around us. MegaSkills provide reassurance and strength in a time of change.

### Confidence

If a computer could really talk and tell us about MegaSkills, this is what I feel sure it would say: "Remember I am a machine. I don't run you: you run me. Don't let me intimidate you. Use what you know about me to learn more. Help others know how to use me."

When you use or buy software for your children, look for the kind that gives kids thoughtful, idea-generating activities, not that one-dimensional click-on "open the door and find the bird" stuff. The software you choose should help your children develop confidence and use the computer on a number of levels.

### Motivation

Think of the word "find." It's right up there on the computer screen and it gives us a big clue to how to use the computer.

Find a goal. Try not to just "surf" aimlessly—it can be a big waster of time. To add direction and motivation to working with the Internet, identify one new area or subject to learn about each day.

Be sure to remind children that ads are still ads, whether they appear on the Internet, on TV, or in magazines. Children need to be just as wary of advertising on the Net as in any other medium.

## Responsibility

Take responsibility for the information you are receiving. Think about what to look at, what to ignore, and what to find out more about. Just because information is on the computer doesn't mean it's accurate or even worth knowing.

Encourage children to use other sources. Check computer-provided information against information from newspapers, magazines, and yes, even books from the library. Remind children to use their best critical judgment.

## Effort

Kids should go well beyond encyclopedia point-and-click when doing homework and other assignments. Information from the computer is a starting point.

Remind children to connect the computer's information to real-life, everyday experiences. Urge them to leave the keyboard to talk with people about what they learn, about questions they have. This is the *real* meaning of "interactive."

## Initiative

Watch out for keyboard addiction. That means spending too much time in front of the screen. It's one step above sitting in front of the television—it's passive and it can take up too much "active" time.

You can add initiative by helping children set up a home page. Keep it up-to-date and link it with others. It's the modern version of a family newsletter . . . the holiday letter that gets sent all year long. Not too many strangers will be interested, but grandparents can be counted on to read it.

## Perseverance

Computers are great teachers of perseverance. They offer untold amounts of frustration that we have to bear with and overcome. One wrong move and the computer is down, and we struggle and persevere to bring it back to life. And just waiting to get on the Web or to print a page or two can be a lesson in perseverance by itself.

Give children a chance to experience these frustrations with you. Don't spare them. Let your children give you the support and solace you need as you struggle to get back on-line.

## Caring

Take care about what you click on to and whom you are talking to on-line. The computer world is not so different from taking walks in all parts of town. There are safe sections and less safe areas. Just as we warn our children about crime in the streets, we have to warn them (but not totally scare them) about bad stuff on the Net.

Work with children to find the safe Web pages and discussion groups. Many youngsters are having terrific, caring experiences with pen pals their own age in different parts of the world.

## Teamwork

Sit with your child in front of the computer just as you are encouraged to sit with your child in front of the television. Find time together for exploring on the Internet. Talk about what you see and share your opinions, observations, and judgments about it.

A computer with its keyboard seems to beckon friends and family to join in.

## Common Sense

Too much of a good thing is still too much. Just as you have a TV-watching schedule, set up a computer schedule.

Use an alarm clock or timer, especially for computer use. When more than one child is trying to use the computer, a timer can help reduce tensions. If the computer linked to the Internet uses the family phone line, another source of conflict arises. Use your common sense to figure out a fair amount of computer time for everyone.

## Problem Solving

Computers are not problem solvers. They don't replace our brains. But they can provide information to help our own problem-solving process.

Use the discussion groups on the parent education Web sites growing apace on the Internet. Many groups offer the advice of well-known national experts, answering individual questions. We learn how other families deal with problems similar to our own. We reduce our sense of isolation.

Sometimes we can get to thinking that we are the only ones with problems. Through the Web, we talk together and form new ideas. We learn about new opportunities and new ways of solving problems that had seemed unsolvable. It's a new community of neighbors and friends.

## Focus

There is so much to be found on the Web; it can seem like a very strange land. When we know what we're looking for, it is a wondrous land. When we don't, we may retreat. There is help. Every day new guides and maps to the Net are appearing in newspapers and magazines. Start a notebook of favorite Web sites: you will create your own map to this new land and you will stay on track, focused and able to meet your goals.

## Virtual Reality is Not Real Reality

Let's not fool ourselves. Reality on the computer is like a copy of a famous piece of art. We're not seeing the real art with our own eyes. It's like seeing a video of the family instead of meeting the family, or looking at pictures of Yosemite or Niagara Falls instead of actually going there. It's better than nothing, but it's still not the real thing.

While we work and wait for the real thing, we can take advantage of virtual reality if we are lucky enough to have a computer and access to the Internet. But, real is better. And that's why MegaSkills activities are so important. Use the pages that follow to experience the real thing . . . MegaSkills activities *are* the real thing.

*Joe DiDio, courtesy of the National Education Association*

## CHAPTER 5

# MegaSkill One: Confidence

## Feeling Able to Do It

## THE NEVER-ENDING REPORT CARD

**The Grades We Get in School**

Gordon enjoys tackling new projects and making new friends.

He shows disciplined work habits.

**The Grades We Get on the Job**

Mr. Smith does not shy away from hard jobs.

He meets challenges head-on and has excellent interpersonal skills.

We know what we're hearing when children say:

*"I just can't do that."*
*"The other kids are better than I am."*
*"I'm scared."*
*"I won't try it."*

We're hearing a child's cry for more confidence. It cuts to the heart. Somehow when our children don't feel confident, it does something to our own confidence as well.

"I remember the potholder I made in third grade, made out of loops that were yellow, red, gold, and orange. It was a present I made to give to my mother, and oh, was she proud. And did it make me feel good!"

These are the words of a man in his late fifties. He has a doctorate and many scientific achievements on his résumé. But when asked about his sense of confidence, he talks about the potholder.

Self-esteem is talked about a lot these days. It is important, but it's a hollow concept until and unless it is based on experience. Self-esteem is not a separate "course": it's mixed and mushed into daily life, a result of ongoing, achievement-building activity.

This chapter involves children in positive experiences right around the home. They don't cost money or take a lot of time. But they increase children's sense of control, build children's courage, build their sense of family, and reduce their fears of the new and unexpected. They work to give children an "I Can Handle That" attitude.

Our goal is to help children develop a sense of self-respect and respect for others, which is the base of real confidence. It's this foundation they add to all through life.

## SMALL THINGS MAKE A BIG DIFFERENCE

I still remember the day I carried my chicken home. I carried Rocky, the rooster, in a crate bigger than I was. It was the last day of first grade. All through the spring our class had raised chicks, watching them hatch from eggs until they were almost full grown.

Then it was time for summer vacation. Who would care for the chickens? Everyone in class wanted them, especially the one named Jewel.

Our teacher, Mrs. Lutz, decided that the only fair way to distribute the chickens was to have a drawing. And the only children who could participate were those who brought notes from home saying that if we won, we would care for the chicken.

Clutching my note (my brother, who was in fifth grade, wrote it, and my mother signed it), I waited throughout the day for the fateful drawing. About fifteen of us lined up to draw slips for four chickens. At last the appointed hour, 3:15, came.

I watched, eagle-eyed, as Mrs. Lutz marked an *X* and the name of a chicken on four slips and only an *X* on the other slips.

Then she started down the row of children. At that moment I realized I was standing in the wrong place. Sally and Sara Quick, the blond twins, stood before me in line, and they plucked the slip with Jewel's name on it. It was disappointing. They were so happy. But I knew even then that if I were to get any chicken at all, I had to pull myself together.

I was next. Now usually I close my eyes during crisis moments. But this time, as I have at times since then, I kept my eyes wide open, and I concentrated, and then I

picked, sliding my hand carefully along the top of the book until I came to a precious slip of paper.

And lo, there it was, "Rocky." Oh, I was proud and happy; yes, disappointed that Jewel was not to be mine, but happy that I was a winner nevertheless.

The end of the school day came, and there I was with my chicken crate and a feeling of success. I struggled with that big box over the six blocks to my home. My brother came by a couple of times to try to help me with it, but I refused. This was my chicken, my achievement, and I would bring him home alone.

For the rest of my elementary school years, my brother and I raised Rocky and a group of chicks from the hatchery. We lived in a small town, and no zoning official came by to tell us not to do this.

I have never forgotten Rocky and the day I carried him home alone. It is a memory of struggle and success that gives me confidence and motivation to this very day. When I have to do something hard and when I get scared, I think back to Rocky and that crate, and even though it has nothing to do with the current situation, I breathe deeper and think to myself, "I can do it."

That's what every child needs . . . experiences that give the message, "I can do it." We all need some version of Rocky in our lives.

## Confidence Practice

Coming up with confidence-building experiences for children can be a challenge. These experiences need to be small enough

Confidence ebbs and flows like a river. It does not run at high tide all the time. There are some days when you know you can manage whatever comes, and there are others when getting out of bed can seem a momentous step. So too with children.

On those more difficult days, it's helpful to be able to think back to a time when something good happened and you managed well and overcame some odds. It provides the strength to keep going on days when confidence is running low.

for children to deal with, large enough to encourage growth, and easy enough for parents to work with.

When children are young, it does not take a momentous act to help them gain confidence. Small actions can have great impact. You can start at home with household objects, such as a telephone or a television.

The telephone, found in almost every home, is ideal for giving children what I call confidence practice. Young children use it to call Grandma or a friend, reaching out socially to get early practice in the art of conversation. Older youngsters use it to keep talking but also to give and get specific information.

Here are three activities, all using the phone, suited for children's needs and abilities at different times in their growing-up years.

## Telephone Time ■ ages 4–6

- **Reading**
- **Practicing Sequence**
- **Following Directions**

For this early reading activity, you need a telephone, seven small squares of paper, crayon, or pencil.

Tell or show your child your home telephone number. Say each separate number aloud as you point to it.

On separate pieces of paper, write down each number. Now show your child how to put the pieces in the same order (left to right) as your phone number. Let your child read this telephone number aloud from the assembled pieces of paper. Provide help as needed.

As a game, mix up the pieces of paper and let your child put your telephone number together. At first let your child match the papers to the number listed on the phone. Then try this without looking at the phone. Now ask your child to write down the phone number, left to right, on a larger piece of paper. You might want to post this for all to see and admire.

When you are both out together, let your child dial home. Do this when someone is at home to give your child the satisfaction of making contact.

## Calling for Help ■ ages 6–9

- **Writing**
- **Organizing Information**

This activity helps your child learn to use the telephone to report emergencies. This is especially important when children are home alone. You need a telephone book, telephone, markers, and paper.

Ask your child to find in the telephone book the numbers for *Fire/Rescue* and *Police,* usually listed at the front of the telephone book.

If you don't already have one, make a list of important telephone numbers to call in an emergency, similar to the one that follows. With your child, fill this in and put it near the phone.

Emergency: Dial 911 or 0
Fire _____
Police _____
Friend or Neighbor _____
Dad's Work _____
Mom's Work _____

Take turns explaining what to say on the phone when you report emergencies. *Examples:* Someone at home is hurt; you smell smoke or see fire. When you use the phone in this practice, be sure to keep the contact button pushed down.

(See Chapter 14, "Problem Solving," for a full range of safety activities.)

### From Michigan . . .

Parents report their own creativity. To help young children remember numbers, they use rhymes. Here's one: "Dial 555-0309. You'll reach Grandma all the time." You can make up your own phone number rhymes.

## Information Hunt ■ ages 10–12

- *Study Skills*
- *Asking Questions*
- *Conducting Research*

Telephones can give children practice in getting needed information, like when a movie is going to start or how late the library is open. For this activity you need a telephone, telephone book, and newspaper.

Let's say your family is ready to make a major purchase, such as a washing machine. Ask your youngster to check at least two newspaper ads and then make a few calls to get additional information from salespeople. *Examples:* What's the guarantee? When will the washer be delivered? Have your youngsters call at least two stores and compare answers to these questions.

Or perhaps your family is planning an outing: You need directions before you start out. Let children pick a place around town to visit and find out, by calling the bus lines, etc., how to get there, how long it will take, and how much it will cost. Picking up the phone to ask these questions may not be an act of bravery, but it does take a measure of courage, and it helps to build confidence.

We're surrounded by confidence-building "tools." A bicycle is one example. For younger children, it's a matter of learning how to stay on it without falling off. For older ones, it's a means of transportation to school or to pick up a carton of milk at the grocery store. Beyond that, it could be an entry into a bicycle race.

## TACKLING TV

Think about the TV set. First a child learns to turn it on. The next step is to figure out what shows to see. Beyond that comes a test of children's confidence when they turn the set off on their own.

A good idea that comes up in most households is that kids really ought to watch less television. Today's children are viewers supreme, tuned into TV on a daily basis for learning and entertainment.

There is an art to using television well, to helping children get the most from it, without the extremes of youngsters who sit before the set six hours a day and parents who forbid any TV for fear that their children will become addicted.

"No TV at all" homes are rare, but where they do exist, it's often because deep down the parents cannot trust themselves with a TV set, afraid that once it goes on they won't be able to turn it off. It's unfair both to turn TV loose on children and to deprive them of it altogether.

Cutting down on TV watching is one of the toughest good ideas to translate into action. Here are TV activities that help chil-

dren show growing confidence—mastering and manipulating their environment.

## Our TV Diet ■ ages 4–8

- ■ *Reading*
- ■ *Analyzing Data*
- ■ *Developing Discussion Skills*

This activity gets the whole family involved in making choices about TV watching. You need thinking minds, a television schedule, and a marker.

As a family, decide how many hours you will each watch TV. Read the TV schedule aloud with your children. Ask what programs everyone wants to watch. Share your opinions about the shows you like. Circle the shows you pick. Children need to hear your judgments. This helps them build their own critical viewing skills.

Together go on a TV diet. If your children are watching four hours a day now, cut back to three hours a day the first week, two hours a day the second week, and so on.

Set young children to thinking about scheduling their own TV-watching time. Every family works out its own plan.

Here's an example of how one family does it. Parents set the maximum daily watching time: one to two hours a day. (Educational specials, which the parents encourage children to watch, may be exempt.) Children choose any shows—equaling that time period—up to eight P.M.

If this diet doesn't work all the way, at least it does part of the job. It raises the

---

**From Illinois . . .**

"Our kids watch the news on TV before we get home. At dinner, they tell us what's going on. They're now more interested in national events. They no longer see TV just as entertainment."

awareness of how much time the family is spending in front of the set. Just learning that number, which is usually higher than we think, is enough to change some TV-watching habits.

## Taking Charge of TV Watching
■ any age

- *Writing*
- *Remembering Details*

This activity actually has youngsters keeping track of the family's TV watching. You'll need a TV set, TV schedule, pencil, paper, and ruler.

Start out by reading the TV schedule together. Pick the programs to watch, alone or together. Then make an easy chart like the one below. Make several copies.

### TV Plan

| Date | Time | Program Name | Who Watched? |
|------|------|--------------|--------------|
|      |      |              |              |
|      |      |              |              |
|      |      |              |              |

Everyone fills in TV-watching choices, date, and time. Let children who can't yet write dictate their choices.

Post this plan in a special place near the TV set. Nearby keep a pencil attached to a string. After you watch the show, fill in **Who Watched?** In this way, keeping track of what is picked and what is watched is easy.

With your child, decide on a reward for keeping to the TV Plan for at least three days. It might be going on a family picnic or attending a baseball game.

## Keeping TV Watching Under Control ■ any age

- *Writing*
- *Discussing Ideas*
- *Creating a Plan*

This activity helps families continue their efforts to manage TV watching. You need a TV schedule and markers.

Talk about different family members' interests and hobbies: Skating? Stamps? Cooking? At the beginning of the week, check the TV schedule for any programs that might be related to these. Together circle the programs the family decides to watch. Children circle their programs with one color marker. Adults circle programs with another color.

If someone becomes interested in a new subject after watching a television program, try to find more information on that topic. *Example:* If the program is about computers, check newspapers or magazines for articles on computers.

Television need not be an ogre to be afraid of or to avoid. Activities like these

**From Florida . . .**

"These activities gave me the confidence to turn off the TV and to know there were other activities I could do with my kids."

use TV as the resource it really is. (Some of the activities in Chapter 21 address TV violence and how to help children deal with it.)

## FROM THINGS TO PEOPLE

In the journey of growing up, children must learn to manage objects and work with people. Confidence comes from both. In the activities that follow, children find out more about their families and themselves, and they get a chance to learn to like each other more.

You'd never guess it from Norman Rockwell paintings of families gathered around holiday tables, but many children pass through a period in their lives when they are somehow ashamed of their family. Some don't get over it. Much of this embarrassment about family may be a normal growing-up rite of passage, when Mother doesn't dress right or Dad never says the right thing. When children want to be just like everyone else, their parents may be different, with "funny accents" or very little money. This "shame" causes a lot of pain for both parents and children. There may be no way to overcome it completely, but I believe that if children knew more about their parents, especially about their early lives, it would help.

My parents have been dead for thirty years. They look out at me from pictures on my wall, but I do not know very much about their lives before I came of age. They came from Europe to make a new life in a new land. I remember a few words of their

---

> **From Pennsylvania . . .**
>
> "These activities helped me understand how important my life, thoughts, and opinions reflect on my child's life, thoughts, opinions. It changed the kind of messages I send my child."

language, but I know nothing of their early lives.

I regret that we did not talk about their past. I didn't realize how important it was to talk together about this, and neither did they. With my own children, I'm trying not to make the same mistake.

## I'M OK, AND SO IS MY FAMILY

Children love knowing more about themselves. Parents like this activity because it not only helps children think seriously about themselves but provides lots of laughs, too. It helps families remember the funny times that sometimes seem funny only in retrospect— the time the big fish got away, along with the fishing rod, or the time friends were invited for a birthday party on the wrong day.

### The Importance of Me ■ ages 4–9

- *Reading*
- *Matching Words and Pictures*
- *Using Picture Clues*

This activity helps children build pride in themselves and their interests. The task is to make a "me" poster. You need markers, poster cardboard or large paper, scissors, paste, old magazines for pictures, and snapshots, if possible.

Together look through magazines. Find pictures of what your child likes—pets, foods, clothes. Cut them out and with paste arrange them on a large sheet of paper. Magazine pictures are fine. If you have extra snapshots, use them.

And be sure to put some words on the poster. Kids might write: "Look at me at four years old!" "See the picture of my brother!" Adults might add: "This is a pretty dress." "Look at the fish we caught."

You might want to take turns and make poster life stories of other family members. Draw pictures of other members of the family and display these about the house.

Hang the poster in a special place for all to see and enjoy. An activity like this one says to your child, "You are special, and your family knows it."

## Family Mobile ▪ ages 4–9

- ▪ *Reading*
- ▪ *Using Visual Clues for Building Understanding of Relationships*

This gives children a greater sense of the family along with pleasure in creating an art object for the home. You need a clothes hanger, some snapshots or drawings of the family members, construction paper, paste, scissors, and some yarn.

Mount the pictures of the family on separate pieces of construction paper. Cut a small hole in the top of each paper and thread a piece of yarn through the hole. Tie these to the hanger in different places.

Lo and behold, you have a family scene that you can enjoy and talk about.

## Now and Then ▪ ages 10–12

- ▪ *Writing*
- ▪ *Listening and Speaking*
- ▪ *Organizing Information*

This activity helps to get generations talking together, especially about those early years. Everyone was a child once. Here's a way to share some of those memories.

In this activity, the child and a parent or grandparent make a Time Line. It's a way to recapture memories of people at certain times in their lives.

You need a roll of shelf paper or large brown wrapping paper, pencils and crayons, and a ruler.

Decide together with your child when to begin the Time Line. This may be at birth or when school started or some other special time. Decide how much space will be allowed for each year. One inch per year or one foot per year? Draw a line for each one of you.

Now try to remember. What was special about age five? Was that the year you began kindergarten? What about your parents? Was there a kindergarten where they grew up? Did you each have a pet? What kind? Fill in the years as each of you has experi-

| Child | 5 years<br>I began<br>kindergarten | 6 years<br>I got my dog | 7 years<br>I went to<br>the circus | 8 years<br>I joined the<br>Scouts |
|---|---|---|---|---|
| Parent | 5 years<br>? | 6 years<br>I started<br>school | 7 years<br>? | 8 years<br>I got my<br>rabbit |

enced them. If you don't remember everything, fill in what you can.

*Example:* This is a very simple version, but it gives you an idea of what a Time Line can look like.

Talk about the memories. Compare similar experiences. Talk about differences. For example, at no time in my life have I experienced such a momentous decision as my parents did when they decided to immigrate to a new, unknown country.

Another way to harvest memories without using a Time Line is to have children interview grandparents and relatives who lived through different periods of American history: the Roaring Twenties, the Great Depression, World War II, or the peace demonstrations during the Vietnam War. Youngsters can record these interviews with a tape recorder if one is available.

These activities provide a framework for beginning conversations. What unfolds are the feelings and the special ties that bind us together.

Young people may want to start their own family archives by putting all these family memories in a book to share with their own children.

## What Do I Do Right? ■ ages 10–12

- *Writing*
- *Collecting and Using Information*

Many of us spend a lot of time telling each other what we do wrong. Here's an activity to help us focus on what we're doing right. You need paper and pencil.

Together think of and write down at least two things you like about yourselves. *Example:* "I have a good sense of humor. I like to share with others."

Talk about what others say they like about you.

Figure out together jobs and activities at home that both you and your child will feel proud of accomplishing. *Examples:* Fixing something around the house, cooking a special dish for the family, teaching the family a new game.

Above all, find some listening time in your daily routine. Even a car ride to the grocery store can be a good time for a chat. Try to set a time every day, if only for a few minutes, to talk about the events of the day.

There are times when children need to share a secret or to ask a question that is

**From Texas . . .**

"Instead of my saying 'You should have tried harder,' I try to think of encouraging words because sometimes my kids try, and try hard, and it still doesn't come out right. They need to know they should keep on going, even when it's hard, even when they lose. That's the only way you can win."

bothering them. If you're available to listen to your children when they are young, chances are they'll continue to communicate with you as they grow older.

## IT TAKES COURAGE

Just as we say the old adage "It takes money to make money," we can also say, "It takes courage to make courage." It can take a parent's courage, or at least the control of fear, to show a child how to be courageous.

We want children to be careful but not fearful. How do we work toward this special "recipe"? How do we help children be careful but not fearful?

You teach this on the street as you're waiting for the light to change, on the beach when you're dodging the big waves, beside the basketball court when you yell to your child to go for a big shot.

Little by little you show, you teach, you let children test themselves—first by letting them ride a bike to the corner, then around the block, then to the store, and then on a trip out of town. You work toward a gradual building of the abilities it takes to be courageous and careful at the same time.

I have a problem with heights. When my young children went to the top of the big slide in the playground, my immediate reaction was to shout, "Stop! Come down! You'll hurt yourself!" They were perfectly happy up there high in the sky. I was the one who was petrified. It took some time for me to pull my own courage together, to let them be courageous and free from the seeds of my fear. They needed to be brave, even if I couldn't be.

Take the case of Peter. A high school junior in his first year as a driver, Peter asked his father if he could borrow the car to take two friends for a day at the beach, three hours away on country roads he had not driven before. His dad was worried. Actually he was scared, but he knew that his son was responsible and that he had shown he was a good driver. The father agreed but laid down certain instructions about when to be back home and what to do in an emergency. Dad was reluctant, somewhat fearful, but knew he had to let go. (Peter made the trip safely, not without a few calls home to ask to stay overnight now that he was "at the beach." This request was denied. The boys arrived home late but very pleased. Dad was pleased with himself as well.)

## CONFIDENCE AND EXPECTATIONS

In California a few years ago, a study showed that "ordinary" students could ex-

## TEACHING TIPS: CONFIDENCE

### Sharing Our Experiences with Our Children

There is not a living, breathing person who is confident all the time. And yet our children can get the idea that everyone else is more confident than they are and that everyone else, even and especially a parent, has never been scared or felt the pangs of loss of confidence.

That's why it is important to share your experiences, to come clean, to tell your child about a time in your own childhood when you felt confident, really able to do something like jump off the high diving board or ace the math test . . . and also about the time when you felt not so confident, when you had trouble standing up in front of the class to give a speech or when you realized you were short on cash at the checkout counter and you had to put some items back.

So tell them. Share as many memories as you can remember.

### Sparking the Conversation: The Shy Kids

Focus on a specific problem. For example, when I first went to school, I had trouble speaking up in class. I felt shy. I guess I was worried that I wouldn't have the right answer.

So I didn't raise my hand and I was the quiet little girl in the corner. It wasn't until the teacher called on me and made me talk that I opened my mouth in class.

When I told my own children about this, they were surprised (I talk so much now) and they were very sympathetic.

They started talking about their own experiences with confidence—when they have it and when they don't. I learned that my older daughter, age nine, a whiz in her classes, was having trouble making friends at school. And my younger daughter, age six, was spending so much time with friends that she was finding too little time for her work. It gave us all a chance to give each other a pep talk.

### Moving to the Bigger Questions

From these specifics, it's easier to move to some of the bigger questions in conversations with your children:

- What makes people scared?
- Does what we say to each other make a difference in our self-confidence?
- What kind of praise do we like to receive?
- How can we help each other feel more confident?

There is no end to questions like these. Follow this road to get the conversation going. Start with your own experiences and encourage children to share theirs when they're ready. Then move to some of these bigger questions that continue throughout our lives.

ceed themselves when expectations for them were high.

Researchers went into a school and tested the students for academic potential. They did not tell these scores to the teachers. Then, ignoring the scores, they randomly divided the students into two groups. They told teachers that one group was made up of "late bloomers" whose academic

---

**From California . . .**

"I think these activities have helped me, in a way, more than my child: I am developing more patience and am having to share with someone who really wants to learn. It's helped me realize that I am, indeed, not too old to learn."

---

"promise" would be realized that year.

At the end of the year the "promise" was realized. This group was comparable with their classmates as far as could be established, but their teachers had expected them to succeed, and they had. These children got a confidence-building message.

As adults, we know what makes us feel confident. It's when we see ourselves doing things, accomplishing, taking action, and having some things turn out right. Not everything is going to work. But we know that nothing works if we don't try.

That's how children learn—by trying. When they try, they build confidence. It's good to tell kids they're wonderful, but it's not enough. When children, and adults, too, see themselves as doers, they develop the ability to do more.

## CHAPTER 6

---

# MegaSkill Two: Motivation
Wanting to Do It

---

## THE NEVER-ENDING REPORT CARD

| The Grades We Get in School | The Grades We Get on the Job |
|---|---|
| Julie is a go-getter, excited about learning. | Mrs. Holbrook always seems to be thinking and planning ahead. |
| She raises her hand and has something to say on almost every subject. | She generates enthusiasm among the staff and provides leadership for the work that has to be accomplished. |

---

When they have it, it shows:

> You see your children wanting to do things, eager to learn.
> They do schoolwork and household jobs without a lot of nagging.
> They make plans for the next day, for the next week.
> They say *yes* more than they say *no*.

In this chapter are activities that help children gain the sense of discipline it takes to stay motivated, to work against discouragement, and to face competition and challenge.

> Sorry to say, there is no medicine that turns an apathetic youngster into one bubbling with enthusiasm. Parents can help with activities that generate a child's excitement in learning. But children have to catch this fire and start fueling up on their own.

- How to break down jobs into manageable "bites."
- How to set and keep to time limits.
- How to give yourself a pat on the back for a job well done.

There was a picture in the paper the other day of a ninety-one-year-old woman who had just climbed Mount Fuji.

Now that's what I call motivation. She was quoted as saying, "You always feel good when you've made a goal. You need goals." Right! But do you get them, whether you're nine or ninety-one? And what does it take to handle competition, to handle failure, to handle whatever comes?

I believe it takes a special ingredient that's found in motivation. This is the ability to work against discouragement and to keep on going.

Attitude counts for so much. The youngster with an IQ of 160 might not study or get good marks while the kid who keeps plugging away receives good marks and goes on

**From Texas . . .**

"A year ago when I went grocery shopping, my son, age nine, had all these excuses. He just didn't want to go. I said, 'When we go to the store, you take care of the coupons. I will give you half of the money we save.' He asked, 'Am I supposed to go find them?' I said, 'Yes, you are.'"

"So he started. He pulled out coupons, and he got paid for half of what we saved. Next he wanted to learn how to pick out good fruits and vegetables. Then he told me to give him the list. He'd find the things. Now, when it's time to give him half the money we saved, he says, 'No, I don't want any.' What he wants now is to help out all the time."

to do what the innately gifted cannot accomplish. Every teacher has students who live out these tortoise and hare stories.

When I look at sports events on TV, as I sit back and watch teams pummel each other, I think, "Gosh, those players are really motivated." And then I think about the students I've had over the years; some were motivated, and some I just couldn't seem to budge.

How do people become motivated? I think it has a lot to do with catching a feeling of excitement, of some one thing that gets us going, has us saying to ourselves, "I want to learn more about this" or "I want to be better at this."

Certainly we can't catch "fire" for our kids, but they can catch some of our fire or the fire of those in the vicinity. We know that youngsters get excited. They can go wild about the latest music or clothes or movies. What we need to look for are ways to help them get excited about developing a skill that, like a good stock, has growth potential. We all need things we can enjoy learning. We don't have to be precocious

Wanda, now a bookkeeper, recalls what got her going with numbers. As a child, she sold candy to neighbors and classmates. Her mother gave her big ledger sheets and showed her how to fill them out so she could keep track of the candy she bought and sold. Wanda loved it. She received an allowance, and using her ledger sheets, she was able to tell how much she had spent and how much was left over. Her sister couldn't, and that edge probably added to the excitement. She felt special.

Years later, when she was tested for job aptitude, she learned what she suspected. The answer was, "Finance, banking, and/or accounting." She thinks it all started with the ledger sheets that she loved to fill out.

That's a neat story with the edges tucked in. For most of us, it really doesn't work that way. We have to be exposed to quite a few excitements in order to pick the one or two that get us going.

math or chess geniuses to catch fire, and the fire does not have to be a bonfire. A slow, low simmer will do.

One way is to share our own excitement. It might be about skiing or cooking or long walks or short stories—whatever it is that excites us. And if we are not excited about anything (which, while we're breathing, is hardly likely), let's find people who *are* excited and put our kids next to them. It might be the neighbor who does woodworking, the dressmaker down the block, the uncle crazy for fishing, the accountant who really gets a kick out of balancing numbers.

## "COACHING" MOTIVATION

Teachers and parents are like coaches on the sports fields—encouraging, urging, and sometimes pushing. Children have to develop their own sense of direction, but we can show them some ways to light the fire.

This chapter provides activities to help children ignite and manage this motivation so that it lasts and lasts, just as it has for the ninety-one-year-old mountain climber.

## BEATING BOREDOM

Children are born motivated, not bored. They come out into the world eager, reaching, looking, touching—and that's what we want them to keep on doing.

Just outside our front door is a world of experiences waiting to delight even the child who complains bitterly, "There's nothing to do around here." What we do doesn't have to be exotic to be exciting. The activity examples that follow prove the old saying, "All you have to do is look." They help children (and adults) see the world with new eyes.

## Just Outside ■ any age

- *Thinking*
- *Storing Experiences for Reading and Writing*

While your children are young, start to share and discover the joy and mystery of the world: a walk as it's turning dark, a stroll through light rain. Talk together about what you're sensing and feeling. Stay up together to see the moon rise and get up early one day to watch the sun rise. Use a magnifying glass to look closely at those small objects that fascinate small children. Listen to the wind and the birds. Smell the rain and the burning wood in the fireplace. Observation and use of the senses are crucial to a scientist and to a poet.

## Shopping Center Stroll ■ ages 4–7

- *Thinking*
- *Building a Storehouse of Experience*

Most of the time we shop at breakneck speed with kids being dragged along. Try a walk with no other purpose than to show your children some of what goes on backstage at the local stores. Go into the florist's and watch the making of corsages. And go "backstairs" in the supermarket, if permitted. That's where the supplies are kept and where the meat is cut . . . where the action that makes the market look good takes place.

## Sitting and Watching ▪ ages 4–7

▪ *Thinking*
▪ *Building a Storehouse of Experience*

There's a lot to be seen and learned while watching the workers at a construction site, at an airport or rail station, or at your own corner.

Look, listen, and talk about what you see. How many different jobs do you see being done? Do you see workers using tools? What kinds? Are others reading plans and blueprints? What do they say to each other? How are they dressed? Do they seem to get along? Who's the boss? How can you tell?

As children watch others working, they become familiar with what jobs are like and what they might like to do when they grow up.

Some of the happiest moments, and the most motivating ones, are the ones in which parent and child sit together and talk about what they see together as the world goes by.

## Local Law ▪ ages 8–12

▪ *Social Studies*
▪ *Observing Civics in Action*

Lawyers are not just on TV. Every courthouse provides an ongoing display of law in action. And the courts are open to all, usually including children of any age.

Check first with the courthouse information office to see what trials are scheduled, what stages the cases are at, whether there are juries, and so forth. Before going, talk with your children about what they'll see, including the courtroom itself, the judge, the jury, the lawyers for the two sides, and the witnesses. Seeing a court in action is eye-opening for everyone.

## Getting Around ▪ ages 8–12

▪ *Social Studies*
▪ *Making Predictions and Testing Them*

Learning to get around without a car can be a valuable lesson. Gather bus route maps and schedules to a place around town. These are usually available by calling the local transportation company. Let children use the schedules to figure out what transportation is available, how much time it will take, and how much it will cost. Destinations might be a library downtown or a movie theater or a park. Once the most economical and fastest methods are identified, put the youngsters to the test. Let them take the trip, if possible, by themselves, or with the whole family.

One of the fastest ways to have youngsters appreciate the service of the family car is to let them take public transportation.

## The Foreign Touch Around Town
■ any age

   ■ *Social Studies*
   ■ *Understanding Diversity*

Visit foreign restaurants and stores in your community. You don't have to buy a fancy meal or an expensive souvenir. Just give children time to browse, have dessert, and perhaps buy a postcard.

When you visit a large American city such as New York or San Francisco, be sure to stroll with your children through ethnic neighborhoods like Chinatown, Little Italy, or the Lower East Side.

Even if your town hasn't got a foreign section as such, it probably has a Spanish grocery or just an old-style delicatessen. Buying rye bread in a deli is both educational and nourishing.

All of these activities have provided a platter of experiences, a smorgasbord to delight and excite the eye and the palate. Now comes the time to move children from seeing to doing.

## BEYOND NAGGING

How do we get people to do things? Sports people say they do it with inspiration (heroes to be imitated) and with competition (get out there and beat the others).

---

> **From Virginia . . .**
>
> "We left notes for each other about what we didn't like. My daughter, age twelve, wrote, 'You never let me explain. You always say no.' And I responded, 'No, I don't.' But then, I thought about it, and I wrote, 'Yes, I do do that. I really do.'"

Teachers do it with grades. Employers do it with salaries.

How can parents do it?

I'd like to think that nagging works because it is such a handy thing to do. But like millions of other parents, I have found that nagging can do just the opposite of what it is intended to do. It can motivate kids not to do things. Cutting down on nagging, in contrast, can be a motivating factor, one that works for both parent and child. Here's an activity that cuts down on nagging because it cuts down on talking.

It uses notes—in words and pictures— as reminders. I wish I had thought of this when my own kids were young. They say I was a terrible nag, and if I had nagged them less, they would have been more motivated.

## The No-Nag Writing System
■ ages 7–12

   ■ *Communication*
   ■ *Writing for a Purpose*

For practice, announce that for five minutes no one will talk. Instead you will send notes. Try this out at the breakfast table. Write short messages such as, "Please pass the toast" and "May I have my lunch money?" If you enjoy the quiet this brings, you can try this for longer periods and at other times of the day.

Ask your child, "What do I nag about a lot?" The answer might be "Cleaning my room" or "Practicing the piano."

Children have been known to nag. Tell them what they nag about. It might be about getting ice cream or using the car, depending on the age.

Choose at least one nagging problem that is important to you and your child. Promise each other that instead of nagging, for one whole week you will send each other reminder notes.

Set up a message center for these reminders. A bulletin board in the kitchen or family room is a good place.

Or post reminders around the house. Leave the notes in the bathroom, on the stairs, or in other places where they will be seen. A note left on the pillow always seems to work!

After the week is over, check to see if the messages have been answered. If they have, you may want to continue to keep up the writing and keep your voices down.

## BUILDING MOTIVATION MUSCLES

There is method and discipline in motivation that can be built from tiny, beginning steps. Here are activities designed to en-courage children and imbue them with the staying power it takes to remain motivated.

### The First Step ■ any age

- *Thinking*
- *Building Memory and Reflection*

The old Chinese saying is true: "The longest journey starts with a single step." The first step in doing something can be the hardest.

We need to get children used to taking those all-important first steps. They need to recognize a first step. One way is to tell them about our own first steps: the first date, the first job. If you can remember it, describe your own first day in school, or any first you feel you can tell your children about. You need not have been a first-time success. It may be even better if you weren't. The point is that you tried and then tried again.

Ask children to tell you about any first times they remember. It might be the first day at school, the first grade they received on a paper, the first time they tried to ride a bike or swim in the pool.

---

**From Delaware . . .**

"I have been more observant about what's been going on with my daughter. We look at things together. Before, I didn't give her a chance. Now, when we cook I say, 'You do it, try it for yourself.' I never did this before."

First steps are hard. We tend to say, "Aw, come on, that's easy," but it's not. Our goal in helping to motivate children is to help them gain the optimism and the courage to take more first steps. That is the lesson we have to teach, and one way to teach it is by sharing our experiences.

Before they do things, children tend to ask two questions over and over:

▪ How long will it take?
▪ What was it I was supposed to do, again?

The following activities for young children can help answer these questions.

## Time Me ▪ ages 4–6

▪ *Mathematics*
▪ *Practicing Estimation*

This activity will help your child better understand the difference between "a few seconds" and "a few minutes." You need a clock or watch with a second hand.

Ask your child to watch the second hand for five seconds. Together count off the seconds. Put this into action. Time it again and see how many times your child can clap in five seconds. Now have your child watch the clock for one minute. Then time it again and see how far you can both count in one minute. Together read a book for five minutes. Time yourselves. How many pages did you read? Hold your breath for five seconds. Let your child time you. Then trade places. Time yourselves as you both say the alphabet aloud. Together time a traffic light

---

**From California . . .**

"My oldest son got to the point where he didn't want to do work. He wanted Mommy to do it. He was eight. I told him, 'We are going to have a race.' I write his words ten times each and he has to write them three times each. We've made a game out of his homework. We time ourselves, and he likes that a lot. We compete to see who finishes first."

---

as you stand at a street corner. Time two TV commercials. How long did each one take?

As you see, there are many ways to help children get a feel for time. Even as adults we often have trouble knowing how long thirty seconds is. A better sense of time helps us anticipate how much we can accomplish in a day—if only we try.

## Tell Me ▪ ages 4–9

▪ *Communication*
▪ *Listening Skills*
▪ *Following Directions*

Teachers in the early grades tell us that children have trouble listening. Perhaps it's because they have been bombarded by so much coming at them all at once on television. Here's an easy activity that can help cut through the multimedia, noisy environment. For this one, all you need are listening ears.

Think of a real job at home that your child can do. It might be setting the table, taking out the garbage, bringing in the newspaper, hanging up clothes. Think of three or four instructions for this job. Ask your child to listen carefully as you say them. *Example:* "Take out four forks, four knives, and four spoons. Put these on the table in four place settings. Put the fork on the left, the knife and spoon on the right."

Let your child give you instructions to follow. They can be as easy or as complicated as you and your child want. In this way, you individualize this activity to suit your child.

By adding pencil and paper, you can turn this into a "write and do" activity. Write down instructions instead of talking about them. Have your child write a set of directions for you to follow.

Hide something and give instructions on how to find it. *Example:* "Take two steps forward, turn right, take three steps back." Trade places and let your child hide something for you to find.

As a special treat, organize an outdoor treasure hunt. Prepare a short list of items, such as a small stone, a branch, a green or red leaf. Give youngsters a paper bag for the collection. Turn this into a game by timing the minutes it takes to find the objects. Use this when you go shopping. At the store, your child can help you find the family's grocery items.

## FOLLOW THROUGH

When children see that they can concentrate and follow through on an action, their desire to do more grows.

### This House Is a Mess ■ any age

- ■ *Mathematics*
- ■ *Recognizing and Creating Patterns*

This activity is really ageless. I don't know anyone who responds to the task of cleaning up with joy and eagerness. Maybe it's because we think we have to do everything at once, and we can't. So we feel discouraged.

Just as in teaching in the classroom, where we divide a curriculum into parts, cleaning up a house can be divided into parts. Then the tasks become doable, and while children may not be whistling while they work, they do know where to start.

For the big job of cleaning house, you might do one room at a time or one task, like washing windows, in several rooms. For children, putting away clothes and toys in their rooms can be a first step. This can be followed by dusting and then by vacuuming.

---

**From Georgia . . .**

"We do this activity at home all the time, so our special messages are usually taped to the refrigerator door. It's also taught the children to leave phone messages and where-we-are messages."

Make the job more pleasant by working with someone else or even to music. Marches are known to be very effective. Rock 'n' roll moves the dustcloth along.

Turn cleaning into a game. Decide how long it will take you to do the job. Then time yourself against the clock.

Set the same task for yourself and your child. You can race each other to see who is the fastest cleaner of them all!

## Excuses Don't Count ■ ages 7–12

- ■ *Study Skills*
- ■ *Observing and Keeping Records*

This activity teaches children that work can be organized so that it gets done and that excuses for not doing tasks just don't count —at home or in school or on a job. You need paper, pencil, and a ruler.

Make a chore chart for the hours between five P.M. and bedtime. Ask children to choose a time to do each chore. Write those times on the chart. The chart might look like this:

| Chore | Time | Done |
|---|---|---|
| Setting the table | 5:30 | _____ |
| Doing homework | 7:30 | _____ |

The next day, children do the tasks at the time planned. When they've completed the job, they put a check mark in the **Done** column.

Talk about when they did the tasks. Did they do them all? If not, did they have real reasons or excuses? An excuse might be that they forgot to set the table while playing ball. Talk about using excuses to avoid doing things. Do we know when we're using them?

Look around the house. Think about the chores that need to be done. *Examples:* Clean out the closet, straighten the drawers, weed the garden. What excuses do adults use to avoid these chores?

(For a related activity, see "A Homework System" in Chapter 7.)

## A PAT ON THE BACK

Every family needs to figure out what it chooses as rewards for doing the dishes or doing homework. Children need our signal. Will they be rewarded for keeping quiet or speaking up? For reading a book or watching TV? For obeying rules or breaking them? And families need their own reward system. It's important that the rules be clear, the system fair and consistently

---

**From Texas . . .**

"I keep a list of positive words in my household bills file. When I open my bills, it's the first thing I see. The list includes: 'proud,' 'super,' 'great,' 'excellent,' and 'marvelous.' I need the encouragement because the bills really pile up. Instead of getting aggravated, I use these words on myself and my kids."

There are some basic principles of competition that every child should learn, or at least listen to. To compete, you have to be able to lose. You have to be willing to fail but not feel like a failure. You have to get up off the floor and try again.

followed. Whether it's a present, a grade, a raise, or a word of praise and a kiss, a reward is very sweet, indeed.

This scene captures for me the power of rewards. It was a hot summer Saturday in a restaurant in a small town. A little girl had just opened the door. Her parents were busy behind the counter. And this child, age eight, was busy, too. Carrying her parents' laundry, she came through the door with a smile on her face that said to all of us, "I'm not bored. I'm happy. I am doing something important." That was her inner reward. Her parents' praise was the external one.

I believe we can help our children understand their strengths. This enables them to feel good about themselves and strong enough to compete with others. Our children need to be able to face competition.

To be competitive, we have to be willing to work hard, but we also have to have a sense of what is special about us. When kids compete in the classroom, it is not the same as competing on the football field. In football, we win or lose. While a lot of talk is given to how we play the game, the result reported on the news is who won and who lost.

In the classroom, there is the possibility for a different kind of winning, based on a child's individuality. A child needs to think about and to hear from parents and teachers answers to "What is special and different about me?" Children who know this are in a better position to compete and succeed than youngsters who do not recognize their unique strengths.

For most of us, there is no one big win and then competition is over. Every day there are wins and losses, and the person who can keep competing without losing heart has more chances to be a winner.

There's a lesson that is taught at every dance recital and ball game. When dancers stumble in the middle of a solo, they get right up and keep on dancing as if nothing had happened. The same is true for football players who miss a touchdown pass.

"To be successful, I have to feel success. Sports has done that for me. While I am in the top 10 percent in native sports ability, my son is in the low 10 percent. But that doesn't mean he can't participate. He enjoys sports and learns from them. I've coached his Little League and soccer games for years. Other parents are pushing to have these kids go on to tougher competition, but I want these youngsters to experience the feeling of success. I know what it did for me. My mother told me, 'You can do anything you want to do.' That's the way I feel today."

## TEACHING TIPS: MOTIVATION

### Sharing Experiences with Our Children

We're worried about our children's motivation today, maybe more than ever. We see so many kids who say they are bored. Boredom used to be considered a problem for adolescents, but now it's striking younger and younger. A teacher tells me about a group of second graders she took on a special field trip to a new museum. After a few minutes in the galleries, they came to her, asking, "Is this all there is?"

These children are used to a new sensation every few seconds on TV; they are used to flitting from one thing to the next at rapid speed. No wonder they get bored.

Motivation thrives on learning enough about something to get really interested in it. And that takes getting into a subject in some depth, and that takes time.

That's why hobbies are so good for children and for adults too. If you had a hobby as a child, maybe making model airplanes, maybe collecting stones, tell your kids about it. Help them develop an interest. When they have an interest and they seek more information about it, they get involved. When they get involved, they get motivated. It's a remarkable cycle.

### Sparking the Conversation: What's New?

Learning is at the heart of motivation. We're always learning but we're usually moving too fast to recognize it:

Think about what you have learned in the past year, in the past week, in the last day. For example, what did you learn about a certain person, about something new on the job? Share a thought or two about this with your child.

Ask children to share with you a "learning" or two from school. They might tell you about a new item on the bulletin board or what they saw on the way to school. These observations can be the stepping-stones to further interests.

### Moving to the Bigger Questions

Children may not know the word *motivation*, but they recognize it when they see it. Check with them:

What are they encouraged by? What discourages them? Are they more motivated with certain people, certain subjects?

There's been no better way invented to encourage children's motivation than seeing their parents as interested learners, excited about an idea. So what's the next thing you want to learn about?

They're competitors because they keep on competing, not because they keep on winning.

We want our children to be competitors who keep on trying. It would be grand if they could always win, but that's not the way it usually happens . . . even for the big winners.

## LOSE AND STILL WIN

A successful accountant tells how he learned to get going and keep going through sports.

In coaching, even when his teams lose, which happens a lot, he talks with the kids about what they did right, about the wins in their loss. Did Tom catch a ball he had never caught before? Did Stephen steal second base, something he had never done before? There is, he says, some success in every loss, and his team members need to know this.

## WHAT KEEPS US GOING CHANGES WITH THE YEARS

We have to keep alert to what fuels our motivation motor at different points in our lives. What works at age five won't work at ten or fifteen or forty. A young child may be motivated by the promise of a star on a chart, an older child by a new pair of jeans. A woman of forty-five tells me she swims an hour every morning before work, driving almost an hour to get to the pool. She does this so she won't have to take pills. Every other member of her family takes mountains of pills each morning to keep blood pressure down. As long as she swims, her blood pressure is fine. "I made up my mind I won't take those pills," she says, "and I'll swim the ocean if necessary."

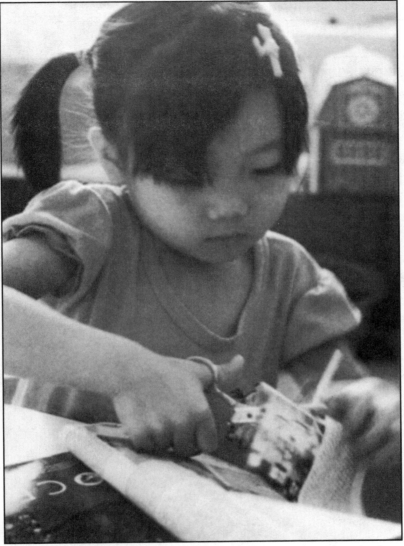

Courtesy of the National School Boards Association

## CHAPTER 7

# MegaSkill Three: Effort

Being Willing to Work Hard

## THE NEVER-ENDING REPORT CARD

### The Grades We Get in School

Alice likes to do a lot and she tries her hand at almost everything. Alice is a doer. She is ready to do the hard work it takes.

### The Grades We Get on the Job

Mrs. Taylor always seeks opportunities to gain new skills and knowledge.

She knows that it takes hard work to make the necessary changes.

We recognize effort when we see it:

> The doctor who takes time to talk to us.
> The waiter who attends to us with just the right amount of care.
> The student who reads a paper over before handing it in.

And we recognize effort when we don't see it:

> The mechanic who lets a car out of the shop without checking to see that all the hoses are attached.
> Household repair firms that make appointments for a certain time and then don't show up.
> Students whose work is so sloppy it can hardly be read.

Do our children know enough about the value of effort and the pleasure of work? What is known about student effort today? What are some ways to encourage it? What about homework, and what is a parent's role? This chapter provides some answers to these questions.

Where do children get the idea that saying, "I'm doing my best," in as plaintive a tone as possible, will excuse them from having to work hard?

Do I sound cranky? Well, maybe I am, but I am also tired of hearing from young people who are doing perfectly inadequate jobs of bagging groceries or writing an essay, "Well, I am doing my best. What more can you ask?"

As for me, a lot. I want more than that pat phrase that gets every adult off their backs. I want their best, and while I don't know exactly what that is, I know when I am not getting it.

I know that this is going to sound terribly old-fashioned. I suggest we stop saying to our children, "Take it easy." This is what I call "education pollution."

When I called for the fifth time to find out where my newly repaired computer had been sent, I was told by the clerk, "Well, it's not here," and I asked, "Well, where is it?" She said, "I'm doing my best." I said, "Well, you'll have to do better."

> The value of believing in effort over native ability is that you can help children do something about their level of effort. It's fatalistic and harder to help them do something about their level of ability. Ability seems set in stone; effort can be influenced; it's open to change.

An hour later she called back to say it was in her office after all. She just hadn't looked. She had not done her best before, and now she had. I praised her for making the effort. I wanted her to know her best when she used it.

Maybe not knowing what effort feels like is a problem today. If so, it's not just a personal concern; it's a national problem.

Recent research has uncovered a difference between American and Japanese students and their mothers, which we can call the "effort gap." Stanford University researchers asked mothers in Japan and in the U.S. to explain their children's achievements in mathematics. These were their questions: "Why does your child do as well as he/she does?" and "Why doesn't your child do better?" Mothers could respond from among these choices: ability, effort, luck, schooling. The groups of mothers gave very different answers.

American mothers voted overwhelmingly for ability and schooling. Japanese mothers voted for effort. The fifth-grade youngsters in the study shared their mothers' views. The American kids agreed that native ability was the key, while the Japanese kids said that if they did not do well in math, it was because they were not making a great enough effort.

What's ironic about the American mothers' response is that the U.S. is supposed to believe in the Horatio Alger story that hard work, in the long run, pays off, no matter what the odds against you. Instead, our children seem to be getting a contrary message—that they need the ability first.

Can we send our children a message about effort that they will listen to? Research says we can.

In Texas, elementary school children having difficulties with subtraction were divided into four groups—A, B, C, D. Each group worked on its own with a packet of materials. An aide checked the work in groups A, B, and C every eight minutes. As the children came to a new section, the aide gave them the new instructions. To group A the aide said, "You've been working hard." To group B she said, "You need to work hard." Group C received no comment.

> Our children, who may look as if they're never listening, do indeed hear one big, "educationally polluting" message. The big message (and it seems to get said at least ten times a day) is this: "TAKE IT EASY! DON'T WORK TOO HARD!" It's often followed by "HAVE A GOOD DAY." It might be assumed that if you do take it easy, you will have a good day.

Group D had no involvement with the aide other than to hear her read the instructions to everyone.

The results make a strong point for telling children they are working hard. The group that was told, "You've been working hard," actually did work harder than the others. They completed 63 percent more problems and got three times as many right on the test that followed this training. They also said that they felt more confident about the test and their ability to deal with the problems they would face.

Across the world, in Australia, a somewhat different strategy resulted in a similar pattern. Aides in this study congratulated the children each time they said that their success in math was due to their own effort or lack of it, instead of blaming it on luck or their ability.

What do these studies mean for families and for effort? They mean that we can talk children into making more effort, that they do not have to be afraid, and that we can help them see that more effort can mean better results. Children can have an effort standard for themselves, and as parents, we can have an effort standard for them.

So how do we do it? It has to be more than a lecture on making an effort. First we may have to help children know what effort is and how they can measure it.

## LEARNING ABOUT EFFORT

Effort has its secrets. And we need to let our children in on them.

If more young people knew what a significant impact even a little extra effort can make, more of them would make it. For example, in an office, one secretary may jump up as if the seat ejects at five o'clock, no matter what, and another will ask if everything has been done for the day.

Inevitably the questioner is told that everything has been done, thank you. The other does not ask the question or get an answer, but the behavior is noticed. When a pay raise is distributed, chances are that only one will get it. One secretary will be asked to stay on and will move up; the other will be encouraged to move out.

When one waiter makes sure that you are happy with a smile or an "Everything all right?" and the other ignores you, guess who will get the bigger tip. It's no mystery. It's the result of effort.

The kid learning magic tricks, the adult perfecting a golf game or struggling with a crossword puzzle, the tennis enthusiast practicing strokes over and over, the aspiring figure skater at the rink at dawn, the

---

There are cases where even a little effort has a payoff. In other situations it takes a lot of effort to see results.

Take the case of sports. It's interesting that often in these areas of extracurricular pleasures people expend enormous effort without having it feel like effort at all. They're working hard and often without a lot of, if any, immediate reward.

marathon runner who practically drops before stopping—these are people making lots of effort, and they think they are enjoying themselves. It feels like enjoyment. The secret is that it is.

We need to let our kids in on this secret. How do we do it? Here are some suggestions on how to give kids the opportunity to know effort when they see it and to practice effort on their own.

## My Day ■ any age

■ *Communication*
■ *Discussion and Listening Skills*

Spend time talking with your children about the pleasures of work and of effort. Try to be as specific as possible. If you enjoy your work, so much the better. If you enjoy part but not all of it, talk about the things you enjoy. Tell about incidents from

Ask children about their day. Urge them to follow your lead in talking about the little successes. They should not have to emerge from school with A's to have had a good day. Ask about the bits and pieces of success along the way: the new friend at lunch, the speaking up in class, the locker that finally opened in time for gym. This list can go on and on, too, and it should. It's these efforts that children recognize in themselves that enable them to make more effort.

work, and not all of them have to be heartwarming. Describe the feelings of satisfaction you may get, even after a very hard day. The reluctant customer you were able to woo and win, the copier at the office or the washing machine at home that just wouldn't work until you finally figured out what was wrong, the meeting that got meaner until you told a joke that broke the ice, the memo that got the boss's applause.

The list can go on and on. It's not made up of big things. Sure, if you get a raise, brag about it. But don't stint on letting children in on the everyday efforts and goings-on at work and at home that illustrate effort and the sense of satisfaction that comes with it.

Not all problems are solved quickly or easily. Let children in on your frustrations. Perhaps it's the car that didn't get fixed, the mail that didn't go out, the telephone that stopped working, the meeting that didn't take place, the bus that didn't come on time, the grocery store that was out of milk.

But when you do talk about the day's problems, try to discuss what you are doing and what your children think can be done to solve these problems. Satisfaction lurks in the nooks and crannies of dealing with manageable problems.

I think of effort as going that extra mile, not taking the easy way out. It's hard to measure. No one can go 100 percent all of the time, and yet we have to expect enough. Here's an activity that helps children recognize levels of effort all around us.

## The Extra Mile ■ any age

- ■ *Thinking*
- ■ *Observation Skills*
- ■ *Drawing Inferences*

Help your children know what we really mean when we say "make an effort."

Take time to point out to children those people who are making that extra effort.

The gas station attendant at a full-service station who actually gives full service, wiping off the windows or even the headlights without being asked.

The supermarket checker who, instead of kibitzing with other checkers, moves directly to take care of each customer without delay.

The salesperson who, when asked if a product is on sale, gives a polite, full answer instead of a grunt that says, in effect, "Why did you bother me?"

You promote your child's sense of effort by pointing to others who are making an effort and showing how much you respect this.

### From North Carolina . . .

"I used a lot of these kinds of 'recipes' before, but this program made me go back to using them. And now I understand why I was doing it. It's been terrific in helping to eliminate a lot of little things in everyday life that cause a lot of stress."

## Do and Not Die ■ any age

- ■ *Thinking*
- ■ *Comparing and Contrasting Information*

It is very possible to make an all-out effort and still not win. But that does not mean do or die. One of the major blocks to all-out effort is fear. Fear of doing wrong, fear of not being perfect. The excuse for not making an effort is often this: "If I don't put my all into it, I can always lean back and say I have not given them my best. I'll never know if I could have won, nor will they, because I held back."

Sports is one place where people can't hold back. There are winners and there are losers, but both have to try like crazy.

Together check the sports pages. Almost every day there is a story about athletes who never said die, who didn't give up the fight until the fight was really over, who played the match to the end with all the strength they had.

These are inspirational stories. Talk about them. They are superhuman efforts, not able to be made every day, not expected every day, but they point the way.

## HOMEWORK AND EFFORT

I am not a lover of traditional school homework, but I don't hate it, either, except homework saved for Sunday nights, which is a downer. I don't automatically think teachers are better because they give lots of homework or terrible because they don't.

One problem with homework is that subjects are different and students are different, but homework tends to be the same: reading that everyone in the class has to cover and then those repetitive exercises that perhaps only half the class needs. But even those drills are not without redeeming qualities. They give youngsters who don't need them a sense of being out in front, of having achieved mastery of the material.

The remarkable school success of recently arrived Asian children who came to this country without even knowing English has prompted discussions about nature versus nurture. A Stanford University survey of San Francisco high school students found that Asian Americans consistently received better grades than other students, regardless of the parents' level of education or income. Actually, the more English spoken in the home, the less well the students did in school. Researchers found that Asian parents are able to get their children to work harder.

The Stanford study measured hours high schoolers spend on homework. The differences are startling. Asian American males spend almost twelve hours a week on homework; American white males spend eight, and American black males spend a little over six.

For females, it was found that Asian Americans spend over twelve hours a week on homework; white Americans, eight hours, and American blacks, over nine hours.

Asian Americans also scored higher on other measures of effort, including attendance and paying attention to the teacher.

A University of Michigan study of elementary school students in the U.S., Taiwan, and Japan found that the American children scored lowest in math. But the study resulted in perhaps an even more revealing finding. It's about homework. American first graders spend about fourteen minutes a night on homework and hate it. Japanese spend thirty-seven minutes and Taiwanese seventy-seven minutes, and both groups say they like homework. What's more, Asian children go to school 240 days a year, while American children go only 180 days a year.

Asians believe that hard work makes a difference, and they let their children know it. I believe that Americans also believe in hard work, and we have to let our children know that we do.

---

There are continuing arguments about whether certain youngsters have a higher math aptitude or even higher IQs to start with. The arguments will accelerate with each new study. But while whatever we discover about inherent capacity will be interesting, it will not effect change for other students and enable them to perform better.

What is measurable now, what we can learn from, is the different effort that different youngsters put into their schoolwork.

## No Substitute for Hard Work

There is still no substitute for hard work and for the time that work takes. Maybe a lot of our stress is caused by our thinking —children thinking—that there are short cuts for everything and that everything should take little time and be easy to do— if only we knew the short cut. But very little comes easily and quickly.

I am not making a case for Japanese up-bringing and schooling over ours (their higher education programs, for example, do not compare with those in the United States)—but they do appear to be able to teach their children endurance, and that is one thing we tend not to teach in the early school years. Our young people need to learn about endurance and to be taught the importance of effort. Homework gives children practice in making effort.

# THE HOMEWORK CONFLICT

Whatever teachers do, there never seems to be a happy medium in homework. Some parents say their kids have too little. Other parents say their kids have too much. I don't necessarily believe kids need to have more homework, but I believe they must pay attention to the homework they are given. Children need to know that their parents feel homework has to be taken seriously. This is true even for homework a parent might think is "busywork" or "a waste of time." Students need to understand that homework is something they must do. It is not an option, even if the assignment is dull or too easy or too hard. If students and parents have an objection to an assignment, they should raise it with the teacher or with the principal, if necessary. But homework, like an assignment on a job, cannot be ignored.

## Taking Homework Seriously

Homework is a student's responsibility, not the parents'. I am troubled by homework assignments for children that are really addressed to parents. If it's too hard or too long for a student, it should not be assigned . . . unless it's clear that it's an assignment parents and children are supposed to do together. How much does a child learn from a science fair experiment designed by a weary parent at two A.M. when the child is asleep? An honest show of hands at PTA meetings would reveal that many parents are veterans of these late-night projects for which children receive grades. This is no way to teach science or to teach honesty.

As an English teacher, I told my students that homework writing assignments were theirs solely to do, that if parents helped them do the writing, I would never know how to help them. I encouraged them to talk over the assignment and to share ideas with their family, but I wanted to be sure

> It can be hard to remember that homework assignments are our children's alone, not ours. The difficulties are theirs, and so are the achievements.

I was reading a student's, not a parent's, paper.

As a parent I worked to follow my "teacher's hat" advice. While I enjoyed hearing my children read their essays aloud after they had completed them, I was not involved in writing them. When it came time for college essays, they wrote and typed their own. I wasn't applying for college. They were.

## PARENTAL INFRASTRUCTURE

This does not mean that as parents we don't have a role to play. We do—as the infrastructure that makes it possible for children to accomplish their homework. The infrastructure I have in mind is like a bridge or a road that makes comings and goings possible.

Providing the infrastructure in homework means providing the base from which children can operate. It's the atmosphere that promotes study and enables children to be students.

Children need parents who think homework is important, who let them know this, and who provide discipline that children can follow and that is enforceable.

At least three kinds of parental discipline patterns have been identified, and I believe they are relevant to homework:

**Permissive:** Adult makes few demands on child and sees child as own self-regulator.

> **From New York . . .**
>
> "When my kids came home from school, I used to say, 'Start your homework!'
>
> "Now we plan the day so that they have time for a break, for some talk. There is more time for everything because we plan how we will spend our time."

**Authoritarian:** Adult has set standard of conduct in mind and sets out to shape child to fit it, using force and punishment to curb child.

**Authoritative:** Adult sets standards and asserts control but sees child's need for reason and understanding.

Parental-authority researchers are all for the authoritative parent. Permissiveness is not as good for children as once was thought. The trick, and it's a tough one, is for parents and for teachers to be authoritative without being authoritarian. It's not easy.

Here are some "authoritative" activities that can help. They provide children with an atmosphere that encourages learning within a structured and supportive environment.

## A Study Place ■ ages 4–9

- *Study Skills*
- *Building Organizational Abilities*

All children need their own place at home to do homework. Even with this special place, they might still use the dining room table. But they gain a sense of the importance of homework from having a place of their own. Fancy equipment is not needed. Use old furniture. Cut it down to size as needed. You need a table or desk, a chair, a light.

Walk through your house with your child to find that special study corner. It need not be big, but it needs to be personal. With your child, find the furniture needed; check the attic, ask friends, or visit nearby garage sales.

Paint cardboard boxes or orange crates for bookcases. Latex paint is easy to clean. Encourage your child to decorate the study corner; a plant and a bright desk blotter do wonders. Save children's artwork from school for the extra touch.

A study place can be a desk, or it can be a modest lapboard for a child to use atop a bed. What is basic to both is their message that studying is valued in this house.

## A Homework System ■ ages 10–12

- *Study Skills*
- *Researching and Charting Information*

There is a better way than nagging children every day about homework. This activity enables children to keep track—on their

> It's a continuing surprise for many parents that this system works as well as it does. Children ask parents to initial the chart when their tasks are done.

own—of what has to be done. You need paper and a marker.

Use a sturdy, large piece of paper to make a homework chart that can be posted on the wall. Here's what one looks like:

| Days | English | Math | Social Studies | Science |
|------|---------|------|----------------|---------|
| Monday | | | | |
| Tuesday | | | | |
| etc. | | | | |

Each day after school, your child makes checks to represent homework assignments. To show completed homework, the check gets circled. Attach to the chart a marker or pen so that it is always handy.

## Talking About Homework

Talk about assignments with your child after they're completed. This is more of a conversation than a checkup. Was the assignment difficult? Easy? Would your child like to know more? Consider follow-up trips to a museum or library. Homework can be a starting point for your child's continuing interests—pursued with pleasure and without assignments.

## Our Home: A Learning Place
■ any age

- *Reading/Writing*
- *Focusing on Good Work Habits*

Help your home (even if it's a small apartment) convey the message that people learn here.

You want children to be reading a lot and using as many different materials as possible. Let there be books and magazines everywhere, including the bathroom. Studies show people do a lot of reading there. These do not have to be the latest magazines or books to be useful. Ask friends and neighbors to save theirs. You can set up an informal exchange so that there is always fresh reading material, just as there is fresh food, in your home. Let your children see you reading, and talk with them about what you've read.

You want children to be writing as often as possible. Put notepads and pencils in a number of places around the house, including next to the telephone, for messages. In the kitchen use them for grocery lists, and keep them next to the bed for putting down that brilliant middle-of-the-night thought.

And you want to show that you value your child's school experience. Use a bulletin board or magnets on the refrigerator to display children's schoolwork and artwork. Or use an indoor clothesline with clothespins. Youngsters enjoy changing these displays themselves as they bring new work home. When parents ask, "What did you do in school today?" children can point with pride to the newest addition in their very own gallery.

## STUDYING: A PERSONAL APPROACH

After years of studying students, I am more and more convinced that what works for one person does not necessarily work for another. There are those who have to do it standing up, those who do it sitting down, those who need complete quiet, and those who do well studying with lots of background noise.

Just because children are sitting down and look as if they are reading quietly does not mean they are absorbing the material. Don't let what looks like studying make you think it is studying. Children will evolve their own personal style of study, but it's important that it be shown to work. If children can't pass tests and master the material after studying in complete quiet, they may want to try some background music. If they can't work with noise, they can go to the library. The beauty of studying at home is that children can have their own personal style, as long as it does not bother others.

## Time for Studying

We know from experience in school that some children are faster to finish classroom work than others. The same is true for homework.

The research on Asian students and math shows that time spent on the task pays off. And as an English teacher, I know that when a student takes time to polish an essay and read it over more than once, it pays off.

When you talk with your children about homework, ask if they think they are putting in enough time to do it really well. When you talk with your children's teachers, ask if they think your child is spending enough time to do the homework carefully and thoroughly.

## TEACHING TIPS: EFFORT

### Sharing Our Experiences with Our Children

Effort is funny. You've probably got lots of examples, as I have, of times when you've made major efforts and nothing worked out. And then there are those times when you made little effort and, bang, big results!

Your children have the same experiences. They write a paper, for example, that takes days and days, and the teacher says, "You should have tried harder." Then they knock off another paper in ten minutes and, bam, they get an A.

Where's the justice? Answer: There isn't much, but there is a law of averages. That means that when we try a lot, some of the ships will come in and some won't, but chances are, there will always be some ships in port.

We have to help our children know the value of effort. Failure is no crime. Not trying is.

### Sparking the Conversation: All-Out Effort

Ask children for their own memories of making an effort and not making an effort.

Do they know kids who respond to low test grades by saying, "I didn't study anyway"? What do they think this shows?

Try to remember a time when you made an all-out effort, maybe to win someone's affections or to get on a team, and it didn't work out. Your children will notice that you are still standing, so making an effort can't be too disastrous.

### Moving to the Bigger Questions

Try these for a lively discussion:

- Is there a fear among students of making an effort, a fear that if you try and lose, it's worse than not trying?
- What about expectations? How realistic are we about winning and losing?

Just as we learn in different ways, different kinds of effort are very useful for our well-being. On any day, we may run the gamut, from jogging to gardening to cooking to memo writing to putting up a roof. These wonderful opportunities give expression to the remarkable variety of human abilities.

If your children are now spending more time watching TV than doing homework, they may not necessarily need more homework, but they do need to cut down on TV watching. TV does not help children feel a sense of accomplishment. Help your child spend time on hobbies—perhaps those old standbys, stamp collecting and model airplanes, or cooking or a new sport. These involve effort, and with effort comes a sense of accomplishment.

Education is hard, daily work. Telling our kids to "take it easy" is sending the wrong message. Our children are being contaminated, and we, as protective adults, must fight back with the words and actions that send the right message. What our children need to hear from us are the old-fashioned words, "Go to school, behave, learn, work hard."

## EFFORT IS PLEASURE

Clearly effort is not all grim and serious. People are made for effort. We function better when we're exerting ourselves. Ask any jogger, swimmer, baseball player. The pleasure of effort comes not just from physical exercise but from mental exercise, too. Our children need to know this.

Talk about the satisfaction a writer gets, an artist, a mathematician, an accountant. There is real pleasure in working with our minds.

It may be harder to feel a rush of pleasure after finishing ten pages of homework than after jogging ten blocks or swimming ten laps, but our children need to know that even their homework can bring them pleasure. It is the satisfaction of using oneself, of accomplishment.

Our children need to know that effort is the path we take to achieve mastery—and mastery is one of the greatest pleasures of them all.

*Courtesy of the National Association of Elementary School Principals*

## CHAPTER 8

# MegaSkill Four: Responsibility

## Doing What's Right

## THE NEVER-ENDING REPORT CARD

**The Grades We Get in School**

Becky gets her assignments in on time.

She seems to know what to do to take care of herself.

**The Grades We Get on the Job**

Ms. Stein meets her deadlines through effective resource management.

She knows when to say yes and when to say no.

Check yourself. When you hear yourself saying or thinking about your children,

"Why are you always late?"
"Where have you been?"
"Why can't you start acting more grown-up?"

you are hearing the need to help your child become more responsible. When you hear yourself saying about your children,

"I can count on you,"
"You are reliable and dependable,"
"When you tell me something, I can believe you,"

you are hearing yourself praise your responsible child.

This chapter is about developing self-discipline in children. It's about children knowing what they have to do and gaining self-respect from doing it.

At the age of twenty-eight, Paul is one of the most responsible young men I know. He is a topnotch printing salesman, a father of three, and a man of his word. I asked him how he got to be so responsible.

*My parents gave me a motorcycle when I was thirteen. They told me I was to care for the bike, that I was not to ride it on the public streets, and that I was to walk it to the biking trails. But I didn't always do what I was supposed to.*

*One day as I came roaring over a hill in the middle of a street, a policeman was waiting for me. I'll never forget the ride to the station in the back of the police car and the meeting with the judge.*

*I received a Juvenile Two form for unauthorized use of the road.*

*My dad said, "I hope you learned something from this." And I did, but it was probably a very risky way to learn it. I learned that there are authorities out there to enforce rules, and you'll be caught — maybe not today, but they will catch you.*

*But that motorcycle kept me out of trouble, too. It kept me in the fresh air, getting mud all over me in the fields rather than getting into drugs on street corners. I subscribed to all the magazines on bikes and read them cover to cover — even when I wasn't reading all my schoolbooks.*

*My parents probably put more trust in me than they should have. They were determined to force me to learn to be responsible.*

*For my own kids, I'd be less risky, probably get them a dog instead of a motorcycle.*

For many parents, giving a teen a motorcycle is both out of the question financially and unsuited to how the family lives.

So it's good to know that responsibility and reliability and trustworthiness can be taught quietly and at home. When I thought about the activities that are useful in teaching responsibility, I realized that they can seem an odd combination. Some are as straightforward as learning to sew on a button or to get up on time. Others are as complex as what it means to cheat on a test or lie to a friend.

Children will probably learn to sew on a button faster than they will grasp abstractions about truth. But the underlying willingness and readiness to be responsible can be strikingly similar for both.

The activities in this chapter seem so unrelated that I began to question putting them together. Then I remembered the broad definition I had chosen for responsibility — *doing what's right.*

Our children become responsible through an accumulation of experiences. The value of mixing tangible activities — using buttons and alarm clocks — with family discussions about an intangible abstraction, such as truth, is that buttons and clocks provide immediate, positive payoff for responsible actions. The payoff on the abstractions can take a lifetime to assess.

Here are some starter activities that span the broad MegaSkill of responsibility. They include the following:

- taking care of children's own property and others' property
- carrying out home and school tasks
- encouraging children to think about choices and values

It can be helpful to think about personal responsibility in this way: how to enable children to *do for themselves* and *do for the family.*

The following activities widen children's sense of responsibility from self to family, and each reinforces the other.

---

Teaching children to be responsible involves finding ways to help children feel competent, to know what's right and to do what's right. If children need to wake up on time, you show them how to use an alarm clock and expect them to use it. If a child lies to you, you let your child know that lying is wrong and that it works to destroy the precious trust you share.

## HELPING CHILDREN DO FOR THEMSELVES

Children need to learn to take care of themselves—even if parents have nothing to do all day but take care of them. When children hang up their clothes or wash their feet, it does not seem like schoolwork. But this practice in self-reliance carries over to the classroom.

Let's start with some activities that help children learn to take better care of their bodies and their clothes.

### Body Beautiful ■ ages 4–9

- *Study Skills*
- *Recalling Details*
- *Charting Information*

For this activity, you need a marker, a pencil, and paper.

Talk with your child about personal cleanliness and why it's important. We're not talking "too clean." We're just talking clean, such as "not smelly." And, it can be pretty easy.

Talk about washing face and hands, combing hair, and brushing teeth. Include any other parts of the body that children tend to get dirty.

Together make a list of what needs to be done to be clean before going off to school. Post the list in the bathroom.

If you and your child like charts, post a simple one like the one below. Your child checks off this chart in much the same way that a pilot goes over a checklist before takeoff. Attach a marker to the chart so that it's easy to do the checking.

To provide incentive, especially at first, you may want to think of a small reward. It might be a new brand of toothpaste that your child picks out or a new toothbrush or a special brand of soap.

| Looking Good | Sun. | Mon. | Tues. | Wed. | Thurs. | Fri. | Sat. |
|---|---|---|---|---|---|---|---|
| I brushed my teeth. | | | | | | | |
| I washed my face. | | | | | | | |
| I washed my hands. | | | | | | | |
| I combed my hair. | | | | | | | |

Check the chart daily at first, then weekly. Pretty soon you won't need a chart. The idea is to make good grooming your child's habit.

## Clothes ■ ages 4–9

- *Reading/Writing*
- *Following Directions*
- *Building Good Work Habits*

Clothes may or may not make the man, but taking care of them helps make the all-important inner man or woman. When children are young, taking care of their own clothes may be among the few areas in their lives in which they can practice responsibility.

### Picking Them

For this activity, you need ordinary clothes. Pencil, paper, and tape for labels are optional.

With your youngster, put clothes together in places where they can be found. One way is to label the outside of dresser drawers.

Talk about appropriate clothes to wear in different weather. Turn this into a game. Pick a thick sweater and ask, "Do you wear this on hot or cold days?" Do the same for shorts, mittens, and so forth.

Before children go to bed at night, ask them to think about clothes to wear the next day. Let them lay out these clothes in advance. Ask your child to check to see that the clothes are clean and ready. This can save time and stress in the morning.

### Washing Them

Mom and Dad are not the only people at home who can wash clothes. This is a skill everyone can have, including young children. For this activity, you need some dirty clothes, soap, water, and perhaps a washing machine.

Pick up any detergent box. Reading it together with your child will immediately broaden your child's vocabulary with words like "formulated" and "cycle."

Whether you are washing an item by hand or in the machine, with your child move through the process step by step, preferably with one or just a few items, treating spots first, if necessary. Talk about separating colors, then talk about the temperature of the water, then the soap suds, then the machine instructions, then the rinsing, then the hanging up or the machine drying. Go through all the steps with your child watching and helping.

Now, with you close at hand, let your child take one dirty item all the way through, either by hand or by machine. What precautions need to be taken? How will you know it's worked?

---

**From Texas . . .**

"For the first time, I let my daughter do some ironing. She started with handkerchiefs. Each day she woke up earlier to ask for more clothes to iron. 'If you keep this up,' I said, 'you can graduate to shirts.' And she is really excited about it."

It may take time to graduate to the washing machine. Next to learning how to drive a car, learning how to use a washing machine and a lawn mower are the most responsibility-building tools in any home.

An iron is also a responsibility-teaching tool. Because we iron less with today's no-iron fabrics, I sometimes tend to overlook it. Show children how to iron safely. Lower the ironing board and give children the chance to show their stuff.

## Fixing Them

What I especially like about this sewing activity is that it not only teaches responsibility but also builds children's hand-eye coordination, an essential for learning to read and write. You need needle, thread, scissors, buttons, and children's clothes that need repairing.

With your child, pick an item that needs a button sewn on. Together select the necessary tools. Look for a needle with a large eye. Show your child how to thread it. Take time to illustrate how to do all this safely. Then show step by step how to sew on a button.

Now watch as your child replaces a button on some old clothes. Don't expect the job to be perfect, and resist doing it over. Children need practice to master this skill. Wearing a crooked button in this case is a mark of honor for both girls and boys.

With some colorful fabric scraps, you can help children move to making gifts and other items around home. For example, a bright patch on blue jeans is easy and fun. Place mats, book covers, and banners are other easy-to-do items. Personal hand-sewn gifts from children are especially appreciated, and they cost only a few pennies.

## A Special Place ▪ ages 4–9

- *Study Skills*
- *Creating/Writing for a Purpose*
- *Remembering Details*

Here's a responsibility builder for the early school years. It calls for setting up a special home-school box to help children keep track of their belongings.

Children generally come into the house and toss their school things every which way. In the morning, with everyone rushing off to jobs and to school, these things are hard to find.

### From Michigan . . .

"My daughter's box was made by her dad. She took delight in decorating and filling it. She is the youngest of four and always wants homework when she sees the others doing theirs after school. So I have been giving her 'assignments,' correcting them, and putting them in a folder in her box. What can I say? . . . We love it."

You can hear your child now: "I can't find them anywhere." ("Them" can be anything from mittens to pencils.) And hear yourself saying loudly, "Well, keep looking until you do."

You need a cardboard box big enough to hold supplies and some clothing. Add some magazine pictures, markers, glue, and scissors, and you're ready to make a Special Place.

Children decorate these boxes with pictures, words, artwork, and their own names in big, bold letters.

This box goes near the front door or in your child's room. When your child comes home, the box is the first stop for school items, hat, toys, glasses. It is the last stop on the way out the door in the morning. Finished homework and supplies needed for school are put in the box at night, ready for the next day.

As a reward for your child using the box, put in a note every few days, praising your child's sense of responsibility: "Hi! This is terrific. Love, Dad." "See you at six P.M. to go to the game. Love, Mom."

At the very least, children now know where their things ought to be. Moreover, the box cuts down on family nagging in the morning. If a little box can help do that, it's got to be worth trying.

P.S. Older youngsters, even parents, can use their very own boxes. I've got one near my front door for my glasses and car keys. It's invaluable on mornings when my head is in four places at once.

Now that we've covered some do-for-myself activities, we'll move to giving kids practice in doing for others.

## HELPING CHILDREN DO FOR THE FAMILY

As parents, we keep saying it—our children need to learn to be responsible. We also have to watch that we don't undermine our good intentions. Our urge is to protect, perhaps even to overprotect. At times we become responsible for our children, often to protect them from unpleasant consequences. We turn in their library books; we feed their pets and water their plants. Sometimes we even do their homework for them. But that doesn't work for very long, and it does not help children grow up.

Overall, responsibility means that we can "count on" our children and they can count on us. Here are some "count on each other" activities.

### Promises! Promises! ■ ages 4–9

- ■ *Thinking*
- ■ *Sharing Opinions*
- ■ *Evaluating Information*

When asked to do a task, children often make promises. They may not fully realize what keeping these promises involves. Their intentions are sincere. They want to please. Here's a way to get children talking about promises and consequences. All you need are thinking minds.

Talk about what happens when people don't do the things they are responsible for. *Examples:* Plants that don't get watered wilt. Animals (and children) that don't get fed whine. Garbage that isn't taken out smells.

Ask children to think about what would happen if parents decided they didn't want to shop or cook meals, if the bus driver stayed home, if the movie projectionist didn't show up for work. Should people do only tasks they like?

Discuss the effects on others when tasks are not done. Is it fair? Is it responsible? Is that why carrying out promises is so important?

## Taking Care of Things ■ any age

- *Reading*
- *Listening and Talking Together*

Children have been known to be careless about property—their own and others. Expensive items can find their way quickly to the junk heap. That's what can happen if parents don't find a way to help children be responsible for caring about what they are supposed to care for.

This activity can help. You need thinking minds, paper, and pencil. Talk with your child, preferably before buying a costly gift, about what is reasonable to expect in the way of care for this gift.

A pet is a good example, even if it doesn't cost money to start with. A pet needs daily care. How much is your child willing and able to do? Get these understandings ironed out in advance so that there will be fewer misunderstandings later. Write down what you have both decided on, and post this list in a prominent place.

Or you may be considering a home computer. These are fragile machines that need careful operators. Make sure that children know what is expected. Take them with you to the store. Read the operating manual together. Go over the steps one by one. Children need to know not only how to run the machine but how to care for it.

In every home there is some property that is "out of bounds." It might be medicines, Mom's make-up, china, CDs, or a treasure box in your child's room. Make a pact with your youngster. You will leave your child's treasures alone in return for the make-up and medicines being left alone. Designate these "untouchables" and keep to the bargain.

## Don't Worry: You Won't Be Late
■ any age

- *Study Skills*
- *Building Good Work Habits*

This activity helps teach children the importance of showing people that they can be depended on, rain or shine. We parents go to work even when we don't feel like it. We call our employers when we'll be out sick or when we'll be late. Children need to know this and need to copy our behavior.

This activity helps kids learn to wake up on time on their own. You'll need an alarm clock, paper bag, and a piece of paper for each family member.

Write "wake up" on one piece of paper and "wake *me* up" on the others. Put the papers into the bag. Everybody picks one piece. The person who picks the slip

> Talk about how people worry when those they are expecting are late. Children worry when employed parents are late coming home for dinner. Parents worry when children are late coming home after a movie. Talk about what to do to cut down on each other's worry. Is there anything that can be done to help us be prompt? This is an investment in other people's feelings.

marked "wake up" will do the job of waking up the others the next morning.

The people who pick the papers marked "wake *me* up" choose the wake-up time. It might have to be early—early enough for everyone to get to work or school on time.

The "wake-up" person sets the alarm clock for five minutes before the wake-up time. You'll find out the next day if the "wake-up" person was dependable. What happens if the "wake-up" person is late? Will someone be late to work or school?

Do your children wake themselves up regularly? If not, invest in an inexpensive alarm clock for each child right away.

## WHAT DO I DO? HELPING CHILDREN THINK RESPONSIBLY ABOUT CHOICES AND VALUES

There are daily dilemmas in life that virtually every child will face. What do I do when . . .

I see others cheating on a test?
I find money?
I know a friend has done something wrong?

These are tough questions. They test our children's ability to tell right from wrong and to do the right thing. And they test our parental ability to help children figure out how to handle these problems in such a way that children feel comfortable with their decisions.

Children need to know what parents think, but moreover, they need to know how to figure out where they themselves stand. This takes time, and it comes through discussion, the chance to open up and talk honestly with parents and close friends. It takes asking questions ourselves: What are the choices? What are my values? How do I want to be treated? What kind of person am I? What kind of person do I want to be?

This takes discussions around the dinner table and while driving in the car; it takes time, but it's worth it. It means talk and a lot of it, but it also means action. As parents, we don't have to be angels, but

> Most of us want to be good; we want to do the right thing; we want to feel good about ourselves. As children grow and define the kind of persons they are, they need encouragement and support in following their impulse to do the right thing. The people most responsible for providing this support are parents.

children need to see parents who are honest, who have respect for laws, who wear seat belts, who do not take drugs.

We can safely assume that our children will be exposed to more temptations, more crime, in their everyday lives than we were. Are they ready? Do your children know what to say when a stranger offers them a lift or some drugs? Do they know what to say when someone they know tries to get them into trouble? It pays to have doubts, it pays to worry about these very real fears.

But it's not enough to worry. You need frank and open discussions with your children. Express your concerns and let them hear their own fears come out into the open. Practice conversation and behavior about how to turn away from a stranger, about how to turn down a friend. Do some role-playing. Put yourselves into difficult situations. These worry savers can be lifesavers. (See the special section on safety in Chapter 14 for some specific activities.)

All the lectures in the world will do no good if children see that it's just "talk." It's hard, if not impossible, to hold children to certain rules when parents brag about breaking laws. It's hard also when parents seem too good to be true. Have we never been tempted to do anything wrong? It can help when we tell about a temptation and how we handled it.

I have my own story about shoplifting. It's my "Sen-Sen story," and it must have impressed my children, because whenever I start to tell it, they say, "Oh, not the Sen-Sen story again!"

I was eight years old, and I was in a drugstore, waiting to make a purchase. As I stood at the counter, I picked up a small packet of Sen-Sen (a tiny package like a sugar packet) and held it in my hand, reading the instructions. Sen-Sen, for those not as old as I, was one of the first breath fresheners on the market. Whether I needed a breath freshener in those days I am not sure, but after walking out of the store with the item I had bought and paid for, I looked down into my hand and found that I was still clutching the packet of Sen-Sen, which I had not paid for. What to do? I walked back to the drugstore, told the druggist what had happened, and paid for the Sen-Sen. I am not sure I ever used it, but I do know I feel virtuous about it to this very day.

Not all such stories have happy endings. Teachers are finding themselves caught in problems involving cheating. It's hard to know whether there is more cheating in school today. Possibly it's discussed more openly because cheating is seen as a reaction to stress, and we talk more about stress than before.

To be sure, cheating occurs in many more places than in school. But school is a place which in large measure determines students' future success in academics and

---

**From California . . .**

"This program helps me know that I am not alone. Other parents have problems, too, and they are just like mine."

## TEACHING TIPS: RESPONSIBILITY

### Sharing Our Experiences with Our Children

The environment—in the past, we never really had to think about our responsibility for it. We knew that litterbugs got fined, but that was all.

Our environment was just there, quietly doing its job, with a solid ozone layer and trees that kept growing and beaches where we could swim. No longer. Now, along with being responsible for ourselves, we actually have to be responsible for our environment.

Times have changed. One of the big differences is that we know a lot more than we used to. We know about dangers, about acid rain, about detergents that don't biodegrade and plastic cups that will live forever.

We need this information and we need to share it with our children—not to frighten them, but to build their awareness of what each of us can do to help. Check with your library and with environmental organizations directly to find out what you can do.

### Sparking the Conversation: What Can We Do?

Ask your children for their ideas on how they can help right around your home: for example, recycling newspapers, moving lamps (which give off heat) away from air conditioners (which work hard to give off cool), keeping the refrigerator door closed more than open, using the back of pieces of paper to get more mileage from every sheet.

Remember that children make excellent nags to keep parents responsible. For example, they might encourage car pools, remind you not to keep the car motor idling, and to start the barbecue with paper and sticks rather than lighter fluid.

Because of increased awareness in the classroom about the environment, chances are that your children will know more than you do.

### Moving to the Bigger Questions

Because your children may have a head start in their knowledge about the environment, let them teach you and lead you in answering questions like these:

- Do people get sick from pollution? What kinds of illnesses do they get?
- Should we do anything when we see a car or bus or a factory spewing pollution?
- When businesses move to recyclable packaging, should we let them know we approve? Should we write them a letter?
- How can we make more people aware of their responsibility in taking care of their environment?

in personal values. That's why "looking the other way" is a real disservice to children. How to handle cheating and cheaters continues to be a problem. To report them or not to report them, to punish them or to counsel them—these are continuing dilemmas for students and teachers. The bottom line is that adults must be responsible so that children can be responsible.

## I LOVE YOU WHEN YOU BEHAVE YOURSELVES

Responsibility is really a two-way street between parent and child. MegaSkills are not just for children; they're for parents, too. I remember a message from my own children that reminded me of my own responsibility, which I was not meeting.

I have this tattered and faded sheet of yellow paper upon which a six-year-old's wobbly print calls out firmly: I LOVE YOU WHEN YOU BEHAVE YOURSELVES!

That note was written by our daughter while an argument raged between her parents in the next room. What that argument was about I cannot recall. What I have to remember, thanks to that note, is that we were behaving irresponsibly.

The note was a "responsibility reminder." It came from a child, so it probably had greater impact than most parental reminders. I'd like to say that this sweet note prevented all future acts of irresponsibility. It didn't. But I'm sure it helped. It's good to let our children know that we parents need MegaSkills reminders, too.

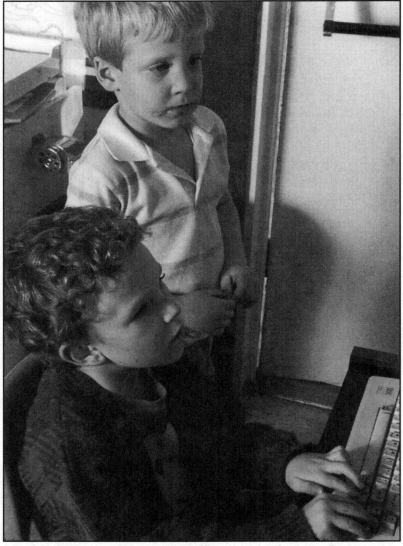
*Debra S. McKay, courtesy of the Association for Supervision and Curriculum Development*

## CHAPTER 9

# MegaSkill Five: Initiative
Moving into Action

## THE NEVER-ENDING REPORT CARD

| The Grades We Get in School | The Grades We Get on the Job |
|---|---|
| Stan keeps coming up with new ideas that the class really likes. | We depend on Mr. Johnson for his creative thinking. He moves the whole office along. |
| He has a good attitude toward teachers and fellow students. | His attitude toward work is positive and productive. |

When you hear yourself thinking or saying to your child,

"What a good idea!"
"You're our spark plug,"
"You're pulling us along,"
"You're always thinking of something new,"

you are hearing yourself praise your child's initiative.

This chapter is about generating and harnessing initiative. It's about energy, vitality, interest. It's about the organization it takes to get started and keep going.

Initiative starts with a good idea, but the idea is not enough. You have to do something to make things happen. Even after you hit a home run, you still have to run around the bases.

Initiative is grounded in first steps and follow-through. Activities in this chapter give children opportunities to build interest and gain practice in taking the initiative to put good ideas into action.

Initiative is really at the heart of science. It gets us asking questions and looking for answers. It has us wondering, guessing, seeking clues, experimenting, figuring out how things work or don't.

The activities in this chapter take us into a science lab, but in this case it's our kitchen, our basement, our back yard. We examine what happens when macaroni goes into boiling water or when we put water into the freezer or when plants don't get sunlight. We help our children get comfortable with guessing, or "hypothesizing," and with science concepts that they otherwise encounter only in textbooks.

These activities get children thinking about cause and effect. They observe changes when the water boils. They get a sense of system by looking at the plumbing in our homes, of organization by sorting and classifying objects. And all of this you and your child do together in daily life at home.

These concepts are at the heart of science. When we help give our children the freedom, the permission, the encouragement, the time, and the environment in which to explore, to question, to ponder, to be amazed and, yes, even puzzled, we are laying the base for a continuing interest in science. Whether or not our children grow up to be Einsteins, they need to be people who say, "I wonder how that works."

## I'LL TRY IT!

You don't have to go outside your home to give your child a world of experiences that build interests and lead to school achievement. These experiences give children ideas on which future interests are built.

I remember how I felt when I tried science in the kitchen with my young children. Let me tell you, they were not the only ones learning. We watched water come to a boil. We timed how long it took to make macaroni soft. We defrosted ice cubes in the sun and in shade. We put wooden and metal spoons into hot water and then touched them, sometimes with a burning surprise. And we talked about what we were learning.

The activities that follow are especially appreciated by younger elementary graders, but older children who have not had these will enjoy them, too. My own kids, now grown, still remember our special "science times" in the kitchen and in the yard. *One warning:* My kids say I lectured too much about what they were

Children who have visited their parents' workplace or have watched the sun rise or have taken a bus to the other end of town are children who, when thinking about taking a new or first step, have a better chance of hearing a soft inner voice say, "It's OK, you know about that," or "It's like what you did last week," or "It's not so different from what you did before. You can handle it!"

learning. So try to avoid my mistake and enjoy these moments together.

Employed parents, fathers especially, may think that to make up for lost time with the kids, they need to sacrifice, to do activities like going to museums or the zoo or a show. Not so. There really is great educational value in activities such as going with children to the bank and to the grocery store . . . or even down to the basement.

## Machines: Look and Listen
■ ages 4–9

■ *Science*
■ *Making Hypotheses and Predictions*

Use the house itself. Go down to the basement and take a look at the furnace. How does it work? What are all those pipes for? Don't forget those plumbing pipes. It really is a shame that some are not exposed so that children can see the activity beneath the walls.

Kitchens make noises. Listen and name them—the refrigerator's hum, the stove's purr, the fan's whoosh.

Look at a bicycle. What's the importance of the wheel? Peek beneath the hood of the family car. Can you name the parts?

Take a good look at all the appliances at home. You might want to tackle the bigger question of where all this electricity comes from in the first place. When traveling past a power plant or a dam, you might mention that little old toaster at home.

## Machines: Please Touch
■ ages 4–9

■ *Science*
■ *Researching and Evaluating Information*

Oh, the joy of taking things apart and maybe even putting them together again. Here are some activities in which you can put parts together wrong and still enjoy them. You need a working flashlight with batteries, a small machine that is broken and dispensable, and some tools.

How do flashlights work? Find out what happens when one battery is taken away or put in upside down. The beauty of flashlights is that they can be made to work so easily.

If you have a small, broken machine, such as a clock or pencil sharpener, and you don't care whether it works again, try

this wonderful activity: Put the machine and some useful tools, such as a screwdriver, on a table. Allow your child to take the object apart. Stand by in case you're needed, but do let your child try to put it back together without your help.

## Water, Water Everywhere
■ ages 4–9

■ *Science*
■ *Distinguishing Between Fact and Opinion*

Water is great for stimulating scientific thinking. For these activities, you need water, ice trays, salt, an egg, and some dishes.

Put water into an ice tray and set it in the freezer. How long does it take to freeze? Try this with different levels of water in different sections of the tray.

Put a few ice cubes on the table. How long do they take to melt? Why are they melting? Put them in different places around the room. Do they melt faster in some places than in others?

**Salty and Fresh Water:** Make some salt water by adding a couple of teaspoons of salt to two cups of water. Fill an ice tray with this water. Fill another tray, but for this one use tap water only. Put them in the freezer and check them after a few hours. What do you see? Is the one with ordinary tap water frozen? Is the salty one jellylike?

Float an egg in both salt and fresh water. Which water holds the egg higher? Salt water is more buoyant. From that you might go on to discuss salt in the Dead Sea and how easy it is for people to float there.

**Evaporation:** Put some water in an open dish in a sunny place. Let your child make a mark to show the water level. Use another dish with an equal amount of water, and put this one in the shade. Which one dries first? Watch what happens, and talk about what you see.

## Hot and Cold ■ ages 4–9

■ *Science*
■ *Practicing Scientific Methods*

Stand by as your children try this activity. You need water, macaroni (or spaghetti), and two pots. Put some water in one of the pots and bring it to a boil on the stove. In the other pot, put a larger or smaller amount of water. Try to use a similar degree of heat and the same size burner. Watch to see how much faster or slower it takes different amounts of water to boil.

Put macaroni in boiling water on the stove. What happens? Ask children to carefully check how much time it takes for the water to boil, and watch the boiling process. Plunge in the macaroni and watch what happens next. Then you can eat the experiment.

To check on temperature around you, use a house-and-garden thermometer. What happens when the thermometer is in the refrigerator? In the freezer? Atop the radiator? In the sun?

## Light and Shadow ■ ages 4–9

■ *Science*
■ *Conducting Experiments*
■ *Observing and Discussing*

For these activities, you need a light, objects of different shapes, a mirror, a glass of water, and a spoon.

When are shadows longer and shorter outdoors during the day? On a sunny day, go outside at different times and stand in the same place. Check to see shadows grow longer and shorter.

Use a strong light bulb indoors. Try some shadow play on a dark background. Try making different shadows with squares, circles, and other shapes. What happens when children jump, skip, wave hands, wiggle feet?

Use a mirror to catch light from the sun. Then move the mirror, throwing the light in different places around the room.

To illustrate how light passes through air and water at different rates, try this experiment. Put a teaspoon in a glass of water that is two-thirds full. Looking at it sideways, children see the "disconnected" parts of the spoon.

> In a number of these activities, you are raising questions to which you might not know the answers. You and your children can go to the library to look up the answers later. The important part is for children to be interested enough to want to know and try more.

## A Can and a Straw ■ ages 4–9

■ *Science*
■ *Practicing Experiments*

You need a can of juice, a can opener, a plunger, water, and straws.

Open a can of juice on one side only. Try pouring. Nothing comes out. Why not? Make another opening. Again try to pour. What happens and why?

Attach a plunger to a wall. It sticks. What holds it there? When will it fall off?

Using straws, suck up water. What holds the water in so that the straws can be twirled about without losing the water?

## Plants and How They Grow ■ ages 4–9

■ *Science*
■ *Evaluating Evidence*

Taking care of plants is a visible cause-and-effect experience. What do plants need? How do they change when they don't get what they need? For these activities you need plants and aluminum foil.

Put two similar, healthy plants side by side. Let your child water one plant but ignore the other for a week or two. What happens?

Using aluminum foil, cover the leaves on one side of a sun-loving plant. Keep this covering on for a week. What do the leaves look like when you take off the foil?

This adventure of growing things can be enjoyed in a window box or on vast acre-age. Green beans will almost always come through, and carrot tops like nothing better than to show off with green growth.

## LET'S GET ORGANIZED

There are mornings when you wake up and you just know it's a day to get organized. Children get those feelings, too. That initiative needs to be captured before it evaporates.

Not only do the following activities for very young children teach organizing skills, but they also get needed jobs done at the same time. Take classifying and categorizing, for example. This next activity will eliminate that mess you've been avoiding for months.

## Nuts and Bolts, Pins and Needles ■ ages 4–6

■ *Reading*
■ *Classifying Objects*
■ *Using Descriptive Words*

For this activity, you need a toolbox, jewelry box, clothes drawer, sewing box, or bookcase.

■ With the toolbox, ask the children to sort nails according to length.
■ With the jewelry box, children can separate necklaces, rings, and earrings.
■ With their dressers, children sort their clothes (otherwise known as cleaning out drawers!).
■ With sewing boxes, children separate thread, needles, pins, etc.

---

**From South Carolina . . .**

"We went through our cabinets together and my daughter helped me rearrange various items. We even got rid of things that weren't needed. She enjoyed this activity because it made her feel important in the kitchen."

---

■ With the bookcase, books can be sorted in many ways: by size or color or in more abstract ways—books children like or dislike, funny books or sad books.

It may not be immediately apparent, but classifying is a key skill in the three R's. Students need to be able to identify things and ideas that go together.

### Everything Fits ■ ages 7–12

- ■ *Mathematics*
- ■ *Estimating*
- ■ *Using Spatial Abilities*

This activity gives somewhat older children practice in putting things in order. Use the kitchen cupboard or refrigerator, the family linen closet, or a closet in your child's room.

First talk about a good way to organize the shelf or closet. In the kitchen it might be by putting containers of the same size together or by putting certain foods together. In the bedroom, it might include sorting socks and making sure they are in pairs. In the closet, all shirts might go together, with pants at the other end.

Let your child organize at least one shelf in the order you have both decided upon. The system may not last, but for at least a day or two the results of this activity provide solid satisfaction.

### IT TAKES PLANNING!

Any parent who has suffered through setting up an elaborate easel for a child who says, "I want to paint," and then hears, "I don't want to paint," a minute after the easel has been put up, will want to be able to say as soon as possible to their dear, dear child, "Honey, you know how—do it yourself. OK?"

The sooner children get used to taking initiative, the sooner they will be putting up the easels for themselves.

When my children were very young, if I announced that we were going on a trip, the kids would be at the door, and even if it was midwinter and they didn't have their coats on, or if we were going to spend a week away, they would delightedly announce, without an ounce of preparation, "We're ready!"

Of course, they were ready; they didn't have to do anything. But it wasn't long before they did. That meant packing their own bags and doing anything else that was needed to get ready, including ironing!

## Gather and Go ■ ages 7–9

- *Thinking*
- *Generating Ideas*
- *Gathering Information*

Teach children how to collect and organize materials. Start a project, big or little: a puppet stage, a dog house, a party, baking cookies. Talk with children about what they will need. (Young children will need your advice.)

List what you have to purchase and what is already at home. Then, with your child, collect the essentials before you start the project.

For another version of this activity, have children collect information about something they want to do or learn more about, a skill or hobby: how to bake a cake, how to start a rock collection, how to tune a guitar. It's good to *know* before you *do*.

## KNOWING WHAT'S WHEN

A calendar in every household is an essential piece of equipment. Yet all by itself, an ordinary household calendar cannot help children become organized.

The extra-ordinary calendar motivates everyone in the house to use it, as a reminder and as a way to be in touch with other family members.

## When Do We Have to Do What? The Family Calendar ■ any age

- *Thinking*
- *Organizing and Presenting Information*

Children seem to be forever forgetting things, especially dates and responsibilities. This activity provides a memory jogger. You need a calendar, markers, or crayons.

Get a plain calendar with large squares for each day. Start any time. Talk about the days, weeks, and months spread out before you.

Start filling in the squares with special days, such as birthdays and upcoming events. Include medical appointments and team practices.

Let your child decorate the calendar. Find ways to personalize it, with special colors for each family member, for example, or with drawings or pictures for special days. Use the calendar for generating children's suggestions; for example, list special foods children want or ideas for places to go on family outings.

Use this calendar to write special messages to each other. Of course, there will always be: "Mom, I need lunch money" or "I really do need those new jeans." But remember, praise is a miracle worker. Here are messages everyone likes to get: "Joe, I like your smile." "Mom, thanks for helping me with my homework." "Dad, you make terrific spaghetti." "Sally, you ride your bike well."

## Striking Back at Sickness
■ all ages

- *Thinking*
- *Developing Categories*
- *Organizing in Logical Order*

Even when children are home sick and in bed, their initiative can make the day brighter and help them feel better. Sure, there are days when nothing but closed shades, long naps, and lots of TV will do. But there are other days in the recuperating period when new skills and interests can be found and developed.

Children will be interested in different kinds of activities, depending on their age. Readers will enjoy the daily newspaper, lots of magazines, and books from the library. Keep in mind that everyone, young or old, enjoys being read to.

Stock a young child's bedstand with provisions for arts and crafts—crayons, paper, scissors. And don't forget puzzles, old greeting cards for collages, and games.

Preschoolers can dictate stories to their parents or older brothers or sisters and then illustrate their own books. They can also dictate letters to grandparents.

Elementary graders enjoy pasting up family photo albums, bringing together the snapshots lying about in an old shoe box. Boys and girls can be taught to embroider, knit, or sew doll clothes. And there's always string and card tricks and paper folding, including making paper airplanes.

Equip your child's bedroom window with a bird feeder, thermometer, and even a weather vane, if possible. While in bed, children can use pencil and paper to keep records of the number and kinds of birds that come and how the temperature and wind change during the day.

Use a notebook with the hours of the day listed on the left-hand side of the page. Attach a pencil to this pad so it doesn't get misplaced when the covers are jostled. Every hour by the bedroom clock, your children can record the temperature, the direction of the wind, and the number and colors, if not the kinds, of birds they have seen. You might want to provide a bird watchers' guidebook.

Set up a bulletin board close to the bed, and a radio, too. Children can post interesting articles, the radio log, or pictures clipped from the newspaper.

Once out of bed, youngsters can work on their cooking, practice learning to type, grow seeds in jars. Activity possibilities are almost endless. Yes, TV is nice when children are sick, but it's the wise parent who seizes on these other learning activities for passing the time.

School should not be forgotten, especially if your child is out three or more days. Contact the teacher to make arrangements for keeping up with the class.

If children are being cared for at home by someone other than you, be sure this person knows about the activities you've planned with your child.

## YOU'RE IN MY SPACE!

All those magazine-pretty houses with separate quarters, even whole wings, for children are nice. But for most families, living in apartments or small houses, even a playroom is a dream, and life among all those things children accumulate and argue over is a nightmare.

We can spend days sidestepping the stuff on the floor and screaming at the kids while they scream at each other. Or we can take the initiative to make living together a happier experience.

First ask children what they think ought to be done to clear up the mess. *A warning:* They may be quite content with their mess, so parents need to be prepared to point to the real problems experienced by the rest of the family.

Ask your children which of these ideas they'd like to try first.

■ **Provide some kind of work space, no matter how small, for each child.** This can vary from a lapboard that children use while they sit on the bed to a piece of furniture to a drop-leaf shelf that is attached to the wall, if apartment regulations allow.

Try the idea of a small piece of colorful rug for a young child's work area on the floor. This helps cut down on the tendency for children to covet the same work space, even in big rooms.

To make communal work space for young children doing artwork, put a heavy plastic tablecloth over the dining room table and an old shower curtain or newspaper beneath.

■ **Give children a place to put their possessions.** This should be an "untouchable" place. No one is to disturb these things. The children's end of this bargain is that they have to put the things away neatly. This place could be a box or drawer that fits under a bed, or a shelf above it.

■ **Label toys with the child's name when these cherished items are brought into the house.** This way there need be no argument over who owns what.

■ **Provide pegs so that children can hang up their own clothes.** Also, make sure that shelves are reachable so that

## TEACHING TIPS: INITIATIVE

### Sharing Our Experiences with Our Children

When I think about initiative, I think about our ancestors, who traveled across oceans with little or no possessions, who boarded wagons and later trains to make lives for themselves in new lands.

Help your children to connect with their own past. Tell about parents, grandparents —grandparents who made those voyages, who took that kind of initiative. Talk about today's new immigrants who continue to come to America to make a better life for themselves and their children.

No matter what generation of Americans we are, the immigrant spirit is part of our nature. We are people of strong ideas and strong action. This desire to make things happen burns within us and, when channeled and focused, it's a powerful force in education.

### Sparking the Conversation: Let's Have a Picnic

Start with some examples of initiative. They need not be big endeavors. Small, everyday ideas will do. For example, let's say it's a weekend day, and you ask, "What will we do? Who's got an idea?" Your child pipes up, "Let's have a picnic."

What happens to this or to other ideas that come up at home? It helps to take your children's ideas seriously. Children know they get serious consideration when the family decides together, Yes, we can do it because . . . or No, we can't because . . . And as many times as it's reasonable to follow through on a child's idea, so much the better. But remember, when the idea moves into action, the child needs a role to play. If it's the picnic, there's food to be bought, made, and packed, perhaps even friends to invite. Kids need this practice in order to show their initiative.

### Moving to the Bigger Questions

Ideas are the wellspring of initiative. They're fun to talk about:

- Can taking initiative too fast get you into trouble? If so, what kind?
- Can waiting too long to take action get you into trouble? If so, what kind?
- Do you get lots of ideas, almost all spilling out at once, or do you wait for the one perfect idea to come along?

There's a wise saying: "The perfect is the enemy of good." So try to recognize the good when you've got it.

children are able to put away toys when they're finished with them.

■ **Use what's in the apartment.** Put a piece of wood on top of a radiator (except in winter), and you have a shelf. Place a large sheet of wood or Masonite over a bathtub, and you have a good-size work area. And use wall space. Hang pegboards to hold carpentry tools and toys.

Organizing our houses in these ways enables us and our children to be ready, to be prepared to take advantage of good ideas when they strike.

## Junk Day ■ any age

- ■ *Thinking*
- ■ *Making Reasoned Decisions*

Some things that look like junk in a child's room are really "treasures." But other stuff is really junk, and kids think so, too. Given some incentive, children will be ready to give it up. This activity rewards tidiness and

---

**From Michigan . . .**

"It was such a busy weekend, we never even got out for a walk. So my son and his friend made a game of picking up the bedroom. They counted objects. They put them away in groups. It's a great way to get a bedroom full of toys cleaned up."

---

provides some math practice, too. You need large grocery bags and a room with junk in it—often a child's bedroom. A bathroom scale is also useful.

Give your child paper bags and these instructions: "Today is junk day. Go through your closet/drawers/bedroom and take out all the junk or give-aways that you want to get rid of. I pay for junk!"

When your child presents the bags, look through them together to determine if everything in the bag is really ready to leave home. Take the real junk and give-aways to the bathroom scale and weigh each bag.

Offer your child so much per pound. This can be determined by both of you. *Example:* Fifteen cents per pound for six pounds of junk equals ninety cents. Let children figure out what's owed them, and then have them deliver junk to the trash can and give-aways to a special box.

We all know that one person's trash is another's treasure. Getting treasures organized is a way to enjoy them more.

## Offering Without Being Asked
■ ages 7–12

- ■ *Thinking*
- ■ *Generating Ideas*
- ■ *Listening and Speaking Together*

This activity provides practice in offering to help without being asked. All you need are jobs to be done around the house.

Ask children to choose one job that

they're often asked to do. Examples might be taking out the garbage, cleaning their room, washing clothes. Suggest that for two days they do this task before someone asks them to do it. Talk about it. Did they get the task done before someone reminded them? Did it make them feel good? Did they offer to help others? How did they feel?

Take a poll of all family members. Ask which household jobs they like and dislike the most. To show your get-up-and-go and generosity of spirit, try one person's most disliked task for one day. Who knows — one person's dislike may be another's like.

## ORGANIZED BUT FLEXIBLE, TOO

There can be a danger in being too organized. I have been in houses so neat, so clean, that I was afraid to put my shoes on the carpet. I have been in too neat, almost sterile classrooms.

We need room in our lives for dirt, for accidents, for changes, for silly mistakes, for missed appointments, and for children who get sick at the last minute.

When I complain to one friend, a very wise woman, about an unpleasantness in my day that I had not planned for or even thought about, she says, "Gosh, that's an interesting challenge." I try to remember those words, even as I gnash my teeth, and somehow it helps.

*Susan M. Vandertie, courtesy of the Association for Supervision and Curriculum Development*

## CHAPTER 10

# MegaSkill Six: Perseverance

## Completing What You Start

## THE NEVER-ENDING REPORT CARD

### The Grades We Get in School

Alan has patience. He wants to keep at a task until it's done.

He is developing a strong ability to concentrate.

### The Grades We Get on the Job

Mr. Johnson is a man who finishes what he starts. In our business, we call him "the closer."

He doesn't turn out the office lights until the work is done.

When you say these words, you know you are trying to teach perseverance:

"First you have to try, then you have to persist."

"If one way is blocked, try another. Go around, go beneath, go over."

"It's not enough to start—you have to finish."

"Even when you feel like quitting, don't."

"Keep at it; you'll get it."

That's what this chapter is about—how to help children get into the habit of following through and finishing.

Perseverance is what some say separates the men from the boys and the women from the girls. It's the steps that follow initial actions.

It almost always takes *more* than:

just sending out résumés to land a job.

just opening the door to have a successful business.

just winning one presidential primary to become president.

Perseverance is the *more*—it's the difference between those who try and those who succeed.

Some people may experience overnight success, but most of them, when the story is revealed, admit that it took a long time and a lot of practice to achieve that overnight success.

We can help our children become perseverers. But this task can be more of a challenge today. Children see everything happen so quickly, or so it seems. I had to wait hours for Jell-O to gel. Even ice cubes freeze faster today.

There will always be others who are more talented than we are, who are better looking, who have more education. Even with these benefits, they still need perseverance in order to accomplish and to create.

> What is worrisome is that we seem to accept the fact that our children have short attention spans. TV shows made for children—even educational ones—are actually built on that premise. No segment is to be longer than a certain number of minutes or seconds. Instead, we should emphasize building our children's level and length of attention and their ability to concentrate over a period of time.

I'm generally fond of the faster pace of life today, glad for instant Jell-O and sometimes even for instant mashed potatoes.

But my own experience has shown that of necessity some goals take longer to accomplish, and that to get there we have to keep working at them. I'm not sure that our children have as many patience-building experiences as they need to prepare them for those long-range goals.

Words such as these encouraging comments do help, and children need them:

"I know you'll make it."
"You're doing a great job."
"You signed up for those lessons, and you need to see them through."
"It will get better. You'll get the hang of it."

It often, however, takes more. Beyond words, there are experiences that by their very nature teach perseverance. They can't be done in a rush because they demand a level of detail and a passage of time. I've chosen the following activities because

even as they teach perseverance, they also get some very important jobs done around home.

## ASSEMBLING LOOSE ENDS

Some of the hardest jobs, the ones that never seem to get done, the ones we avoid doing for as long as possible, involve keeping track of things and putting the pieces together. Here are some activities to make these seemingly impossible jobs a little bit easier to handle.

### Our Very Own Photo Gallery
■ any age

- *Reading/Writing*
- *Comparing and Sequencing Information*

This activity reinforces family feelings and keeps track of precious moments that are too important to lose. You need a notebook or photo album, family photos, and pen and paper for writing captions beneath the pictures.

On a large tabletop, distribute pictures so that they can be talked about individually. Figure out a way to organize the photos. Most of the time, it's done in chronological order: What happened first? Second?

Attach the pictures to the album pages, along with captions (explanations) that children can write. *Example:* "I am in my first bathing suit." Young children can dictate these lines. Not only does it take time to do this activity, but the activity itself illustrates the passage of time.

You might want to make up a yearly collage of family photos and put it in a frame. One wall can be the family gallery. As the years go by, these memories become even more precious.

## Family Directory ▪ ages 4–9

- ▪ *Reading/Writing*
- ▪ *Classifying Information*
- ▪ *Using Descriptive Words*

This activity combines writing and alphabetizing practice for children in a task that cries out to be done—assembling important family telephone numbers. You need a store-bought or homemade telephone book for the phone list, and pencil or pen.

Find all the important telephone numbers that would be useful to have in one place. Include numbers of the school, the car repair garage, the pizza parlor, along with the usual emergency numbers. (See "Calling for Help" in Chapter 5.) Ask your child to think of names of family members. Remember aunts, uncles, cousins, and friends. Use scrap paper at first to list these names.

Names are easier to alphabetize when all names beginning with the same letter are listed together. Put the last name first. Help your child alphabetize this list. Double-check this sheet. Then enter the names and numbers in the family telephone book.

This home directory can be decorated with pictures children have made, or they can cut out from magazines pictures that show families doing things together. Put the directory in a handy place, and encourage family members to add new numbers as needed.

## Home Health Records ▪ any age

- ▪ *Study Skills*
- ▪ *Researching and Charting Information*

In most homes, family health records are every which place, and it's hard to remember who got what shot when. This activity helps make sure the information gets collected in an ongoing way. To be very honest, this activity is probably the least liked one in the book. But it's so essential that even though you may not like it, I urge you to work with the children to do it.

You need the family's health information records. These can include summaries of clinic visits, immunization dates, and physical, dental, and eye reports. You also need a notebook or folder for each family member.

Find your youngster's health and immunization records. If you have no records, call your doctor to have them sent to you. Together make a record of childhood diseases and immunizations for each child. There's a sample chart on page 97.

Talk with children about changes in their weight and height as they grow older. This helps them understand the pattern of growth. Talk about the various childhood diseases they've had, and how each disease made them look or feel. You might even

| Immunization Record: Johnny | Date Received |
|---|---|
| Diphtheria-Pertussis (Whooping Cough) _____ | |
| Tetanus (DPT) Vaccine _____ | |
| Oral Polio Vaccine _____ | |
| Measles Vaccine _____ | |
| Rubella Vaccine (German Measles) _____ | |
| Mumps Vaccine _____ | |
| DPT Boosters (1) _____ (2) _____ (3) _____ | |
| Oral Polio Boosters (1) _____ (2) _____ (3) _____ | |
| Other _____ | |

have a snapshot of Sally when she had the mumps.

weight, learning a new skill, and preserving their health.

## LEARNING TO WORK AND WAIT

Time is a big element in perseverance. Children can practice getting beyond the need for immediate gratification, showing that they are willing to work and wait for results.

Among activities that call upon children to wait are growing plants, watching their

## Our Special Garden ■ ages 4–9

■ *Science*
■ *Following Directions*
■ *Comparing and Evaluating Evidence*

Everyone enjoys watching seeds sprout and come up through the earth. When they don't, we can start again. The important point is that this activity helps children get practice in finishing a project they start. You need two or three packets of seeds, small pots or milk cartons cut down, a ruler, and, depending on the season and your household space, a sunny windowsill or outdoor garden.

Buy seeds or use seeds you have saved. Empty a few on the table beside each packet. Ask your child to look at the seeds and examine their size and color. Feel how

### From Tennessee . . .

"We did this activity in steps. First we got a cup and put holes in the bottom. Then we put in the dirt. We already have a bean that's fifteen inches high. The kids have had so much fun watching their plant grow a little more every day."

hard they are. Talk about the differences. Ask children to fill each pot with about two inches of soil. Plant a few seeds in each. Place the pots on a sunny windowsill. Together read the directions on the seed packet. Talk about what you have to do to be sure the seeds grow.

Water the seeds as the directions say. Then, day by day, watch for the seeds to begin to sprout. Seeds grow slowly. It will take about ten days to see them.

Plants have a way of saying, "We love you and we care." Share one or more of these homegrown plants with a sick friend, a neighbor, or an older person in a nursing home.

## KEEPING HEALTHY: AN EVERYDAY JOB

Getting and staying healthy is an ongoing job that takes daily perseverance. At the same time that so many Americans are on the health kick, others are ruining their health with addictions that cripple the body and the mind. The following activities help promote the real pleasure of good health.

Even kids know it's no fun to be sick.

### Good and Good for You ■ ages 4–9

- *Science*
- *Weighing Evidence*
- *Setting Up Categories and an Action Plan*

This activity helps young children get into the habit of eating healthy rather than junk foods. They learn that good food need not be boring. You need pencil, paper, a bathroom scale, and nutritious snack foods.

Talk about the reasons to eat right— good looks, more energy. But do more than talk. Actually try out some new, better, different snack foods at home.

Nutritious snack foods include carrot sticks and raisins, bananas rolled in chopped peanuts, celery stuffed with peanut butter, tomato or cucumber slices topped with cheese, raw vegetables with cheese dip, and raisin and nut mixes.

Check family weights. Who's the heaviest? The lightest? Try recording weight changes in a week's time. This is good math practice, too.

Ask your child to think of good, interesting food combinations to try. Add these to the grocery list. Set aside part of a refrigerator shelf for children to use for these special snack foods. In this way children can make their own healthy snacks.

### Exercise Plan ■ any age

- *Thinking*
- *Researching Information*
- *Organizing a Plan*

Children spend a great deal of time sitting, and it's bad for their health. It takes some effort to plan and carry out a family exercise program. This activity can help. All you need are thinking minds. Willing bodies come later.

Together talk about what would be a realistic exercise plan for the family. Think

> **From Virginia . . .**
>
> "For the past month, I have been dieting with the help of my doctor. I intended to start an exercise program on my own, and this activity gave me the push I had needed. It also gave me the chance to explain my need to diet and exercise to my child."

about these questions: Do we prefer to exercise alone or with other people? Do we prefer to exercise indoors or outdoors? How much time can we spend on exercise daily?

List one or two exercises each person can do regularly. *Example:* Jog fifteen minutes daily in front of the TV set. Take the stairs at the office instead of the elevator.

Think of what you do that may hurt your health: Smoking? Drinking? Not eating fresh fruits and vegetables? Can you name one thing you will try to start doing? Make up a plan for a weeklong, practical exercise routine. Figure out a reward if you stick to the plan. Then plan for the next week, and the next. Children will be inspired by your perseverance.

## False Friends: Alcohol and Tobacco ▪ ages 10–12

- ▪ *Thinking*
- ▪ *Understanding Consequences of Decisions*

Youngsters sometimes give in to pressure from friends to smoke or drink or take drugs. These are dangerous to their health and prevent them from using their minds well and excelling in sports. Being informed and aware of the negative effects of alcohol and tobacco can make it easier to resist these temptations. This activity helps youngsters face up to the problems of drinking and smoking. You need newspapers, scissors, and good conversation.

Together talk about as many reasons as you can think of why people drink and smoke—boredom and curiosity, for instance. How can we avoid these traps? It's not easy. Getting involved in sports or club activities can help.

Be sure your children know what you think. Remember, they see what you do. It's harder to make a case for not smoking when parents are heavy smokers. What we ask our children to do is what we must be willing to do. That involves sacrifice. But it's worth it.

Often there are articles in the paper about rising sports stars who get hurt not on the sports field but with drugs in their homes. Over a period of a week, cut out newspaper articles telling about these athletes or about accidents or fires caused by drinking or smoking. Talk about these. Could they have been avoided? Does your family know of an actual case of someone who was hurt because of alcohol, drugs, or tobacco?

Look for ads that show glamorous people drinking and smoking. Is what they say true? What don't you and your youngsters agree with? Try to listen more than talk. Try to create a climate where your youngsters' views can be expressed and discussed.

## Practice Makes Almost Perfect
■ any age

- ■ *Communication*
- ■ *Building Discussion Skills*

This activity helps children understand that learning something new and difficult takes practice and time. You need thinking minds.

Talk together about activities that you each do in free time: swimming, sewing, bike riding, reading novels. Try to remember when you learned to do these and how long it took to learn. Did you make mistakes? Do you still make mistakes?

Each of us has a lot to learn and a lot to teach. Choose something that you each do well. Think about teaching this to a friend or to a member of the family. Teach one thing at a time. If it is baseball, it might be how to hit the ball. If it is sewing, it might be how to thread a needle.

When children hang up their clothes or put away the dishes and keep doing it night after night—it does not seem like schoolwork. But it is, in a most fundamental way.

Making a bed regularly or taking the dog for walks conscientiously has a lot to do with success in school. School achievement depends on a child's ability to see a job through to completion. Taught this early, children will continue to want to complete a job and will get pleasure from doing it.

Is it easier to do an incomplete job than a complete one? I am not sure. When I see students who have to think of all kinds of excuses for why their papers are late, I see them squirming and feeling uncomfortable. Think of the effort they're putting into coming up with the excuses. I wonder if they wouldn't find it faster just to do the complete job.

Increase the difficulty of what is taught each time. Try to offer helpful, not harmful, criticism. Helpful tells what to do *without* tearing down the learner. Avoid put-downs: the goal is to build up.

Make some realistic choices about what new skills to tackle and about how to teach them. A teenager, for example, might want to learn how to drive a car but may need a teacher or a car to practice on. Ask friends or family members to help, if necessary. This builds team spirit into the effort and passes along experience and skills from generation to generation.

## WHAT'S SO EASY ABOUT INCOMPLETES?

Students can get into the habit of taking an incomplete and of not finishing what they start, but it's not necessarily the easier way out.

I am not convinced that we always have to finish what we start, but we have to learn to finish many things. A lot depends on the

## TEACHING TIPS: PERSEVERANCE

### Sharing Our Experiences with Our Children

Who among us hasn't had daydreams that go something like this . . . ?

You're playing the piano on a concert stage. All eyes are upon you, admiring you. Guess what you forgot to do? You got it—*practice.*

You're standing at a podium, before a crowd of thousands, about to make the most important speech of the decade. Guess what you forgot to do? You got it—*write it.*

So share these dreams with your children. The dreams are wonderful and your children will probably be surprised that you *(you?)* dream them. But that's all they are, dreams, until and unless you have the perseverance to try to make them come true.

### Sparking the Conversation: Sharing Our Daydreams

Focus on a "what-would-you-like-to-see-happen? dream" that you tell each other about:

For example, a parent might sit down to a banquet every night (all right, once a week) without having to pay for it, shop for it, or cook it.

A child might come home with an all-A report card without having read the books, written the papers, or studied for the tests.

Oh, how we wish these dreams could come true, just like that. But reality is different. Talk together about how to realize your dreams. Who can help with that banquet? What books and papers need to be read and done to get those good grades? To have that banquet, to get those grades, takes time, effort, perseverance, sticking at something until it is accomplished.

### Moving to the Bigger Questions

From these specifics, try this move to these kinds of questions:

- Is the journey to something really the best part, or is the best part finally getting there?
- Is stubbornness always a bad thing? Can it be good sometimes?
- How do we force ourselves to do things that we don't want to do?

Can we share any of these "secrets" with children or do they have to learn it all by themselves, all over again?

**From Illinois . . .**

"My child folds clothes with me and will do *all* the socks or *all* the towels. She feels a real sense of pride when she finishes because she *stuck with it* until it was done."

situation: As an adult, if I don't like a book that I am reading for pleasure, I'll stop reading it. But as a student, I have to finish all the assigned readings, and as an employee, I have to finish tasks assigned to me.

When I was a child, I was given piano lessons. As the old saying should go, you can lead children to the piano, but you can't practice for them. Maybe I sensed that piano playing was an option in my family. What was not an option was doing homework and getting it done on time.

Every family needs to decide on its own options. But there should be some that children know they have to complete. For example, if they sign up on their own for ten-

nis lessons, they should not be able to quit after the first lesson. Just as you can't expect penicillin to work after the first dose, your children need to understand that they need to give things a chance to work. And when they do this, they need and deserve praise!

Rome wasn't built in a day, but if you are a watcher of TV, as our children are, you might believe it was built in an hour, or in a mini-series, at most.

Perhaps more than other generations, our children need to learn that things don't happen all at once, and sometimes not even very quickly. Reaching a goal may take time and long days of effort and continuing work, but it's worth it! Practice may not *make* perfect, but it *makes,* it builds, it creates, it accomplishes, it completes. And in doing that, it makes us feel good about the job and about ourselves.

*Gary Kubat, courtesy of the Association for Supervision and Curriculum Development*

## CHAPTER 11

---

# MegaSkill Seven: Caring

## Showing Concern for Others

## THE NEVER-ENDING REPORT CARD

| The Grades We Get in School | The Grades We Get on the Job |
|---|---|
| Don befriends everyone in the class. He lets them know he cares how they feel. | Mr. Stovall is fair and encouraging. He makes his staff feel appreciated. The morale in his office is high. |

Are you worried about your child's ability to care about others, to show affection, to be thoughtful? If so, you'll hear yourself saying or thinking:

"Don't be so selfish."
"You've got to care about other people."
"Do you think you're the only one in this world?"
"Do you think you are the only one in this house?"

This chapter is about how to help your child practice caring. It's about considera-

### From New York . . .

"I didn't really believe doing these activities would make much difference. The other day my neighbor walked in and saw us doing an activity, laughing and talking together like she had never seen. That was different! But the big surprise came the next morning. Into the kitchen walked not the chip-on-the-shoulder daughter I'm used to, but someone who gave me a friendly 'good morning' and some nice talk."

tion, about being interested in others, about listening to and learning from them.

**I, I, I. Me, Me, Me.** These aren't musical notes. They're the sounds children make—before they get tuned into **You, You, You** and **Us, Us, Us.**

When I put "caring" on the list of Mega-Skills, I had to face the question of how caring fits into the definition of MegaSkills. How does it, like the other MegaSkills, help children learn and want to keep on learning more?

Caring, I believe, belongs on the list not just because it's "nice," but because caring helps us learn from each other. It enables others to help us. People don't function well in isolation. Caring connects people. It gives us and our children a sense of community.

Knowing how to care is especially needed today. Children reared in smaller, separate households may need to learn caring more than those who come from larger families and who know from birth that they aren't the only ones around.

Growing children are naturally wrapped up in themselves and in their needs. But parents and teachers can teach caring in ways that are meaningful, even to the young.

## A WORLD OF CARING

In this chapter are personal caring activities within the family and with friends, and broader caring activities that extend beyond the home to the wider community. These activities emphasize "talk"—sharing ideas and feelings, using small moments to connect and communicate.

> Most of us live, work, and care in the concentric circles of family, friends, school or job, and community. These are like circles made by a stone tossed into a pool, causing new, ever-widening patterns. The center is the family, and it's in the family that children learn caring skills for the other circles in which we live.

### Family Notes ■ ages 4–6

- *Writing*
- *Sharing Information*

Tell your child that each day for three days, you will send each other notes. You need pen or pencil and note paper.

Each note will be a special message that will say something nice. The "something nice" will be something true that one of you has noticed about the other. It might be, "You have a nice smile" or "Your dinner last night

> **From Colorado . . .**
>
> "I'm a noncustodial father, seeing my kids only on Sunday. And it seemed as though every Sunday night when I was driving back home to their mother, we got into a terrible fight. Now I use Mega-Skills activities while we are in the car together. Frankly, they have changed the whole atmosphere. We leave each other smiling and kissing."

was very good" or "I like the way you cooked the chicken." Let children who do not yet write dictate their messages to you. Children enjoy figuring out nice things to say. Not-nice things might come to mind first. After a few laughs, the kids settle down.

Decide on a place to exchange daily notes. You can put them on the refrigerator, stick them in lunch bags, or pass them out at the dinner table.

As a special touch, ask a surprise "mystery guest" to send your child a note. It might be a message from a best friend, from grandparents, or from a neighbor.

### How Does It Feel? ■ ages 4–8

- *Thinking*
- *Observing and Discussing*

This activity helps children get a sense of how other people feel—an essential for work in school or out. All you need are thinking minds. This is a "talk about" activity.

Start by helping young children describe someone else's appearance. Ask your child to describe how a certain person—a friend or a teacher—looks. Use drawings. Where adjectives fail, a picture usually helps. Even when children are not artistic, they are generally more confident at first with drawings than with writing.

Ask "how do they feel" questions. *Examples:* "Jane has just won a race. How does she feel?" "Bill has just fallen down. How does he feel?" "What might each of these friends do, based on how they feel?"

Tell children to try to visualize themselves in your place. How do parents feel when mud is tracked into the house? How do parents feel when they have to nag children about homework or chores?

Trade places. Try to put yourself in your child's shoes on the first day of school or when the big test comes back or when kids are picked or not picked for a team.

## Greetings for Friends and Neighbors ■ ages 4–8

- *Writing*
- *Using Language Arts Creatively*

This activity has children making greeting cards. It gives children a chance to be cre-

> Children will believe you really do understand when you share some "emotional" memories of your own—not just what happened on your first day at school, but what you felt.

> Right near where each of us lives is someone who can use the help your child can provide. It doesn't have to be a big kind of help.

ative, even if they don't think they're artistic. It saves money and lets friends know how much you care. You need paper, pencil, scissors, markers, old greeting cards, and magazines.

For ideas, you and your child might take a few minutes to look through the greeting card section in a drugstore or stationery store. Decide who needs a greeting card. Does someone need cheering up? Is a friend having a birthday?

Together pick someone to receive a homemade greeting card. Fold the paper so that there will be a front, back, and inside for writing a message. Cut out a picture from a magazine or draw a picture for the front of the card. Ask your child to think of and write a message. For ideas, read old greeting cards and poetry books. Then address, mail, or hand-deliver the card.

Some of the people who would most appreciate those greetings may live nearby. Do you know a senior citizen who is living alone? Do you have new neighbors who have just moved in?

Not only will the greeting be welcome, but it is a good way for your child to get to know the neighbors and for the neighbors to get to know and care about your child. (See "Our Block" in this chapter.)

## How Can I Help? ■ ages 9–12

- *Thinking*
- *Researching Information*
- *Creating a Plan*

Do you have an elderly neighbor or relative living nearby? Suggest that your child perform an essential task for this person on a regular basis, once or twice a week. Depending on your child's age, it could include some marketing, going to the post office, answering mail, or reading the paper aloud.

Of course, it's important to know and trust the person your child is helping. Start by asking your friends for names of people they know and can vouch for.

## All in the Family ■ ages 9–12

- *Communication*
- *Listening and Speaking Together*

To know how to behave, it helps to know how we affect others, especially family members. This activity helps youngsters get "feedback" from the family about their behavior. You need thinking minds. This is a "talk about" activity.

Let family members "rate" each other. The object is to think positively and to avoid put-downs. What you hope to build is more of an "I care about how you feel" atmosphere at home. This can be done anywhere—at the dining table or in the car. Ask:

"How well do I listen?"
"How well do I help around the house?"
"Do I ever make you feel sad? How?"
"Do I make you feel happy? How?"

Think of two things that make each of you happy and two things that make you sad. Think of at least one thing you can do easily that would make your family happy.

Talk about these and about how easy or how hard it is to make other people happy. Small things can go a long way. A kiss, a cookie, a flower, an encouraging word, can give a big, quick lift. Children need to know this so that they can form the habit of making other people feel good.

## About Ourselves ■ ages 7–12

- *Thinking*
- *Building Self-Knowledge and Concern for Others*

This activity helps children learn more about others and share more about them-

---

### From Havre de Grace, Maryland . . .

Children have very strong caring feelings not so different from adults. Here's what children said "About Ourselves." Try these with your children at home. What do they agree and disagree with?

| I'm happy when | My wish for my family is |
|---|---|
| I win. | |
| I get good grades. | to win the lotto. |
| I get my favorite toy. | to go to Disney World. |
| Good things happen. | to be healthy, love each other, and |
| I have my birthday. | help others. |

selves. This is a personal activity, so you may want to save it until you have warmed up with a few of the other, more impersonal activities. You need pencil and paper.

Finish these sentences separately and compare answers.

I am happy when _____ .
I am afraid of _____ .
I am sad when _____ .
It's funny when _____ .
My favorite things include _____ .
When I am alone, I _____ .
I really care about _____ .

Talk about your responses. Share a few examples of happy and sad times. There may be some tears and more than a few laughs. It can be a very special moment.

## Our Block ■ ages 4–6

■ *Social Studies*
■ *Learning About the Community*

Young children especially need to know their neighborhood and their neighbors. This is important for their physical safety as well as for emotional reassurance. Help children know who lives where by drawing a neighborhood map together. You need paper, scissors, markers, ruler.

In the middle of the paper, draw your own home. That is the center of your child's world. Mark it with an *X*. Then list all the names of the people who live next door on either side. If you don't know them, make a note to find out their names and introduce yourselves.

Then extend the map to include the entire block, the route your child takes to and from school, and the route to and from the grocery store.

Draw with a free hand. Don't worry about exact distances between places. Fill in street names and telephone numbers for places and neighbors. Use a telephone book for information and a community map if one is available.

Post this map for everyone in the family to see. If you and your child have not yet taken a walk around your neighborhood, make a date to take this walk very soon.

## From One to Another ■ any age

■ *Thinking*
■ *Identifying Strengths of Diversity*

This activity helps youngsters appreciate differences among people. You need thinking minds for this "talk about" activity.

Think of ways in which people make themselves different. Examples include the way they dress, the way they talk, the way they do their hair, the way they have fun.

Think of ways people make themselves similar. Examples might be the way they dress, the way they talk, the way they do their hair, the way they have fun. (Notice when they are the same.)

Can each of you think of someone who has difficulty getting along with people? Could there be reasons for this that no one knows about? Is there anything you might do to help this person?

Talk about handicaps and about people who have them. Help children build a sense of empathy, of understanding what it's like.

Together read aloud some stories about the bravery of the handicapped. Better yet, make sure your child has some firsthand experience with a handicapped person at school or among your friends, relatives, or neighbors.

Making fun of differences is known as childish, but it may be childish because no one has bothered to talk with children first.

## People Scavenger Hunt ▪ any age

- ▪ *Social Studies*
- ▪ *Learning About Others*
- ▪ *Decreasing Bias and Stereotyping*

Together go on a people scavenger hunt. You need thinking minds.

Do you know anyone who speaks another language? Has been in a play? Has a relative who is more than ninety years old?

### From Florida . . .

"My kids are learning that people who look different are not so different after all. Every supermarket, every classroom, is filled with what used to be called 'foreign.' We eat Spanish, Italian, and Chinese foods. The whole world is right here in America and it makes our daily lives more exciting and interesting."

Think about someone you saw recently who is different. *Examples:* A street person carrying old bundles, a person in a wheelchair, a blind person. Try to imagine what it feels like to be that person. Talk about the problems these people face and how they cope with them.

Seek out people from other countries to talk to. Many of our own communities have become miniature United Nations. Help children take advantage of this opportunity by talking to neighbors who may be immigrants. When you hear a foreign accent, take time to stop and talk. Ask what we need to know about their native country, and share a tip or two on what they need to know about the U.S.

## Who Can Help Me? ▪ any age

- ▪ *Writing*
- ▪ *Purposeful Writing to Obtain Information*

There is always something that other people can help us with. But first they have to know we need help. For this activity you need paper and pencil.

Make two columns on the paper. At the top of the left column, write: HELP NEEDED FOR. At the top of the right column, write: WHO CAN HELP? Post the paper. Those who can help will write their names.

*Examples:* Mom's clock might be broken, and a friend who comes to visit and who knows how to fix clocks offers to help. Sally may need someone to help her check the spelling on a term paper, and her older brother offers to help.

The idea is to get children in the habit of using skills to help one another. This puts some organization into the give and take needed to manage a household.

## Heroes Among Us ■ any age

- *Reading*
- *Relating Main Ideas*
- *Recalling and Sharing Details*

This activity encourages kindness and provides reading practice, too. You need newspapers, pen or pencil, and scissors.

Cut out newspaper articles about heroic acts by ordinary individuals. *Examples:* Someone rescues a person from a fire; a neighbor stops a robbery; a youngster saves a child from being hit by a car.

Think about and remember a time when you were particularly helpful to someone.

### From Tennessee . . .

"I ask my kids, 'Do you think people help each other enough these days?' And then they ask me about the 'old days' and I try not to say how much better things were then. But I do talk about a sense of community and about how much we really need each other. They kind of squirm, but we all realize even more how much we depend on each other."

Share your memories with each other. Talk together about good deeds that have been done by other family members. Don't forget grandparents and great-grandparents.

Think together about one or two caring, unselfish people, famous or not, whom you admire. What do you like about them? Are there ways to become more like them? What have they accomplished? Share these thoughts and think about realistic efforts that each of you can make to be more like these heroes.

## The Gift of Time ■ any age

- *Communication*
- *Developing Time Concepts and Personal Responsibility*

Gift giving provides an opportunity to think about what would make someone else happy.

Talk about gifts that people love to receive but that don't cost much money, if any. Think about making gifts at home. What materials are needed to bake cookies, to sew a potholder, to construct a model plane?

Think about the people you'd like to give gifts to and what would suit each person. Pool ideas and make some choices. Try to think of gifts that aren't "things." You might share a special skill in order to help someone.

For children, it might be: "I will play ball with my younger brother for one hour." "I will make my sister's bed for three days." "I'll weed the garden for Mom for a week." "I will polish the car."

For adults, it might be: "I will read to you for at least fifteen minutes every night before bed for the next week." "I will take a walk with you this weekend."

Some of the best things between parent and child are still free! And one of the best and most surprising things between brothers and sisters is the caring they can show toward each other.

When Brian was nine, illness forced him to be bed-ridden for six months. Every day, his sister, Eve, age seven, would come bouncing in from school, ready for some outdoor play. But first she would go in to see Brian and ask, "Want to have my day?"

Then she would launch into funny vignettes about classmates and teachers and special events. They would laugh a lot. It was a good time for both of them— the giver and the receiver.

Where had this little girl learned this secret for sharing her day? It was what she saw at home. Both of her parents worked. When they got home, they each told a story from their day, usually a funny one. She listened and she learned.

---

### From California . . .

"In our house when the going gets tough, we take a little time to say, 'Let's think of at least two ways we can be nice to each other.' It sounds corny, but it works. And it's actually easier to think of two ways than it is to think of one."

---

## CARING AND LISTENING

Children truly need people who care about them. After my mother died, my father had to be both father and mother. It was very hard for him, not only because he commuted to work three hours every day, but mostly because, until my mother's death, he had not been involved in taking care of his children.

Friends told my father about Millie, an unmarried, middle-aged woman who had just come from England to work in the U.S. and who needed a place to live. Millie wanted a family. She probably wanted to get married and have her own children, but what she got was me. We had an extra bedroom in our house (my brother had gone off to college); she moved in and started keeping an eye on me. Maybe the real purpose was to get my father to marry her. That didn't happen, but what did happen was that Millie cared for me at a time when I felt very uncared for.

Millie did not try to function as my mother, but she showed me in many ways that she cared. She worked in a dress store that had discounts for employees and their families. I was often there, trying on dresses, and I bought some with the discount she got for me. We went out for dinner and the movies together when my father worked late. She needed my companionship, and I needed hers.

Millie was lonely for England and her sister's family. I can still see the mirror of the dresser in her bedroom. Tucked in the

## TEACHING TIPS: CARING

### Sharing Our Experiences with Our Children

It's easy to see the headlines in the newspaper and hear them on TV and get the idea that people just don't care for one another anymore.

But all of us who are out here in the world know that there are both very harsh and very soft, caring events happening every day. The soft ones just don't make the headlines.

That's why I never tire of telling about the leaders in the MegaSkills workshop program, volunteering to help fellow teachers and fellow parents. If I read the news as a barometer of how people really felt about each other, I would have never predicted this outpouring of help and, yes, love. Because these stories of caring don't make the news, it's all the more important for us to make sure children know that caring exists and to have examples of caring, not grizzly headlines, as models for their actions.

### Sparking the Conversation: Nice and Not Nice

In your own experience, you see caring, unsolicited: the boss who boosts your confidence; the neighbor who watches out for your child; the teacher who sends home the note telling you what your child has done right.

Ask your children for examples of niceness: Have they been nice to somebody lately? Who has been nice to them?

Ask children for examples of being not nice, any they want to share. Any you want to share?

Talk about brothers and sisters: Do they fight more than friends fight with each other? If so, why? And what can be done about it?

### Moving to the Bigger Questions

The subject of caring prompts lots of big thoughts:

- Does caring for others, giving to others, do anything special for the carer, for the giver?
- What does it mean to act selfishly? Who is an unselfish person that you both know?

There is a saying that the more we give, the more we get back. How have you experienced the pleasures of giving? How have your children? Talk about the special returns that come from giving.

edges around the glass were pictures of her family and friends. They stared out at her every time she stared in. When I went away to college, she put my picture up there, too.

Now, decades later, Millie is gone. And I remember her presence more than anything she did for me. She was there when I was alone, and she listened. When it comes to caring, that's the bottom line.

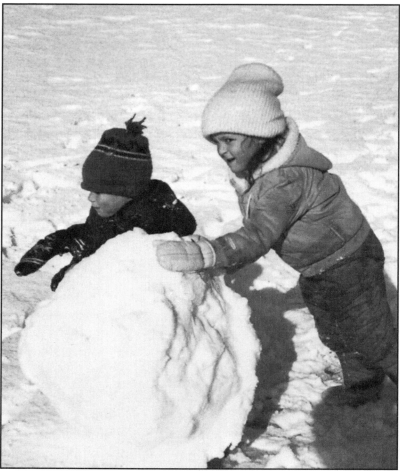

## CHAPTER 12

# MegaSkill Eight: Teamwork
## Working with Others

## THE NEVER-ENDING REPORT CARD

### The Grades We Get in School

Jim stands up for himself, yet he works well with the group. He doesn't always have to get his own way.

### The Grades We Get on the Job

Mr. Samson is a loyal member of the company team, working with and on behalf of the other members of the firm.

We know team players when we work with them:

> They don't always have to get the credit.
> They have spirit, and they share it with others.
> They laugh with others, not at them.
> They pitch in and make sacrifices.
> They are helpful, not helpless.

This chapter is about building a child's ability to work with others, as part of a team, cooperating to achieve a common purpose.

Teamwork is essential not just on a sports field. It's essential in business and in a family.

There may be no greater need for teamwork today than in the new configurations in family life, including blended families and step-families. No one says that nuclear family life is always easy, but reports from living rooms and kitchens across the country reveal the need for even greater teamwork when two different families come together to live under the same roof.

The activities in this chapter build children's abilities to cooperate and to be part of a team.

It's not easy. An uneasy balance exists between individualism and group work in this country, especially in our schools. Students are expected to perform and to be graded as individuals, competing rather than cooperating with each other.

It's different outside the classroom walls. On the football field, not even the best player can win the game alone, and an orchestra needs a stage full of cooperating players. Job evaluations make it clear that to receive good "grades," employees are expected to work together, collaborating to get the job done.

Teachers increasingly emphasize the need for teamwork, but the school as an institution is basically just not a hospitable place for this. That's why it is so important for parents to pay special attention to teamwork.

# WORKING TOGETHER

There are few cows in the back yard for our children to milk. While there are still chores for kids to do, with dishwashers and washing machines, there are fewer of them. So increasingly, the only way children can succeed and feel needed is to bring home top grades from school. All children will not be able to receive those good grades. They need other ways to show what they can accomplish. Activities at home, even chores, can help. They provide a sense of getting things done, and they help children feel more needed, more important in the life of the family, even when they gripe.

## Together and Alone

There are at least two kinds of teaming— one, where we are next to or near each other, doing the same job together, as in a bucket brigade to put out a fire, and another, where each of us does a different job as part of a larger team effort, such as cleaning the house.

In looking back, I don't think I did enough of the bucket-brigade kind of teaming. In our house, we usually divided the labor. There I was in the kitchen, scrubbing, while my kids were down the hall, vacuuming. They didn't actually see me doing my job. And I didn't see them.

There is something special about being in the same place, doing a job together. Before sending children off to do a job on their own, I'd start by having them do jobs right with you, next to you. This isn't just to keep an eye on them; it's to build the spirit and the sense of teaming, to see ourselves accomplishing a task together.

My friend Ruth remembers bringing her children up on the roof with her and her husband, and together they tackled the job of repairing roof shingles. The children passed the nails; they held the ladder; they felt part of the team.

This same spirit prevails when families bake cookies together or read aloud to each other or change a tire together or shovel snow together or rake leaves together.

My own children disliked housework chores but found them more agreeable when we were all in the same room together, one doing the dusting, another doing the polishing or the sweeping.

Outdoors, they loved to rake leaves, but not alone. They liked it when we did it together, one holding the bag, another putting in the leaves. It's the being together that they really liked.

My children do not have pleasant memories of the Saturday mornings when I insisted that they check the chore chart

Most of the time, most people like to be with other people. We get strength from each other. We don't feel so alone. But today more than ever, it is not always possible to be together. To accomplish a large task as a team, we divide the labor, and each of us goes off to do part of the task. This is the way we make dinner, run a house, or manage a business.

before going out to play. This was especially hard when the other kids were waiting for them outside, without having done their chores at home. I will be forever grateful to the "really mean mother" on the next block who didn't let her children go out to play until they had cleaned their rooms and taken care of the chores for the rest of the house.

My own mother was a compulsive cleaner, plumping up the cushions on the sofa, for example, the minute someone got up from sitting there, and not leaving the house for a family outing until the kitchen floor had been cleaned, even if it was clean to start with. So I was reluctant to be too clean. Maybe that's why I did not insist that my children's bedrooms look the way I liked. I tried to be content with a shut door so that I did not have to see their version of order, which I called mess. Even so, there were times when my children felt I was too demanding, and I was.

I think we all would have been better off with more do-it-together activities, especially at first, and a more democratic approach to handling tasks. The activities that

follow do divide the labor, but they still build the important feeling of teamwork.

## WHEN THEY SAY, "LET ME!" . . . LET THEM

Many young children plead to do chores around the house long before their parents ask them to. Young children will beg to fix dinner or wash the car. Parents often turn down these offers because letting your children help usually means more work—at first.

### Real Work, Not Make-Work
▪ ages 4–6

- *Study Skills*
- *Building Relationships Between Schooling and Career Goals*

Talk with your children about jobs that need doing at home. Ask what they think they can do. It can be surprising how willing and eager they are to tackle jobs . . . when they're still young and not expected to enjoy working.

Set attainable goals with your child. Start with easy tasks and work up to harder ones. *Example:* A four-year-old can bring in the paper every day and wipe the kitchen table.

Turn jobs into games. Set the same task for you and your child. Race each other to see who wipes the table or retrieves the newspaper faster. Chances are, your child will win, on the up and up.

> It's true. It does take more time and patience to teach children how to work, to show them a job step by step, to encourage them, and then to step back and let them take over. It's easier to do the work for them.
>
> But as with much of parenting, efforts when children are young are an investment in the future.

Remember, show children how to do the work—but do *not* redo their work. *Example:* The first time a child uses a vacuum, show how to do it and what to pick up. One mother turned a six-year-old loose without instructions, and within thirty seconds a new baby bib was in the sweeper. It was a lesson for both of them.

## Divide and Conquer ■ ages 7–9

- *Study Skills*
- *Developing Work Habits by Sharing Tasks*

One of the best ways to organize a household task is to divide it into parts. Teach children to accept and carry out household responsibilities as a member of the "family team." You need paper and pencil.

Pick a job that has several parts. A good example is preparing a meal. What do you do first? What do you do second? Your list might look like this:

Plan the meal.
Shop for groceries.
Prepare the food.
Set the table.
Clean up afterward.

Ask everyone to choose from the list one job to do. Some coordination is needed, just as if the family were a football team driving to the goal line. A team spirit is built when each person does part of the bigger job. And don't forget to pass around a heaping helping of praise!

## Organizing Household Chores
■ ages 10–12

- *Writing*
- *Categorizing Information*

Here's a writing activity that helps family members remind each other in a positive way about jobs that need doing at home. You need paper and pencil.

Together make a list of all the jobs that need to be done around the house. You might separate them into weekly jobs and daily jobs.

**Weekly Jobs:** Doing laundry, vacuuming, grocery shopping, mowing the lawn.
**Daily Jobs:** Cooking dinner, making beds, taking out garbage, feeding pets.

Decide together when jobs will be done and who will do them. Write down names next to the jobs. Family members can switch with each other later. Try to avoid labeling work as "girl's" or "boy's." Talk about a job a youngster usually does around the house, such as setting and clearing the table, and a job an adult usually does, such as washing clothes. If possible, trade places and do each other's jobs at

---

**From Missouri . . .**

"My child helped me put away the laundry and when we were done, he said to me, 'Mom, that's a lot of work you do every day. I think we should pitch in and help more often.' I almost fainted."

least once. Did you do these jobs differently or the same way?

When children say to a brother or sister, "Let me help you," it's music to a parent's ear. But it's a tune some of us don't hear very often.

To spur these generous outbursts, think of ways to do activities together.

Use stories to make a point about helping one another. Among the classics for young children is "Cinderella." Those mean stepsisters who never helped got their comeuppance, and Cinderella, the great helper, got the prince. Real life isn't a fairy tale. But we know that teamwork is highly rewarded in sports and business. Point to the examples reported in the media. For older children, tell the story or show the film *It's a Wonderful Life*. In this classic, Jimmy Stewart sacrifices for his family, stays home from college, and manages to keep open a small bank that helps poor people get homes. With the help of an angel named Clarence, he learns that he has indeed lived a wonderful life.

## TALKING AND THINKING TOGETHER

In teamwork, not only do you have to do things together, but you have to be able to think as a team.

The goal is to help children express their thinking so that the family as a team has a better understanding of the "wavelengths" everybody is on. In this way, we generate respect for everyone's ideas.

## What Do We Think? ■ ages 7–9

- *Communication*
- *Listening*
- *Organizing Information*

Help children practice finding out what others think. Take a poll at home about household products. You need pencil and paper.

Ask your child to take a poll on a product the family is using, such as toothpaste or soap suds. Should we buy more of this? If yes, why? If no, why not? What could the family buy instead of this product?

To do this, your child must be a good listener. When everyone has been polled, ask your child what he or she has learned. Does the family like these products? What changes are asked for? Talk about the poll results at the dinner table.

As a reward, on the next shopping trip you might buy some of the new products the family suggested. In this way your family sees its wishes come true.

## What Are We Watching?
■ ages 8–12

- *Writing*
- *Formulating Questions for Purposeful Writing*

This activity helps youngsters ask questions and get answers about a subject on which everyone in the family has an opinion—TV. By hearing how others use TV, children develop their own judgment about whether a show is worth watching. You need paper and pencil.

Decide with your youngsters on two or three adults to interview about their TV watching. (These might be a parent, a neighbor, an aunt.)

Together think of three questions to ask. Your youngster should write them down and leave space for the answers. *Examples:* "Do you watch TV each day?" "For how long?" "Do you have favorite shows?" "To improve TV, what would you change?"

Talk about the answers your youngster receives. Suggest forming a team effort to keep each other "on the road" to more activity and less TV watching.

## What's Your Opinion?
■ ages 10–12

■ *Communication*
■ *Identifying Problem-Solving Alternatives*

*Yes, we can. No, we can't.*

Children often disagree with their parents about rules, seeing only their own points of view.

This activity makes it easier for children to see both sides of an argument. It teaches them to think as a team member. All you need are thinking minds.

Choose one rule that causes family arguments. *Examples:* When to do homework? How late to stay up on school nights? What TV shows to watch?

Ask your child's opinion of the rule. If it's about bedtime, that opinion might be, "Having a bedtime is a bad rule. Kids should go to bed whenever they want." Ask your child

to give at least two reasons for this opinion. These might include, "I miss the best TV shows when I go to bed early." Listen carefully.

Now ask your child to give two arguments for the other side. One might be, "Kids need sleep to keep awake in school."

Coming up with pro and con arguments is an excellent way to help children learn to consider alternatives before making a decision. While your child is working on these pro and con arguments, you do the same. Explain your points of view. Talk over your differing opinions. Does everyone have good points? Do you need to change any rules? Actually, children have been known to be very reasonable team players when they get involved in helping to make family rules.

## MONEY—DIVIDING AND SHARING

A handy tool in teaching teamwork is money. It can prompt families to pull together to save it, figure out how to divide it, and get together to spend it. Here are three activities that illustrate this.

## Down the Drain and out the Window ■ any age

■ *Mathematics*
■ *Building Awareness of Math in Daily Life*

This activity helps children team together to save family money on utility bills. Children may be wasting electricity and water without even knowing that they cost money. For this activity you need some utility bills.

Take a house electricity tour. Check whether lights, radios, or televisions have been left on. Talk with your children about ways to save on utility bills, such as turning off the air conditioner when nobody is home or lowering the heat at night when people are sleeping.

Take a house water tour. Think of all the ways you use water—for dishes, for bathing, for cooking. Then talk about ways you can conserve water.

Look at the bills in the next few months to see the results. Use a set of bills you and your youngster can follow.

## What's My Share? ■ ages 10–12

■ *Mathematics*
■ *Recognizing Relationships*

This activity gives children practice in learning about and paying their fair share of a bill. It builds a child's sense of individual responsibility within the family's larger financial effort. You need newspaper, paper, and pencil.

Think of at least one thing the family wants or needs. Find an ad for it in the newspaper. Pretend that everyone will share the cost of this item equally. *Example:* The family decides to buy a new CD. Perhaps it costs twelve dollars. If everyone in the family shares the cost, how much will each have to pay?

---

**From Alaska . . .**

"Our son has worked at times with us in our fishing business. He has learned a lot about earning, spending, and saving money. As a result, he is understanding when we can't buy extras. He also takes pride in items, such as clothing, that he helps buy for himself."

---

Think about your own daily living costs. Lunch and bus fare are good examples. Calculate these for a one-week period. Are there ways you can save on these costs?

You might think even bigger. How about a pretend vacation? Figure out where to go and how much the holiday will cost. Look in the newspaper travel section. Pick a spot. Read the ads and see if your child can get an idea of how to plan a family vacation you can afford.

## Shopping Around ■ ages 7–12

■ *Mathematics*
■ *Connecting Reading and Writing with Math*

This activity helps children learn how to compare prices in order to shop carefully for an item they want. You need newspaper ads for new products, classified ads for used items, and pencil or crayon.

Ask children to select an item to "buy" from a newspaper ad and from a classified ad. This might be a bicycle or a television set. Together mark the ads that sound like the best buys. Talk about the items and urge the "consumers" to discuss the ads with other members of the family. Which do they consider the best buys?

Compare classified prices on really large items, such as houses or cars. This helps children begin to think about big sums of money. Go to an auction. Visit some garage sales listed in the paper. These are fun, and the prices provide math practice. You don't even have to buy anything!

## LEARNING ABOUT TEAMWORK

Good examples are good teachers. The news media provide us with examples, many bad, but some good. Use the good ones to show children how people working together can make a real difference.

And look to the living examples you have near you, perhaps right next door. These are neighbors, friends, relatives, who, if prompted, have a great deal to share and teach your children about how they work with others in the community and on the job.

### People Helping Each Other
▪ ages 8–12

- *Reading/Writing*
- *Working with Visual and Print Media*

You need current newspapers, a television, pencil, and paper.

Together find at least two articles that tell of events affecting families in a foreign country. *Example:* A drought in Africa leads to food shortages.

Talk about these events. Could they happen here? Together look in the paper or think about a situation that affects the area in which you live. *Example:* A neighborhood school closes. Talk about this. What, if anything, can you do about it?

Ask your youngster to pick a news event to follow for several days. Try to find a topic that involves people helping each other. Follow it in the paper. Listen to the radio. Watch the news. Discuss it together.

Take action: Help your child write a letter to the editor about something affecting families in the area. *Example:* Suggest an after-school center for kids. Explain that this is one of the ways to make your opinions known and to change other people's views.

### How Have Others Helped You?
▪ ages 10–12

- *Communication*
- *Relating with Adults*
- *Building Discussion Abilities*

**From Indiana . . .**

"On Saturdays, Jimmy helps his grandmother put her groceries away. He puts cat and dog food on the bottom shelf, big cans in the back, small cans up front. Jimmy says he likes helping his grandmother like this . . . and he's starting to help me more at home, too."

Many of us owe a lot to other people. These are our "mentors," people who worked with us, helped us along. Often these are our parents, but not always. A mentor might be a friend, a co-worker, or an older person who became interested in us. This is a "talk about" activity, designed to help children learn about the people who have guided them in the best sense of teamwork.

Invite a few friends in and ask them to tell your children about the big influences in their lives. Trade places and share your experiences with their children. Sometimes we listen better when the story is being told by someone we don't know as well as we know our own family.

And your children may even pick up some new mentors.

## WHERE TEAMWORK IS TAUGHT TODAY

Among the most vivid examples of family teamwork seen today are the small businesses run by families of newly arrived immigrants. Everyone appears to be working together. Whether that can be or will be continued as these families become "Americanized" is unknown. To someone like me, who was raised in the Depression, when we did spend time working together in the store—not always harmoniously—watching such closeness brings back bittersweet memories. This teamwork may look better than it actually is. And the current situation for most of us, where the lack of teamwork is lamented at home and at school, may look worse than it really is.

Among the most visible and positive signs of communities caring about children —and among the most successful programs—are clubs or groups designed specifically to help youngsters grow up. I'm talking about the Four-H Clubs, the Boys Clubs, the Scouts, the Big Sisters and Brothers, the athletic leagues, and the church groups. These groups exist in almost every community, small and large. The MegaSkill they teach remarkably well is teamwork.

It may be a problem for employed parents to find the time to participate with children in these groups. But just as banks are now open at different hours and doctors now accommodate working parents' schedules, it is likely that these groups can also work out ways for busy parents to ensure that children can come to the meetings and to be involved themselves.

When your children want to join, it's a good sign. You may need to ask around to find out about these groups and where and when they meet. First check with your school, then with a nearby recreation center. The local United Way or Community

---

**From Florida . . .**

"Now, on Saturday mornings, my kids work with me as a team to do the housework. They pitch in because they know that saving time in the morning means that we can put in two hours of play every Saturday afternoon."

## TEACHING TIPS: TEAMWORK

### Sharing Our Experiences with Our Children

It seems that everybody's talking about teamwork. We see articles about it in the sports pages and the business pages. It's the key to success. Some folks call it the most desired MegaSkill today.

Many of our children know what it means to be part of a sports team. But they often don't know what it means to be a team player at work and in the family.

That's why it is so important to share your experiences about teamwork on the job and at home, too. Not all your memories will be wonderful. You may recall, for example, the times on the job when your boss or your fellow workers didn't pull their load of the job, instead pushing work off on you.

And you may recall the times when it was as if you'd won the World Series, as a team. Share as many experiences as you can for as long as the kids will listen.

### Sparking the Conversation: Moving Day

You may find it helpful to focus on a specific problem. For example, if you've gone through a move recently, packing and unpacking and being generally uprooted, your family knows firsthand the need for teamwork.

When a household moves (no matter how little we think we've collected), it works a lot better when everyone pitches in. If you've gone through a move recently, talk about what everyone had to do. If you're thinking about a move, and dreading it (who doesn't?), now is a good time to think aloud about what everyone will have to do to make it work well. Who knows, it might just nudge your children enough to start throwing away some of the junk that's piling up in their rooms. The thought of having to pack it is awesome.

### Moving to the Bigger Questions

From discussion of specifics, you can move to questions like these:

- When do we like working with others?
- When do we like to and need to work alone?
- What jobs do we do at home as members of a team?
- What jobs at home should we turn into teamwork jobs?

If any one member of the family is still doing all or almost all of any one job (for example, Mom cooking), then teamwork is the right MegaSkill at the right time for your home.

Chest office is another good source for information about these groups.

> Having a sense of humor about ourselves is an essential life skill, perhaps the twelfth MegaSkill. There's a big difference between laughing at ourselves and laughing at others. Laughing at ourselves without tearing ourselves down is a sanity keeper. It's a connector, a bond to other people and their experiences.

## HUMOR HELPS

Working together with others, whether in small or big organizations, can be a headache.

We all have moments, often at meetings, when we want to stand up and shout, "I quit!" or "All of you are fired!"

That's what I do in my daydreams and my nightmares. At difficult meetings I have found another way. It seems to help—because it's humorous.

In the meeting room at my office, I keep a very large aspirin. It's about six inches across, and I found it one day at a specialty store in New York. When the meeting is going nowhere and everyone seems to be getting a headache, I thrust that aspirin onto the table, and we all get a big laugh. It helps.

If we can gain some perspective in the middle of an argument at home or on the job, we're bound to see something funny in the scene that will give everyone a good

laugh. It might come right then or a day or a week later, but it's delicious at any time.

## THE IMPORTANCE OF TEAMWORK

When I asked a top-management public relations executive what his firm looks for most in new employees and in advancing others, without hesitation he said, "People who can work with other people. We need people we can count on, people who are loyal, who are team players."

Jobs today depend more than ever on people-to-people skills—not just in public relations, but throughout the economy. Projections indicate that the majority of job seekers will find this to be increasingly true.

Beyond the practice of the activities in this section, the daily news is filled with articles that can supply ongoing discussions about teamwork. Teamwork pervades all sections of the news, from the sports pages to the business pages. Everyone, it seems, is working as a member of a team, including scientists. Rarely can one person perform a major task completely alone. Writing a book might be an exception, but publishing it requires people working together. The challenge is to ensure that every member of the team has the opportunity to contribute.

> The search is for team players, not as yes-people but as strong contributors helping one another to be stronger.

*Elvira Crocker, courtesy of the National Education Association*

## CHAPTER 13

# MegaSkill Nine: Common Sense
## Using Good Judgment

## THE NEVER-ENDING REPORT CARD

### The Grades We Get in School

Joan knows how to divide her time so her assignments get done, and she still has time left to read over her papers before handing them in.

### The Grades We Get on the Job

Dr. Thornton has the ability to keep things in proportion. Even when the pressure is on, she doesn't get rattled. She keeps on doing her work carefully.

---

Do your kids have common sense? If they don't, you are not alone.

We all want our children to:

■ Know about cause and effect, including understanding that what they say will have certain effects on others.

■ Show balance and judgment about handling the irreplaceable resource of time and the scarce resource of money.

And, along with these grander ideas, we want them to put on their seat belts and resist the seduction of sitting in front of the TV all day.

This chapter provides practice activities to help children develop this kind of common sense. Gaining common sense is an evolving, long-range process. When parents ask in exasperation, "Where in heaven's name is your common sense?" the truest answer a child can give is, "It's coming."

Common sense is not so common. A reason children may not be using common sense is that it is not a sense we are born with. It is built through experience and practice.

I pride myself on my common sense today, but I didn't always have it.

When my brother, age eleven, invented a chair that would go to the top of the tree next to our house, he asked me, age seven, if I wanted to ride in it. I was delighted. The next thing I knew I was rising into space. The chair was attached to ropes that my brother and his friend Ivan had thrown around one of the tallest tree limbs. They were experimenting to see if they could pull on the ropes to carry me and the chair to the top.

It worked. The chair and I reached that limb. But I looked around from my perch in the sky and I began screaming, "Let me down! Let me down!" Hearing my pitiful pleas, they let go of the ropes. We all learned about gravity very forcefully and very quickly, especially me. Had I not landed on the grass, I would have been in pieces. I think my fear of heights began that day. I ran crying into the house to complain about my mean brother, and my mother asked, "And where was *your* common sense?" I didn't know, but I think at that moment it was more in my hurting bottom than in my head.

Can we teach common sense, or at least a few of the basics, and avoid our children having to learn it all through bitter experience and trial and error? I believe we can.

Unlike a subject such as reading or math, common sense has no curriculum. The best we can do is to find areas in which common sense is needed and then figure out ways to give children practice acquiring it. That's what I've done in this chapter, with activities in very different areas for which there is wide agreement that common sense is needed. Inch by inch, we coach children to common sense.

## GATHERING INFORMATION

When you have common sense, you try to see more than one point of view. When you have common sense, you have perspective.

To get this, children need to know how to acquire information, and not just from textbooks. Information helps kids make decisions and avoid hasty conclusions, as enticing as they might be. In this section are activities for gathering information not only from things around us but also from and about people.

The activities may look like fun. Actually, they are, but they're more. They help reinforce children's innate information-acquiring abilities.

## The Careful Eye ■ ages 4–9

- *Reading/Writing*
- *Vocabulary Building*

Look around the room and ask children to name everything they see. This activity builds observation skills. At first the list may be short, but encourage children to name everything from floor to ceiling.

Put several objects on a table. Ask youngsters to look hard and then close their eyes. Remove one or two of the objects. Let children name the things you took away. Turn this game around and ask your children to play it on you.

Ask children to observe everything on their way home from school to see how many things they never noticed before. *Examples:* a broken tree limb or a stop sign.

Noticing is important. One of the fathers in our program, now a single parent, says of himself, "I noticed everything at work and nothing at all in my relationship at home." Noticing in relationships is discussed later in this chapter (see "People Common Sense").

---

**From Florida . . .**

"I was very surprised that my daughter did *not* know the names of a lot of objects in the house. We had so much fun that the babies joined in, too."

---

## Memory Stretching ▪ ages 4–9

- ▪ *Thinking*
- ▪ *Recalling Details*
- ▪ *Practicing Sequences*

To encourage information gathering, try questions like these:

Does your back door swing in or out?
Do you put your right or left sock on first?
Who's the slowest eater in your house?
What did you have for breakfast? For dinner last night? Go back meal after meal to see how far you can remember.

Ask your children to make up questions for you to try to answer. You'll probably have more trouble answering these questions than do your children. It's an exercise in humility, even for high-powered executives.

## Guessing ▪ ages 4–9

- ▪ *Science*
- ▪ *Formulating Hypotheses*
- ▪ *Checking Evidence*

Everybody has to be able to guess. The fancy word for it is "hypothesize." The better guesses are ones based on as much information as you can pull together beforehand. For this activity you need a yardstick and a scale.

Ask "guessing" questions and let children ask them of you. How wide is this room? How long is the driveway? Get out the yardstick and check these guesses.

> **From Illinois . . .**
>
> "We take the *MegaSkills* book with us to the dentist. While one of the kids is in the dentist's chair, I do activities with the other one who is waiting to go in. It gives each of the kids something to look forward to at a painful time."

Talk about weight in general terms. Then guess how much different things weigh. A typewriter? A book? Mother? Brother? Put them on the scale and check.

These activities help children make judgments based on what they know to be facts or guesses.

## Checking ▪ ages 7–12

- ▪ *Thinking*
- ▪ *Evaluating Information*

Checking is common-sense practice, and it can be taught in a straight forward way with a series of questions.

Have we checked to see, for example, that:

There's gas in the car before starting out on a trip?
There are no cracks in the eggs that we buy at the supermarket?
The seams are tightly sewn in clothes we're planning to buy?
There are no cars coming before we start across the street—even if the light is green?

We can get children in the habit of doing these checks. With all the checking in the world, there will still be plenty of surprises, but some of the everyday, unpleasant ones can be avoided this way.

To keep kids on their toes, try this. Show youngsters the good side of a wormy apple. Ask, "Is this a good apple? Can you eat all of it?" Then turn the apple around. It shows children they have to know both sides of the question. It's a trick with a valuable lesson.

## Using Clues ■ ages 4–8

■ *Thinking*
■ *Deductive Reasoning*

Help children use clues. This is an easy activity that gets children used to seeing small but important details. This ability is important in reading, mathematics, and science, and it's basic common sense. Use any day, any house.

Begin by saying, "I'm thinking of something—an object—that is in this very room." Then give hints, one at a time. Tell about the object's size, color, or use. *Example:* If you are thinking of a saucer, you could say, "It's the size of a big pancake," "It's blue and white," and "It is used under a cup." After each clue, let your child try to guess the object. Continue giving clues until your child guesses it. If necessary, make the clues more obvious. Switch places. Let your child give you clues. Explain that the purpose is not to fool but to give just

enough information so that the object can be named.

Try describing an object in another room. Ask children to guess what it is. Have them go to that room to check the accuracy of your clues. For example, was your description of the sofa's color accurate? For variety, send your children into the room to draw the object that's been described. Try trading places for these activities, too.

## Asking Questions ■ ages 9–12

■ *Study Skills*
■ *Researching Information*

This activity gives youngsters practice and confidence in getting information from people around them every day. This is a "talk about" activity.

Ask parents, relatives, and neighbors about their jobs. How did they choose them? Do they enjoy what they do?

Talk about how jobs have changed over the years. What jobs did your grandparents and parents hold? Where did they live? Is it really all that different today?

"Using Clues" and "Asking Questions" illustrate differences in children's abilities to gather and understand information as they grow older. The older youngster's activity asks that the child have a sustained information-seeking conversation with another person, perhaps even leading the conversation and keeping it going with questions. When youngsters can do this, they show growing maturity.

## PEOPLE COMMON SENSE

There is such a thing as people common sense. It involves concern for others, but it also means seeing things from other points of view, putting ourselves as best we can in other people's shoes.

To help children do this, here are scenes of real people having a choice of what to say to one another. Common sense dictates that one of the three choices for each scene is the preferred response. It may jump right out at both you and your child.

## WHAT SHOULD WE SAY?

Read these scenes aloud with your children. Before reading the bank of possible answers, think of what you might answer. Ask for your children's answers and the reasons why they picked them. If the answers seem obvious, so much the better. The curious thing is that while we "know" the right responses, we often have trouble using them. Getting into the habit helps.

---

**From New York . . .**

"Because of my encouragement, I think, my son is on his way to becoming a professional baseball player. He gets up at bat and says to that pitcher, 'I can hit anything you pitch to me.' He's tiny, but he says to himself, 'I can do it.'"

---

### 1. The Report Card

Anne had always received top grades—all A's and B's on her elementary school report card. For her first report card in seventh grade, she brought home three C's. Her father looked at the card and felt these words rising in his throat: "How could you get these C's?" Instead, what do you think he said, and why did he say it?

a. "When are you going to settle down?"
b. "Your sister never even got one C."
c. "Being in a new school is hard. Soon you will get to know your teachers and the other students, and it will get easier."

### 2. The Kitchen Floor

Tom, age eight, came in to get a cold drink from the refrigerator. The floor was still a bit wet from the scrubbing Mom had given it that morning. With the bottle of juice in his hand, Tom slipped, and sticky liquid went flying everywhere. Mom walked into the once-gleaming kitchen, now a mess again. She felt like screaming. Instead, what do you think she said, and why?

a. "Why are you so clumsy?"
b. "OK, accidents will happen. I'll help you clean up this place."
c. "You're always doing things like this."

### 3. The Boy Next Door

Leah was only nine, but she really liked Michael, the boy across the street. The boy's family had been away for a year in South America. In the month before their return, Leah had crossed off each day on the calendar. She told that to her friend Margo. Finally the big day arrived. There they were. Leah and Michael said hello shyly. Margo was there, too, and what do you think she said?

a. Nothing.
b. "Boy, did Leah miss you!"
c. "Leah's been counting the days."

### 4. The Rained-Out Birthday Party

Amy had been looking forward to her tenth-birthday picnic for weeks. The morning arrived, and with it, the beginning of a daylong rain. Her brother Sam, age fifteen, who was helping plan the party, woke her. What do you think he said?

a. "Why does something like this always happen to us?"
b. "Don't worry. We're going to have a great time inside."
c. "I'm never going to help you with a party again."

### 5. The Bike Race

David was participating in the fifth-grade bike race. He had trained with his father for months. As he started, his bike went over a rock, and he pitched sideways. When David picked up the bike, he saw that the bike frame was out of alignment. His dad was on the sidelines. What do you think he said?

a. "Let's get a tool so we can straighten the frame, and you can use the bike for the next race."
b. "We might as well go home."
c. "Why did you have to do that?"

## Answer Key

The answers below are so commonsensical that they make us wonder why we ever use put-downs. Maybe we need to practice these positive answers aloud so they come out more easily.

| Scene | Response |
|-------|----------|
| 1 | c |
| 2 | b |
| 3 | a |
| 4 | b |
| 5 | a |

## WHY WE SAY WHAT WE SAY

Talk together about why people say what they do. Without using a fancy vocabulary, talk about motives, defensiveness, and hostility. Make up your own scenes with new sets of responses that include both words and actions.

Children benefit from hearing parents' answers and by practicing positive responses themselves. It's never too early or too late to start.

## COMMON SENSE ABOUT TIME

We never have enough time, or do we? We encounter either a drought of nothing to do or a deluge of too much. Children always seem to be at one end or the other. They say, "I'm bored, there's nothing to do," or "Gee, I don't have time to do that," especially when "that" is a chore around the house. The activities that follow attempt to give children some common sense about time.

## How Much Time? ■ any age

- ■ *Mathematics*
- ■ *Making Predictions and Estimating*

For this activity you need pencil and paper.

Take time to talk about how the family spends time. *Examples:* How much time do we spend watching TV? How much time do we use for sleep? How much time is spent on jobs around the house? How much time for homework or activities with friends or for talking on the telephone?

You're estimating, not measuring. You're making educated guesses based on the time you spent yesterday or last week. Jot down these different estimates next to each person's name.

This can be the beginning of your discussion about time. The activity gets children thinking about how they spend time without making judgments about whether they spend it in the right ways. Actually measuring the time spent and making judgments about it can come next.

## How Time Flies ■ any age

- ■ *Mathematics*
- ■ *Observing and Keeping Records*

Time may fly, but it can be measured. The ultimate goal is to try to manage it. But first let's see how we spend it. You and your

**From Vermont . . .**

"The activities help give me structure and help to organize my time. I have a three-month-old and a kindergartner. Before, I didn't seem to have time for my older child after school. Now we set aside a special time with a special activity each day. She looks forward to it and so do I."

child will each keep track of your time for one day. You need two pieces of cardboard —one for each of you—a ruler, and a pencil or marker.

Draw a very large circle on each cardboard. Tracing that circle against a big round plate helps. The object is to mark off this circle into twenty-four equal parts, one for each hour of the day. First divide the circle into four quarters. Each of these quarters represents six hours. Within each quarter, you and your child should mark off six equal spaces, like slices of pie.

Pick any day, preferably a weekday. You can do Saturday or Sunday later. Start by shading in the hours spent in sleep, then the hours spent at school or on the job. What's left? Time alone or with friends? Time spent in travel? Time spent on homework or chores? Time before the TV? Time for meals? Time for hobbies?

These pictures of your days will be interesting to compare and will give you both a lot to talk about, and maybe even to complain about.

## My Time Wish ▪ any age

- *Communication*
- *Presenting Information*

For this activity you need the time circles from "How Time Flies."

Take your time circles and see what you would change if you could. What's your ideal day? Would you spend more time sleeping and less time traveling? Would you spend less time eating and more time on hobbies? Would you spend less time alone and more time with each other? Talk together about these ideal days. See what little changes you can make to bring your current days more in line with your ideal ones.

## Time Your Plan ▪ ages 7–12

- *Thinking*
- *Organizing Information*

This activity provides practice in making a plan. You need paper and pencil.

Ask children both to think about what they would like to do and to predict the times they will begin each activity. Saturday is a good day to try this. Together write down the time your child thinks each activity will begin. *Examples:* Wake up at 8:00. Get dressed by 8:30. Finish breakfast by 9:00. Play baseball at 9:15.

As children begin an activity, they write down the time next to the prediction on the plan sheet. How close are the estimates to the actual times?

This planning practice can be very helpful in a couple of ways. It helps children

begin to manage their time, to take more control over how they spend it. And it helps give children step-by-step skills for handling major school assignments with distant due dates, such as term papers, which just can't be done (well) the night before they are due.

## DELICIOUS TIME

There is increasing concern that we over-schedule our children, that we want them to be busy all the time, that we "hurry" them along to adulthood before they have had a chance to be children.

I don't think children need be busy or even look busy all the time. The same is true for adults. Both children and adults need time for looking at clouds, for taking a bubble bath and reading a potboiler, for playing with a pet, for sitting with each other, even when we're not talking. This is time for what used to be called smelling the roses.

The common-sense activities provided above give us not only a better sense of how we spend time but also a better chance of saving more time for those delicious unstructured hours.

## MONEY COMMON SENSE

Money isn't everything, but it is a daily concern of families, and it's useful in developing common sense. Giving children practice with money is important because it gives them a sense of competency that carries over to their other work, in school and out.

**From Tennessee . . .**

"My oldest child is twenty-one years old and I was successful with her, but the things that worked with her sometimes don't work with the younger children. I like the different approaches that I learn with MegaSkills."

Kids do funny things, even with their allowance. Maybe that's all right, but I have this attitude about wasting money: I don't like it. Neither does my husband. I asked our younger daughter recently if she remembered wasting money when she was young, and she said she certainly did, and we certainly got angry.

It seems that when she was six, she invested her entire weekly allowance of seventy-five cents (not a small sum then) in chewing gum. Perhaps worse yet, she opened all the packages and put the naked little gums out on a plate in the center of the dining room table. I don't recall this at all, nor does my husband. But our daughter tells us that when we came home from work and saw the dried-out gums, we both became angry and used such famous parental comments as "Have you no sense?" and "Why did you do this?" The upshot was that her allowance was cut back to thirty-five cents, since it was apparent that she did not really need the larger sum and had only wasted what she had left.

In retrospect, we probably overreacted. What our child did was precocious (gum hors d'oeuvres), but it was foolish. Maybe it was then that I decided she ought to learn

about the value of money; the activities in this chapter are the result. In her mid-thirties now, our daughter reports that she has learned about money. She says she never unwraps gum until it's ready to be chewed.

Handling money is serious business, but it can be taught in easy, commonsensical ways.

## Money in Print and in Pocket
▪ ages 4-6

- ▪ *Reading/Math*
- ▪ *Checking Newspaper Ads*
- ▪ *Counting Money*

This activity helps children reading newspaper ads figure out both how much one dollar buys and the different ways that pennies, nickels, dimes, and quarters add up to a dollar. You need newspaper grocery ads, scissors, glue, paper, and a variety of change: five nickels, five dimes, four quarters, and the more pennies, the better.

Ask your child to look with you through the ads to find items that can be bought for a dollar or less. Cut these out and paste each ad to a separate piece of paper.

To teach children how to make change, try this. Put pennies, nickels, dimes, and quarters in different sections of an ice cube tray or an empty egg carton. Hand children a quarter and let them give you that amount back in different coins. Use this with other combinations. As a reward, let your child buy a surprise, using the correct coins, from a vending machine.

As a variation, use children's allowance to teach number combinations. One week, present a dollar in four quarters; the next week, in ten dimes, and so on.

## Yesterday and Today ■ ages 7–9

■ *Thinking/Math*
■ *Using Household Bills to Understand Prices*

This activity gives children a clearer understanding of daily living costs and how they have changed over the years. It also helps them get to know about your childhood. You need grocery receipts, current bills, and paper and pencil.

Gather together some household bills. List each service and the amount owed. Put the name of the bill on the left side of the paper. Put the cost on the right side.

Fold the paper so that the cost side is hidden. This turns the activity into a game.

Ask your child to predict the amount owed for each bill. Write down the guesses next to the items. Then unfold the paper to show the actual costs. It may surprise you that your child has very little idea of the costs of rent, groceries, and telephone use.

If sales tax is charged in your state, explain the tax and how it works.

Talk about how prices have gone up since you were a child. Share your memories. *Examples:* "I remember when candy bars cost twenty cents" or "I remember when seeing a movie cost less than a dollar." Tell what you saved for when you were a child and how you did it. If you had an allowance, tell how much you received.

On a trip to a grocery or department store, talk with your child about how you used to be able to buy more with the same amount of money not so long ago. Of course, don't forget to mention that salaries are now higher, too. Sharing these memories is a good way to help your child know you and your past better.

## Eating Well for Less ■ ages 4–9

■ *Reading/Thinking*
■ *Using Ads to Plan Healthy Meals*

This activity helps children practice math by planning nutritious family meals that cost less. Use newspaper grocery ads, pencil, and paper.

Talk together about what the family might eat this week. Make up a menu of meals for two days, with your child taking charge of the choices for one meal. Check the advertisements together for coupons or sales on these or substitute foods.

Judge with your child the amount of food needed. Total the prices for the planned meal. Divide by the number of people who will be eating. This gives the cost of the meal per person.

Together check your cupboards and refrigerator before going to the store. See what you have on hand. Let children go to the store with you, if possible. Let them choose certain foods and pay for them. Two tips: Remember to go grocery shopping when you're *not* hungry. If your stomach is empty, you'll buy more than you need. To find the best buys, use unit pricing, which helps you and your child compare prices on the same types of food offered by different companies and in different-size boxes or cans.

> At home, put a sign on the cupboard or refrigerator. It might say, "(Child's Name) found best buys for our meals this week and saved us money." (If you know how much you saved, indicate the amount.)

## Clothes for Less ▪ ages 10–12

▪ *Math*
▪ *Using Ads to Build a Budget*

Preteens buy clothes a lot, or at least they want to. They might as well know how to save money on them. This activity helps. You need store catalogues, newspaper ads, pencil, and paper.

Pretend you each have $250 to spend on clothes. Pretend you have absolutely *nothing* to wear. Make up a complete season's wardrobe from top to bottom. Use newspapers and catalogues. Compare "purchases." How well did you do?

Talk about the advantage of buying clothes and other items out of season. Think of an item each of you wants. When would be the best time to buy it? How expensive is it? Set up a plan for saving (at home or in a bank) so you will have the money when the time comes.

Each of you make up a clothes budget. Include your total monthly income from allowance and any jobs. Figure out when you'll be able to buy the item you want. Make sure there is a little left to put away.

## Saving and Banking ▪ ages 10–12

▪ *Math/Reading*
▪ *Working with Bank Materials*

This activity helps youngsters learn about bank accounts and provides tips on how to save money. You need pencil, paper, and perhaps even money with which to open a savings account.

Visit some banks to get information and pamphlets about services. Read the information together and discuss it. Decide which bank is most convenient. Which offers the highest interest rate? What are the bank's charges? Consider opening a savings account for your child. (The bank may require a minimum balance.) Let your youngster answer the bank officer's questions and fill out the application. Try to see that the bank statement is addressed to your child or you and your child jointly. It is important for your child to read and check the statement.

For a special item your youngster wants to buy, suggest a savings plan. You could work out a "matching grants" arrangement. For every dollar your child puts in the bank toward the item, you might give a dollar (or part of a dollar). This can inspire your youngster to a greater savings effort. Help your child set goals for regular deposits. How much will be added each week or each month? Will there also be

## TEACHING TIPS: COMMON SENSE

### Sharing Our Experiences with Our Children

"I just have to have those shoes. I can't live without them." That's your sweet child talking.

Those wonderfully named shoes probably cost over $100, and while asking for them is a remarkable demonstration of your child's motivation, it doesn't say much for common sense.

How do you talk common sense to your child? One way that doesn't seem to work well these days is to recall how it was when you were a kid, when your parents went to the store and bought the most sensibly priced brand and it all worked out fine.

The pressure on your kids to have what their friends have is overwhelming. How can they resist? How can they help preserve the family budget and get some common sense at the same time? They have a chance if they get the chance to talk to you, not about the old days, but about today and the pressures you yourself experience.

### Sparking the Conversation: Parents Under Pressure

What are you as an adult under pressure to do? To buy? To think? . . . when your child's request goes against common sense? How do you fight back? When do you give in? What do you do? What do you say to yourself?

What advice do your kids have for you? Can they see some of the same pressures they face in the pressures you face as an adult? Encourage them to name some of the pressures on them just as you have named some of yours. You may find that your children have some good advice that, once they've said it to you, may even be useful to them.

### Moving to the Bigger Questions

Young children will probably not recognize the idea of pressure . . . but they *are* being asked to do whatever everybody else does. To a great extent, being like everybody else is a form of security, and everybody likes to feel secure. Questions like these can help your children get a sense of the pressures they face without even knowing it:

- Who sets the fashions? Who tells us what to buy?
- When we hear product claims on TV, are they always true?
- Do we know anyone who has bought a name brand product but has not been satisfied?
- Can we each remember a time when we used our common sense?
- Can we remember a time when we didn't do what everybody else did and it turned out all right? Sometimes it turns out even better.

regular withdrawals? Talk about any basic expenses you expect this savings to be used for.

## JOBS AND MONEY

Parents have been worrying more and more about the impact on teenagers of jobs that take too much time away from schoolwork. The money earned from these jobs is often spent not to help out the family at home but to buy teenage luxury items.

Preteens need to have impressed upon them that schoolwork, now and into their teen years, is their main job, and that it demands and deserves a great deal of time. Most jobs they would be able to get as teenagers, as young and inexperienced as they are, would not provide them with much opportunity for learning. It is more important for young teens to do well in school than to spend a lot of time on a job.

## ARGUMENTS ABOUT MONEY

People probably argue more about money than anything else. While many of these arguments are really about money, I suspect that many are really about other things, such as self-respect, power, recognition, affection, and security.

I remember an all-evening argument with my husband when we were first married. It was over a two-dollar can of furniture pol-ish that he had bought and that I thought we didn't need. In retrospect, I don't think the argument was about the two dollars. I think it was about values and whether that purchase showed that we shared the same set of values.

I was never able to bring myself to use that can of polish, and I don't think he used it, either. When we moved several years later, I saw it sitting alone in the back of the cabinet under the sink.

Maybe some good does result from arguments about money. Maybe they give us a chance to know more about each other—and ourselves. My daughter remembers that when she was five, she had a boyfriend, also five, who lived across the street. He never had any money. She had an allowance, so she bought him treats every time the ice cream truck visited the block. He said he would pay her back, but he didn't. We moved a few blocks away, but she never forgot his debt.

When she was ten years old, she walked back to his house and said, "Michael, you owe me sixty cents." He paid her almost everything he owed, but she's sure that the moment signaled the end of their friendship.

They had grown apart, and it probably wasn't because of the money at all. But arguments about money have the strangest way of being about more than money, a common-sense lesson she learned at an early age.

*Joe DiDio, courtesy of the National Education Association*

## CHAPTER 14

# MegaSkill Ten: Problem Solving

Putting What You Know
and What You Can Do into Action

## THE NEVER-ENDING REPORT CARD

### The Grades We Get in School

Jess is always coming up with new ways to solve old problems. She gave the class ideas for setting up the science exhibit.

### The Grades We Get on the Job

Ms. Short is a woman of ideas. She figured out how to substantially increase company revenues by designing a new product distribution system.

Do your children say "I can't" instead of "I can"? Children are not born problem solvers. They learn how, and they show they're learning when they:

Know how to ask questions and get answers.
Have the ability to identify and face a problem.
Generate ideas that could be solutions.
Show that they can make a reasonable decision.

The activities in this chapter are designed to encourage children's problem-solving abilities, helping them put what they know and can do into action. And they have proven to be remarkably helpful to parents.

### From Massachusetts . . .

"I didn't have all the answers, and didn't need to have them. I learned that there are other ways to do things, not just one."

A special section focuses on safety, an issue of great concern to families today. We cannot be safe for our children. They have to know on their own the questions to ask and the steps to take. They need to be able to deal with problems and potential problems calmly and effectively.

The smartest thing I probably said to my children when they were growing up was, "Try to be one of those people on whom nothing is lost." I think one of the James boys said this—not Jesse, but Henry, the writer.

Problem solving depends on not losing ideas. It requires thinking. When I taught in high school and even in graduate school, the hardest question I could ask students was, "What do you think?"

Because they had so much trouble, I began to consider how thinking could be taught, not just in the classroom but in the home.

Thinking is not a subject all by itself—it's what you *think about* that is the subject. We need children who can begin to think

> **From Montana . . .**
>
> "Talking with my children about Mega-Skills has helped me open up and talk with them about really tough subjects like sex, AIDS, drugs. The lines of communication have opened."

about serious subjects; with encouragement and the proper skills, they can do this.

My recipe for problem solving is made up of two basic ingredients:

- Practice in asking and answering questions.
- Practice in making decisions.

That's what the activities in this chapter emphasize.

It's intriguing that these activities cross age and ability levels without a scratch. I've used many of them with success from the elementary grades to graduate school. Of course, the results are different. We should expect college students' responses to be more sophisticated and complex than those of second graders—but sometimes they aren't.

## QUESTIONS, QUESTIONS, QUESTIONS

Asking and answering questions takes a lot of practice and time. In school, children don't really get enough practice. There isn't much time for "thoughtful" questions and answers. Sure, children answer true-and-false questions and questions for which there is one correct response, such as, "What is the longest river in the world?" But what they need more of, and what schools —for very good reasons—have trouble providing, are thought-provoking questions, such as, "What do you think about . . . ?" or "How could this be made better?" or "What would you do to organize this differently?"

These are open-ended questions. They are not used as often in class as even many teachers would like. They take a lot of time; there are no "right" answers; they often elicit "I don't know" from students; and they might generate answers that teachers find troublesome to hear and difficult to handle. I have asked a number of them in my time as an English teacher, and sometimes I berated myself afterward for not going for the multiple-choice, single-right-answer quiz.

## THE "THOUGHT-FULL" HOME

There is a growing movement afoot to encourage more "thought-full" schools, but it will probably take more time than today's students can wait for.

What parents don't have to wait for is the "thought-full" home. By this I mean a home where children get the practice they need in asking thought-provoking questions and in coming up with "thought-full" answers. Any parent can do it . . . and do it now.

**First,** it means asking questions that you really want answers to and that you really care about hearing the answers to.

For younger children, you might ask questions about the stories you read together: "What do you think will happen next?" "How do you think the story will end?" "What makes you think so?"

For older children, you might use situational questions. When the TV konks out, ask the kids, "How do you think we should handle this?" "Should we get it repaired?" "Should we buy a new one?" "What do you think?" "Why?" (Also see "What's Your Opinion?" in Chapter 12.)

When the TV is on, you might ask, "Should we turn it off?" "What is this show telling us?" "What are we getting out of it?" "Should we think of doing anything else instead?"

**Second,** it means listening to children's answers, even forcing yourself to listen, if you have to. If necessary, ask your children to remind you to listen when they find you aren't. We're not talking about thirty-minute presentations, but answers that may extend over a minute or two.

**Third,** it means letting children know how really smart they are. Preadolescents may know more about the working of a TV set than any parent suspects. We have to be sure that our children know when they give us their thoughtful answers that we are not only listening but learning.

**Fourth,** it means letting your children ask you questions that they want answers to and your taking the time to respond thoughtfully. They might ask why they have to do the chores at a certain hour every evening or what is making you so upset about their hair style or their friends or their report card.

**Fifth,** it means that your children listen while you talk and that just as they are expected to keep within reasonable time limits in their answers, so are you.

## THE "CREATIVE TOUCH"

Even though all problem solving is creative, some questions elicit more "creative" answers than others. When you ask a child, "What do you wish would happen?" you can expect a more imaginative answer than when you ask about the broken TV set.

Encourage children to imagine. What would happen if the automobile had not been invented? A whole new world opens up. Ask children to name five inventions the world could use that have not been invented yet.

Try designs on paper to elicit ideas. Put a blob of ink on paper, fold it, rub, and blot.

> You can spur children's inventive thinking with questions that limber up the brain. Ask how many things can be made from a paper plate. From a rubber band? From a paper clip? How can ordinary stairs be improved?

Ask children to tell you all the things the blob reminds them of. Trade places and try it yourself.

Place circles or squares or triangles of various sizes on a sheet of paper. Then ask children to name and draw as many different objects as they can think of using these figures.

Help children think ahead about what they would change and what they would do if they had their wish:

What do you want more time for?
How would you use more money?
What is a waste of time?
What makes you feel really happy?
How do you wish the family would be
    different?
What would you like to keep always the
    same?
Whom would you like to be friends with?
What would you like to do tomorrow?
    Next week? Next month?

Encourage children to ask you some of these, too. The list is as endless as are wishes. Asking the questions may be one of the first steps in having these wishes come true.

## YOU KNOW MORE THAN YOU THINK YOU DO

For some people, the hardest answer in the world is "I don't know." But for many children, I think one of the easiest answers is "I don't know."

We can't let our kids get away with this. They are smart. They know more than they think they do. Street-smart kids, for exam-ple, are problem solving all the time. They get in the classroom and they're often struck dumb. They need the chance to show what they know and how they go about solving problems. Home, where there is no worry over wasting classtime and covering a certain curriculum by the end of the month, is a good place to let kids show what they know.

What you'll be talking about for the most part are open-ended questions. There are no right answers. You are not in the class-room, so there are no other hands waving in the air, no other children eager to give the right answer. It's a relaxed atmosphere of give and take. It's a time for exchanging ideas, feelings, hopes, dreams. It's a time that only a "thought-full" home can provide.

## MAKING DECISIONS

Decision making is not easy, but it becomes less painful as children:

- Become increasingly aware that they can help to solve problems.
- See that a problem can have more than one solution, but that one may be better than others.
- Learn about restraint and to think about a problem before acting.

### Not to Decide Is to Decide

Decision making generates a lot of fears. I know it does for me. Years ago, I brought home a poster that was helpful to me. It said, "Not to Decide Is to Decide." Finding this in a bookstore made me realize that I was not alone. Since they had printed so many of these, other people must have been having the same trouble. This was comforting and provided me with more courage to make decisions.

> Involve children actively and early in decision making, especially in family decision making. They can be active participants or can just listen in. In this way they come to know, and to identify with, the process adults go through making up our minds.

## Thinking and Choosing
■ ages 4–7

■ *Thinking*
■ *Generating Choices for Decision Making*

Children can use practice making small decisions before they have to make large ones. You need thinking minds.

Ask your child to pretend the following things are happening:

■ You can't find your key and no one is home.
■ You get lost on your way to a friend's house.
■ You are teased on your way home from school.

Ask children to think of as many ways to solve these problems as they can. Don't reject any ideas, even if they sound far-fetched.

After children have mulled over three or four different solutions, let them pick one way that seems best.

For more ideas, try out these scenarios with your children:

■ Mother calls you to go on an errand to the neighbor's house next door. But before you start out, a friend comes by and says, "Let's play." What do you do?
■ You're in a terrible hurry to get to a costume party, and just as you're putting on that special costume, it rips. What do you do?

Let even young children decide how to arrange their own room or at least part of it, and include your child in the choosing of the decor and furnishings.

Ask for children's ideas to remedy a problem they cause (not necessarily at the time when you're upset about the mess). *Examples:* Mud on the floor, coats not hung up, milk left out. This way, instead of having a solution imposed on them, children have a hand in making it—and, we hope, a stake in seeing the solution work. (For more examples, see the special section on safety that follows this chapter.)

## Decisions Aren't Easy ■ ages 9–12

■ *Thinking*
■ *Judging Decisions and Consequences*

As kids grow older, they need to be aware of the many decisions they make every day . . . about clothes, friends, jobs. You need thinking minds.

Talk with your youngster about some important decisions you have made in the past. *Examples:* Buying a car, changing jobs, getting married. Tell about the things you considered before making these decisions. Were there good and bad consequences? Were you happy with your decisions? Would you make the same ones again?

Making decisions usually involves looking at the pros (the pluses) and the cons (the minuses) of a situation. Together consider the pros and cons of skipping school, eating a lot, spending money. What is gained? What is lost?

Whenever possible, try to let your youngsters bear the consequences of their own decision making—good *or* bad! Talk about what could be done next time.

Encourage children to become planners: What would they do if they were teachers?

---

**From Oklahoma . . .**

"We go to this large supermarket, and I use coupons a lot. I never used to take my kids to the store because they always seemed to be getting underfoot. Now I take them because my son has helped me solve the problem of how to find the items I was having trouble finding before. He wrote down all the aisle numbers and what you can find in those aisles. Now I give him the coupons, and he finds the items. I can hear him now: 'Do we want the cookies or can we go with the crackers?'"

---

Fathers? Mothers? Exchanging roles gives them a glimmer of teachers' and parents' points of view.

Ask for children's advice in choosing the best place for a vacation. Discuss the reasons for their choice and the factors that determine the ultimate decision, such as time and money. Children need to face these realities of life. Providing this practice will help.

## THE MATTER OF CHOICE

Since choice is basic to problem solving, real choices must be available to children. For young children, limit the number of possible choices. Don't give children decisions to make that you believe are yours alone. There is danger when children are given decisions to make that are really not theirs to make or when children are told they can make the decision and then find that their parents really didn't mean it.

Choose the real decisions that children can make and be prepared to live with their decisions. The ones our children make are not always the ones we would make. If you say, "This is *your* decision," you have to mean it.

## SAFETY—EVERYDAY PROBLEM SOLVING

### Supervising the "Latch-Key" Child

Security is safety, but it's more than that. It's feeling safe. Many young children say they don't feel safe at home when an adult is not there.

Studies show that children feel safer and less alone when they *feel* supervised.

While it is still impossible to be in two places at one time, there are ways to help children feel supervised, even when parents are not at home.

Just being home doesn't always do the job. It's possible to be at home all the time and not have children feel that their parents care.

Use your problem-solving abilities to come up with ways to make sure your child knows you are supervising—no matter where you are.

*Examples:*

Set up a call-in, check-in time as soon as your child gets home from school.

Leave messages for children all around the house: on the calendar, the front of the refrigerator, the pillow, the back door.

Use a tape recorder or answering machine to leave and pick up messages from one another. Hearing an adult voice is helpful in itself.

Make sure that children know what they are supposed to do. Go over their after-school time with them the night before.

Ask around to see if there is a neighbor —perhaps a retiree at home—who can be called—just in case.

> Children need to know that parents care about what they are doing.

> Help brothers and sisters get along without your being right there to break up fights.

It can be more dangerous for siblings who don't get along to be home together than for one of them to be home alone. It's comforting for parents to think the darlings at home are taking care of each other. But that's not always the case. Efforts need to be made to help siblings be civilized; these include providing separate activities that keep kids out of each other's hair, and separate study areas as well.

(See also Chapter 24, "Parents and At-Home Child Care." Tips provided for helpers can also be useful for children on their own.)

Make sure that the house is safe and that children know how to keep it safe. The activities presented later in this section focus on basic household safety strategies.

## WE CANNOT BE SAFE FOR OUR CHILDREN

Children have to know the steps to take on their own to be safe. Of course, we can and should warn kids not to step in front of speeding cars and to turn off the stove after using it. But children have to do these things themselves. We can't watch kids from morning to night to prevent them from doing something unsafe.

One way to tackle this problem is by building children's own safety habits. Without becoming overfearful, our youngsters can be taught about decisions they need to make to protect themselves.

## WHAT'S THE PROBLEM?

A solution is good only when it's carried out. It doesn't help when the front door is not locked, when heaters remain on after children have departed the room, or when purses are left out for all to see. That's why it's important for children to be part of the problem-solving process. They're the ones who will be putting the solutions into place.

Take children through these activities by asking questions before coming up with solutions. You can ask the following questions first or go straight to the solutions suggested in the activities. In any event, make sure that your children know the problem they are being asked to prevent. Here's a four-point system to try:

1. What is the problem?
2. What solutions can we try?
3. What are the good and bad points of these solutions?
4. What do you think of the solution in this activity?

Helping children go through some step-by-step thinking is just one way to get them into the habit of problem solving. This is not an automatic, sequential program. Good ideas can come in the strangest way,

like bolts out of the blue. When faced with decisions, many of us say, "I want to sleep on it." Somehow or other, good ideas germinate in the middle of the night, and by the next morning, we know what we're going to do. It's not clear we have employed step-by-step reasoning to get there; it seems that some wonderful, mysterious process is at work.

## THINKING THROUGH A PROBLEM: STEP-BY-STEP EXAMPLE

Here are questions keyed to the system above. They can lead you through the activity "Warning, Warning," which follows. The activity is about poison prevention.

1. Children accidentally eat or drink poisons and dangerous medicines lying around the house. Many youngsters become ill and die.
2. What can we do here at home to prevent this from happening? Let's name a lot of ideas.
3. Are there any good or bad points about the ideas we've listed? For example, if we are going to hide everything, will we be able to recognize new, dangerous medicines or products in other settings?
4. How about giving the following activity a try? In a few weeks, we'll check to see how it's working. (*Note:* To check, you bring in a new medicine and see how your children handle it. Can they tell it's

dangerous? Where do they want to put it?)

Make up your own questions as you work through all these safety activities. In this way, your children will know that they have a role to play in keeping themselves and their home safe—and you will feel a lot safer when you are away from home.

## Warning, Warning ■ ages 4–6

- *Reading*
- *Understanding Vocabulary in Context*

Children have ways of finding everything, so it's best to instill in them their own understanding of how to prevent poisoning. This activity helps children recognize the warning labels on medicines and household cleaners at home. Early readers get practice reading the labels. You need a sturdy box with four or five household products and medicines. (Use only those with warning labels.)

Take one product out of the box. Help your child find the warning label and say it or read it aloud. Point together to the words that mean WATCH OUT. Some of these are *caution, poison, danger, warning, hazard.* Point out the skull and crossbones symbol.

Ask your child to read the labels of the other products in the box and to list these words. Talk about why these cleaning products and medicines are kept out of reach.

Discuss what can be done if these products or medicines are swallowed accidentally. The labels tell us what remedies or antidotes counteract the poison.

Put your child's list of warning words in a special place for the family to read. The refrigerator door is a good place. Make warning signs for your house. *Example:* "Poisons are stored in this cupboard."

Remind your children to take medicine only with your approval. Twice as many children die accidentally from taking drugs and medicines as from swallowing household cleaners.

## Household Danger Spots
■ ages 4–6

- *Thinking*
- *Building Observation Skills*

Here's a way to help children learn how to recognize home repair danger spots, so that when they see one, they'll avoid trouble and let you know what needs to be fixed. You need ordinary household objects, including paper bags and rags.

Take a walk around your home with your child. Check in each room to see that electric cords are not frayed, that throw rugs don't slide, that old papers, rags, and paints are stored properly, that sharp edges of knives and tools are covered.

Make a list of items in the house that need to be repaired. Separate the list into two sections—those that can be repaired at home and those that have to go to the repair shop. If items are repaired at home, try to involve children in helping.

## Appliance Checklist ■ ages 4–6

- *Reading/Writing*
- *Creating a Safety Checklist*

This activity helps children learn how to use appliances safely. Have children find lights and appliances with OFF marked on them. Practice turning appliances on and off. *Examples:* Light switches, CD players, irons, portable heaters, televisions.

Show children how the stove is turned off. If the stove is not to be used at all, explain why. Talk about why children should never play with matches.

Together with your child, make an OFF chart to post near the front door. Here's a model to follow:

### Have We Remembered to Turn Off:

| | |
|---|---|
| ____ TV? | ____ Heaters? |
| ____ Stove? | ____ Lights? (Leave |
| ____ Other electrical appliances? | hall light on for safety.) |

*Note:* Use symbols on the list for children who cannot yet read.

## Keys to the Kingdom ■ ages 4–6

- *Thinking*
- *Testing Household Safety Measures*

Children need routines to follow, limits that they understand and that can be enforced, and structure for use of their time. This is the essence of feeling secure, of feeling supervised, of feeling cared for. This is what parents can provide, even from afar. Studies of children who report in to their parents after school and who say that their parents know where they are all the time indicate that they feel well supervised. And they behave that way.

You need working locks and keys for this activity.

Take a walk around your house. Show children how to lock and unlock all doors and at least a few windows. Point to exits to use in case of fire or other need to escape.

Let children try using all house keys. Have keys made for each family member and put these in special places for safekeeping.

Try to make your home as burglarproof as possible. Make sure there is a strong chain on the front door so that it can be opened only partially. Many parents tell children never to open the door for people they do not know.

Tell children never to enter the house after school if the door is ajar, a window is broken, or anything looks unusual. Give instructions to go to a neighbor's or to a store, then to call Mom or Dad and wait for an adult to arrive before returning to the house.

## Community Safety Tour
▪ ages 4–6

▪ *Reading/Writing*
▪ *Checking Signs in the Neighborhood*

This activity helps children feel at home in the community, and it teaches them the meaning of important signs, even if they can't yet read them. You need thinking minds, paper, pen, and some change.

Walk with your child or drive through your community. Point out the many signs you see. Which are the signs for safety? What do the other signs tell you? *Examples:* BUS, YIELD, WALK, and CAUTION are some signs that children need to know.

Show safe and less safe places to walk. Identify and introduce yourselves to neighborhood safety personnel, such as policemen and crossing guards. Talk about safe

Prepare a safety kit for your child to take everywhere. It can include an identification card, a list of important telephone numbers, change for several phone calls, and perhaps enough money for bus or cab fare. Tape the kit inside your child's lunchbox or knapsack.

places to go in case of danger. *Examples:* a neighbor's house, a business office.

## Dealing with Strangers ▪ any age

▪ *Communication*
▪ *Practicing Speaking on the Phone and Taking Messages*

Children must learn to protect themselves against strangers at home and on the street. Here's how. All you need are thinking minds.

Give instructions to your children on how to talk to strangers on the phone, at the door, and on the street.

Make up a set response to use on the phone. *Example:* "My mom can't come to the phone now. May I take a message?"

Teach children how to take careful telephone messages that include the caller's name and phone number. Buy a phone pad or make one out of scrap paper. Practice handling phone calls. Use a play phone or the real phone. Take turns being the caller and being the child at home.

Warn about accepting rides and gifts from strangers. In view of the tragedies that have occurred, be absolutely firm in your warnings. Do not assume that children know the dangers. Role play some typical situations such as, "Do you want candy?" "Can I give you a ride?"

It's wise to avoid calling attention to money. Advise children not to carry thick wallets and to keep them out of sight. Girls who carry shoulder bags should hold on to them firmly. If youngsters are carrying large amounts of money, tell them to divide the money and to carry it in at least two places.

## Street Smarts ■ ages 10–12

- ■ *Communication/Reading*
- ■ *Talking Together About Safety*
- ■ *Reading Community Materials*

Safety rules have a tendency to be over-looked by older youngsters—once they feel old enough to take care of themselves. Use thinking minds for this one.

Talk together about at least three things to increase safety outdoors. *Examples:* lock cars, keep personal items out of sight in parked cars, avoid deserted areas.

Ask family and friends to tell about one special safety rule they practice at home or outdoors. Are there any good ideas your family had not thought of?

Use city transportation schedules to figure out a trip to a specific destination, such as a concert hall. How long will it take? Is it a safe place to go? What safety precautions, if any, are needed?

## In Case of Fire ■ any age

- ■ *Reading/Writing*
- ■ *Learning Emergency Words and Creating a Plan*

Help your family know how to leave the house quickly and safely in case of fire.

You need thinking minds, pencil, and paper.

Show children the emergency numbers for Fire, Police, and Poison Control listed in the front of the telephone book. Tell children to dial "0" for the operator in case of an emergency. For children who can't read, make a picture chart with the numbers. Buy a small fire extinguisher to keep in the kitchen and a smoke alarm for your home.

Practice leaving the house quickly, using different exits. Make these sessions family affairs so that everyone will know exactly what to do in case of fire or an accident. Practice until you are sure children understand what to do.

Children are much more likely to stay calm in a crisis if they feel they know what to do.

One of the differences between teaching about safety and teaching about money, for example, is that you really can't teach safety in stages, waiting for children to grow up and handle more complicated details. A six-year-old needs to know as much or almost as much as a twelve-year-old. It's as if you want to teach everything at once, especially now that young children spend so much time alone at home.

## TEACHING TIPS: PROBLEM SOLVING

### Sharing Our Experiences with Our Children

"You dummy!" That's what kids said to me when I told them about my foot getting caught in the spokes of my brother's bike. I was riding on the back of the bike and even though my parents told me to put on my shoes, I didn't. I was barefoot, the bike hit a bump, my foot went into the wheel; it came out with a spoke in it.

I've lived to tell the tale, and nobody has to remind me again. I wear shoes when I ride a bike. That's one way to learn, painful but not deadly.

Children like to hear stories like this. And it opens doors to conversations about far more deadly consequences for children who today don't listen to the warnings about how to be safe . . . safe from drugs, safe from AIDS, safe from crime. While no one can promise complete safety, there are precautions that help.

### Sparking the Conversation: Getting Kids to Talk and Listen

Today children have to listen and learn before they experiment. There is a lot of information around. Early elementary graders are hearing about AIDS, about smoking, about drugs. Are they learning?

Talk to your kids about all those other kids, the ones who need the lecture. Ask, How can we reach them? What's the message they'll listen to? Brainstorm ideas. Come up with a bunch of alternatives. What's good about each one? What are the pluses and minuses?

This form of problem solving is really a habit of the mind. Even young children can get into the habit. For example, "How can we get Uncle Jim to stop smoking? Any ideas?" And the ideas will come. Some will be better than others. Those are the ones you save, and you keep one handy to try out the next time you talk to or see Uncle Jim. It might even work with a parent who smokes.

### Moving to the Bigger Questions

Try some of these with your young problem solvers. They might have an answer that's escaped the rest of us:

- To reduce crime, will it help to have more police?
- To stop the spread of AIDS, what kind of education will it really take to reach kids? What will get them to listen?
- To get more kids to say no to drugs, what will it take? How do we keep our friends from being "dummies"?

Ideas build on one another. They have a terrific ability to keep flowing as long as we keep drawing from the well.

## SAFETY: AN ALL-AT-ONCE SKILL

Children don't know all the safety problems and hazards in advance. They don't start out knowing which items at home are poisonous and what to do in case of fire. And you don't know when and if they will face such problems. Thanks to the growing number of good books on children's safety as well as the activities in this chapter and others that you will think of, your children can be prepared.

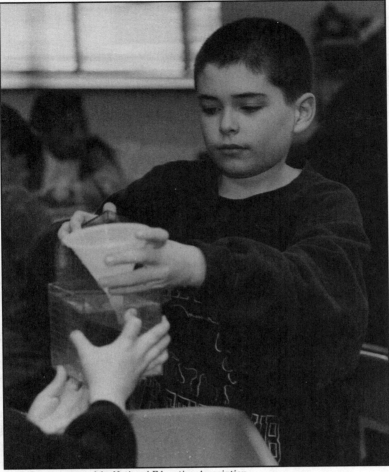

*Joe DiDio, courtesy of the National Education Association*

**CHAPTER 15**

# MegaSkill Eleven: Focus

## Concentrating with a Goal in Mind

## THE NEVER-ENDING REPORT CARD

### The Grades We Get in School

Jon is learning how to set goals and work to meet them. He tries hard to manage his time and keep at the assignment that must be completed.

### The Grades We Get on the Job

Jonathan Barry has a wonderful ability to focus on the work to be done, to examine the situation, to set priorities and keep working until the goal is met.

Focus is the newest MegaSkill. In the earlier MegaSkills editions, focus did not emerge as an indicator for the Never-Ending Report Card. Today, however, more and more of us are talking about the need for focus.

Do we really have to worry about this? Haven't people always been distracted? The poet Wordsworth over a century ago talked about "getting and spending, we lay waste our powers."

The need for focus is not new. What's different is that "wasting our powers" is more dangerous today. We see increasing levels of individual anger and frustration as people struggle to manage change in their lives. Crime on the streets and anger in the school halls may not be necessarily related

When our lives become complicated and life is coming at us too fast, self-discipline and focus are more necessary and more important than ever.

to change in the larger society. Yet there is growing evidence that young people are having more and more difficulty coping, and therefore are turning to drugs and becoming increasingly antisocial.

Focus has always been important, but it's almost been assumed that we have it or can be counted on to develop it. In slower times, that was probably the case. But today, when so many of us, children included, feel caught in the whirlwind of so many choices and so much to do, the call for focus is being heard in schools and in the workplace as never before.

For the very lucky few, focus is not a problem at all. Those are the folks we read about in the newspaper who as kids knew they wanted to swim across the Atlantic or become a rocket scientist or a chess master. They just *knew*—they were focused as all get out. However, for most of us, focus is a continuing problem and a challenge.

Some of the obstacles standing in the way of focus are so obvious that they get overlooked. For example, it's hard to get

- Parents have been heard to mutter, "Our kids need focus. We'd like to see them keep their mind on one assignment, one idea, just to get it done."
- Teachers are weighing in with, "Kids just don't seem to be able to pay attention and listen."
- Employers complain that employees make mistakes over and over, that they don't seem to be able to keep their mind on their job.

focused in the midst of stress and disorganization. Focus demands that children and adults get enough sleep and food. It demands a level of structure in our homes and classrooms so that we can focus our minds. We can't take this for granted, yet in many homes today, even affluent homes, there is a basic lack of daily structure that children crave, even when they don't know they crave it. A time to eat, a time to sleep, a time for homework, a time to be together.

Our children need to be able to control their impulses and to see the adults around them controlling theirs. Our children need to become what psychologists call self-regulating. This gives them the ability to be calm enough to be attentive and focused.

This is the basic level of organization that is vital to get the most from the activities in this chapter. Each family functions in a different way. We don't have to be tightly scheduled, but we do have to provide our children with the sense of security and organization that makes it possible for them to focus.

This chapter provides twenty activities to help children figure out systematic ways to set goals and to meet them.

The particular strength of focus as a MegaSkill is that it connects so well to meeting goals. Goal setting has the remarkable ability to keep our minds and our thinking centered. When we work toward a goal and measure our progress along the

### The MegaSkills Focus-Building Process

The step-by-step focus-building in this chapter is designed to become automatic once we get used to it. The exercises provide the practice it takes to turn goal setting and goal meeting into a habit. It becomes part of us, part of our way behaving and thinking.

#### WHAT DO I WANT TO ACCOMPLISH?

Finding a Goal
Selecting an Objective
Moving into Action

#### WHAT DO I HAVE TO DO?

What Do I Have Going for Me?
What Do I Do to Get There?
What Do I Have to Watch Out For?
How Will I Know That I Am Making Progress?

way, we use our MegaSkills and feel more productive, more involved.

## WHAT DO I WANT TO ACCOMPLISH?

This is no easy question. Much of the time, even as adults, we can't get our hands and minds around what we really want to do. A goal does not have to be lofty and far-reaching to be important. Even young children can become goal setters and meeters. When children have at least one goal to work on, they are off to a fine start. Try these exercises.

### Goals: All Sizes, All Kinds
■ any age

These activities teach a basic strategy for finding a goal that "fits." You might find more than one. You need paper, markers, a calendar, and thinking heads.

### A. Finding a Goal

- *Thinking*
- *Generating Ideas*
- *Listening and Speaking Together*

Caution: Do not begin with a question such as "What's your goal?" It's bound to be met with the classic answer, "I don't know."

Instead, start with a potpourri of subjects or categories. Goals can be created in all of them: school, family, sports, friends, hobbies, clothes, music, movies, food, toys, and so on.

Working with your child, make a list of these ideas, with each of you suggesting topics as they come to mind.

### B. Selecting an Objective

- *Writing*
- *Organizing Information*

Once you have your list of at least five topics, rank them based on your child's interest in them. You can start at either end, from least to most interesting. Write the number 1 next to the topic that takes top billing.

Now the task is to narrow the subject. Let's say your child is interested in hobbies. What hobby? model airplanes? collecting stuff? games? computers? Together, rank the hobby of choice in the same way you ranked the subject, from least to most interesting.

### C. Moving into Action

- *Study Skills*
- *Researching and Charting Information*

Now your child moves from words to deeds. For example, if the hobby your child picks is magic tricks, think about how many magic tricks will be learned by what date. Set goals for yourself along with your child to inject a sense of teamwork into the activity. Try to keep the goals realistic and doable. Remember to talk about what it takes to meet the goal you've selected. Do you need books on magic tricks? other supplies?

Check your calendar. Pick a date to mark with your child for the presentation of the magic show or other event. Keep the date within reason, not too far off. For young children, a week is forever. For older children, a month may be workable. By keeping a goal short range and manageable, it is possible to gain a feeling of accomplishment without having to wait too long.

## WHAT DO I HAVE TO DO?

### What Do I Have Going for Me?

Once we select a goal, we ask ourselves, "What have we got going for us? What strengths and abilities can we draw on? What are my *resources?* What *obstacles* need to be overcome?" We don't say it in these words, but this moves our thinking.

### Taking Stock ■ any age

- *Thinking*
- *Comparing and Contrasting Information*

This is a discussion and memory sharing activity.

How is your child's attitude? Ready to move forward or somewhat frightened? Try to reassure your child that it's OK to be scared. It's good to know how we feel so that we can use this nervousness and not be discouraged by it.

How about your child's previous experiences in developing new skills? Have there been successes? If so, point them out and indicate how similar they are to what your child is trying to accomplish now.

### One Obstacle at a Time ■ any age

- *Study Skills*
- *Building Good Work Habits*

Talk together about the fact that there are always obstacles on the road to fulfilling a goal. Instead of thinking of all of them, start with one. Identify and talk together about just one obstacle in the path of meeting the goal. It might be how to keep nervousness under control. Focus on it and forget the others. Ask your child what to do about it. Think of several ways to deal with it. Keep talking about this one problem, not any others. Tackling one obstacle at a time makes success seem possible, even likely.

### Keeping Going ■ any age

- *Study Skills*
- *Building Good Work Habits*

Kids (some adults too) can get the idea that successful people always have success. Talk together about the reality, which is sharply different. Tell your kids what it was like when they were first learning to walk— they fell down a lot as they began to take steps. Tell as many of these experiences as you can think of. What makes successful people successful is that they know how to keep going and keep trying.

## What Do I Do to Get There?
■ any age

■ *Study Skills*
■ *Building Good Work Habits*

When traveling, it helps to have a map. That's what it's like when we work toward a goal. We need to keep on the road but also to be able to see the interesting sights along the way. We have to keep our eyes on the prize, be organized, and set specific rules for ourselves that keep us as focused as possible.

## Paying Attention ■ ages 4–9

■ *Study Skills*
■ *Remembering Details and Charting Information*

Most of the time, when we look at something, we browse. We aren't really paying attention. To work on a goal we have to keep focused. This starts with paying attention.

Try these exercises that help to focus attention. These examples are gradual on purpose. The idea is to help children focus attention over a longer and longer period of time.

■ Watch a construction project, day by day. Try to detect what's different one day to the next.

■ Play long games such as Monopoly in stages. Start at some point and pick up the game at exactly the same place the next day. Remember where you and other players left off.
■ On a map of the United States, find all the state capitals. Do this in stages, finding ten capitals each time. Remember which ones you found the last time you played.

Think of your own attention focusing games. It might be to remember which foods you ate last week or what clothes you wore. Tell about the content of the books you read and the TV programs you watch. Extend the descriptions each time, longer and longer. Focusing our attention is truly a basic skill today.

## Getting and Keeping Information

It takes information to achieve most goals. That can be almost any goal, from buying a bike to giving a speech. Here are some discussion activities with questions we can ask ourselves and each other as we gather the information we need.

## Where Do I Get the Information?
■ ages 9 and up

■ *Study Skills*
■ *Researching Information*

What do I need to know? topics for a speech? how to judge good bikes? Jot down the questions. Where do I get the information? from books? ask friends? use the Internet?

## How Can I Remember It?
■ ages 9 and up

- ■ *Study Skills*
- ■ *Organizing Information*

How do we file and keep this information? in our heads? in notes? in file folders? We need to ask, "How does what I am learning connect to what I already know?" This helps us remember and recall new information.

## How Do I Know I Know Enough?
■ ages 9 and up

- ■ *Thinking*
- ■ *Making Reasoned Decisions*

Have I checked more than one source? Opinions will differ. Have I figured out which opinions make more sense? Am I satisfied that I know enough? At some point, we have to call a halt and say that this is it!

**How About a Planner?** A growing number of schools today are distributing versions of Daily and Weekly Organizers to students. Children lead busy lives, and they often forget what they have to do, including and especially homework assignments. While the homework doesn't always get done, even with an organizer, at least the lame excuse of "I forgot" gets lamer.

Why wait for schools to hand out the planners? If you and your child believe that an organizer can help to keep track of what has to be done, go to a stationery store together. Pick one that's not too thick, that your child can comfortably use regularly.

## Making a Plan ■ ages 8 and up

- ■ *Study Skills*
- ■ *Organizing a Plan*
- ■ *Listening and Talking Together*

OK, now you're ready to buy the bike or make the speech. What do you do first? second? third?

A plan doesn't have to be written in some fancy document. It does need a semblance of order. This order varies based upon each person's idea of order. There are the neatniks and the not so neat. Our kids do not have to use the same 1,2,3 model we use.

For this activity, use paper, pencil, and thinking minds. Together, choose a goal. Then separately write down your plan for meeting it. After you have jotted down your ideas, talk about how your plans of action are similar and different.

For example, to buy a bike: 1) I have my information. 2) I am ready to visit the stores. 3) I am ready to ask my questions. 4) I am ready to pick the brand(s) I am most interested in. 5) I am ready to check out comparative prices at other stores. 6) I am ready to make the purchase.

For example, to make the speech: 1) I have chosen my subject. 2) I have information. 3) I sit down to write my outline. 4) I revise it. 5) I practice it at home. 6) I time myself. 7) I go into class, as ready as I will ever be.

Developing strategies to meet goals is very exciting learning, for younger and older students. The older we get, the more we enjoy the strategizing. We can all learn how to do it and enjoy it.

## What Do I Have to Watch Out For?

Stress, Discouragement, and Distraction . . . these are among the great enemies of focus.

We have to be able to recognize these enemies and fight them. We need to share these strategies with our children. Here are some talking together activities.

**How We Battle Stress.** We count to ten, we take a walk around the block, we talk it out, we take a cold shower or a hot bath. We try as many ways as possible to maintain self-control and a sense of balance. Children need to hear us talk about these and need to practice with us these stress battling strategies. They may not always work but they help put us on the right track.

**How We Battle Discouragement.** We accept the fact that we will have disappointments and make mistakes. We try to forgive ourselves, to learn from the mistakes, and to move on. Children need to hear from us that yes, we do make mistakes. We live through disappointments. We need to share some of these experiences and tell what we learned and what happened afterward. We have lived through them and so can our children.

**How We Battle Distraction.** We struggle to stay focused. We try to keep from getting sidetracked. For children, this often means having the strength to resist peer pressures. One of the better ways to deal with these pressures is to have plans and to try to stick to them. We figure out timelines for reaching goals. And if they don't work the first

> Today, more than ever, it's easy to get distracted. We put blinders on horses so that they see only straight ahead. No such easy gimmick for humans. We have to do it the hard way.

time, we start again. Courage is not just for singular heroic moments. Battling to stay focused takes courage.

**Keeping Focus in Balance.** Can we ever be too focused? The answer can be yes. While we need to know how to keep our attention on a task, we also need to know when to shift our attention. Over-focus can become obsessive. The key is in balancing focus.

Driving along a busy highway, we dare not take our eyes off the road. Cooking dinner is different. We can walk away from the stove for short intervals. When we care for a young child, we can look away at least for a short time, when a child is in a playpen. But we have to keep our eyes glued on a baby who is crawling freely across a room.

The right amount of focus depends on the situation and how much focus it really takes. Measuring this out is an art. Like learning how to cook, like learning how to drive, it takes practice and experience.

## How Will I Know That I Am Making Progress?

We need to know and to show how we are doing, and we shouldn't always have to depend on others to grade us and to evaluate our progress. We can more simply and effectively measure how we are doing when we focus on setting and meeting goals.

Any goal will do. For younger children, the more tangible the goal the better. When the goal is to read ten books in a certain period of time, children can measure and keep track of their progress. For older children, the goal might be more abstract, such as to make more friends and get more comfortable in class . . . and even that can be assessed.

Keep the following activities in mind to share with your children.

## Promises to Ourselves ▪ any age

- *Communication/Writing*
- *Listening and Talking*
- *Charting Information*

We make promises to others a lot. But among the most important promises—perhaps *the* most important—are the ones we make to ourselves. These are the source of strength for the plans we make and the steps we take. You need paper, pencil, and thinking heads.

Share with your children two promises you are making to yourself. Ask them to share two promises with you. As much as possible, let these be measurable so that you and your children can assess whether and how they are being met. These don't have to be grandiose: one might be to spend ten minutes each day reading to your child.

For your child, the nature of the promises will depend on your child's age, but one could be to spend five minutes each day for

a week talking about what happened in school.

Make your choices. You can post them on a chart and give each other stars or check marks. In any case, pick an easy and clear way to indicate your progress in action.

## How Am I Doing Chart ▪ any age

- *Writing*
- *Creating a Plan*

This is an ordinary piece of paper with three columns. One lists the steps to take to meet a goal. The second lists dates for taking these actions, and the third is for the child (or adult) to mark the completion of each step. You need paper, marker, and a ruler.

Let's say the goal is to read a certain number of books. On the left-hand side of the paper is the list of numbers—one through ten. Next to each is the name of the book. If these aren't picked yet, just list the numbers. Use the calendar to fill in dates. It's especially important to keep track of each step as it is accomplished. Use a marker to check it off. Be bold. Give yourself credit for what you are accomplishing!

## Grading Myself Report Form ▪ ages 8 and up

- *Thinking/Writing*
- *Evaluating Evidence*

Why should we wait for others to give us grades? We can do it ourselves and improve our own work in the bargain. Use the How Am I Doing Chart and add a fourth column or make a brand-new form. You need paper, pencil, and thinking heads.

Ask your child to think about the ten books. Give yourself grades on how much and how well you are reading. Pretend you are the teacher and you are making judgments about your work. Think of questions you would ask: Do you know most of the words? Can you read aloud fluently? Can you read and then explain the story to someone else? Does your reading improve as you move along from book to book? This report can be kept private or shared with the family. The important point is that it helps our children evaluate their own progress—but we must remind them not to be too hard on themselves.

## MegaSkills Moments ■ any age

- *Communication*
- *Listening and Talking Together*

Cheering ourselves, savoring what we do, rewarding ourselves . . . traditionally, we don't do enough of this, yet it's especially important for setting and meeting goals. When we identify a goal and meet it, this is truly a MegaSkill moment. Let's savor it. Let's identify it, tell others about it, and reward ourselves.

All the steps along the way in meeting a goal are MegaSkills moments and all of them can be celebrated. Every family will have its own way of making MegaSkills moments special.

Focus has the quality of becoming a magnet. When we focus on a topic, suddenly we see connections all around us. The clues are there. There are answers everywhere. It's another miracle of focus.

Focus heightens the experience of all the MegaSkills. It targets and sharpens the moments so that we notice them and pay attention to them. Children (and adults also) gain a heightened sense of self-respect.

It's important to remember that paying attention is a personal thing—we pay attention in our own ways. When we tell our children to pay attention, we may look for the traditional signs—sitting still and looking straight ahead, narrowing the eyes, or furrowing the brows. However, these signs can be deceiving. Research studies indicate that we often pay closer attention when we move about, when we look at a problem from different perspectives. I know that there are times when I look very attentive and I'm not paying attention at all, and vice versa.

Take some moments together to talk about how you and your children pay attention, the signals you give yourself to get more focused, and what you can do to remain focused.

We deserve to applaud ourselves, not necessarily in these words but with similar kinds of thoughts: "I have focused my energies. I now know more about what I can do. I now know how I can use all of my MegaSkills more effectively. I did it, and I can do even more!"

# Readiness to Learn: Translating "Educational Goals" into Practical Action at Home

The most crucial ability that parents must encourage in children is their continuing readiness to learn. Children are remarkable learners from birth. A parent's biggest job is to feed a child's appetite for learning. This conveys the message that education is very important, that you believe in it and in your child's ability to succeed.

## CHAPTER 16

# Getting Ready for School

## We Have a Little List

"Ready or not, here we come" . . . to school.

The first goal of the federal government's America 2000 education strategy is that "all children in America will start school ready to learn."

But many of our children are not ready.

Readiness to learn is the toughest educational goal: the hardest to measure, by the usual measures, the most significant for the long haul, and the one on which all families have the greatest impact.

Every other goal—literacy, reading, math—falls into place when students are "ready." While readiness is usually associated with the preschool years, it really never ends. A child needs to be ready for kindergarten and every other grade along the way.

While knowing the alphabet or being able to count are useful skills to have, they are not the foundation on which school success rests. What this section concentrates on is readiness for academics. Academic readiness rests on children's learning habits.

## NO MORE EMPTY HEADS

Getting ready for school used to be considered relatively simple: a matter of buying a new notebook and a new pair of shoes. Today we know that it is far more complicated.

School used to be the place where it was thought that children with new notebooks went to have their heads filled with knowl-

> "*MegaSkills*, with its new emphasis on readiness, is especially important to national education goals and to literacy so that children will enter school ready to learn and eager to read."
>
> — Susan Roman, Ph.D., Executive Director, Association for Library Service to Children, American Library Association

edge. They were seen as empty vessels, blank tablets.

Those were the dark ages in education, and it was not long ago. We really didn't know what was going on before kids entered school. We thought they started to learn in kindergarten or first grade, when they crossed the schoolhouse threshold.

We now know that children's heads (and hearts) have lots of stuff in them long before school starts. Their tablet is about half full as school begins. When it comes to what can be measured on tests, the eminent educational researcher Dr. Benjamin Bloom found in studies published in 1964 that what knowledge children have acquired by age four, which primarily is language, accounts

> With so much riding on the early formative years, this chapter looks at what children really need to be ready to do well in school from the very beginning. And it's not knowing the ABC's or being able to count to ten.

for 50 percent of what students show they know on tests at age seventeen.

It's no wonder that preschool is now acknowledged as a critical learning period.

## The Usual List

There are all kinds of advice on how to help children get ready for school. Most comes in the form of the traditional checklist. It often reads like this: "Make sure your children know their colors, know their alphabet, can tie their shoes, can go to the toilet themselves."

There is nothing terrible about these lists, but, aside from learning to use the bathroom alone, which does take time and needs to be done at home, there is nothing on this list that can't be taught lickety-split in the classroom.

Kids have to be ready for school every year, every day of their school career. There is a continuum of readiness skills through the grades. For example, while kindergartners may need to learn to be quiet, older students may need to learn to speak. What's easier and wiser is to build habits for learning when children are young, so they can get the benefit from them throughout the years.

> What does take time to teach and what makes all the difference in the classroom, whether it's preparation for kindergarten or for the sixth grade, are productive habits for learning, not the specific bits of learning themselves.

> The key question: What has to be and can be taught before school, at home, to help to ensure that children get the most out of school?

Some checklists are beginning to move in this direction, but they are still so general that it's hard to know what to do to help children get ready.

Here are a few examples:

"Be a role model."
"Establish family rules and limits."
"Let children do things by themselves."
"Demand the support our schools need to thrive."
"Join with other parents to improve the school."

Making such lists is almost like waving a magic wand and hoping that all will be well.

What I hear from parents today is that they don't need more generalities. The generalities are mostly known. What isn't known, parents say, are specifics to back them up.

## The Three-Big-Questions Checklist

I've identified three big questions that are key to children's readiness for school. And every parent can take specific action to help answer these questions:

**1. How Are My Child's Social and Group Skills?** How can I help my child learn to respect the rights of others, sit down, pay attention, follow directions, take turns?

**2. How Are My Child's Organizing Skills?** How can I help my child prepare for the methodical nature of schoolwork? What can I do to help my child work in an orderly, systematic way?

**3. How Do My Children Handle Themselves Personally?** How can I help my child handle disappointment, tolerate frustration, and get his or her own needs met, even in a large group?

In the next few pages I outline "starter activities" to provide home practice in these major areas of school readiness.

## 1. SOCIAL AND GROUP SKILLS

### Learning to Sit Down ■ ages 3–5

While modern classrooms don't require that children sit down all day, much of the work is done sitting down. So young children, unused to having their bottoms on chairs, have to get used to it.

This takes practice, but you can make it into a game. You need a few chairs, a watch with a second hand, if possible, and a radio or CD player.

This game is a version of musical chairs. Once you sit down, you have to stay seated for a period of time. Start with a fifteen-second sit-down; then increase the next sit-

You want your children to speak up, but you have to help children get practice in waiting to speak, in waiting to get needs met. Otherwise children are in trouble in the group setting of the classroom.

down to thirty seconds; then all sit down for one minute.

Have as a goal a five-minute sit-down during which you can talk, read, or just sit quietly together. This activity is ideal for tired parents.

Getting from fifteen seconds to five minutes can take weeks of musical chairs activity. And there is one hard rule: both parent and child must sit on similarly hard chairs. There are few pillows in school.

### Learning to Take Turns ■ ages 3–5

It can be easy for children in small families (especially only children) to get the idea that whenever they want to talk, they talk. Whenever they want something, they ask for it and maybe even get it.

Not so in school, where there are other children who have similar ideas.

### And Now We Will Hear from the Other Side of the Table

This is a mealtime exercise. Use the trusty clock again and make sure everyone gets a chance to have a say about some general issue of family interest, such as dinner menus, television, friends, and so on.

The point is to get young children (and older ones, too) in the habit of listening to others and of taking turns.

Start with thirty seconds of talking and listening. Then increase the time to one minute, two at most. Any longer encourages speechmaking that even grown-ups can find hard to listen to.

Try different versions of this game. For example, decide together about what to watch on television. This group activity helps children learn what others think.

## Learning to Pay Attention
■ ages 3–5

Teachers report that one of the greatest problems young children have in the classroom is their inability to listen and to follow directions. Good habits are learnable. Here are activities to provide pay-attention practice at home.

## It Actually Happened . . . on TV

TV activities can actually help children learn to listen and pay attention. Combine television watching with pay-attention practice. Children adore these activities. Sit with your child to watch a certain show you both agree you can stand.

Let your child know in advance that this is a pay-attention activity and that you'll be asking questions about the show. For example, what are the names of the lead characters? What are they wearing? Then let children trade places with you and ask you to recall certain details. This is also an excellent way to teach children the questioning skills they need for school.

## Now Hear This

You give three or four directions and your child must follow each one in turn. It's a game, but it's serious business. Make up easy commands, such as "Walk to the sink," "Turn on the cold faucet," "Let it run while you count to five," and "Then close it tight." Follow up by asking for a glass of water.

---

### From Indiana . . .

"I have three children, ages six, nine, and twelve. The youngest thinks that what she says is not as important as the others because they're older. So I ask them each to stay at the table until all three have talked about their days, each listening to the other."

---

### From Michigan . . .

"I started Now Hear This and received an overwhelming response to continue. It became a bit challenging to keep the directions flowing fast enough. The following day, our daughter wanted to go through all the directions again, and we did."

Then let children give you directions to follow. Make the commands easy or hard to suit children's ages and listening abilities. Start short and go longer and longer.

## 2. ORGANIZING SKILLS

Teachers do a lot of organizing for children: "This is your assignment and it's due tomorrow." But children themselves, ready to do well in school, must have their own organizing skills.

### Reasonable and Expectable Routines ■ ages 3–5

Adults may get bored with routine, but children crave and need it. When is bedtime? When are mealtimes? What times are set for TV watching? The more regular these routines, the better. They help children to learn what to expect in school and of the world around them, of others, and of themselves.

We can help show children how we tackle problems that demand organization. For example, children need to see how adults get ready to do a job. If we paint this room, what do we need? When we wash the car, what do we need? When they have a homework assignment, what will they need?

Here are home ideas to help children get organized. Thank goodness we don't have to be efficiency experts ourselves to help children acquire organization skills.

### A Quiet Place for Study and Reading

All you need is a chair, a table, a lamp. Additions can include a plant, a drawing, a colorful blotter. This can be a corner, as large as a study or as small as a lapboard on the bed. Abe Lincoln didn't need a den to become a reader and learner.

### Books, Magazines, All Around Us

Children need to see parents reading, and they need to be read to. Children need to be able on their own to find a book and magazine at home that they can pick through and basically get comfortable with.

Reading needs to be everywhere, as part of our daily lives, in the living room and in the bedroom.

Recently I spoke with an educational reformer about what had to happen in schools to make significant educational change for children. Finally I asked, "How did you learn to be so interested in so many things?" He thought a while and said, "You know, now that you ask that, I remember that almost every day I spent forty-five min-

---

**From Pennsylvania . . .**

"I think these activities have helped me, in a way, more than my child, in that I am developing more patience and am having to learn to 'share' my kitchen with someone who truly wants to learn. Thank you for helping me realize that I am, indeed, not too old to learn!"

utes in the bathroom, reading the encyclopedia. That's where we kept the old ones. I loved the quiet and I loved looking through them. I guess," he said, "that's really where I learned almost everything I know today."

This revelation takes nothing away from the need to improve schools, but it shows once again how important every home is in the educational lives of our children.

## Paper and Pencils Abound

Let there be pads and pencils throughout the house so that children get writing and organizing practice as part of their everyday experience.

Put paper next to the telephone for messages, in the kitchen for a grocery list, next to the TV for a list of shows to watch.

## "Tools" for Planning Ahead

Your calendar need not be fancy, but it should have big empty squares and a marker attached for notes. Children need to see a regularity in certain events and to enjoy the surprise of special events.

All children can use a calendar of their own. These are easily obtainable and inexpensive, often free. It takes organization to keep calendars up-to-date. When children see parents working with calendars, it becomes second nature to keep theirs up-to-date, too.

Just as with a calendar, children can use address-telephone books for friends, for

the school, for the library . . . all the places children go and need to know about. These too are inexpensive, sometimes free. Look for the ones with the largest spaces in which children can write.

Kids should see not only that we are ready to tackle problems, but that there is a method that adults follow (or try to follow). By being invited to the process, children get the sense of how they too can master the skill of organizing.

> Let kids in on the secret: as students, we parents weren't always number one in the class. We've had our share of frustrations, but look, we're living; we're getting through.

## 3. PERSONAL ATTITUDES

Schools can be encouraging places but very often they are places where our children have their discouraging experiences: a low grade, the day the teacher yelled, friends who aren't friends anymore, the part in the play we didn't get, the essay that we had to do over. We can add to the list.

Is there any way we can prepare our children for handling these everyday kinds of trials and disappointments?

While we can't protect our children from feeling disappointment itself, and from feeling hurt, we can help them acquire some understanding to help them handle these disappointments.

> Nobody is totally organized; we are always on the way to becoming organized.

Here are five basic messages our children need to hear from us:

- **These things happen.**
- **They don't kill us.**
- **There is always another day.**
- **Have courage.**
- **Remember, we love you.**

---

**From Delaware . . .**

"I'm a school principal now, but when I was a kid, I was not a very good reader. The teacher used to tell us that if we could read the words from the blackboard, we could look into the big mystery box at the front of the classroom. I never did get to look into that box and I don't want children today to be excluded like that either. That's why I think this program is so important."

---

## You Have to Have Heart

It can be hard to get positive attention in a classroom, where so much of the teacher's time is spent in disciplining children who are acting up just to get attention. So how can we help well-behaved youngsters say politely to the teacher, "Pay attention to me."

First, of course, urge your children to raise their hands. But they may find that others are yelling out the answers or that the teacher is still calling on others. Try to avoid saying, "That teacher doesn't like you."

The most effective approach is to encourage children themselves to speak with the teacher, telling how they feel about not getting called on, or if they feel they are being unfairly criticized, and how it hurts. This approach, I believe, and I speak from experience, is the surest way to a teacher's heart.

This assignment is not easy for children. They may need your help in practicing what they'll say to the teacher. This puts you into the teacher's shoes and provides you with the teacher's point of view as well.

We need to prepare children for life in school, an institution that is really basically good but that in addressing the needs of the group can be mighty hard on the tender feelings of individuals.

School is also the place where kids receive honors, win awards, make friends, experience achievements. Somehow we take to these experiences more easily; they need less preparing for. But when the awards do come, it can be useful to help children with an appropriately modest acceptance speech.

We talk a lot about the head when it comes to schooling. But the heart, that mysterious organ that does more than pump blood, may be responsible for even more of the story.

Kids have to have "heart" to do well in school.

---

School is the place where kids have to say to themselves, almost every day, "I can do it. I will keep trying."

---

Joe DiDio, courtesy of the National Education Association

**CHAPTER 17**

# The Three R's: Before School

Even before children go off to school, parents worry about the Three R's: "When will my child read? Write? Do math?"

It's natural to be anxious, especially now when there is so much concern about academics and whether our children are learning enough.

The Three R's, especially reading, are the make-or-break skills that children are expected to do well with early in school, often in first grade. This pressure to excel is hard on children; it is hard on parents; and it is hard on teachers. Rather than dwell on how to change the time schedule within our educational system, this chapter focuses on activities that help children get comfortable with reading, writing, and arithmetic even before they come to "real school."

The focus in this chapter is *not* on duplicating school activities, but on using the unique resources of the home and community. Parents can do a lot to help children with academics, and I don't mean using flash cards and workbook exercises. There is a world of ways to encourage academics at home without the use of traditional school methods, which I believe are best left to the school. Children need a different, informal, individual reading environment at home. (See Section D, "Strengthening the Three R's at Home," for activities in the school-age years.)

## WORKING WITH SHAPES

To read, a child recognizes shapes. The alphabet is a collection of shapes that stand for sounds. To read, children see similari-ties and differences among shapes. Here are some easy and effective shapes games.

### Shaping Up

Cut from colored paper, or even newspaper, large duplicate circles, squares, rectangles. Put one of each shape on the floor. Ask your child to find and put the matching ones on top of them.

Then ask children to match smaller and more intricate shapes, including alphabet letters, capital and lowercase. Make the letters large. You might want to start your game with three, expand to ten, then fifteen. Your child will eventually match all twenty-six letters in one game.

Play a similar matching game with numbers, starting with number one and working up to a hundred, if your child is so inclined.

### Finding Shapes

Look around your home to identify shapes all around you: the circles in drinking glasses, the rectangular tables, rugs, and windows.

### Let 'Em Eat Shapes

Here's a tasty accompaniment to the "Shaping Up" and "Finding Shapes" activities. You need sliced bread, peanut butter or some other spread, and a dull-edged knife. Cut the bread into different, duplicate shapes. Ask children to find a pair of matching shapes, put spread on one piece, and place the matching shape on top for a tasty sandwich.

These activities are great for older children to play with younger children in the family and those for whom they baby-sit. They're easy and cost very little.

Children really interested in these shapes games may want to trace or make their own games of model letters to play themselves or to share with friends.

> Would you believe that putting away dishes teaches reading? It does—by teaching classification skills. Match plates with others of the same size, forks with forks. This is similar to recognizing the same alphabet letter in different words.

## LISTENING TO SOUNDS

To read, children also need to listen—to hear the sounds that certain shapes make. Try thirty seconds of silence. Then have children tell you what they hear: a car down the street, a bird twittering. The moment of quiet is a wonderful treat for parents too!

### Name That Sound

Children close their eyes and tell what sounds they hear. *Examples:* a key jangling, a tongue clicking, a faucet running. Then turn the tables and let your child make sounds for you to name.

### Rhythms

Tap out rhythms with a fork on a tabletop. Ask children to repeat the rhythm back to you. Vary the style: slow, fast, loud, soft.

Use more complex rhythms and patterns as your child's ability to respond develops.

## Phonics Bingo

Combine heightened listening ability with alphabet sounds. To help children associate sounds with letters, make a grid of consonants on a piece of cardboard. Here is a sample:

| S | D | F | M |
|---|---|---|---|

Keep the grids simple at first, with perhaps only three or four letters. (The more recognizable, noisier consonants are B, D, F, J, K, L, M, N, P, R, S, T, V, Z.) Call out a sound and ask players to cover the letter with a button, a bean, or a small cardboard circle. Say the sound with a word. *Examples:* "puh—pat," "mmm—mat."

> When children are young, getting ready for reading is not a quiet, solitary activity. It tends to be an activity that generates lots of talk between parents and children. Talking and reading together early helps to ignite the desire to read alone later.

## GETTING COMFORTABLE WITH WORDS

### Hidden Letters

All around the kitchen, from the cupboard to the refrigerator, from the stove to the sink, there are letters—A's, B's, F's, P's—on soup cans, on cat food, on cereal boxes, even on soap.

Make a game of finding these letters. Tell children to find (without tearing up the place, of course) five A's or three C's or any combination appropriate to your child's skills. Start easy and build up to letters that are harder to find. Children can then write down those they find or just share the objects on which the letters had been "hidden." You're building reading observation skills as well as having fun together.

### The Grocery Store Eye

Reinforce your child's concepts of color, shape, size, and numbers with this activity at the store. While shopping, ask your child to locate a box of soap powder, perhaps a large orange box with blue letters. Then ask for eggs in a white container or green beans in a yellow can. With a little practice, your child will be able to locate and bring you the right item. For children who can read, provide a shopping list.

### The Daily Rounds

Take time on errands to point to letter sounds in the signs you see each day. *Examples:* S—STOP, STORE, SCHOOL; B—BUS, BANK, BEAUTY SHOP; F—FIRE, FLOWERS; G— GO, GAS, GROCERIES.

Reading is all around us, all the time. While riding in a car or bus, read the signs aloud and encourage children to sing them out as they see them.

### Stop! Look! Rhyme!

"Sock" and "clock," "bed" and "head," "floor" and "more"—rhymes are all around

> Encourage your child to say words aloud with you. Children who speak and write well enjoy the sounds words make. A baby babbling in a crib begins a love affair with words that need never end.

the world, even in the bedroom, and they're good for going to sleep with and for learning to read.

### Labeling Home Objects

Just as in the schoolroom, where teachers label doors and desks, parents and youngsters at home can label beds, sofas, rugs. *Note:* Masking tape leaves no scars on walls and furniture.

### Dress Me

There are words for clothing—"shirt," "blouse," "sock," "shoe"—and words for body parts—"foot," "arm," "head," "knee." The bedroom is a fine place to learn these words: Say the words aloud as clothes go on and come off. Print the words on large pieces of paper. A large poster with a child's silhouette on it can be tacked onto a bedroom wall to carry the words for parts of the body, and it's comforting for children going to bed to see "themselves."

### Roomfuls of Words

Look in newspapers and magazines for pictures of furniture and objects that belong in different rooms of a house. Divide a large piece of paper into sections labeled "Living room," "Bedroom," "Kitchen." Children paste the pictures in the appropriate section, or "room." This activity builds vocabulary and teaches classification skills.

## Story Telling

Almost any time can be story telling time—but this time let your child put the ending on the story. Tell a story that poses a problem, and let your youngsters tell how to solve the problem. If necessary, use plot ideas from stories they know, perhaps "Cinderella" or "Jack and the Beanstalk," and be sure to stop before the end. Once children get the hang of making up stories themselves, encourage them to come up with plots that you'll have to solve.

Turn waiting time into reading time. Look through the pictures in the magazines you find at the doctor's office. Remember to take along storybooks or magazines whenever you might have to wait.

## Getting Comfortable with Numbers

### Matching and Piling

Laundry contains numbers. Match the socks and count them. Count the sheets and fold them into fractional parts: one half, then one quarter. You'll find all the socks and have a neat linen closet, too!

### My Own Calendar

There can be one in every child's room. Use the promotional ones given away at the end of the year; they often have big numbers. Check off the days until different events happen. How many days and hours until that special day?

---

**From Colorado . . .**

"We found it so easy finding the numbers that we made it harder, by looking for them in sequence: (1, 2, 3, etc.). It worked."

---

### What's Your Size?

Equip children with rulers, yardsticks, or string to check the length and width of their hands and feet. Talk about the family's sizes for shoes, dresses, and suits. Who has the biggest hands? The shortest feet? The longest legs?

### Egg Carton Counter

Save those old egg cartons. In the bottom of each egg section, write in a number. Make some of these negative numbers to get the excitement going. Egg cartons are great for matching or pitching games with two or more people. Give each person an equal number of pennies or stones. Try to land in the sections that have the highest values. When the pennies or stones are used up, total your scores.

### Playing Store

Save milk cartons and boxes. Use play or real money. (Real is more fun!) Have youngsters price items. How much for a quart of milk? For a can of corn? Young readers can check prices using newspaper ads.

### Math in the Bathtub

Water play for a young child can provide fun, cleanliness, and solid math instruction.

Equip the tub or sink with plastic containers of various sizes: cup, pint, quart, liter, gallon.

Fill the tub with bath water. Then in go the children to experiment. Ask questions: How many of the small cups fit into the larger ones? How many quarts are in a gallon? It's not necessary that children memorize the names of the measures. What is important at this point is that they experiment and enjoy the experience with numbers.

## Measure for Pleasure

The world is filled with things and spaces to measure. How tall is the lamp? How wide is the room? Use yardsticks, tape measures, string—anything that measures. Jot down the results to share with the family.

### From Missouri . . .

"We used our freezer. I was really surprised to see that my son could show me on the clock where the hands were when we put the ice cube tray into the freezer. And I had never realized before how much water it actually takes to fill the tray. We measured it together."

Look around. Count the windows and doors in any one room. Then count the number of rooms and make a guess about how many windows and doors are in the entire building.

### From California . . .

"It's fun, it's easy, it passes away the time on a long trip. Learning can be so much fun without even trying. . . . You can motivate your children and then there's no stopping them."

## Games = Learning

Math is basic to indoor games, from simple bingo to complicated bridge.

For young children, make connect-the-dot puzzles using different number sequences: 1, 2, 3, for young children; 3, 6, 9, for more sophisticated players.

A storehouse of games—lotto, bingo, dominoes, hopscotch, crazy eights, Parcheesi, jackstraws, go fish, beanbag tosses, war, Cootie, tenpin, I Win, darts, Uncle Wiggly, casino, Monopoly—all build number comfort and skills.

# Strengthening the Three R's at Home

The role of the parent is critical because the home environment is vital to children's educational achievement. Not even the best school can do the job alone. Parents can, and should, take advantage of opportunities at home to teach their children in an informal way, developing strong one-on-one relationships. As children continue in school, parents, grandparents, and all adults in children's lives, must remember that they are vital partners with teachers in the education of all children.

*Courtesy of the National Association of Elementary School Principals*

## INTRODUCTION

# MegaSkills and the Three R's: The Chicken and the Egg

What comes first—the chicken or the egg? When it comes to MegaSkills, it doesn't matter.

Educational life for children is school, but it is more than school. In this section are activities that empower children to use what they have learned in school in their lives beyond the classroom.

There's reading, writing, math, and there are also adaptations of activities to illustrate how to spend productive, enjoyable vacation time together and how to focus on different ways children learn.

> From eggs come chickens, from chickens come eggs. And so with MegaSkills and the academic skills. One leads to the other. They go back and forth in an ever-renewing, exciting cycle.

These activities do not take the place of school homework, but they make homework more manageable for children to do and want to do on their own. They fire up children to want to learn more.

They set the base for learning all through life!

The child who learns to write can prepare an essay, conjure up a story, and, later on, create a love letter.

The child who reads can handle a test, devour a novel, and, later on, understand an insurance policy.

The child who learns math can figure out the text problems, bring home the right change from a grocery errand, and, later on, manage the family budget.

**The three R's are tools that use the capacities and qualities of MegaSkills, inside and outside the classroom.**

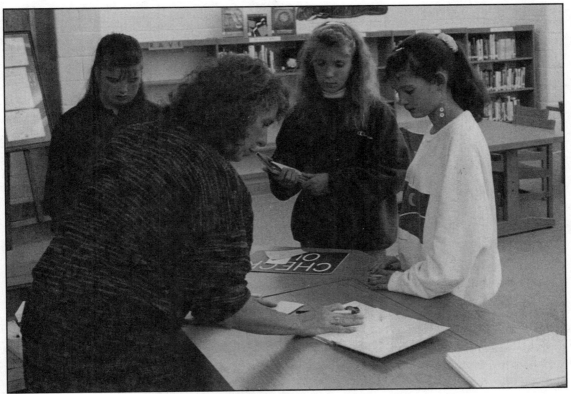

*Michael Lydick, courtesy of the National Education Association*

## CHAPTER 18

# Reading: Moving Along with Books

As parents, we may do some things wrong, but if we have helped our children gain a love of reading, we have done a lot of things right.

> We have given our children trips to the farthest reaches of the earth and to the sun and the moon and the stars.
> We have opened the doors to knowing their own heart and the hearts of others.
> We have given them maps for their voyage through life.

One of the early children of divorce, my husband has bittersweet memories of his childhood. One memory, however, remains forever sweet. His mother would come home from work and read to him almost every night before he went to bed. It turned him, he says, into a lifelong reader—an enduring present from his mother.

We know a lot about reading. We know that the vast majority of children take to it like ducks to water. But unlike ducks, who keep swimming for the rest of their lives, many youngsters do not keep on reading.

Let me tell you what's in this chapter and what's not. It contains many activities for home use that help to build children's love of reading and learning. This chapter assumes that parents know the importance of reading aloud to children. What many parents may not be aware of are other everyday activities that help with reading. This chapter does not contain a simple answer to the question of whether children should read before entrance into regular school. There is no simple answer; experts often oppose each other. This chapter also does not contain a discussion of phonics versus the look-say method of teaching reading. It's my view that in teaching you need to take advantage of all the methods you can lay your hands on to suit the changing needs of every child, every day.

## FOR THE LOVE OF WORDS
### Mystery Word Box ■ ages 5–9

I think that just about the best reading activity I did at home with my children was one we called the "Mystery Word Box." It was a vocabulary activity, but it was more than that. It was a bedtime activity, a parent/child lovefest—and it was about words.

We used a recipe card file box, three-by-five-inch index cards, and alphabet dividers. It worked like this. Each day, my daughter, who was five at that time, got to pick up to five mystery words of the day. She didn't have to know how to spell them or what they meant. She could choose any words that she had heard and that appealed to her in some way. The mystery lay in what words she would pick. My job was to write them down in big print on the cards. She

---

A major concern about reading is not how to teach children to read but how to ensure that they will continue to read, enriching and broadening their skills and interests.

would say them aloud, "reading" them from the cards. We would talk about what they meant, and then she would file them away in the box.

I remember only a few of those words—how I wish I had saved that box. It would have been better than a time capsule. What I do remember is that the words were emotional or funny sounding—words like "love," "death," "accident," "crocodile," and a word from *Mary Poppins*, one I still have trouble spelling: "supercalifragilisticexpialidocious."

During the day I would sometimes find my child on her bed, the contents of the mystery word box set out before her. These were her very own words, and she would be playing with them, saying them aloud, caressing them with her voice. Some days she would put the cards around the wall of her room so she could look at them at night as she went to sleep.

This word box is really a treasure house of favorite words. They become a child's very own precious possessions, and delight in these treasures lasts a long time.

## Doing and Reading ▪ ages 7–9
### Scavenger Hunt

Make up some home reading games, and encourage children to do the same. In our house, "Scavenger Hunt" was made up by our older daughter (age eight) to provide reading practice for her sister (age six). She wrote out clues and deposited them around the house and yard. The younger child

delighted in finding them and kept asking for more of this reading "work."

### Read and Do

Give each child a list of things to do. *Example:* "Roll up a sheet of newspaper, fold it in half three times, tie up the roll with a piece of string." These can be far-fetched, plain fun, or actual chores that have to be done around the house.

### Letter to My Child

Letters that you write to each other and actually mail or just slip into your mailbox are another good reading device. These, too, can gradually be made more challenging to read.

Send your child a letter in which you "hide" new words. Keep most of the letter in easy language, but insert several new words that your child has to find and ask about. This pairs the delight in new words with the joy of receiving a letter.

### Cooking Up Directions

You don't just cook a dish—you have to read directions to know what comes first, second, and so on. Select a simple recipe with your child—perhaps Jell-O, instant pudding, or canned soup. On every package is a set of directions: Either read them aloud to the pre-reading child or ask young readers to do it on their own. You're coming up with a tasty dish and reading at the same time.

### Morning Messages

Leave notes for each other. Children enjoy receiving surprises and take pride in writing notes to someone else. Here's one you might tape to the bedroom light switch: "Dear Susan: When you get up, please gather up the things lying on your floor. Put them away where they belong. Love, Mother." (*Note:* I can report that while these items are not always picked up, children do get practice in reading.)

The message should be written so that the reading is well within your child's ability. For a very young reader, it could be: "I Love You. See You Soon." One morning when I got up later than usual, I found a note slipped under my door: "Mother, don't worry. I have had my meal and I have gone out to play. Love, Jessica." (Jessica had just turned seven.)

## INVOLVEMENT TO SPARK THE ZEST FOR READING

Just because children are on holiday from school doesn't mean that they're taking a vacation from education. I am not talking about remedial exercises or catch-up homework. I'm talking about the time for discovery and the joy of learning that take no holidays—and may, in fact, be enhanced during holiday periods.

Vacations are a great time for families to reinforce and extend children's learning—without it looking or feeling like school. These activities feel special because they provide fun and learning at the very best times of the year.

## What Can I Do Now?  ■  any age

This is the often-asked vacation question. Answer it with a **Vacation Bulletin Board** or Vacation Family Calendar, a way to stimulate your child's ability to plan and be responsible for having things to do.

Ask the family to post ideas about what they'd like to do during the holidays. Children can cut out articles from the newspaper and write notes suggesting their ideas.

Use large sheets of paper, leaving plenty of blank space for each day. Talk about what everyone wants to do. Make plans not just for outings but for home projects, too. As children get ideas, they pencil them in. This gives children practice in doing independent research and in working out compromises with family members who have different ideas.

Parents should write in their own schedules so that children come to understand and sympathize with parental obligations and responsibilities, even during holidays.

Suggest that youngsters choose new activities to try for the first time or that they

> Not all time needs to be scheduled, nor should all family members have to do everything together. Children need time during vacation to relax, to be free of the usual fast pace of school. It's a good idea to encourage youngsters to get their homework done early in their vacation to avoid having it hanging over them every day.

develop old ones further. Perhaps it's ice skating or cookie baking. Seek out active experiences, especially those that offer opportunities for success.

Make an effort to be alone with each child for some time during the holidays. This might be going to a movie or taking a walk in a shopping center. Use this opportunity to talk, and try to listen more than talk.

## Home Interest Center ■ any age

On a tabletop or bookcase, put out books, articles, or pictures on a particular subject. Spark breakfast conversation and encourage newspaper reading with "My Picks in the News." Get these by asking everyone to clip pictures or articles for discussion.

## A Summer Trip Around the World—Without Leaving Home ■ ages 7–12

The long summer vacation can be hard on everyone. Even kids get bored after the first flush of freedom wears off.

Here's a solution: Take the youngsters on a trip without leaving home. With imagination, your living room trip can smack of the grand tour, especially in the social studies education it will provide.

Tack up a large (the bigger, the better) map of the world. With the family working together, chart a travel course. Lightly pencil it in at first, until all controversies (such as whether to visit Rome or Naples) are resolved. Once these are settled, apply the trusty felt-tip pen. Use a contrasting color to mark your progress as the trip goes on.

On the wall next to the map, post your itinerary of dates and places. Here's an example:

| | |
|---|---|
| July 15 | Depart by air to London |
| July 16 A.M. | Arrive in London |
| July 20 | Leave for Paris |

This trip can last all summer. Spend some time on it each day or refer to it once a week, depending on the time you can spare and how much it interests the children.

Avoid a textbook approach to the study. Try special nights: "An Evening in Paris," with the children planning a French meal and singing French songs; "An Evening in Beijing," with Chinese food and chopsticks. These evenings need not be elaborate. The important point is that the children themselves do the preparing, and that involves getting information.

> Gather material—and much of it is free —on what it's like to live in other lands. Check with travel agencies, embassies, tourism offices, and the Internet if you have access.
>
> The library is a great resource, with everything from geography books to fairy tales of other countries.

While this trip is not the real thing to be sure, preparing for it may be at least half the fun, with lots of reading and learning.

## Reading: A Habit ■ any age

Not even the best school can take care of all a child's reading needs. A diet of textbook reading has not been known to turn people into lifelong readers.

Visual, listening, and talking activities prepare a child for reading, but children need to *want* to read. That is where the home environment supportive of reading comes into play. The object in teaching reading is not to turn out readers who read only when they "have to" but to turn out readers who enjoy reading and who continue to read even when the homework is over. Here are some ways parents can encourage reading as a habit at home, above and beyond the school assignment.

## MY READING CORNER

All children need their own bookshelf and reading light. These need not be elaborate or expensive. A bookshelf can be a painted crate or cardboard box. The point is to make reading convenient and enticing and, above all, to build children's images of themselves as readers.

---

**From South Carolina . . .**

"I think MegaSkills is great. My fifth grade teacher never liked me, so I never got that extra reading when I needed it."

---

## PLEASANT DREAMS

Encourage your children to decorate their sleeping area. The more appealing it is, the easier it may be to get children to go to bed. Ask your children what will make their sleeping arrangements more comfortable. *Example:* an extra pillow can make reading in bed easier and more enticing.

## CARRY BOOKS ALONG

Try family read-alouds on summer picnics or even while you're driving in the car. People can get carsick when they read, but some find that they can build up a tolerance and that it is a good time for reading.

## TAKE TURNS

Try reading aloud to others who are doing household chores. Encourage children to read to you while you're cleaning the refrigerator, cooking, sorting the laundry, and so on.

## READING WITH KIDS

Instead of always reading to children, read *with* youngsters who are able to read. Take roles in plays; act out dramatic poems. When possible, tape-record your voices to give reading added glamour.

Let your children dictate stories to you and then draw pictures to accompany the

> Everyone reading this book probably knows how important it is to read to children. Even so—and let's not forget to say it—you may have to *make time* to do that reading. It is so important that it is a matter of *making* time, not finding it. Even five to ten minutes a day can make a big difference.

words. They'll be able to "read" their words back to you. Older brothers and sisters can take turns as secretaries.

When children read on their own, it's tempting to say, "Thank goodness, we can forget about this now." Reading, however, is more than a skill. It needs to be nurtured and encouraged to have continued meaning in your child's life.

## THE LIBRARY

Try to go with children to the library at least once a week. Give youngsters unhurried time to browse, to make book discoveries. Let them take books home, even if you think them too hard, too easy, or not "worthwhile" reading. You can quietly check out another book considered worthwhile or just the right level; read it if the ones your child has chosen do not work out.

Check Appendix C for MegaSkills book selections. They illustrate MegaSkills found in stories and novels for children. Encour-age your children to try some of these, and use them for read-aloud times at home.

## WHY BUY?

Why bother to buy books when you can go to the library and take them out for free? Probably because borrowing is not really the same as owning. (We don't use the rationale of "why buy?" for CDs.) Some books should just always be around the house, like old friends, to be looked at, to be underlined or starred if a reader feels strongly about a part, and to be read over and over. Many parents have noticed that their children do read certain books over and over, and they ask them why. The answer is, "I like them a lot." Which is all the more reason to have those special books around.

Thanks to public libraries, a home library need not be vast or expensive. But choosing books to stock the home larder can be difficult, just because there are so many to choose from. Where do you begin?

### Start with the Children

If they are already reading, they may have some favorite books, ones they'd like to own. If children are not yet reading, ask what kinds of stories they especially like: What subjects? What would they like to learn more about?

Talk to your child's teachers or the school librarian. They often have lists of good books and are delighted to share

> When the books are home, a parent's job is not over. Books can often use introducing. Even for children who already read on their own, it can help to read a first chapter aloud. And if you know something about the book, you can lure your child to it, just as when friends tell you about a good book they've read lately.

them. Look carefully at school book fair displays and take notes about those books that interest you and your child. It's helpful when schools and organizations set up samples of good, inexpensive home libraries for children of different ages.

Do some comparison shopping before buying. Books, like dresses, come in different prices. One publisher's edition may cost $4.95 while another edition of the same text sells for $8.95. You may choose the more expensive one because of its illustrations and paper quality. Sometimes the less expensive can be the better buy, comparing favorably in pictures and type sizes.

Look for books that have an appealing "come and read me" look. In nonfiction, check for up-to-date accuracy; look at the copyright and revision dates on the front inside pages. Read a few paragraphs to see if the writing style is clear.

Find books that tie in to your child's interests and needs. A very shy child may gain more than good reading from a book about a shy child who found courage to do some big deed. You can also find books about youngsters of different racial and cul-

tural backgrounds with whom children may identify. (See The MegaSkills Library for Children, Appendix C.)

## The Home Reference Shelf

It is probably wiser and cheaper to wait until children are able to read at the middle elementary school level before investing in a set of encyclopedias. In this way you can buy a more advanced set in print or CD-ROM that will last longer. The value in having different reference texts at home, such as almanacs, is that children get used to using more than one book for research material.

## READING TROUBLE? CATCH IT EARLY

Children want to read, and they will if they can. If children aren't starting to read by the end of first grade, then there is some reason why, and it's not because they are "lazy" or "ignorant." Either the instruction is not appropriate, or the child can't handle what is being taught.

The situation needs thorough examination. Often the causes are physical. Poor eyesight is obvious but sometimes overlooked. Subtle coordination problems that may occur even in "athletic" children can be a cause.

Both parents and teachers need to watch for early signs of a child having reading difficulties. Many of these difficulties are now commonly classified as dyslexia. For any number of reasons, the child is unable to break the reading code. A growing number of special programs are now available to provide specialized help. Check community organizations and ask at your child's school for programs near you.

Some children's inability to read can be connected to poor self-esteem. Children may see themselves as people who can't do things. Home activities help children see themselves as people who can accomplish things. Self-esteem is crucial for the child to feel like a doer and to be a doer—in all activities, from learning to jump rope to learning to read.

## MEETING SPECIAL LEARNING NEEDS

Education, unlike pantyhose, does not fit one size for all. While we know that our left foot is usually larger than our right, both shoes, except for those sold in the fanciest stores, are the same size, and the left foot always pinches. The same is true for bathing suits. Many women need one size top and another size bottom, but because they come in the same size, one part will fit, and the other won't.

Special education is like those different-size shoes. It gives children a special fit for their special learning styles.

More than likely what special learners need at home is not more of the same drill and practice that they are already having trouble with in school. They need and want activities that offer opportunities for success through alternative or different kinds of learning.

## The Home Education Plan

In school, Individualized Education Plans (known as IEP's) are developed for special education students. The following is an example of what I call a Home Education Plan (HEP); it provides specialized help for children at home, to extend and reinforce but not duplicate what children work on in school.

The activity is divided into **Look, Listen,** and **Do** sections. They separate out from the home learning recipe single activity strands that focus directly on visual, auditory, and coordination skill development.

- The Look section provides practice in:
  **Visual Discrimination**—the ability to see differences between similar objects.
  **Visual Memory**—the ability to remember what was seen.

- The Listen section provides practice in:
  **Auditory Discrimination**—the ability to hear differences between similar sounds.
  **Auditory Memory**—the ability to remember what was heard.

- The Do section provides practice in:
  **Visual and Auditory Integration**—the ability to combine the skills worked on in the visual and auditory areas. Emphasis is on creativity and on eye-hand coordination.

*Note:* Additional examples of Home Education Plans are included in the writing and math chapters. They illustrate how activities can focus on different learning styles.

As you do the examples in the writing and math chapters, refer back to the definitions of **Look, Listen,** and **Do** above.

## TV or No TV? ■ ages 7–9

Here's an example of an activity that helps children develop reading skills through exercises that appeal to a variety of learning styles. This activity helps the family make choices about TV programs to watch by reading the TV schedule in advance. You need a TV set, a weekly TV schedule, scissors, paste, and paper.

At the beginning of the week, post the TV schedule. Read it aloud. Talk about why one program might be better to watch than another.

## LOOK

**Visual Discrimination.** Look at the TV schedule. Point out one channel's number. Ask your child to find two other channels with different numbers.

Point to a television show that begins with the letter *T*. Is it a good show? Ask your child to try to find one or two other shows that begin with the same letter. Are they good shows? Why? Why not?

**Visual Memory.** With your child, look at shows listed at the same time on two different channels.

Ask your child to name the shows at seven P.M. on channels four and nine. Which one might the family watch, and why was it chosen?

## LISTEN

**Auditory Discrimination.** Tell your child the name of a television show you watch regularly and why you watch it. Ask your child to name this show.

Now name this show again, this time in a list with three other shows. Ask your child to listen and signal when the show you first mentioned is named again.

Trade places. Ask your child to name a favorite TV star. You listen. Then your child names other TV stars, including the first one. Now it's your turn to listen and raise your hand when you hear the first star's name.

**Auditory Memory.** Pretend you are a TV announcer. Your job is to announce the names of three shows. Your child listens and repeats the names of these shows in the same order. Which is a favorite show?

Watch a television commercial together. Ask your child to listen and recall. Was music used in the commercial? What product was advertised? How many people appeared in it?

## DO

**Eye-Hand Coordination.** Save a few TV schedules so that they can be cut apart . . . and put back together. The task is to construct your very own guide of favorite TV shows for at least one day.

Talk about and compare the choices of different family members. What shows would you run if you managed a TV station?

## WE ARE NEVER DONE WITH READING

After children learn the basics of reading, some go on to become voracious readers, devouring everything from novels to almanacs. Others go on to become specialized readers, reading a diet of biographies or history or even poetry. The great majority go on to become readers of newspapers, magazines, and cereal boxes.

But there isn't a person who can be done with reading.

We all need to keep on reading, even to protect ourselves. Reading can be more effective than a weapon. Our children will need to be able to read forms and contracts before they sign them. They will want to read movie and play reviews before spending money at the theater. They will need to read about supermarket specials to save money at the store. This is functional read-

---

Reading is not just looking. It takes all our senses to master the Three R's. By mixing and matching our learning styles for all our children, not just special learners, our students stand a better chance of learning what they have to know now and what they will need to know in the future.

---

ing. It doesn't elevate or inspire, but it's part of the daily routine, like brushing teeth.

I don't know how some people can get through breakfast or start the day without reading or at least taking a look at the morning paper. I grew up before television became a morning companion. For me, reading a paper in the morning makes me feel ready for the day. I'm so addicted that when I don't have the actual day's paper, I will scavenge through the garbage to find an old edition that I will read again.

## CHILDREN AND PARENTS: READING TOGETHER

Teachers can teach children to read, but they cannot keep them reading. Encouraging children to continue reading is the job of the home. Setting an example helps. Children—at least when they are young—imitate their parents.

My father was surrounded by newspapers wherever he was—they were next to his bed, on the floor by his reading chair, in the car, in the bathroom. I feel sure that's how I came by my own addiction. It seems natural to have reading material by my side at all times. Once a habit takes hold, it's hard to break it. Becoming addicted to reading is one of the better habits.

Before I leave this chapter, I want to share a few ways that parents who may not be great and voluminous readers themselves can help children get the reading habit.

Most parents will happily read to children but some cannot. My own immigrant parents were not able to read aloud in English to me, and I did not understand Polish or Yiddish.

But I did understand that reading was important. That's the message every parent must and can give.

It's good for your children to see you reading, but this doesn't have to be a diet of masterpieces to do good. It's important to read with your children, but that, too, doesn't have to be *War and Peace*. It can be the kind of reading that an adult has to do every day—a form, an ad, a newspaper article, a recipe, the TV schedule.

One of the best at-home reading exercises for developing comprehension is to read directions that come with a new piece of furniture to be assembled. By the time you get the piece put together, you've also had a lesson in overcoming frustration.

Or try reading a computer manual together. It's not Shakespeare, but it can test your level of understanding in similar ways.

The point I am trying to make is that to get children reading, they have to read. There is a lot of reading besides Shakespeare and textbooks. I devoured comic books and movie magazines as a child. Maybe it wasn't "good" reading, but it kept me reading, and that was the important thing.

If you have a mortgage, take out the contract and read it together. Find your insurance policy and try to read it. It may be the first time you have actually read it.

If you have credit agreements, look those over. Read bank statements. You may be spending money for service charges at one bank that you could save if you moved your funds to another.

Let children follow along as you go over a tax form. They might see a deduction that you've missed. Everyone gets junk mail. Before throwing those mailings away, read them. Some of it provides good laughs as well as reading experience.

So read those menus, read the ads, read maps, read medicine labels, read the big print, read the fine print—but READ.

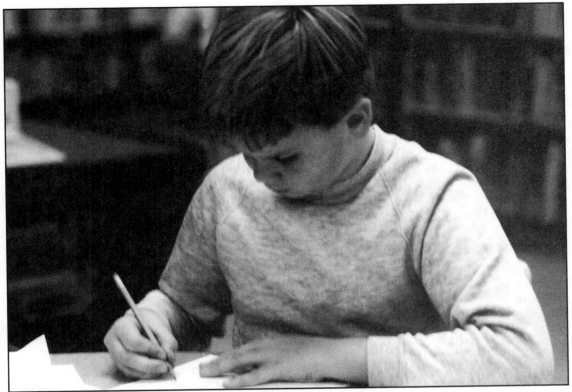

Helen S. Craymer, courtesy of the Association for Supervision and Curriculum Development

## CHAPTER 19

# Writing: Everyone Can Do It

Every class I have ever known has so much to say until the teacher announces it's writing time. Then students get very quiet. They're scared. Writing is scary if you don't get practice at it. Like learning to ride a bike or drive a car, writing takes practice.

Most of the activities that follow are really good at any age. Look them all over and pick the ones that you think will work for you.

> There is a great deal that every parent can do at home to help children both want to write and learn to write. It's not necessary to know a participle from a gerund. The point is to help children write more and feel more comfortable writing. Even essays can be easily taught.

In doing these activities at home, worry more about doing lots of writing and less about spelling and grammar. I want our children to use correct spelling and grammar as much as anyone else. But you can't teach everything at once. In these activities, you're teaching the pleasure of writing.

I looked into the shoe box where I have kept young children's writing—samples from those I have taught and those others have taught. As I describe the activities for young children, I'll include some of these writings so you can see what delights are in store for you when you try these early writing activities at home.

## Getting Started: Scribbling
■ any age

Getting started is tough. The piece of white paper without a scratch on it can be daunting. It looks as though everything you write has to be perfect. So put a few scratches on it.

Sometimes young children don't need these scratches as much as older ones who have gotten scared of the empty page. The scratches I'm talking about are scribbles. They loosen up the muscles and lower the inhibitions.

## Pictures and Words ■ ages 5–8

Use magazines and newspaper pictures worth ten thousand words. Any popular magazine is a gold mine of good pictures. Start keeping a file of appealing pictures from advertisements you come across. In this activity, everyone selects a colorful photograph. The idea is to look at it,

### From a Preschooler

*Going Places*

Once upon a time, there was a little girl.
She Lived in a pretty house
I am at the park    the park is nice
I sit down on a bench
now I go home to the house
A nice warm fire
I go to bed dreaming

observe the details, and figure out what's happening in the picture.

Ask the following: What's happening here? What do you think happened just before this picture was taken? What do you think happened afterward?

Everybody jots down ideas. Read these aloud and compare answers. If there are preschoolers looking on, let them dictate their versions. The flow of ideas doesn't have to make complete sense to be completely helpful.

## Story and Sequence ■ ages 5–7

Sequence can also be learned with those trusty pictures (see "Pictures and Words"). Everyone selects three or four or five pictures (depending on your child's level) that together tell a story. Paste these on cardboard pieces. Then number the pictures.

Using the pictures in numerical order, your child then tells a story. Even preschoolers can take part without very much extra help. Then shuffle the pictures and try again. It's fascinating for kids and grown-ups alike to see how the stories change.

Here's an example:

### The Story of the World's Fair
*There was a fine lumberJack. one day*
*They are very smart I hope you like*
*    them*
*I went on a ferris wheel. Do you like*
*    ferris wheels?*

*I was on a rollercoaster one day.*
*The dinosaurs are nice but not so nice*

Children can write down or scribble their tales. Very young children, it's been shown, remember what their scribbles say. Prewriters might dictate their stories, perhaps to an older sibling. This provides writing practice for the older child.

## Summarizing ■ ages 5–9

Children need to develop the ability to tell stories that have beginnings, middles, and ends. I don't really enjoy those long, rambling stories that children delight in going on and on with. I know I am supposed to say I enjoy every word. But after about five minutes, I take refuge in asking, "How does it end?" It's good for children to know that even a good story has to have an ending.

---

This is another sure way to get ideas rolling. Start a first sentence, "Once upon a time," and everyone adds a sentence to keep the story moving. Some of these will be silly, but the point is made about how to build a story.

*Get kids talking—and from this talking comes writing.*

## Finishing Unfinished Stories
■ ages 5–9

Start out with one person, probably an adult, telling a story. But stop before coming to the end. Let children finish the story, at first perhaps working together, then alone.

Before finishing a story that you're reading aloud, stop and ask your children how they think it will end and why they think this.

## Logical Order Puzzles ■ ages 7–9

Clip paragraphs from the newspaper. Or ask children to write their own about any subject that comes to mind. Paragraphs written by professional writers in large advertising print work well for this exercise.

Cut and separate the sentences and mix up the pieces. The challenge is for the youngster to work these sentences back into a logical order. Elementary graders enjoy this game and particularly enjoy having parents participate. The cut-up sentences are hard to keep together, so it's a good idea to put them in a little envelope. The activity is enjoyable on its own, but what's being taught is the important understanding that sentences need to follow one another logically.

## Writing Memories ■ any age

Among the most prized mementos of my children's growing-up years are the scraps of paper containing their early writings.

In many ways, writing is like making the pieces of a jigsaw puzzle fit together. The puzzle pieces are thoughts. They need to connect. These activities provide practice in making these connections.

There's the invitation to the fifth birthday party: "Be a Smarty—Come to My Party." There's the excuse note to the teacher: "Dear Mrs. Field, Please let me stay in today is that OK. By the way, I get too wet outside. Sincerely yours, the Riches." It didn't get sent, but it provided good writing practice.

And there are poems and stories about the little mouse, the snow, the cuckoo clock, our flute. We didn't have a flute, but that didn't matter. What matters is that they got a chance to write, and the pleasure was both in the writing and in the reading of it decades later.

## Looking at Advertisements
■ ages 8–12

Use those glamorous, colorful advertisements to illustrate the idea of a main point, or "thesis." Ask the following: What's the main idea in this ad? What's it trying to persuade us to do? A strong, handsome man drinking a certain soft drink in a fancy car with a beautiful girl at his side is telling us something about that soft drink. Even young children get the message. All of the details are organized to back up the ad's message, main point, or thesis. For now, look at and discuss these pictures. The time to write will come.

## Connecting Ideas ■ ages 8–12

Good writing needs not only ideas but ideas that are united, combined, and tied together to make a logical whole. Try the following activity. It can become a bit silly, but it helps teach the pulling-together formula. You need a blackboard or a large piece of paper.

Everyone jots down an idea or name of a thing. The goal is to combine these items into a logical sentence. Let's say you get the words "toys," "trip," "sunny," "teachers." You might come up with this: "On sunny days, teachers often let their classes take toys with them on school trips." Even when your ideas defeat logic, putting them together is good mental exercise and gives everyone lots of laughs.

## Subject Bounce ■ ages 8–12

In this activity you toss subjects and statements from youngster to parent and back to youngster. *Example:* Jan names the subject, "Cats," and turns to Jim to come up with a statement about cats. His might be, "Cats are mean," or "Cats are pretty," or any other statement he can think of. The statement giver then gets to come up with a subject for someone else to make a statement about.

The game pulls together listening and writing skills. It's best to encourage chil-

dren to make "big" statements about a subject. Take, for example, the subject "mother." The statement, "My mother likes cereal for breakfast," is a relatively narrow idea. It is easier for essay development, later, to make a broader statement, such as, "My mother is busy all day."

The younger the children, the more help they may need at first. But the game itself, once under way, has never failed to involve everyone and, more important, to teach these two basic skills in writing: (1) Having a subject, and (2) Having something to say about it.

## Brainstorming for Subjects ■ ages 8–12

Working together, even if it's just a group of two, jot down all the things you can write about. It can be anything at all, from parents to ice skating to cooking to homework to baseball.

Pick one of these to be a subject that you and your child will work on. Let's say, for example, you've picked "family." Keep on brainstorming. Think of all the possible things you both can say about the family. Don't try for any particular order. Jot them down as they come to mind.

Now you have a list of what you might write about the family. Decide what you would say first, second, and so on. You may find some items on the list, as you examine it, that shouldn't really be there, or you may think of others that you should have included. As you go down the list, decide what should come when, and eliminate those items you can no longer use. Add the important new ideas. After all, you may have forgotten to include Aunt Lily!

At this point, you have a list of what you hope to include in your writing, and you have them identified in numerical order. You're almost ready to write (and most of your work has already been done)—but not quite.

There's one more important step that will help. I call this "The Umbrella."

## A Recipe for Writing Essays: The Umbrella ■ ages 8–12

Even as an English teacher, I had been assigning essays for years before I ever really thought about how to teach them.

The day I had to think about how to teach them was the day my own daughter came home with her first essay assignment and asked, "What's an essay, Mom?"

The usual definition from *Webster's*— "a short piece of writing on a single subject" —would not do. She'd already heard that at school.

So I thought a bit. My eyes came upon an umbrella in the hall that, luckily for me, was not in its right place. There it was in the middle of the floor—just waiting to be discovered.

The open umbrella (if you're superstitious, open it outside) provides a visual form for the structure of an essay—really, for any direct, informational piece of writing.

The umbrella provides a structure to help young writers organize their thoughts. I have used it in both the early elementary grades and graduate school, and it works in both places. It will delight you to see how easily it works and how much it helps.

### The Subject

First you have to have something to write about. This is called the "subject." Let's say, for our first example, that the subject is "ice cream." On the umbrella, it fits in here:

We all like that subject. Now, having a subject is nice, *but it isn't enough for writing. You need to say something about your subject.* That's called "making a statement."

### The Statement

Here are some statements children might make about ice cream:

> I love ice cream.
> Ice cream comes in many flavors.
> Ice cream is better than spinach.

We'll pick one to show how the statement fits in the umbrella:

*Everything goes together—like the parts of an umbrella.* First comes the subject. The statement is about the subject. The proof explains the statement. It would be pretty silly to write, "I love ice cream," and then go on in the same paragraph to explain the love of roast beef. But that is the kind of silly thing that happens to writers who forget to stay under the umbrella.

## The Proof

Having a statement is nice, but it isn't enough. You have to explain your statement to the reader. That's called "proving the statement."

Everything you tell about loving ice cream must fit under the umbrella statement.

The proof can be something like this:

Subject — Ice Cream

Statement — I love ice cream.

Proof — It is sweet and cold.

Ice cream comes in many flavors. There are chocolate, vanilla, strawberry, chocolate chip, vanilla ripple, and many more. Ice cream in any flavor cools me on hot days.

## A Broken Umbrella ▪ ages 8–12

Here is another example to help illustrate, one by one, the three parts of the umbrella and how they need to match.

**Part One:** Start with the subject or the topic of the umbrella. The subject in this case is "dreams."

**Part Two:** This is the statement—what is being said about the subject. This is the part that fits in the umbrella itself. The statement in this umbrella is, "My dreams are silly."

**Part Three:** This is the proof. It has to tell about the subject "dreams" and it has to explain how your dreams are "silly." It has to stay under the umbrella. It can't go off to tell us about something different from silly dreams.

Ask your child to read the following paragraph aloud.

### Dreams

*My dreams are silly. Two nights ago I saw a gorilla flying south. Last night I saw a flag waving at me. Tomorrow I will probably see shoes running down the street.*

Ask: "Is this a good umbrella?" "If not, why not?" We don't see umbrellas in the paragraphs in the books we read, but the umbrella parts are there—even when we don't see them.

Soon children will be able to write paragraphs without the umbrella to help. But in the meantime, try the umbrella to make thinking and writing easier.

## Simple and Complex Umbrellas
▪ ages 8–12

You might have an umbrella like this: "My family is wonderful." This is a big, broad, simple umbrella. A more complex umbrella would be, "Having a big family has its advantages," or "Our family home is the place to be at holiday time."

These more complex umbrellas narrow the topic and ask that the writer prove a very definite point. This is what good umbrellas do: They actually make essay writing easier by limiting the subject, making it possible for even an inexperienced writer to write well.

## A WRITING FORMULA

So you see, it's really pretty easy to teach and to write a formula umbrella paragraph. It gives every child the recipe to write a paragraph. Once that has been learned, a child can go on to bigger and better writing projects. As students go through school, they will be able to move beyond formulas to writing with a developing mastery of usage, form, and style in order to put across ever more effectively what they have to say.

### Combine History with Writing
■ ages 8–12

Use famous persons. Everybody writes a pretend page from the diary of a famous person. You can all choose the same person, or everyone can choose someone different. The choice is fun in itself: Clara Barton or Helen Keller, Buffalo Bill or Michael Jordan, Mick Jagger or John F. Kennedy.

A variation of the activity is the interview. One person poses as a famous person, and everyone else interviews him or her. Usually the person picked is in the news.

This exercise is fine incentive for current events class as well.

### Details Make a Point of View
■ ages 8–12

What we write is governed by our point of view, as is illustrated by this exercise. You and the children write two contrasting paragraphs about the same subject. *Example:* Jim describes the living room as though he's feeling sad and gloomy about everything. In his second paragraph, he describes the same room, but this time he's feeling joyous, on top of the world. The details he picks and his choice of words should make clear the point of view. In the happy paragraph, for example, the blue wall may be "the color of the sun-filled sky."

A similar selection of particular details and their wording can be done with people. Writers are always doing this to make us like or dislike a character. If Spencer Jones has a "long, funny nose," we tend to like him. If his nose is described as "long and bony," we distrust him.

This is a sophisticated exercise that illustrates the many choices that writers make.

> Try writing some parent-child conversations about typical household problems. *Examples:* tracking mud into the kitchen, making time for homework, children refusing to do chores. These dialogues are tremendously revealing for both parents and children, and they're great writing practice.

# MEETING SPECIAL LEARNING NEEDS

## Thinking of You ■ ages 7–9

Here's an example of an activity that helps children develop writing skills through exercises that use a variety of learning styles. Children who don't yet write can dictate their ideas. You need paper and pencil.

## Look

**Visual Discrimination.** Write two good things about your child, each on a separate slip of paper. *Examples:* "Bill smiles a lot"; "Bill minds his manners." Ask your child to write two good things about you on two other pieces of paper.

Exchange these slips of paper, read them, and return them. Write a new compliment about your child on another piece of paper. Include this one with the others and give them to your child. Your child's task is to read and find the new compliment.

**Visual Memory.** Jot down three names, each on a separate piece of paper. Write a compliment to go with each name on three other pieces of paper. Read these to your child and then match the compliments to the names.

Mix up these slips of paper. Taking turns with your child, draw out a slip of paper from the pile and read it aloud. Your child's task is to guess who is being described or to provide the compliment for the person named.

## Listen

**Auditory Discrimination.** Use the compliment slips you wrote for your child. Add one more word to each. *Example:* If a word on the slip is "happy," put the word "very" in front of it. Read these new compliments aloud.

Ask your child to listen carefully to the words and to name the new word.

**Auditory Memory.** Make a list of four friends, neighbors, or relatives that you would like to compliment. Read the list aloud. Ask your child to listen and to repeat this list.

Tell one thing you like about each of these people. *Examples:* John is a good driver; Tina tells good jokes. Ask your child to listen and to repeat these compliments.

## Do

**Eye-Hand Coordination.** Send written compliments to friends or relatives. Some can be hidden to surprise them. Leave Mom's under a pillow. Put Brother's in his dresser drawer.

Let your child choose stationery and write notes or even scribbles to friends and family members. Handwritten notes are always a delight to receive. Talk about how it feels to get a compliment or to give one.

## Homemade Poetry ■ any age

Probably almost every poem in print was written outside of school. Yet seeing poems in bold, black type in big, thick anthologies makes many people hesitate to write poetry, as if it were something produced by superhumans in some out-of-this-world place.

There's poetry in everyone, just waiting for a chance to show itself. One of the nicest things about poetry is that it takes many forms: long, short, happy, sad, rhyming, free form, unrhymed. It's Lewis Carroll and haiku and Emily Dickinson.

Even if poetry is unfamiliar territory to you, your children are not strangers to it. They've been playing delightedly with words:

*A dream with dew all*
*over the trees.*
*All was on new years day*
*A wonderful day in the forest was*
*to have this bright holiday.*
*And the wind was blowing*
*all through the trees.*

Poetry is word play and word feeling. Delight in words and in the pictures they evoke is the key to poetry at home. If both you and the children are exploring poetry for the first time, get hold of a children's anthology of verse from your library. Read some of these poems aloud. Take turns reading to each other. Make a game of picking the poems by closing your eyes and letting your fingers land at random on the table of contents.

Music sparks imagination. Especially good are those selections that tell a story, like *The Sorcerer's Apprentice* or *Coppélia*. Compare your children's interpretations of the music with the original story versions available in most libraries.

## You Have a Poem! ■ any age

Practice a game of associations. Ask questions: What does yellow remind you of? A big yellow sun? A sweet, spring flower? An infected sore? How about love? Mother? Sister? Your bed? The morning alarm?

Take one of these as your subject: spring, insects, trees, flowers. Anything from nature is a fine takeoff point. Jot down all the descriptive phrases about them that come to mind. Encourage children to use words that "paint" pictures.

After you have about ten phrases, stop. You have a poem! It may not be terribly artistic. But it has the basics of poetry — words that paint pictures and convey feelings.

A parent's aim in helping children with poetry writing is not necessarily to turn

Parents who have some favorite poems are in a good position to work with poetry at home. That old-fashioned image of those quiet minutes with children seated around their parents is worth preserving. And when you share your favorite poems, fill the children in on your experiences with them — how your father read that poem to you, or how a certain poem was your third-grade teacher's favorite.

children into poets but to increase their overall ability to use expressive language freely.

Here is an example of homemade poetry written on paper grown yellow on my kitchen wall. Our daughter Rebecca composed it while on a Sunday walk in the country:

> *Whenever the woods I walk among—*
> *Are very green and very young—*
> *The trees in the woods*
> *They wave so nice—*
> *With a little*
> *Path that*
> *I follow.*

All right, I know it isn't Shakespeare. But I treasure it, as would any parent, as a masterpiece.

## GAMES HELP, EVEN WITH GRAMMAR

In grammar teaching, from the middle elementary grades through the senior grades, the student is taught and retaught the making of a sentence. There may be a few additional refinements in each year's curriculum, but by and large it's a program taught in a similar way, usually from one text series.

Some students learn their grammar rules first time out. Others continue to have trouble, no matter how many English classes they sit through.

## Getting the "Feel" of the Sentence ▪ ages 7–12

The important point in grammar is to help children get the "feel" of a sentence and to help them enjoy experimenting with different kinds of sentences. You can teach the feel of a sentence without going into subject-verb technicalities. But if you know them and your child is receptive, it won't hurt to point out that every complete sentence has a subject and a verb. This subject-and-verb combination is sometimes called a "kernel" sentence. Here's one: "Boy runs."

The fun is in elaborating and building on this kernel: A boy runs; A small boy runs; A small boy runs quickly; A small boy runs quickly to the swimming pool; and so on. Children enjoy doing this. You can do it both orally and on paper.

## Where Is Joe's Cow? ▪ ages 7–12

Imitating sentence patterns is good grammar practice. Start with the simple statement, "Joe has a cow." Children, depending on age and ability, can either repeat what you say or come up with the same structure by using their own words, such as "Sally has a horse," then "Joe and Ted have a cow," and so on.

Now change to the question form: "Where is Joe's cow?" Move to the command: "Joe, bring me that cow!" And, of course, the exclamation: "Wow, what a cow Joe has!"

Fill-in exercises can be helpful in teaching grammar. They work best when read aloud, so that the "feel" of the sentence sinks in. Parents can make up paragraphs, being sure to leave some spaces blank. Children enjoy filling in the blanks, perhaps with humorous words. This makes it more of a game.

Older children with some knowledge of grammar will enjoy the "string of letters" game. This consists of giving children a group of letters—for example, *a, d, f, m, p, r, w*—and then asking them to make up a sentence using words that start with these letters. These strings are then exchanged. This provides lots of laughs. Who says writing has to be grim?

## Meeting Famous People— Without Leaving Home
■ ages 7–12

For another unique way of traveling around the world without leaving home, collect famous people.

I know a man in his forties whose hobby is writing to ask for pictures and signatures of famous men and women. He's been doing this since his early teens. He's not just an autograph hound. Each of the letters he sends is individual, and he receives individual answers from presidents, from famous people in prison, from religious leaders. His is an astonishing collection—file drawer after file drawer. You can see young Richard Nixon and a young Pope Paul. It's more than a collection. It's a trip through history, and it's a hobby available to all.

## Writing, Writing Everywhere
■ any age

Encourage writing practice around the house wherever and whenever you can.

Let children write your notes to the mail carrier, to anyone who needs reminders or greetings. Keep paper and pencils all around the house.

On trips, provide each child with a notebook in which to keep a travel log or diary. Children can take notes on what they've seen, things they've liked, foods they've eaten. At home, you can frame some of these remembrances along with a marked map of where you went and some pictures of what you saw.

## BUILDING THE MEMORY BANK FOR WRITING

### Going Places ■ ages 7–12

Outings are more than fun. They put into practice the educational theory that people

> Start a library of homemade storybooks. The books themselves can be made by stapling colored paper as a cover over several sheets of folded lined or unlined paper. Prewriters can dictate their stories, with the parent putting down a sentence or two at the bottom of each page. Children can fill in their own drawings. Don't forget the all-important bold print for the author's name.

learn best from actual experience—by going and doing.

Do some planning. Take the calendar off the wall and discuss dates and budget. Together with your children, decide where to go. Seek out some less-traveled places, especially when you're on trips. Parents can get tired of the same old places, and so do kids. Industrial sites often have special tours for visitors. I recall going with my children through a beer factory in Milwaukee and through a car assembly line in River Rouge, Michigan. They were as fascinating to me as they were to the kids.

All trips need not be planned in detail. Spontaneity and flexibility are important. For a touch of excitement, try a mystery-trip journey to a nearby location with the children blindfolded in the car, not knowing where they're going.

For new ideas on what to see, give each child a map of your area (often available at gas stations) so they can find places they'd like to visit.

The best outings for children are neither extensive nor expensive. For a young child it can be a walk to the library or a browse and a small purchase at the drug store. For an older youngster it can be a trip to a bowling alley or a visit to a factory. The trick lies in using the potential of even an everyday type of event.

## PLANNING THAT'S NOT BURDENSOME

Planning can enhance even the most modest outing, and it doesn't take a lot of time.

**Before.** Preparing children for what they're going to see helps them see more when they get there. For example, if you're going on a picnic and you'll be scouting birds, tell children what they might expect. They like to anticipate what's coming and to recognize it when it appears.

**During.** Encourage children to collect souvenirs as you go: pictures, menus, postcards, for a scrapbook later on. Children may enjoy keeping a trip diary that they write themselves or dictate to you.

**After.** Build on the particular interest the outing inspired. After a tour through a cookie factory, for example, your children may come away eager to bake new kinds of cookies on their own. Whenever possible, tie up new interests with trips to the library for books.

Don't be discouraged if an outing, even though planned, doesn't live up to your expectations. The idea is to go on so many that even when one is disappointing, others will make up for it.

## THE POWER OF SPECIAL TIMES

Going places together creates the stuff of which memories are made. My mother died when I was young. I cannot hear her voice any longer, but I remember very vividly where we went together. She never drove a car, but we went many places on the Greyhound bus that stopped across the street from our house. She liked to shop, and even when we didn't buy, we went at least once a week from our home in Monroe to the big city of Toledo. I remember those trips with a special joy not because they were exotic or expensive. We were alone together, exploring streets and places. Oh, the power of these special times, and how long they live within us!

> The need for children to learn to communicate through writing has never been greater. In the past, there was more dependence on oral communication. Today, you have to be able to put words on paper.

## KEEP THE PRAISE COMING

Try not to overcriticize a child's initial writing work. The aim of these exercises is to build writing confidence in an atmosphere of shared experiences.

Standard English is still standard English—it is the English that is rewarded with a job, with a place on the payroll. This is English that all children can learn.

This chapter on writing is designed as a start. It is a takeoff point for your family's ideas. And do remember that the best medicine for writers, young and old, is steady encouragement and honest praise.

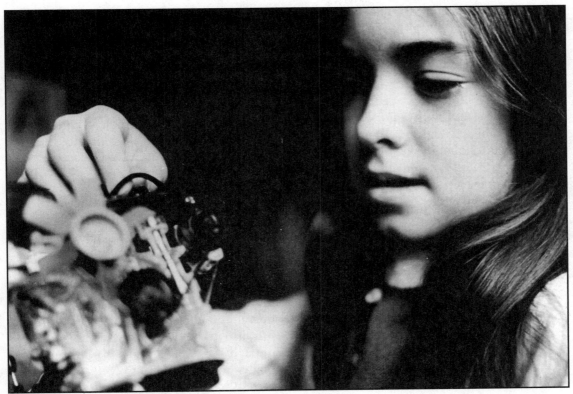

*Joe DiDio, courtesy of the National Education Association*

## CHAPTER 20

# Math: No More Excuses

I would rather read a story than a column of numbers. I would rather try to write a poem than fill in a ledger sheet. I am number-averse, and it is a definite handicap. I remember my high school math with deep feelings of failure, even though I passed. In college I skipped math altogether. I feel for people like me, and I suspect there may be a lot of us.

I was in a drugstore the other day buying a pair of pantyhose on sale—"20 percent off" said the sign. The reduced price was not marked on the package, nor was it stored in the cash register computer. So the young man (he told me he was a college student) who was collecting the money had to do his own figuring. The hose were originally $2.50. He struggled and struggled. At one point, he said I had to pay $2.75.

Finally I showed him how to do it. I had made it through percentages before my number problem took over in algebra and geometry. I think I could have told him I owed him a dollar, and he would have taken it. Here was a fellow sufferer.

Over the years I have become friendlier with numbers. Actually this came about through "number sense" activities I did with my children. Many of these activities are in this chapter. (See "Money Common Sense" in Chapter 13 for activities using money.)

---

No more excuses: Math is at the top of the education agenda today, and we'd all better get comfortable with numbers without delay.

---

To succeed in math, a child really needs not a storehouse of math tricks but rather a storehouse of math experiences to call on. These are all around us.

---

The idea is to help children feel comfortable with numbers. Even with calculators and computers to help, we still have to cope with numbers. And we have to be able to face them as fearlessly as possible.

Here is what I mean by number sense. This example may seem far-fetched, but it is a real one, and it's duplicated many times in homes and classrooms across our nation. A fourth grader was asked to estimate how much his parents would pay for three nights in three different hotels. The first night would cost $32.00. The second night would cost $28.00, and the third night would cost $30.00. This youngster immediately jumped to the answer: $9,000.00!

His parents asked, "Don't you think that's a high price for three nights' lodging?" It was not until his parents added up the bill with him that the youngster understood the difference between $90.00 and $9,000.00. It's just a matter of decimal points—but oh, those decimals!

## A MATH WALK THROUGH THE HOUSE

The plan for this chapter is for families to take a math walk. This is literally a hunt for numbers in our everyday environment.

Keep a pencil, small pad, and tape measure with you. There will be many occasions to use them.

## KITCHEN

### Around-the-Stove Math ▪ any age

Math is good in the kitchen at any age. For the prereader: Set the table and count the settings. For the early reader, measure ingredients and read recipes. For the older elementary grader, divide and double recipes.

### Napkin Fractions ▪ ages 7–9

Make fractions fun to learn and get the table set differently every night. Paper towels or napkins can be folded into all kinds of big and little fractions. Start with easy halves and move to eighths or sixteenths. Use markers to label the parts.

### The Long Receipt ▪ ages 7–9

Check grocery receipts against your purchases. Have your child match prices on items coming out of the bags with the numbers on the receipts. Did you get everything you bought? Sometimes you paid more for an item at the store than you realized.

This old standby is still effective: Let's say you have three for dinner and only two hamburgers. How will you divide them? What about five eaters and only four baked potatoes? Everyone can still eat—but they'll be digesting fractions, too.

### What's in the House? ▪ ages 8–12

Before going to the store, ask children to help you figure out what's needed by looking at the fractions of items you still have.

What's left of the sugar? All gone? Two pounds? How much bread is on hand? A quarter of a loaf? How much milk? Half a gallon? How many eggs? A third of a dozen? You don't have to actually measure. You're estimating and "talking fractions."

### Food Label Numbers ▪ ages 8–12

There's a lot of math on food labels, mandated by law. What's the expiration date? How heavy is the can? What percentages of different foods are contained? It comes as a surprise to many to learn that the first ingredient listed is the predominant one in the container. If water is listed first, that's what you get most of.

Ask older students to read for natural versus additive ingredients. The long, hard-to-pronounce words are usually the additives. How many and how much of them are included in your product? They are not necessarily bad. Your children just have to know what they are buying.

## Math Concepts ■ ages 8–12

### Who Ate the Cake?

Do this with foods that can be cut up, such as cupcakes, apples, or oranges. Cut them into pieces that can be reassembled. The concept is that the whole can be divided into parts and reassembled to form the whole—unless someone eats a piece or two.

### Is Taller Bigger Than Shorter?

Find two containers of different shapes that hold the same amount of water. These might be two measuring cups or coffee cups with the same capacity.

Illustrate this by filling one of the containers with water and then pouring the water into the other container. Chances are, your young child will guess that the taller container holds more water than the shorter one. Up to a certain age (about age eight or so) children tend to say that the taller container holds more water than the shorter one—even when they see you put the same amount into each cup. The eminent Swiss psychologist Jean Piaget identified this as a lack of operational understanding, which children tend not to acquire until the middle elementary school years.

### Can an Orange Be an Apple?

Illustrate this by cutting up two different items, such as an orange and an apple. The parts of that orange put together again will combine to make a whole orange. The parts of the apple can be reassembled into a whole apple. But try putting parts of an orange together with parts of an apple. They do not combine, at least not readily.

## LIVING ROOM/DINING ROOM

### Number Talk ■ any age

There are memories, often about numbers, that bless and burn. They provide revealing topics for family conversations—discussions that even adolescents find interesting.

Can you tell about a time when knowing fractions (or not knowing them) made a difference to you? Was there a recipe you ruined or a deal you botched when you thought that four eighths was more than one half?

Have you been to a restaurant and had the problem of trying to figure out who owed what and how much the tip ought to be? When you paid the bill, did you sometimes pay less than your share or come up with a tip that was too big?

Do you agree that ability with math helps in coping with the demands of everyday life? Talk about this. Tell about a time when someone in the family used math to solve a problem. This does not have to be a "big" deal. It can be an overdue traffic ticket or a refund from a department store.

Keep the talk about numbers flowing. It builds the comfort level for work with math, in school and out.

### Newspaper Numbers ■ ages 7–9

Open almost any page of the paper, and you'll find numbers galore. As a starting point with young children, ask them to circle every number they see. Start with one column at a time to keep the task from seeming endless.

Move on to more sophisticated assignments: Find all numbers over fifty or over one hundred or over one thousand.

Ask children to look at ads for all those specials that end in ninety-eight or ninety-nine cents. Let them get practice in rounding off those numbers by estimating, for example, what four shirts that sell for $7.99 each will cost, or what five pounds of potatoes that sell for eighty-nine cents a pound will cost.

## Practice Percentages ■ ages 8–12

Look around the room. Figure the percentage of people in the room who are wearing sneakers. Look outside. Count the cars on the block. Figure the percentage of black or white cars of all the cars on the block. Figure the percentage of time (number of minutes) that commercials take during radio or TV programs.

## Math Words ■ ages 8–12

There are three M's and an R that students will hear about whenever a lot of numbers come together.

Bounce the ball (if indoors, not too vigorously) to show your math answers. What's twelve minus nine, divided by one, or six plus eleven? Children get exercise and give their answers by bouncing the ball the right number of times.

It can be hard to keep these apart. It was for me. So I make up sentences to help.

**Mode:** The number that appears often. As in: "That jacket this year is really the mode, just the style you want."

**Median:** The middle number in the list. As in: "The median line divides the highway."

**Mean:** This really measures the average. As in: "The mean temperature for July was eighty-five degrees."

**Range:** The limits; how far the numbers extend. As in: "Our family ranges in age from four to forty."

A good way for children to get comfortable with these words is to use them and to hear them used.

Try out this activity at a restaurant as you're waiting for a meal to be served. Ask to hold on to the menus after you've made your choices. Look at all the prices for the appetizers or entrées—keep to one category—and ask these questions: What's the range? What's the median? The mode? Some can be eyeballed; that is, the answer can be arrived at without calculations on paper. The mean usually takes pencil figuring.

## Family Age, Weight, Height ■ ages 8–12

Another activity for the three M's and the R is to figure family ages or weights or heights. In a young family, you will find a mean age in the teens. In an older family, you will get up into the forties.

## Direction Words ■ ages 8–12

When you tell a person how to go from your house to the school and you talk about walking "parallel" to this street, "perpendicular" to another, and crossing at a certain "intersection," you are using words important in math. Help children become comfortable with these words and encourage them to use the words as they give directions.

## Sports, Stocks, and Numbers
■ ages 8–12

Children who balk at math in class are often youngsters who figure out batting averages in their spare time. Some even understand the financial pages.

Capitalize on these interests to help a child overcome math resistance in class. Try questions such as these: Which team has won the most games this season? Who are the high scorers? How much higher are they than the others? Use the newspaper to get the answers.

## MATH IN HOBBIES

## Photography ■ ages 8–12

Shopping for a camera is an experience in mathematics, and it's not just in the initial cost. Compare film prices: How many pennies per exposure? Is it cheaper to buy a roll of twenty exposures than to buy twelve exposures? How much do you lose when a picture doesn't turn out?

## Gardening ■ ages 8–12

Figure out what you need: How many rows will fit in a four-by-four-foot garden plot if they are six inches apart? Eight inches? Twelve inches? If seeds are to be placed two inches apart, how many can you fit in one row? How much fertilizer is needed for a lawn of one hundred square feet? It's mind-boggling how many numbers are involved.

### How Late Is Late?

There's little we can do, once we're waiting, to make a person show up on time for an appointment. But we can spend some of that time figuring out just how late "late" is. Check your watch. How many minutes or hours? What fraction or percentage is that of an hour, a day, a week, a year?

This solid math exercise passes time productively. Of course, when that person shows up, there will be some other words to deal with.

## Ask the Calculator ■ ages 10–12

Certain questions are made for the calculator, and they build the love of numbers and the excitement of estimates and projections. I know there is concern that once kids start using the calculator, they will stop using their heads. But that can't happen if they are asked to use their heads to ask the questions and to know the steps they're taking to get to the answers.

For example, take this question: How many miles do you think we will drive this year in our car? To get the answer, you first have to figure out how many miles you drive in a week or in a month and then multiply appropriately to arrive at your answer. The key is to keep kids talking about what they are doing as they try to figure out the answer.

Try other questions like these: How many dozen eggs do you think this family will eat in a year? How many quarts (or gallons) of milk will we drink in a year? How many steps do you take in a week? In a month? In a year? How many hours or minutes in a month? How many hours until Christmas? Making up the questions is almost as much fun as coming up with the answers.

## BATHROOM

### Weigh Me ▪ ages 5–9

Bring out that bathroom scale and start weighing—anything and everything. First let your children make guesses about how much different things weigh, including themselves. Weigh the wastebasket, the clothing just taken off, a full glass of water.

### Weight Watching ▪ ages 8–12

This is a national pastime that provides useful math practice. Every day for a week, have children read the scales for a family member. Can your youngster find the heavi-

> As long as your children know how they get to the answer, the calculator is more to be loved than feared.

est and lightest family member (or any two willing participants)?

Does someone in the family weigh double another person's weight? If you weigh 130 pounds and in the next two months gain 5 percent of your weight, how much will you weigh? These are intriguing questions that are fun and provide math practice.

### Tile-a-While ▪ any age

Often there are tiles in a bathroom. How many and how wide and long are they? Start counting and come up with some hard data. You can even find out how much area the tiles cover by multiplying the size of one tile by how many there are. This can be lively information at the dinner table if you first ask for guesses from the family. Who comes closest to the correct answer?

## BEDROOM

### Ingredients in Clothes ▪ ages 8–12

What are our clothes made of? These days labels rarely read "100 percent" of anything. Check them to figure out what percentage of ingredients are in the garments you see before you.

## Watch the Clock ■ ages 7–9

Practice estimating times: How long before Mom or Dad gets home? How long will it take us to get ready for this trip? How long will it take to get to school?

## Family Fractions ■ ages 8–12

Think about different people you know and their ages. By what fraction are little brothers and sisters younger than you, and by what fraction are your parents older? If you are twelve and your mother is forty-eight, what fraction are you of your mother's age? (*Answer:* one fourth.) Make up these fractions for other people in the family and for friends.

## MEETING SPECIAL LEARNING NEEDS

The reading and writing chapters showed how to divide an activity into different learning modalities to meet different learning needs. Here are some ways to apply the same approach to mathematics.

## Saving Up ■ ages 7–9

This activity can help children save money and increase their knowledge about banks. You need the usual papers that accompany bank transactions. Even if banks do not use the old bankbook, they all have brochures, deposit slips, and statements.

First you may want to call or visit banks to get information about services. Check which bank is most convenient and which welcome small depositors. Ask about fees and interest on savings accounts.

## LOOK

**Visual Discrimination.** Point out and read the name of the bank on the bank materials. Ask your child to find the name of the bank on the deposit slip.

Using the deposit slip, point out the account number and the space for writing the depositor's name. Your child then looks at the deposit slip and finds these sections.

**Visual Memory.** Show your child the account number on the deposit slip. Ask your child to look at it carefully, turn over the slip, and then try to recall the account number.

Write down the account number and two other numbers. Put each on a separate piece of paper. Point out the account number. Mix up the papers. Now your child's task is to pick out the correct account number.

## LISTEN

**Auditory Discrimination.** Say the name of the bank where the account has been opened. Your child listens and repeats the bank's name.

Give your bank's name and the names of banks with similar names. *Examples:* First Federal, First American, First National.

Your child listens and signals upon hearing your bank's name.

**Auditory Memory.** Look at the bankbook and name the date that the account was opened. Ask your child to listen and to repeat the date.

Give three dates on which deposits were made. Your child tries to repeat these in the order given.

Name the amount of the deposit and the date of the last deposit. Again your child's task is to listen and to repeat the deposit amount and date.

## DO

**Eye-Hand Coordination.** To save up for deposits, children can keep money in a special place or container—such as a piggy bank. They can count the coins and put them in the paper coin wrappers provided by the bank. Then these coin rolls go to the bank.

Notice what happens in this activity. To provide practice for **Look,** we use our eyes. To provide practice for **Listen,** we use our ears, and so on. We all need different ways of learning different kinds of subject matter. Use your own ideas to dream up new ways to reach children through all of their senses.

## DON'T WAIT FOR THE ROBOT

The increasing use of computers by government, industry, and business demands an awareness of computer uses and limitations. An expert in artificial intelligence (the subject of programming knowledge into computers) recently confided that it was much easier for a computer to "learn" calculus than for the computer to stack blocks—a task most people consider children's play.

Involved in stacking blocks are hundreds of steps that children understand and learn by watching adults. The computer's universe is far more limited. Within those limitations, programmed by a person, the computer may work more efficiently than a person. But in the world of almost unlimited and unprogrammed daily choices, the computer can't cope.

---

Numbers can relieve anxiety, not just make it. In a recent film, a basketball coach from a very small town brings his team into a huge fieldhouse for the big championship game. It's clear from the boys' faces that the massive fieldhouse awes them and that they feel there is no way they can play and win there.

The coach takes out his tape measure, holds it to the basket, and lets it drop to the floor. He asks the team to look at the number. Then he measures the distance from the free-throw line to the basket. He asks the team to look at the result. They are the very same measurements as in their little gym back home. The boys' faces register their reassurance, and sure enough, they go on to win the game.

Managing a household, for example, is far more difficult to program than managing a factory job with a limited number of tasks. A household robot will take longer to develop than a factory robot. There's just so much going on in a home all at once.

Math may look cold and calculating, but it is full of feelings and sometimes anxiety. No robot can take the place of a teacher or parent. What robot can tell a funny story about how that "bargain" really proved to be a "lemon"? Even in math, the human factor plays a critical role. That's why friendly feelings for numbers are so important.

*Susan M. Vandertie, courtesy of the Association for Supervision and Curriculum Development*

## CHAPTER 21

# Transitions: To the Teen Years

Beyond the confines of the elementary school years is an emerging adult world that is at the same time both exhilarating and discouraging for children. Fortunately our youngsters, with even a few developing MegaSkills, bring enormous strengths to these challenging years. But like plants, which need water to grow, children need ongoing support from their environment, their family, and their teachers in order to continue their healthy growth.

In these activities, which cover a range of topics from shyness to job applications, children look at themselves, and they look to others and to their community for assistance and information. They get help in being themselves and in resisting peer pressure. Each is another step in their evolving maturity.

## Speaking Up ■ ages 10–12

Shyness is a painful condition that affects many youngsters. It may cause them to miss out on important times with their friends. This activity will help youngsters learn ways to accept their shyness and to develop strategies to overcome it. All that's needed are thinking minds.

Together make a list of three or four situations that cause your youngster to feel shy. This could be speaking up in class or talking to classmates of the opposite sex. Pick one to work on.

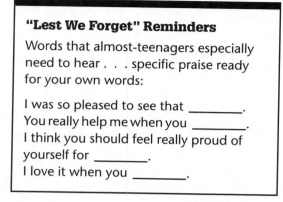

**"Lest We Forget" Reminders**

Words that almost-teenagers especially need to hear . . . specific praise ready for your own words:

I was so pleased to see that _____.
You really help me when you _____.
I think you should feel really proud of yourself for _____.
I love it when you _____.

Make up a pretend situation with a believable set of events. *Example:* A group decides to go for pizza after school. Your youngster wants to go but doesn't know the kids very well. He doesn't go. He feels unhappy.

Discuss some ways to deal with this kind of situation. *Examples:* Walk along with the group. Start a conversation with another person, and say, "I'd like to join you, OK?" Taking this risk of possible rejection is no worse than thinking you've already been rejected.

Make up a list of "overcoming shyness" exercises that your youngster can do without running great risks. *Examples:* Ask a policeman for directions; ask a teacher a question after class; praise someone's new clothes.

Rather than having your youngster be overwhelmed by shyness, suggest taking small steps such as these. The small successes will add up and will give your youngster confidence to try again.

## Under Control ■ ages 10–12

Everyone gets angry at times. Our children need to know that it's OK to show feelings but that starting a fight rarely solves a problem.

This activity helps youngsters face up to and control their anger. You need thinking minds.

Talk with your youngster about what to do when, for example, a friend calls at the last minute to cancel an appointment, or you find that your baby sister has broken your favorite CD.

Choose a TV program to watch together. Look for situations that make people angry. Most of the responses include the use of guns and knives. Because there is so much of this, children might get the idea that these are realistic responses. That's why it is so important to talk together about what to do in real life. Ask children to think about their behavior when they are angry. Do they try to cool off before speaking? Do they talk things over with someone? Do they start a fight or scream? Would you like to change any of this? If so, what would you change? Encourage children to watch people's faces, hands, and legs when they are angry. This is called body language. Sometimes you learn more through body language than from the words people say.

## You Be the Judge ■ ages 10–12

This activity gives children an understanding of how we sometimes let others make decisions for us. This might be how drinking alcohol or taking drugs starts. Sometimes we try to please other people so much that we don't please ourselves. For example, children might buy clothes and CDs because friends have them, not because they like them. This activity gives youngsters practice in thinking for themselves. It starts by talking about clothes. It can move to a conversation about pressures to drink or try drugs.

Ask your child to choose a favorite piece of clothing. It might be something for school or an outfit for special events.

Start with questions like these: Why is this piece of clothing your favorite? Is it the color? Is it because someone special bought it for you? Do your friends own clothes like yours? Would you wear these clothes if you knew your friends didn't like them? Would you wear them if they weren't popular?

### From Virginia . . .

"When my daughter, now thirteen, was little, I did special things with her around the house. What this program reminded me of is that there is still a lot I can teach her—going to the bank, to the drugstore. Whatever I am doing, I can talk with her about it at that moment. We have conversations about the activities in the car, wherever we happen to be. The importance of this program is in the communication that it sparks."

Now you might talk about the judgment your child needs to face peer pressure about alcohol or drug use. Does your child know anyone who has been hurt? Is there anything you can do to help? Share a mistake of your own. Tell about a time that you bought something or drank something you didn't really want just because it was popular. Was it a good or bad decision? Why?

## Today in the News ▪ ages 10–12

Young people need to realize that what happens anywhere in the world today can affect their own lives.

This activity provides practice in following news events and talking about them. It helps children become aware that half a world away is not so far away after all. You need a current newspaper.

Find at least two articles that tell of events in a foreign country. *Examples:* Winners announced in European bicycle race. Drugs seized at the border.

Talk about these. Could any of these things happen here?

Find in the paper or think of a situation that affects your area. *Examples:* Proposed shopping center adds to traffic problems; neighborhood school to close.

Talk about these happenings. How do you feel about them, and what, if anything, can you do about them? What's interesting about the news? Is it relevant to your lives? Can children tell others about it? In this way, they show they understand what's happening around them.

## Volunteer and Learn ▪ ages 10–12

Volunteering in the community is a fine way to help children gain work experience and to learn about the needs of others. Many nursing homes and hospitals recognize the value of having young people around to mix and mingle with the elderly.

Check also with neighborhood recreation centers. And there are local fairs, church groups, and community functions that need help.

When you find an organization to work for, call to set up a meeting with the volunteer coordinator. Because of your child's age and transportation needs, you will probably be involved in making the volunteer connection. But it will be worth it.

In advance, work out with your child some questions to ask: How long will tasks take? How many hours a week will training be offered?

Volunteering is not without pitfalls. Sometimes an institution is delighted to welcome a volunteer but does not provide support and supervision. After one or two visits, a youngster can become discouraged with just sitting around and doing nothing or not enough. Before signing up, make sure that there will be sufficient direction for volunteers to enable your child to work and to learn.

---

You have such a special quality of _____.
It's so good to be able to count on you for _____.

---

## Reaching Out to Others
▪ ages 10–12

It is important for children to get the sense of themselves as helpers, able to reach out to others to do something to make them happy. This activity combines reading with volunteering.

Select an elderly person in a nursing home or hospital to whom your child can read. A local social service agency will have names of shut-ins in your area. If you belong to a religious group, ask your pastor, priest, or rabbi for names.

Find out the older person's special reading interests. Your child should be able to read the material well. Before beginning, discuss how long your child should stay. Ten to fifteen minutes a session may be a good length of time. Decide on this before your child reads so that no one will be disappointed.

Contact the person to whom your child will be reading and make a date for a first visit. Let your child tell a little about your family and then ask about the other person's childhood. Suggest that your child read only a short time the first day. Later at home, practice the reading selected for the second visit. You will probably have to accompany your youngster at least for the first trip.

In between visits, your child can write notes or cards. Everyone loves to be remembered, and this gives your child practice in letter writing. This activity could count as a service project for scout groups.

By helping others, children help themselves. They realize that not all happiness is

> I especially want to thank you for _____.

tied to things like toys or clothes. Some of the best things in life really are free.

## Help Available Here ▪ ages 10–12

This activity helps preteens get experience in securing jobs right around home—jobs that fit into student schedules. One of these is the age-old profession of baby sitter. Really, a better name is child care helper.

Together make a list of friends or neighbors who may need child care. Help your child write a flyer that includes the following information:

▪ Name, address, phone number
▪ Activities you do with children (play games, teach songs, practice good safety habits)
▪ What you charge and when you are available

Distribute this flyer to the people on your list. Post it in supermarkets and community centers.

There are other jobs near home besides child care. Among them are raking leaves, washing windows, shoveling snow, walking dogs, addressing envelopes, and so forth.

Ask youngsters to keep track of the calls they get and to write down when they are expected on a job and what supplies they may have to bring along, such as a rake or shovel.

Remind them to ask about how long the job will take and what pay, if any, is being agreed upon. This is really valuable experience, and it can be put on a résumé as a first "real" job.

---

> It's wonderful to see you growing up so _____.

---

## THE NEED TO KNOW

Kids learn a lot from their peers. Everybody says so. They give each other needed support. The problem is that they also give each other a lot of immature ideas, too. This immaturity needs to be seasoned with some adult thinking in order for kids to start having adult ideas.

The possibilities for ten- to twelve-year-olds to learn from adults—even from those who are not their parents—is enormous, but first the adult world has to let them in.

One of the entry points is to talk about jobs and to help kids get a taste of what the "real world" is like. Here are a few activities that help.

### Jobs Ahead ■ ages 10–12

The job world is changing. Driving a truck used to be a man's job; being a nurse was always woman's work.

This activity helps youngsters start thinking and talking about what they might like to do when they are older. It helps them understand that men and women today have more job choices.

---

> You are terrific to have _____.

---

Together make a list of as many family members, friends, and neighbors as you can. Next to each name write that person's job. Are any of these jobs unusual for men to be doing? For women?

Suggest that your youngster cut out articles and pictures of people doing different jobs that might be interesting as a career. *Examples:* flying a plane, farming, working with children. Ask your youngster to talk about these choices. And share your views, too.

For a change of pace, have each member in the family do a job at home that is usually done by someone else. Boys might try doing the things the girls (or Mom) have been doing. Girls could do the boys' (or Dad's) jobs.

### What Do You Do? ■ ages 10–12

In this activity, children talk to adults to gain an understanding about jobs. They also get a "handle" on how to get conversations going with adults by asking questions and getting information. You need willing friends, neighbors, parents, other family members. This is a "talk about" activity.

Ask your child to prepare some questions in advance. *Examples:* "How did you choose your job?" "What are the advantages and disadvantages?" "Did you need special training?" "Did you have to pass a test?"

Do they have any advice for young people who are thinking about jobs? Nobody has all the answers in a crystal ball, but talking with others helps youngsters sense what questions they need to think about for the future.

## LETTING GO

All parents would like to be able to protect children so that no one pushes them around; so that they make good judgments, avoid costly and hurtful mistakes, sort out the phony and false from the right and true. But we can't.

As children start their trip into adulthood, most of us parents will do a lot more watching and talking together rather than telling and yelling. It can be very hard to pull back. But having helped our children pack their suitcases with MegaSkills, we can be more confident that they'll have a good trip.

# The MegaSkills Support Network: People Helping People

In a sense, we are all raising and educating children today in new territory. We are explorers and innovators; we are pioneers and discoverers. It may not be the moon, but it sometimes feels like it. We need friends and allies in this major effort to help ourselves and our children.

## INTRODUCTION

# Beacons in the Fog

My father and mother came to the New World, America, from Europe in the late 1920s. They were part of a great wave of immigration. From their small community in Poland came about a hundred others. Some were relatives, but most were not. They called each other "landsmen," people from the same land.

They came from the same old place to many different, new places. They did not all stay together. They scattered across this new land to earn their way. But they acted to help one another, even if they were miles apart.

My parents came to a small town in southern Michigan. The closest place any landsman had settled was Detroit. When I was a child, every Sunday we packed into the car and traveled what seemed like a very long journey—about forty miles—to Detroit to be with landsmen. There my parents talked Yiddish, and I heard stories exchanged about what had happened to whom

"When families get involved in education, our children and our communities are stronger. This book not only tells parents how to be involved at home and in school; but moreover, it connects families to community organizations which can provide a support network for the entire community in working together. Educating children is a community-wide responsibility."

—Gordon A. Raley, Executive Director, National Assembly

In a sense, all of us now raising families are in new territory. We are explorers and innovators. We have to be.

Just as businesses are learning that the rules for success are changing, so, too, is family life changing. We are involved today in new patterns of family life, new relationships, different responsibilities and opportunities. Like a dark, foggy night, it is scary.

during the week. It was pleasant talk—but it was more. I heard people arranging ways to help one another. They were making connections. It was about money—but it was more. It was support. It gave these landsmen the strength and courage to face another week in a strange place. I did not understand this then. I thought it was a terrible thing to have to go to Detroit every week, and I got carsick to prove it.

But the feelings of the connections must have seeped into my imagination. I remember that as we made our way back home in the dark, especially on the foggy nights that scared me, I envisioned the taillights of the cars in front of us and the headlights of the cars in back of us as part of a great chain winding along the highway. I recall this vision still. It gave me comfort then, and it continues to do so today.

One of the brightest beacons in this fog is the chain of connections, like lights in the dark, that we form with the people—parents, teachers, child care helpers—with whom we come in contact every day. This is a coalition, the support network, that helps us and our children build and keep MegaSkills.

In this section are specific ways we can help each other get through each day a little more easily and happily—

*How parents help other parents*
*How grandparents "connect" across the miles*
*How parents form a real team with child care helpers*

*What teachers and parents need to know and understand*
*How single parents and schools can help each other*
*What children need to know about school*

We are pioneers and discoverers in a new landscape. It may not be the moon, but it can feel like it. We need friends and allies in this major effort to help ourselves and our children.

**CHAPTER 22**

# Parent to Parent: Looking to Each Other for Help

> Almost the first place—maybe it *is* the first place—families go when they come to a new town is the school. If you have children, the decision of choosing a place to live is often based on what schools your children will attend.

Having grown up in a small town, I find myself not quite at home in a big city, even when I live in one. It feels lonely to walk down a crowded street where you don't know anyone. The tall buildings seem impenetrable and uncaring. When I go into a large school building or a gigantic supermarket, I feel the same way.

Maybe that's why I try to turn almost every place where I am into a small town. I try to bring things down to a scale I can understand and manage.

I need to know my neighbors, whether they live in the house across the street or work down the hall. I need to share and give tips: Have you a doctor to recommend? Do you know a good, cheap restaurant that welcomes children? Who's in charge at the playground? When do we register for school? It's a parent-to-parent support network that many of us depend on and more of us could use.

The activities in this chapter focus on how to help create and structure this network. The core of the plan is the school. I use the school for three very good reasons: (1) There's a school in almost every neighborhood, and it might be free after three P.M. and on weekends; (2) It's the place where children come together; (3) It's

a natural place for parents to come together to assist each other and to learn new ways to help their children.

School is central in the lives of families, and not just between the hours of nine and three, half the days of the year. We need to capitalize more on that centrality to provide parent-to-parent support for dealing with the larger, colder world.

## WHO'S GOING TO DO IT?

If you think I'm talking about teachers taking on this work, you're wrong. This is for parents helping themselves and each other. Join your PTA/parent-teacher organizations. They are doing important work, and they deserve and need more hands. Activities in this chapter illustrate how it can be done. They do take some time and effort. Good things just don't happen by themselves—someone has to take the lead. And it can't always be the same people.

The activities that follow are carried out by parents, but they require the cooperation

> We are an educated, democratic society, and we need more people to say, "I'll start. Let's check with the school. I'll call five people. We'll get the ball rolling."
>
> We're all busy, and there will always be excuses. But if we want better lives for ourselves and our kids, these efforts have to be made—and not just by others, but by ourselves.

of the school. Administrators are responsible for what goes on in the school building. Invite them early in the planning, and expect questions. They need to authorize the activities. It's helpful to meet first with the parent group, whether it's the full PTA or a committee, to discuss what activities to propose, how they will be conducted, who's responsible for what, and what costs, if any, are involved. Administrators want to open the school doors, but they can't do so until details have been worked out.

## INFORMATION CENTRAL

The school is an ideal source of information, for parents as well as children. Here are three information-sharing activities that respond to parents' need to know. They move from very easy to more complex, in step-by-step stages.

### Q-and-A Brown Paper

The easiest parent information exchange consists of a long sheet of brown paper. Ask the principal where it can be displayed. It can have these headings: *Date, Question, Answer, Contact.* Parents don't even have to know or see each other to make this activity work. In the *Question* section you might ask, "Where can we buy furniture?" "How do we find reliable child care?" A few days later, check to see who has filled in an answer. It might be a student, a teacher, a school visitor, or another parent. *Contact* tells whom to call for more details beyond what can be written directly on the brown paper.

Attach next to the paper a marker that just cannot be removed. Put up a new sheet every two weeks. But be sure to save the old ones. You may want to refer to the old answers. There may be enough good answers for the school principal to want to produce a compilation of "Brown Paper Answers" as a booklet for all parents.

### Café Parent

Some schools have empty classrooms. One of these can be set aside for Café Parent. (Grandparents are welcome, too.) Volunteers—perhaps senior citizens—can open the door and set up the coffee pot. Request donations of easy chairs, a table, a bulletin board, lamps, a rug, and other amenities. Special programs can be arranged, or the room can be open for parent use. It's an ideal place for a parent reading shelf with books and materials that can be checked out for home use. Teachers may want to display class materials so that parents can learn what's going on in different subjects. The Café needs to be kept open at least one evening a week and perhaps on Saturday mornings. This is a low-key operation, but it may be what's needed to identify a corps of parents who want to continue to work together in more intensive ways.

### The Family Learning Center

This is a parent center in the school with a multifaceted approach serving a variety of parental needs. Like Café Parent, it uses donated furniture, books, and materials, but it requires at least a part-time staff person. It may evolve from Café Parent or spring full-blown in response to community interest. All of the services listed below may not be needed in every community, but they provide a sense of the range of activities that a Learning Center can offer.

> Every parent needs someone to brag to as well as a shoulder to cry on. Parents need a place to get together to talk, share experiences, have a cup of coffee, put their feet up.

**Book/Toy Lending Library.** This is a collection of toys for children and materials and books on parenting, schooling, and family issues that parents can check out for use at home. The collection is made up of toys and books that families no longer want. These are brought to the library to be exchanged for toys and books that other families have finished with. (An adaptation of this is the "Toy Market" in this chapter.)

**Parent Workshops.** Parents get together to learn together. Parenting is a subject none of us knows very much about—especially before problems arise. You don't always need an expert to run these sessions; we all have good ideas to share. Talk about discipline; talk about balancing work and family responsibilities; talk about how to keep kids off drugs, away from sex, and into their books.

**Child Care.** This service can be offered while parents use the center. Ask administrators about involving upper elementary or teenage students. In this way child care is available and the older youngsters gain job experience.

Teachers can be invited to use the center so that parents and teachers meet informally in this informal place.

## DOING TOGETHER— PARENT TO PARENT

It feels so good to join together with people to do something. The sense of team effort and accomplishment can almost be touched and felt.

Here are three easy-to-do activities that generate these feelings. These are not major school fairs or extravaganzas. These are ways in which neighbors help neighbors.

In each of these activities, people are in "business," selling and buying toys or books or homemade crafts. Tables to hold these goods are set up in the school gym, cafeteria, or auditorium. Every family is responsible for its own business. There are two ground rules: (1) The items for sale must be from one's own house (used but not abused), or they must be gifts or crafts made by family members; (2) the tables are to be manned by the family—parents, grandparents, family friends, and children.

Because each family is responsible for setting up and taking away the tables, pricing the goods, and selling them, no one else is burdened. Unsold items, such as toys no longer wanted and books that did not sell, can be donated to the school or to a charity.

To raise money to cover flyers, postage, refreshments, and a small honorarium for the event coordinator, each family can contribute two dollars or so.

## Toy Market

This is a way for families to sell toys their children have outgrown. Children and parents together find the toys, clean them up, price them, and bring them to the sale.

With children handling the sales, they gain communication as well as money management skills. They can lower their prices as needed to make sales and then figure out how much has been made after the sale is over. This is an ideal event to precede the winter holidays. One family's trash is another family's treasure.

## Book Fair

This provides adults and children with good low-cost reading material, and it can also increase the library collection. With each family handling its own table, these books don't need to be collected or priced in advance. On the day of the fair, families come in with their boxes and begin to display the books. If possible, books should be priced from a nickel to fifty cents so that every child can buy some. The school librarian can be given the choice of the books left over for additions to the school's library. Once again, children handle the sales themselves, negotiating with buyers on the spot and also sharing opinions—"That book was good," or "That one is not so great!"

## We Made It Ourselves

This activity provides incentives for children and parents to produce handmade items and to pursue hobbies for pleasure and profit.

If children can bear to part with their treasures, from model airplanes to candles to soap sculptures to jewelry, here is an opportunity to share, show them off, and perhaps sell them. Remember to bring along children's paintings and any place mats and paperweights they've made.

This is a time for children to garner praise. At an adult art show recently, I admired a potter's wares and saw her young son at the side of the table with his hand-lettered sign: MAGNETS—50¢. He had painted designs on her leftover pieces of clay and had attached small magnets. The paint was still wet. I asked if I could buy two. He seemed very pleased and very shy. As I left, his mother came up to me and whispered, "Thanks." I had not bought them from her, but it was as if I had.

# TALKING TOGETHER— PARENT TO PARENT

## About Schools

To judge whether a teacher is good, bad, or in between, you don't need to be an expert on education. As a teacher, when parents visited the classroom I tried to give them clues on how to look at my work. First I urged parents to give me and the school a fair chance. Then I made the following points:

> Two major topics parents worry about are (1) teachers and schools (how do we know they're good?), and (2) discipline (how can we help our children grow up and avoid trouble?).

■ Don't be impressed with the bulletin boards, with whether the desks are neat and the room is quiet. Some of the best learning in my classroom goes on in what probably looks like minor bedlam, with students moving about, making noise, even laughing.

■ Try to sense the atmosphere of the room. Is there a feeling of security among the students? Are they waiting expectantly for my pronouncements as teacher? Do I encourage divergent opinions and answers, or am I "answer pulling," looking only for the exact one I have in mind?

■ How do I treat "wrong" answers? Do I discard them? Do I try to point out reasons why one answer is better than another?

■ How are my assignments? Are my directions specific and clear? Do I ask the whole class to do the same assignment, or do I sometimes try to provide for some individual, independent work?

■ How do I treat "difficult" children, and what do I define as "difficult"? Chances are, you won't see many problems since we're all on company behavior. But if you do, it's possible that your children, on their problem days, may get similar treatment.

■ Look carefully at me and my personality. It's natural that you'll take more to some teachers than to others. I need not be beautiful, but like all good teachers, regardless of whether I'm bubbling over or reserved and shy, I need to convey to students the qualities of optimism and encouragement. Do I?

■ Don't base your opinion of me on just one visit. Try to come back to see me more than once. If you come away pleased with what you've seen, tell me. Teachers need praise, too. If something upsets you, discuss it with me.

Then I urged the parents of my students to pass along these tips, if they found them useful, to other parents. It helps to know what to look for when visiting a classroom in action.

## About Discipline

I wish we'd all share more tips about discipline—what has worked and what hasn't worked in our houses. I want us to give each other advice and stop worrying that no one wants to hear it. We can discard

> For the best evaluation, parents should look to their children. Are they interested in learning? Are they eager to go to school each day? When this is happening, the school year is good. When it isn't, there is trouble . . . trouble that everyone—students, parents, and teachers—needs to look into.

what we don't want or can't use. We might think that what happens in our house is nobody else's business. Well, not everything is, but if others can help us, wouldn't it be grand if we could let them?

Here's an exercise I call "A Piece of My Mind," from our Parent-to-Parent programs. We say what comes to mind when asked the following questions:

What one piece of advice would you give to a new mother? To a new father?

What's one thing that you wish your parents had told you?

What's one thing you are especially glad your parents told you?

What do you wish your parents would have told your teachers?

What's one thing you would do differently in disciplining your children?

What do you think you should tell your child . . . that you're hesitant to tell?

What kind of information about your children would you welcome from the parents of your children's friends? From your children's teachers? From your neighbors?

What do you think your children would tell you . . . if they had the nerve?

This exercise works when you're thinking to yourself, when you are with one or two friends, or when you're in a larger group. Even if you never talk with someone else about these questions, think about and "listen" to your own responses.

A number of years ago as I was driving down the street, I saw a neighbor's young teenage daughter. I knew her only to say hello, but I saw that she was lighting up what looked to be a marijuana cigarette. She was alone. I was tempted to stop the car, get out, and yank the cigarette out of her mouth. I didn't, but maybe I should have. That night I picked up the phone to call her mother. I put it back down, thinking, "I don't really know this woman. What will she say? Will she say it's not my business? Will she be upset?"

I backed away, and yet I have not forgotten that day and have often wondered what I should have done. Knocking the cigarette out of the girl's mouth probably would have been too dramatic. But I think I should have called, no matter what the mother said to me.

That teenager got into some scrapes not long afterward. In a little while, the mother and daughter moved away. No one on the block has heard from them since. I wonder if what I could have done that day might have made a difference.

As parents, we need each other; we need to learn from one another. There's a lot we can do to help each other. We need to be part of a neighbor-to-neighbor exchange. In some ways, it can be constricting and oppressive. But it's also comforting. It's good to feel that you know people who care about you and what you and your children are doing.

> What can we tell each other that we need to know? What do our friends know about our children? Do we have to wait until someone says, "I knew that all along, but I didn't say anything"?

*Courtesy of Olmsted Studio*

**CHAPTER 23**

# Grandparents: MegaSkills
# Across the Generations

Who is there who does not love being a grandparent?

I can't find one . . . but no matter how glowing grandparents' words are about their grandchildren, there is gnawing concern.

I hear increasingly from grandparents across the country. Because I am almost but not yet a grandparent myself, perhaps they can really level with me. What I hear is that grandparenting today is wonderful and troubling, simple and complex, reassuring and challenging.

> What's new are the problems of distance, divorce, single parenting, blended families, and stepfamilies.
>
> What's old is the strength, the stability, the caring, the common sense, and the kind of love that only grandparents can provide.

Grandparents offer extraordinary potential for strong MegaSkills support. Readers of this chapter may want to pass along the activities and approaches in this section to their own parents or suggest that they read this chapter themselves, using the ideas and building on them in their own creative ways.

## WHAT'S THE PROBLEM?

Grandparenting in song and story harks back to a trouble-free time, a time when the generations could really enjoy each other and spend more time together.

So what's the problem? For many families, it's distance, in miles and emotions. Grandparents, their own kids, and their kids' kids no longer live together or even near each other. How do you stay in touch and keep involved across the miles?

For a growing number of grandparents, however, distance is not the problem. They see their grandchildren almost too much. In these days of divorce and single parenting, many grandparents who thought retirement would be time for relaxation and new interests are involved not just in grandparenting but in parenting itself, all over again.

Recently in Sarasota, Florida, Mickey Knox invited me to talk with a group of grandparents to learn what they were experiencing and to share with them MegaSkills activities to use with their grandchildren. As I talk with grandparents around the nation, it's clear that the joys and the worries of grandparents today are remarkably similar, from Florida to Alaska.

A colleague of mine says that if you look into her mouth closely, you will find a bitten-off tongue. And she is not alone. Many grandparents and in-laws are giving advice when it is not asked for, are stopping themselves before saying that the house is messy or that the kids are misbehaving. They know that it is better to have a bitten-off tongue than a severed relationship.

This does not mean that grandparents need to stifle themselves. It does mean knowing the difference between ongoing, haggling criticism and important messages. Grandparents can be mighty important in putting across the message about the importance of learning, the value of education, and the value of the grandchild.

These are the keys to the activity ideas that follow. Grandparents and grandkids move on from these ideas to ideas of their own.

## MEGASKILLS ACTIVITIES AND APPROACHES

The **Activities** that follow are useful when grandparent and grandchild are together, face to face. The **Approaches**—the ways to say things, to get the message across—are both for when you are there and for when you are communicating across the miles.

### Confidence Activities: Reading and Confidence Building

**Reading Together.** For younger children, there is no better confidence builder than reading with an older person, even when children do not yet read themselves. Young children learn about reading and writing in their preschool years. What joy can replace the proud child's exclamation, "I read the book to you, Grandma!" When children pretend to read the book you have just read to them, this is "early literacy."

**Reading the Fine Print.** For older youngsters, reading aloud life and health insurance policies, even mortgages, provides important practice for students and an important service for grandparents who may have trouble with the fine print. Letting children do this builds their confidence.

### Motivation Approach

**Helping Children Say Yes.** Many grandparents report a lot of naysaying from grandchildren, particularly as they get older. Here is what an experienced granddaughter (she has five grandparents) has to say:

"When I was younger, all my grandparents seemed to want to do was to take me shopping, and I found this hard. They always wanted me to want something.

"Maybe when richer grandparents are with their grandchildren they should pretend they don't have that money and find other ways to show that they care. I would have liked sharing hobbies, hearing stories, reading books."

### Effort Approach

**The Joy of Work.** What about children who feel that nothing they do is good enough? These are the children who fear making the all-out effort it takes to do well.

Check to see how the family feels about its successes. Is there a self-defeating tendency to feel that nothing is quite good enough?

To combat this danger, recall situations with children in which they remember suc-

> **From California . . .**
> "I would have liked being read to—they never did. They thought that reading was to be reserved for bedtime, and bedtime was when parents were with me."

cess. Have they learned to swim? Are they able to locate a number in the telephone book?

Take pride in successes, even the little ones. Guard against "Oh, you can do that better," and "What, not finished yet?" Success ought to feel good.

## Responsibility Approach: All My Grandchildren

Grandparents who are not near their own grandchildren, or those who want to be grandparents but aren't, should follow the example of a remarkable seventy-four-year-old Hispanic grandmother.

Every day, as a school volunteer, she rides the school bus with the children. She takes part in parent workshops; she helps serve school breakfasts; she is committed; she is involved. "My special contribution to the children," she says, "is patience. I learn a lot from the children and they learn about me."

## Initiative Approach: Building Enthusiasm

Provide jobs and activities that grandchildren can do and will feel proud to accom-

---

**From Texas . . .**

"Some people say, 'I don't see why you do what you do.' My answer, I need people and I know they need me. The school does not knock at your door and say, 'We need you.' You have to go to the school and say, 'I want to help.'"

---

plish. These can include building something needed around the house, taking care of a special corner in the garden, cooking a meal for you, teaching you a favorite game.

Involvement is such a powerful approach that it can't be overestimated and must not be overlooked.

## Perseverance Approach: Finishing a Job Without Nagging

Make sure that you convey to children your expectations that they will start and complete the task or project. Help children to think in terms of first, second, and third steps, in everything from cleaning a room to doing homework assignments. After they start, encourage them to keep going, taking one step at a time. Be optimistic, and check that your children have what they need to complete the job.

Try to avoid preconceived ideas of how the task should be accomplished. *Example:* "Please wash the dishes. You should do the glasses first and be sure to soak the silverware before washing." One method may work best for you while another method works best for others. As long as children get the job done, there's no reason why they have to do it your way. They might even come up with a better way.

## Caring Activity: Greetings and Gifts

Help children learn to give as well as receive. They can save for and select their own purchases at the store or make gifts at home. Homemade presents that can be produced by the very young include cookies, paintings, collages, jewelry made from shells. Older children can embroider, design games, and write poems and stories. With colored paper, scissors, crayons, and paste, even the youngest child can make decorations that will add to the festiveness of the holidays. Try paper place mats and door and window paste-ups. Older children can make place cards and homemade favors for the guests.

Encourage children to create their own greeting cards and thank-you notes. Resist grading kids on their writing. If they miss a capital letter or a comma, so be it. Then youngsters stamp and mail the notes. It may take a little longer, but it's worth it.

## Teamwork Activities: The Pleasure of Involvement

Involve children in the work and accomplishment of planning and cooking holiday dinners. Together, make up a list of all that has to be done, from the shopping trip to the cleanup.

Make out the dinner menu together, discussing the time and costs involved. Let children who read well enough look up the recipes and list the ingredients. Have them check the grocery inventory to see what's already at home. Then ask them to check the newspapers to find the stores with the best prices.

Not all of this will work, but parts of the plan will. Children who are self-starters will be delighted with the opportunity to do projects on their own. Others who've had less practice with independent projects may need encouragement and help in gathering

The cookies may come out a little burned and the pencil holder may be a bit crooked, but a child's personal satisfaction will be first-rate. You're providing your grandchildren with the thrilling sense of personal accomplishment unobtainable from any toy.

necessary materials. But once they get going, it's time to get out of the way.

## Common Sense Approach: The Intergenerational Legacy

When you go into a toy store and there's so much to pick from and you don't know what to buy, think back to the toys that your own child loved. Choose these no matter how small they are or how inexpensive: a red pencil, a brown truck, a book of paper dolls.

Most of all, remember the books. By remembering certain books and passing them on, you create a wondrous chain of shared experiences.

When you are not there to do the reading, tape the story and send it along with the book itself. You can add beeps to your tape to indicate to your grandchild when to turn the pages. And if you happen to have a picture of your child at about the age when he or she read that very same book, send it along, too, with a note about that special time.

## Problem-Solving Approach: Make Up Your Mind

Children need the kind of decision-making practice that they almost never get in the hustle-bustle of daily life. This practice takes *time*, a scarce resource in many homes today. That's why decision-making practice with grandparents is so valuable.

Start with small decisions. Encourage children to make a list of pluses and minuses when they are trying to make up their minds. Your child may be trying to decide whether to go to a movie. A plus might be, "I like it because I can be with friends." A minus would be, "I need the money because I'm saving up for a bike." Encourage your child to choose the more reasonable decision and to try to stick with it. Eventually this kind of careful decision making becomes a good habit.

## THE BASICS STILL WORK

Probably the major MegaSkill of them all for grandparents is teamwork. Grandchildren report that they like nothing better than jointly making things with grandparents, getting involved together, being productive, whether the activity is going fishing or making a new dish for dinner.

The experienced granddaughter put it well: "I want to know what my grandparents have to tell me. Grandparents need to make sure to share what they have so that it is not forgotten, so that it is known."

---

Involvement doesn't cost a lot of money; it uses the resources of people and interests that are already there; it binds the generations with constructive activity.

*Joe DiDio courtesy of the National Education Association*

## CHAPTER 24

# Parents and At-Home Child Care

## Making Sure Sitters Do More Than Sit

"I wish I could clone myself so that my child is not deprived of me when I am away, and I wish my household help would do just what I do."

You don't just sit, and neither should your sitters. The chain of MegaSkills support is only as strong as its weakest link.

In this chapter are common-sense responses to the increasingly common desire for sitters who do more than sit.

To work or not to work—that is *not* the question for the majority of mothers today employed outside the home. The result is often talked about in extremes—it's awful or it's great.

Reality is currently somewhere in between.

"In between" is precisely the difficult place many parents today are in. Families are on the front lines of social change, waiting for reinforcements—changes in institutional policies and attitudes—that have not caught up with their lives. For example, schools still generally open and close regardless of normal work schedules, and jobs start and end regardless of children's school hours.

> In the short run, things do appear harder (even with Pampers) than they were in the sentimentalized post–World War II period, when mothers were at home, concentrating on child care. But evidence now emerging indicates that for parents and children the present is not as bad as some would have us believe, and the future looks a lot brighter.

Parents, especially mothers, are caught in between.

The spotlight on the role of the mother in this chapter is in no way meant to exclude the responsibility of the father in the care and education of children. However, there would be little concern about latch-key children and after-school care if mothers were not employed. Therefore this chapter attempts to deal with the different responsibilities for household management that have resulted because of mothers' outside employment. Fathers' help is not only welcome but greatly needed.

## NO MORE "CONVENTIONAL WISDOM"

Conventional wisdom would have children of working mothers performing less well in school. But a recent two-year review of studies by the National Academy of Sciences says that's not so. In general, the achievement of children of employed mothers differed little from that of nonemployed mothers. There are some studies, including those of the U.S. government, that suggest caution in making quick deductions about these effects. But the common-sense summary of the National Academy review reflects much of what is now known: Don't ask if working mothers are good or bad for kids because the answer is: It depends. It depends on the parents, on the child, on the circumstances, and so forth.

What "it depends" on, to a very great extent, are parent at-home management skills, whether or not additional help is available. Families fortunate enough to have household help are in a strong position to gain MegaSkills support from these people, but, once again, it depends. This chapter discusses what it depends on and provides suggestions on what to do.

> In analyzing current research on the effects of mothers' work on life at home and on children's achievements, a picture that defies conventional wisdom emerges. The information is new and sketchy—until recently there was no data on the working mother—but it points to children doing well academically even though mothers work, and to mothers feeling less—not more—strain when they work outside the home.

## MAKE SURE SITTERS DO MORE THAN SIT

There is more to child care than finding someone to do it. Even if your children are in schools or day care centers, they usually spend some time with child care help at home in the evenings or on weekends. This is precious time in the lives of children, and it pays to be concerned about how it is being spent.

When you choose a center, you are not really in the driver's seat. The activity schedules are set by others. But when you hire someone to care for your children at home, you are the employer and manager of the program.

Here are some tips for dealing with this responsibility.

### Define the Job

The majority of children today whose mothers work full-time are cared for by a helper other than a relative. Chances are, you do not know as much about this person as you would know about a relative. And this helper does not know you and your family values. That's why you need to spend time talking with applicants about how you want your child's time spent and what you expect of each other.

Decide how much of your helper's time you want used in child care and how much in house cleaning. Your priorities have to be made clear. Your helper cannot be washing windows and walking with your child in the park at the same time. Provide a clear message of what needs to be done and when.

### Look for Doers

The kind of helper you want is also determined by the age and interests of your children. Ideally you want a responsive and friendly person who is willing to listen and who enjoys being with children. For infants you may want more warmth and patience

> You really don't want "sitters." You want your child care helpers to come up with activities and projects, to take pride in this educational work with your child.

than is needed for older children. For children ages six to twelve, for example, you want care givers who can respect a growing child's needs for independence and privacy while still being able to set limits.

Look over applicants and check their references with these goals in mind. In the interview, give applicants sample problems to solve. *Examples:* A child is cranky and bored. What do you do? A child wants to eat dinner, but it's not yet time. What do you do?

Ask your potential employee to try out an activity with your child—while you watch informally. You'll get a sense of your helper's teaching style and know right away whether active care or just sitting is what this person wants and is able to do.

## Make a Plan: Stock Up on Activity Ideas

List activities for different days. Try to vary quiet activities, such as reading, with vigorous activities, such as playground games. Look for shorter and longer activities. If you know, for example, that making a school box (to hold all the child's school supplies at home) is being planned, you'll know what materials to get ready. Let the helper and your child have a hand in gathering the materials—box, paper, crayons. If you know that each day they'll be reading together, go to the library with your child to pick out books.

Encourage helpers to compile an informal list of activity ideas as they come to mind. Keep a notepad handy to jot down such ideas as, "Try collages with Sara";

Talk together. Ask for your helper's ideas on what to do with your child. And ask your child, too. How long should all this planning take? Probably no more than thirty minutes each week. And think of the worry that you'll be saving and the constructive activity this planning will make possible.

"Help John bake cookies." A list of ideas can be really helpful when it comes to the challenging job of varying activities for several children in one home.

Children themselves are resources for activities. For example, an eight-year-old can read stories to preschoolers; an eleven-year-old can help cook the family dinner.

Even if they are able to, helpers shouldn't do all the work. Some work should be saved for the kids. This capitalizes on their early offers to help and enables children to feel purposeful and to acquire good work habits.

Jobs given children must be real and not make-work. Even a very young child can recognize a phony job. Short jobs (see examples below) that children can finish fairly quickly are very satisfying.

Preschoolers love water play. In the summer they can do water work: sprinkling the lawn, washing bicycles, hosing down the front porch. Older children can help with grocery shopping, cooking, and even polishing shoes (their own and their parents).

Helpers may need tips on how to set up and arrange the work area. Preparing for the after-effects of the work is important. Newspapers, plastic drop cloths, or old shower curtains should be spread down before work starts, so that quick cleanups, not screams, follow a child's efforts.

TV can play a part in this schedule. But to be effective, TV time should be limited. In a three- to four-hour period after school, it's wise to plan for no more than one hour of TV watching. To make this limit more appealing to your child, let your child choose the shows. (See "Tackling TV" in Chapter 5 for related activities.)

Be sure your helper knows what to do in case of household emergencies. Keep your emergency phone list up to date and a stocked first-aid box handy. The activities found in Chapter 14, on "Problem Solving," in the special section on safety, will also be useful.

## Prepare a Special Child Care Box

This is an all-purpose box that needs to be kept stocked and ready. For its all-purpose use, it needs the traditional arts and crafts supplies: crayons, pencils, paper (several colors and textures), round-edge scissors, glue, scraps of cloth, washable markers, ruler, string, old magazines with pictures.

Beyond these basics, it can be more imaginative, with even a surprise now and then. For older children, add something to talk about . . . an article, a surprise book, a treat to eat. Leave word of a household chore to be done. Or leave a note about a game to be tried. One that's always good is "What's Missing?" Five or more objects are put on a table. Children look at them and

then close their eyes. One is taken away, and the children then try to figure out which one is missing. You can keep taking away more and more objects. Everyone takes turns. This game is fun and builds skills needed for reading.

## Follow Household Rules

Your child care helpers will, generally speaking, be better off if they can stick to a minimum of rules—ones the family needs, ones that are reasonable and enforceable.

Each family's rules will probably be a little different from the neighbors', and those differences may cause friction. Children will say, "Susie gets to stay outside until supper"; "Tommy can go to the supermarket alone." That's why it's good to have reasons to support rules. Share these with your helpers so they can speak in your voice to your children. Children, grudgingly or not, tend to listen to reason.

Assure helpers that it's normal for a child to test, to see whether or not they are really serious about sticking to rules. It may be that this testing will, after discussion, reveal that the rule isn't a good rule. For example, children may legitimately object to an inflexible demand that they have a bath before supper every night. Nobody loses face if the child mounts an argument so persuasive that the rule is changed.

Adults should try not to go back on their word. This includes helpers. If children know they can't go out until the work is done, then it's important to stick to this, unless a really important reason for changing it comes up. Children, even young ones, can assist in setting rules and seeing that they are followed.

What happens when children don't follow the rules? How is your helper going to punish your children? If nothing is to be done other than the issuing of a stern warning, such as, "Wait until your parents come home!" make sure this is clear. If something is to be done, such as withdrawal of TV privileges or sending children to their room for a certain period, make sure this is clear. If corporal punishment is out of the question, be sure your helper knows this. In short, don't leave these decisions up to the tensions and emotions of the moment. Make sure everyone knows what to expect.

### Talk About "Talk"

There is no denying that a helper who speaks clear and correct English is a strong asset. Increasingly, however, many families have very reliable helpers who do not have strong English skills. Many are immigrants who speak another language. If a helper is bilingual, of course it is possible that a child can pick up two languages. But by and large, fluent bilingual speakers are not in child care work.

Here are tips on what parents can do to assure that young children hear English every day.

- Encourage your helper to take your child to the playground or community center in order to be with others who speak English.
- Tell helpers to take your child out into the wider community. Walk through a shop-

Young children are learning language. It's vital for your helpers to talk as much as possible with young children—even with babies, who may not seem to understand. Helpers can talk as they cook and as they vacuum. They should keep young children near them so that children can watch and listen. Helpers can talk as they push the stroller and as they roll a ball back and forth to a child. Language is the critically important ingredient in early learning, and it starts and continues at home.

ping center. Go into a store to look at and talk about the merchandise. Explore new blocks. You can probably map out a month's worth of walks.

- Use a tape recorder. Record your own voice and those of others your child knows. Read a story. Send a greeting. The idea is to have your child hear English spoken daily. Show your helpers how to record your child's voice. When you come home, you can hear the message your child has sent to you.

### Working as a Team

Introduce your helper, if possible, to other workers on your block or in the neighborhood. Encourage them to share ideas and activities.

Establish a back-up system. When you are depending on one person to show up at your home each day, you run into the difficulty of what to do when that person or that person's child is sick. Look into the possibility of connecting with an elderly person in your neighborhood who can pitch in. Be sure, even on those days, that your substitute help knows what you expect and has the materials to do the job.

One of the pitfalls as well as the strengths of having household employees is that they are indeed a real part of your household. This means—whether they live in or not—that there is a greater likelihood that you will come to know their personal

> Don't worry about losing your children's love to this wonderful helper who knows all these terrific activities. Studies show that children know their own parents and gravitate to them. There's a wonderful and sometimes frightening bond between parent and child. These activities strengthen that bond. They show that you care, even when you are not there.

lives—their joys, their sorrows, and their concerns about their own children.

Providing the schedule and support outlined in this chapter offers the possibility of helping your employees in their own lives. Knowing how to organize time with children is a useful skill for their own homes.

Keeping mothers at home, even if it were possible, wouldn't solve all the problems of our children's growing up. It's not known whether intensive mothering is good for children over the long haul.

Today's employed mother may well be providing as much or more care and concern for her child as did the traditional mother of the past, who spent a great deal of time running the house rather than focusing on the child. The answer about which type of mother is better may never be fully known and is not relevant. What is relevant is dropping outdated, conventional wisdom and finding approaches that work for parents and children today.

*Joe DiDio, courtesy of the National Education Association*

## CHAPTER 25

# Parents and Teachers
## Superpowers, Not Superhuman

The trouble with schools today is not that teachers and parents don't care anymore. That's the usual complaint, but it's not true. Caring is as intense, perhaps more intense, than ever. The trouble is that there may be so much focus on the school as an institution that there is not enough focus on the needs of the adults, within and beyond the school walls, who must work together in order for schooling to succeed.

I did not say the needs of *children*. I said the needs of *adults*. We know that we have to meet children's needs. What we sometimes don't realize is that in order to meet the needs of our children, we have to meet the needs of the adults who make schools work.

Education is a very human partnership. It depends for its strength, to a great degree, on how teachers and parents feel about one another and what they do to meet each others' adult needs.

This is a new era for families. It is a new era for teachers, too, and not necessarily a worse one for either. But it is a time that presents some new problems for us to solve. Some involve institutional changes, such as how long schools stay open. Much of the change, however, is at the personal level of parents and teachers as people, as partners.

This chapter focuses on what parents and teachers can do now to provide stronger adult-to-adult support for each other and on the obstacles we have to overcome so that we can work as a team to help our children achieve.

I know there are a lot of smiles at Back-to-School nights, and I know that parents and teachers are supposed to get along. But it doesn't take a Geiger counter to detect the fears and frustrations beneath the smiles when parents and teachers meet— and perhaps, especially, when they don't meet.

I think the meanest thing a teacher ever said to me happened when I brought my first child to school to register her for kindergarten. I was nervous and wanted to make a good impression. Being a teacher, I was concerned about not being a bragging parent. But I was also concerned that this teacher know about my child.

So I told the teacher that this youngster entering kindergarten could already read, and I asked what provision would be made for this. The teacher put her arm around my shoulder and proceeded to reassure me in this way: "Oh, don't worry, Mrs. Rich, they all *even out* by third grade." Evening out wasn't what I was concerned about. It was not what I or any parent would want to hear.

The nicest thing a teacher ever said to me came in a telephone call when my

> In this complex world, it takes more than a good school to educate children. And it takes more than a good home. It takes these two major educational institutions working together. To bring this about demands a restructuring of how teachers and parents relate and connect to one another.

younger daughter was in fourth grade. She had been absent from school for three days. Her teacher called to ask about her. "How is she? When is she coming back? We miss her." This teacher knew how to make students and their families feel important. The other teacher did the opposite.

The meanest thing I ever said about a teacher—that she didn't like her students—is something I probably should have said to her face. Parents of students were talking behind her back, and so was I. Something about this teacher made every child in her third-grade class feel unloved. It's an unfortunate attribute for any personality and a devastating one for a teacher. Maybe if I had said something, she might have made some changes.

A grandmother who was a PTA president in 1937 has never forgotten this fifth-grade teacher's remark: "You are as essential to this school as the bricks in the walls." But she also remembers the principal, who said, "Why don't you let the school educate your child, and you stick to your business?"

We do hurt each other. And it's not just teachers ganging up on parents. As a

> Probably the most important thing teachers can do for parents is to make them feel important and needed, and the most important thing, as parents, that we can do for teachers is to let them know how important they are to our families.

teacher, I have seen a wide variety of parental anti-school behaviors. Among them:

- Hard-to-please parents who march into the school office with a daily complaint. At the other extreme are the scared, "helpless" parents who somehow can't bring themselves even to visit the school.
- Parents who use the school in a way that destroys any good feelings children may have about schooling. Is it any wonder a child would balk at going to school after hearing, "Just you wait till you get to school—they'll know what to do with you!"
- Parents who hope, even expect, the school to do for their child what it never did for them, or who expect it to do all the things their home is unsuccessful at. They grow increasingly bitter against the school with each passing day. When the miracles do not occur, they tend to infect their children with this attitude: "That school's no good—what's the use of trying?"
- Parents for whom any change from what they knew as schoolchildren is threatening, whether or not they liked what they had. Some parents get upset when they see children actually having fun in the classroom. I think of this as the "iodine theory" of education—it has to hurt if it's to do any good.
- Parents who identify so closely with their children that they see themselves, not their children, walk into that school.

These parents react to every teacher's comment and every award won or lost as if reliving their own school days.

All this isn't to imply that parents should not criticize teachers or schools. Constructive criticism is essential. But stale attitudes from a parent's own school days are worth recognizing as such and then discarding.

If you like your child's teachers, you won't be tempted to put them down. In fact, you'll probably say nice things about them at home and thus encourage your child to have a good relationship with them, too.

The real test for how well you can handle yourself vis-à-vis school comes when you don't like a certain teacher. What can you do, what should you do, in a ticklish situation like this? First of all, try to examine your attitudes to figure out if you are suffering from an old case of school phobia. Without knowing or wanting it, parents can infect children with certain immature and self-defeating attitudes about school. School is a place where a lot of adults start acting like kids again, perhaps because of their own school day memories.

One way to find out if you're suffering from a form of school phobia is to check your physical responses to school.

> Does your stomach tighten when you walk through the school door?
> Do you sleep well the night before a parent-teacher conference?
> Do you find yourself trembling when you talk casually to your child's teacher?
> Do you sit brooding for days, biting your nails, pondering the deeper significance of a teacher's offhand comment about your child?

Many parents remember school days with burning resentment for what school did to them. It's time to say, "This is a new day!"

## GETTING ALONG WITH THE SCHOOL

Schools need to hear from parents but not be besieged. Schools have an unwritten hierarchy of appeal. Always start with the classroom teacher. Classroom teachers have legitimate cause for anger if you bypass them and go straight to the principal without giving them a chance to brief you and work out the situation. Principals have a right to

---

Try not to tear down teachers in front of your children. This doesn't mean you need to whitewash the school and blame children when they come home complaining about something. But agreeing with the child that the teacher is "stupid" or "dull" defeats any good purposes. Watch out especially for your phone conversations, when children can overhear you complain about the "boring" homework they have been assigned. Instead talk to someone at the school, where it can do some good.

be angry if you come to them before trying to straighten things out at the classroom level. If both the teacher and the principal are unable to work things out or balk at your concern, you may then proceed with clear conscience to the director of elementary education or district superintendent.

These examples illustrate when a complaint is called for:

- You have a right to assume the school cares about your child. If you ask for a conference with the teacher, it's legitimate for you to expect the conference to offer specific details about your child and not generalizations about how wonderful or difficult all seventh graders are. Keeping parents informed is a function of the school. You should raise the roof if you are not told before the end of the year that your child is having trouble.
- You should let the school know when children are at the mercy of erratic homework schedules that may dump four hours of homework due the next day and then give none at all for days.
- You should let teachers know when your youngster feels overlooked or picked on in class. A ripple effect of discouragement can set in. Sometimes teachers are not aware of the effect they are having on students until they hear about it from parents.

Above all, parents have to stop griping behind the school's back—over the back fence or cocktails. It's unfair to complain that the school isn't helping if you haven't asked for help.

## FACE TO FACE: THE PARENT-TEACHER CONFERENCE

One of the great difficulties of the parent-teacher conference is getting through to each other. Teachers say that parents take everything said about their child as a personal attack. Parents accuse teachers of lecturing instead of listening, accusing instead of understanding.

Too many parents come out of parent-teacher conferences having learned only that their child has a problem and nothing more, with no suggestions from the teacher on how to help the youngster. Too many teachers come out of those conferences gnashing their teeth about parents who refuse to act and who want to be helpless.

Getting along with the school isn't easy. It probably never really was, but it seems harder today. Parents are more involved with their children's education. While parents are critical of schools, many are afraid to utter a critical word. Many's the parent who's said to me, "If I ever said anything was wrong, my child would suffer."

> It looks so benign, but don't be fooled. Among the most challenging and emotional encounters in history is the typical parent-teacher conference, complicated by hope, desire, worry, and defensiveness.

It would be Pollyanna-ish to say such things never happen; they do happen, but far less often than parents think. Schools may not be able to reassure a really fearful parent, but it would help if they repeated at frequent intervals that their doors and ears are open, and that parents have nothing to fear.

Schools are beginning to give teachers help on how to relate better to parents at conferences, but often it's the parent who needs help.

Here are some points used with success in our Institute programs:

1. Start out by saying something positive about the teacher or the classroom. There must be something that's good— artwork displays, books lying around invitingly, science corners. Teachers need good words, just like anybody else.
2. Tell the teachers about any special family situation affecting your child: divorce, death, illness, a new baby, a recent or impending move.
3. Discuss your child's talents, skills, hobbies, study habits, and any special sensitivities, such as weight and speech difficulties.
4. Tell teachers about areas in which you think your child needs special help and about any undesirable habits you hope will be overcome.
5. If your child has already received some grades, ask what went into these marks and how your youngster is being evaluated. (See Chapter 27, "Parents and Stu-

dents," for more information on this point.)
6. Ask for a general outline of what will be covered this year. Some teachers, but not enough of them, provide this at the beginning of the school year. Ask about specific ways to help your youngster at home.
7. Don't leave the conference unsure of what teachers have said. If you have questions, ask them. One way to clarify in your mind what a teacher means is to put in your own words what you understood. This gives everyone the chance to clarify issues if any misunderstandings have taken place.
8. At the conference, *really listen.* Some teachers complain that it doesn't matter what they say to parents. Some parents, they believe, have their minds made up before the conference begins, and

> "Parents are reporting changes in their own behavior and are seeing MegaSkills developing in their children. At least 90 percent of the parents have reported that they are better able to understand and communicate with their children's feelings and ideas. Most parents reported to be 'unlearning' destructive responses. Best of all, a strong group of MegaSkills parents is emerging."
>
> — Barbara Chittick and Mary Veasey, MegaSkills workshop leaders, Louisville, Kentucky

nothing a teacher says makes any difference.

9. Follow up on the conference. If the teacher indicates some areas in which your youngster needs improvement, don't sit fearful, waiting for months to find out what's happening in the classroom. Check back—not the next day, but in a few weeks—to see how things are going.

A conference early in the school year can prevent serious academic and social difficulties. Some elementary schools have started the excellent practice of mandatory conferences at the time of the first report card.

In the secondary grades, parents may have to take the initiative and persevere to schedule a conference. In junior and senior high school, parents wanting to see teachers are often thought of as "babying" their children or "pressuring" the teacher for

Remember that a teacher's evaluation of your child, even though carefully considered, can never be completely right. Teachers once classified Thomas Edison, Charles Darwin, Oliver Goldsmith, and Winston Churchill as "dull" boys. Their parents probably knew all along from the exciting things they did at home that they were bright kids. With early homeschool conferences, their parents and teachers could have shared this knowledge.

better grades. This is no reason for any parent to be deterred from asking for a conference. Students should participate in the discussion whenever possible.

## WORKING TOGETHER AS A TEAM

Parents may complain about the inflexibility of the schools, but school people trying to initiate change often find that parents are the big obstacles.

Teachers can get mighty discouraged. Parents, for example, talk about being interested in curriculum; but hold a curriculum meeting, and three parents show up.

Parents and teachers are in the same difficult situation together, besieged by outside experts usually pointing all too clearly to what is wrong. Not enough is said about what is right, both at home and in school. This has to be pointed out and sought just as carefully as the problems are.

Schools will attempt open-discussion meetings, but parents often won't open up. I recall moderating a school forum during which we pleaded with parents to raise all their doubts, to ask any question. A few came from the audience, but I overheard more questions—"When will my kids learn to read?" "How will they learn discipline?"—whispered in the hall afterward than I had in the meeting. I asked one father why he hadn't asked his question so he could get the school's answer. He shrugged.

Parents have to be willing to engage in meaningful dialogue with teachers, coming together to talk about such questions as these: What can we realistically expect of one another? What is the role of the school today? What is the role of the family? How are these different from yesterday's roles? What can we do to help each other and the children?

I look to the day when teachers get the help they need to work with parents in an educational partnership. Teachers need training in working with adults so that they don't talk to parents as if they are children. And they need to be given time and extra hands to do this important job of connecting with the home.

Let's praise each other. We need to hear in word and deed how important we are in each other's lives. And we have to trust each other more. In talking with teachers and parents across the country, I hear a message from each that says, "Trust me; re-

spect me." Parents have got to tell teachers what they need to know. Teachers cannot be left in the dark about difficulties at home that affect children's work in school. Teachers need this knowledge to be able to help.

## WHEN THE BLAMING STOPS . . .

I also look to the day when the blaming between parents and teachers stops, when more parents turn to themselves and to other parents for help, when parents stop looking to the school to solve their problems.

I promise to keep working with teachers to help them understand and treat parents for what they really are—their most important allies. But parents have responsibilities, too, and these have to be met.

Teachers are discouraged by parents who don't want to face up to their responsibilities, who act like kids themselves, who want teachers to do the parenting for them. When one teacher called home about a student's habitual tardiness, the parent said, "I tell him to get up. He just doesn't do it. What am I supposed to do?" And what's a teacher supposed to think?

We teachers and parents are not yet sufficiently tuned in to each other and each other's needs. It's getting better, but in the meantime, let's be good to one another. We don't have to be perfect to be good.

---

Let's share affection. It's difficult to be a parent, to juggle a lot of conflicting demands. Teachers, too, have similar problems. Let's be gentle, forgiving, and loving.

*Courtesy of John C. Lei Studios, Inc.*

**CHAPTER 26**

# Single Parents and the Schools

## Making the Connection

The ad shows a woman in an ice cube, and the caption reads, "Feeling isolated?"

I don't know what product is being advertised, but I am struck by this graphic image of isolation and how much it reminds me of experiences recounted by single parents. The difference is that the ad is funny, and isolation isn't.

There is a lot still to learn about families and about what goes on in two-parent homes. But divorce has come under study, and it has been found that the pain of divorce is an isolating experience that has a negative effect on children's work in school—at least for a while.

This chapter is about what single parents can do to lessen the sense of isolation by making connections with the school and building a network of support.

Up to now, schools have not been known for their support of single parents. At a conference our Institute conducted on single-parent families and schools, the concerns expressed were almost a cry of pain:

■ School personnel are insensitive. They stereotype our children and expect less from them.

> Not too many years ago, it was said that what happens to the family is not the school's business. But the importance of the family in children's education is now known. Schools are in a unique position with single parents, because schools are the continuing, stable institution in their children's lives. The very regularity of the school day can be a comfort.

> Single parents can help themselves and the schools at the same time by following through on the suggestions in this chapter. The activities combine three elements: they bring single parents together to lessen isolation; they provide support for children's upbringing; and they save money.

■ Schools do not provide the before- and after-school care that our children need.
■ Parent-teacher conferences are scheduled as if parents do not work and there are still fathers/mothers in the home.

It is hard for schools to change. Families change a lot faster. For some years now, schools have been playing catch-up. When it comes to meeting the needs of today's family, schools have not yet caught up.

But I know they want to. Teachers themselves are employed parents; they are single parents. They want to help, but knowing what to do is not easy.

## INFORM THE SCHOOL

One of the very first things to do if you are going through a divorce or separation is to get in touch with the school and set up a conference. Many teachers say they can spot troubled students even before parents file for divorce. Major signs that show up in school are loss of concentration, daydreaming, and sadness. Boys appear to be more affected than girls. Children of all ages—not just the young ones—need extra support. Adolescents, who may act as though nothing is bothering them, especially need parental love and guidance in this hard period.

During the conference, try to be as honest as you can about what's happening to the family. Don't predict what terrible behavior you expect your child to develop, but let teachers know you will want to be kept informed and will work closely with them to solve any problems.

Request that your child's report cards and records be sent to your child's other parent, too. Let the school know of any change in address, phone number, or job so that they can always reach you. Schools wait for you to volunteer this information. Be sure it's complete.

## ASK FOR THE SCHOOL'S ATTENTION

Single and working parents should ask that conferences be set up in the late afternoon and early evenings, rather than during the workday. Suggest that the PTA sometimes hold meetings on the weekends so that employed parents can attend. Encourage programs especially for single and working parents on such topics as how to meet the demands of home and job life.

Find out if child care can be provided during meetings for parents. A high school's family-life class could provide child care while parents attend school functions.

Anyone can start a single parents' group.

> Start thinking about and working with the school as a community resource center. Single parents need special services. They need to meet each other in groups for a chance to develop parent-to-parent support systems. The groups can meet at the school. The idea is to set the action at the place where members' children are involved and to bring families together.

It does require the cooperation of the school; you don't just charge in and take over. What's needed are the school facilities once or twice a month and a list of the school's single-parent families. Ordinary but important details need to be addressed; find out the fees, if any, for covering insurance and a custodian. These concerns are not insurmountable and should not take forever to clear away. Usually the fees involved are (or should be) modest. If not, and support is needed to cover costs, the matter should be brought up at school-board meetings. Schools cannot be shut tight when their facilities are needed by the community.

A small group of families can band together and set up their own activities at the school. Once a week you could have a potluck supper, with everyone bringing a dish. Movies borrowed from the school or library can follow dinner. Other family outings can include roller skating, hiking, and amateur-night shows. On weekend evenings, members can take turns sitting for children in the group.

## THE SCHOOL AS A PARENT CENTER

Here are details on school-based activities that parents can conduct for each other.

### Movie Nights

This is a way to provide low-cost family entertainment, expose children to films of good quality, and make money for the PTA or school. You need a movie projector, a film rental catalogue, and someone to sell tickets and snacks.

Order films from the catalogue. Select and publicize the movie series. Schedule the films for suppertime or just after supper on Friday evenings. It's an ideal kickoff for the weekend. Charge a reasonable admission fee. Encourage parents to attend with their children.

### Family "High Brow" Outings

This activity gets families together at a cultural event in the community.

Select a play or museum exhibit to see. You'll need one or two organizers to arrange for tickets and transportation. Some funds will be needed for tickets, which can usually be obtained at discount. Tickets might even be donated. A bus or private cars are needed for transportation.

Announce the event with a flyer from school sent home with the kids. Include a response form. When tickets are distrib-uted, provide the play or exhibit program, if possible. The group can meet for a potluck dinner and travel together to the theater.

Fees can be charged to raise additional revenue for the school, the PTA, or as a stipend for the organizer. Money paid by theatergoers above the cost of tickets is tax deductible if proceeds are used for school purposes.

### Eat a Lot for Little

This activity is a gala family eating at "a dime a dip." You need food donations and some volunteers to set up tables, serve, and clean up. A few dollars are needed to purchase paper plates, utensils, and cups.

Choose a date, gather volunteers, and announce the event in the local paper and school newspaper. Ask each family to donate one dish to feed four persons— meat, vegetables, salad, or dessert. Provide a response slip at the bottom of the newspaper notices. Request that food be brought to school thirty minutes before the event.

Plan for two serving lines, each with several food choices in every category. Serve a dip of each item as requested. At the end of the line, the cashier, who can be a student, totals the number of "dips" and multiplies by a dime. It's possible to eat a balanced, big meal, including dessert, for seventy cents. A family of four can be fed for under three dollars. This event might precede a Back-to-School night or other special event.

### Family "Follies"

This activity gives children a chance to meet and know adults beyond their own family. Plus, it's a showcase for family talent.

Announce the Follies and advertise open-house auditions. The show can be an informal, spur-of-the-moment event or a more elaborate affair. If more elaborate, use a parent/student committee to select acts for the program, and form committees for invitations, programs, publicity, tickets. If possible, video-record the show for later screenings.

## Come to My House

This activity gives parents an opportunity to get together in an informal atmosphere to share mutual concerns about their children. Even though this event is held on "home ground," it's about school and education-related issues.

Parents are asked to "sponsor" a meeting by inviting neighbors into their homes for an informal get-together. This builds personal ties between neighbors. At the meeting, one member might tell about good, inexpensive places to go with children, while another might share tips on getting chores and homework done.

The value of such meetings is that they are help, not gripe, sessions. One family's good idea helps another family. What works in one house might work for someone else. This is truly self-help based on mutual support.

## Raincoat and Boot Exchange

This activity is a real money saver, good for all families but especially for single parents who may have tighter budgets.

When have you had a raincoat or boots that have worn out? They don't—they just get outgrown. Here's a way to keep them in circulation.

Early in the school year, ask parents to bring outgrown rainwear to school. Designate certain days for the exchange. To save administrative work, ask all parents to put their own prices on the items. What isn't sold can be returned or donated to local organizations. To keep costs low, ask that no item be priced over two dollars. In this way, the exchange becomes a real bargain.

All parents—not just single parents—should be encouraged to participate. A single-parents club may want to conduct this exchange and other activities in this chapter to demonstrate its commitment to the school and to the community.

## HELPING OURSELVES

The message of this chapter is *Don't wait.* Don't wait for institutions to change. Don't wait for others to come by to help you. No activity in this chapter is so difficult or costly that it can't be done in every neighborhood in this country.

*Joe DiDio, courtesy of the National Education Association*

## CHAPTER 27

# Parents and Students

## Helping Children Feel More at Home in School

Schools are complex worlds, with rituals, routines, and practices—a way of life that may at first appear frightening, imposing, and difficult for children and adults to figure out.

Some parents tell me that years after they've graduated, they still haven't figured it out and are glad they no longer have to. There's an old joke (is it a joke?) that comedian Henry Morgan used to tell: "I'm forty-four years old and every day when I wake up, I thank my lucky stars I don't have to go to school anymore."

## THE CHOICES WE MAKE

When I talk with groups of teachers, I remind them that we may be the only ones who really liked schools. We went back into them of our own free will. That's the choice we made.

Increasingly today, there are many more choices being made in education by parents and students, not just teachers. Almost everyone now, from union leaders to business folks to parents, agree that families should have a choice about where to send their children to school, at least choice among public schools. In a growing number of communities that is already happening.

Choice is not all peaches and cream. It can give you headaches. Many a family gets near migraines just from trying to figure out what courses students ought to take. Choice about what school to select, including charter schools, really becomes a major

and often difficult decision. It involves visiting schools, talking with teachers, and talking with other families. Parents grapple with the almost philosophical question "What is a good school?" to the more pragmatic "How can I identify it for my child; how do I know it's right?"

The point is that having a choice is good, but it is not enough. Choice has to be followed by thinking through your child's needs and strengths and trying to match them with a school and the people in the school, teachers and principal. Picking a school is almost like getting married, so you want to know as much about it as possible in advance. But, just as with marriage, there is no foolproof way to know everything.

In this chapter you'll read about specific strategies to help build the "connection" between student and school. Whether it's a new school or old school, in reality, for every student, it's a new classroom, with new choices and new teachers every year.

## ABOUT THE SCHOOL ITSELF

School buildings are not immediately congenial-looking places. Why they look the way they do I will never know. Many generate a forbidding atmosphere guaranteed to harden the heart of the most eager first grader. Older school buildings can pass for mental asylums, and new ones, though much improved, are large and have an institutional look. To be sure, more and more

I know what it's like to move to a new school, to be an unknown and feel unknown. It's not a good feeling. I spent my early school years in a small school in a small town, where everyone knew me and I knew everyone else. After my mother died suddenly, my father decided to move the family to a large city nearby. I entered a very large school where I knew no one. This was in my high school years. It was a tough time, and one I have not forgotten.

In a way, my experience was not too unlike the move all children must make when they enter school for the first time or move on from a smaller elementary school to a large junior high.

schoolrooms do exude warmth, using bright colors, but most won't win prizes for their welcoming quality.

Children can be prepared for the look of the school and how a school works—even before they enter one or move on to a new one.

Any new entry is hard. It's easier in the early grades, in a small school. But it's still hard. And so I urge parents to help children feel as comfortable as possible as early as possible in a school year, in any new school situation. Help children try to visualize themselves in this school. Get information about the school, talk about it, make choices, and be ready to make this coming school year as terrific as possible.

If this is a new school for your child, whether it's for kindergarten, sixth grade, or tenth grade, visit the school with your child before the term begins, if possible. Walk through the halls, stop into the front office, introduce yourselves. What kind of greeting do you receive?

Ask to meet the principal. If not at that moment, when? Set an appointment. Have some questions ready—about special programs, about test scores, about the principal's interest in parent involvement. The National Association of Elementary School Principals is working to stimulate parent involvement in every school. Ask about school parent programs, including MegaSkills, and how you can participate.

I have resisted the temptation to present you with a list of questions to cut out and carry with you to the school. It can add an unnecessary confrontational quality to the meeting. Jot down your questions in advance and carry them with you in your pocket, pulling them out as needed to jog your memory. But try to make your appointment a conversation, not a multiple-choice examination. When you leave the school,

As you go through your questions from curriculum choices, to the safety of the neighborhood, to the stability of the teaching force, to the times that parent conferences are held, be sure to listen and watch. It's not just what is said that is important but how it is said. And if the school has a plan and lots of pieces of paper to share, ask that one critical question, "How is it working in practice?"

if your memory needs help, as mine does, take a few notes to recall what was said.

If classes are in session, ask to stop by. Try to walk along the very corridors your children will be walking along when they are students at this school.

In short, get the feel of the place. Start to feel at home there. Ask about and discuss the curriculum: What will be covered this year? What are the possibilities for extracurricular clubs and activities? When do these have to be chosen? How do bus transportation schedules fit in with before- or after-school programs?

It's important to try to feel as comfortable as possible with the school in advance. Once the hectic pace of the school year begins, it's harder to get a reassuring first impression.

> "There has been a tremendous difference in the pupils since the MegaSkills program began. Fighting has decreased. The percentage of pupils referred to my office has dropped from 45% to 8% within a year. We have completely changed our discipline program, going from negative to positive. The children are reinforced for good behavior and showing kindness to one another, and expressing themselves in positive ways in the classroom, cafeteria, and throughout the building."
>
> — John D. Roschy, former principal, Meadowvale School, Havre-de-Grace, Maryland

## ABOUT TEACHERS

Today's sophisticated children are ready to understand that teachers are human beings and that, like anyone else, they can be right and they can also be wrong. In the past, respect in the classroom and often at home was one-sided; all from the child to the adult, and no back talk. Respect today has become more two-way.

Urge your child, right from the beginning, not to hesitate to question the teacher. This need not be done in a smart-alecky or disrespectful way. Students have to know how to stand up for what they think is right. You may want to do a little role playing at home, acting out a scene in which your

children question a teacher politely yet firmly. Most of these questions will probably deal with grades, but students may also question a teacher's point of view.

In trying them out, urge your child to avoid a personal attack. It's like asking for a raise without threatening to quit or being overly humble to the boss. It can be hard to maintain this composure when your feelings run high, but practice can help.

Lest you think that teachers don't alter grades when solid evidence is presented that changes their thinking—you're wrong. Teachers are generally reasonable people who want to be fair. I have changed a number of grades in my time. By the way, I have never known a student to complain about an unearned high grade. And there are

> There are good teachers and bad teachers; a teacher's personality can make or break a class. No magic wand will alter how teachers conduct classes and the personal characteristics they bring to them. Children need to recognize that there are less than wonderful situations for which they are not to blame. And they need inner strength to live through these.

always some of those, along with the ones that are too low.

Just as parents aren't always wonderful, neither are teachers. The only reason to make this obvious statement is that children, especially young children, can tend to believe or want to believe that teachers are always right. When they find that teachers are not perfect and can be unfair, they can be terribly disappointed and disillusioned.

Children should not need to have teachers love them every day in order to feel good about themselves. A child's self-confidence should not have to depend on a teacher's constant approval. Sometimes even the best teachers get angry.

It's possible to prepare children for the realities of teachers as people without undermining children's confidence in school. It can be helpful for children to know that teachers can be rejecting, bullying, dull, lazy, uncommunicative, unhelpful, and discouraging. Teachers can also be enthusiastic, supportive, smart, helpful, imaginative, caring, understanding, and sincere.

I really do believe that the good teachers outnumber the bad ones. And since children have so many teachers in their lives, the chances that they will have their share of good ones is strong. (For more details on this subject, see Chapter 25, "Parents and Teachers.")

## ABOUT FRIENDS

School can be the place where children make lifelong friends. Or school can be a very lonely place if children have no friends. Children who have trouble making and keeping friends need help.

Help children sense that friendships have ups and downs—today you're angry, tomorrow you make up—and that the friends will change. At five they may need someone to go on a swing with; at fifteen, someone to discuss books with. At any age, they may want different kinds of friends at the same time.

Fears often handicap friendship. Some children, like adults, are afraid even of

> Teach youngsters that friendship is like a seed. It must be planted and tended. It demands loyalty, affection, and a willingness to go all out, to keep promises, to be considerate. Use specific examples to explain these ideas. You may want to recount some of your own experiences in school. Tell about when you were popular and when you were lonely, too.

> Older students have trouble when they try to be what they're not, conforming to some popular image of whom they ought to like and what they ought to do. Often they'll tag along with a crowd whose company they don't even enjoy. Adolescents need to be reassured that their judgment is sound and reminded that they needn't worry about what other people think.

trying to make friends, afraid of being rebuffed. Expecting to be excluded, they set up barriers they don't even see, such as excessive shyness or overaggressiveness. Once contact is made, they may be afraid to get close to a friend, avoiding this by spreading themselves thin over many acquaintances.

When you see these fears and the immaturities of always needing to get rather than give, discuss them with your children. Try to avoid "Nobody likes me" explanations and stick to "How can we work together to help you have the friends you want?"

The friends your children want may not be the ones you'd choose. Try to respect your child's choices, but watch for any unhealthy situations that crop up. These include youngsters exploiting each other: social butterfly Sue using bookworm Ann to write all her book reports; aggressive Tom consistently venting anger on passive Jim.

When you see these patterns, bring them to your children's attention. They may know what's happening, too, but continue

the relationship because they don't think they can attract anyone else. Talk about this.

Encourage children to bring friends home from school and to invite some along on family outings. Make youngsters feel welcome in your home. Try to avoid nagging about moderate noise and dirt. Try to set aside a place for children to entertain in, and work out arrangements for their cleaning up after everyone's gone.

Really shy children may need specific help to start friendships. If you hear your children mention a friend at school, help them set a date and make the first difficult phone call. With junior and senior high youngsters, a parent plays a less active role, but you can help direct them to the activities and clubs where they can make new friends.

## ABOUT REPORT CARDS

Except for the few students who bring home all A's (and their parents), nobody really likes report cards, not even teachers. Teachers will admit that no matter how hard they try, they cannot accurately judge what a student has learned. But even while report cards themselves are flunking, they continue to exert a mighty influence. The difference between a C and a B can determine whether a student goes to a certain college or gets a certain job.

Anyone who's been to school, and that's almost all of us these days, knows the abuses grades are heir to. One teacher gives a C to a paper; another teacher might give it an A. The same teacher grading the same paper over again may grade it differently. Some teachers use low grades to make students work harder. Others use high grades for the same reasons.

Specific injustices rankle in the memories of anyone who's ever sat in a classroom. More harmful in the long run, however, are the attitudes that can surround grading: grades that become ends in themselves so that nothing is remembered when the exam is over; children labeled early as poor students unable to break the chains of low marks; threats about grades that cripple children with a fear of failure; grades given but unexplained, so that parents and children are left to wonder and guess what they mean and why they were given.

Yet despite all that is known about the errors in grading, grades continue to be regarded as prophetic, all-knowing measures of children's abilities. If the school says so, and says so in black and white, it must be right.

Ironically, parents who question many other things about the school may hold this belief in grades. In practice, most parents don't object to grading systems or even question them. Parents rarely even ask teachers why they grade as they do. Even when a parent knows better, a low grade will tend to make parents think less of their child.

This is dangerous, and efforts need to be made to avoid this trap. Here are some ways:

- Work with your child to see the report card for what it is. It is an attempt by teachers to assess what a student has learned. It is an administrative convenience in school record keeping. It is not an evaluation of the child as a human being—"you're good"; "you're bad." Grades are not all-knowing. The grade itself, whether an A or D, is a mixture of test scores and teacher reactions. All this can be discussed with your youngster so that grades are put in proper perspective without being discredited.
- Try to figure out with your child what's gone into the mark. Refer to school guidelines, check lists, and other comments on the card. On the secondary level, the mark is more mysterious, as it usually arrives without comments. Because these grades are run through computers in large schools, they often can't even have pluses and minuses. If the grade remains

> Children can be helped to get the best, not the worst, out of report cards, no matter what the grades are. This is important because it appears that report cards are here to stay.
>
> Parents can provide support for children who must receive grades by helping youngsters see the report card in perspective—what it is, how to view it positively, what dangers to avoid, and what changes can be asked for that schools and teachers are in a position to provide.

a mystery to you, discuss it with the teacher.

■ Instill in your children the idea that regardless of the grades they receive, they continue to be accepted and loved. Anxiety about grades can give youngsters the dangerous idea that their value in life and their love from you depend on whether they bring home A's or C's. Since most children will bring home C's, whether they or their parents like it, it's dangerous business to make a C student feel less valuable as a human being because of a little letter that may be wrong.

■ Treat failure in a subject not as a total disaster but rather as a sign of a problem that can be helped. Before nonpromotion, parents and teachers should get together for an in-depth discussion. If learning difficulties are revealed, the student's sight and hearing should be checked. An anti-schoolwork, emotional block may call for counseling.

---

And when your child does finally bring home good grades, bite your tongue before asking that awful question, "Why don't you do this all the time?"

---

Grading as a reward system is not bad in itself. Educational research confirms that rewards, many and frequent, help students learn. The problem with the present grading system is that not many students ever get any of the rewards. Too few of our children receive a real sense of achievement from school.

The answer to this problem is not to give everyone all A's. This would debase grading as a reward altogether.

Forward-thinking schools are experimenting to come up with better report cards. It's up to forward-thinking parents to reassure and encourage teachers to continue this experimentation.

In the meantime, we must come up with more ways, both in school and at home, in which students can excel and feel their worth.

The activities throughout this book provide opportunities for children to excel at home. Through them, children get a sense that they are achievers and succeeders in ways that go well beyond the classroom walls. This sense carries over to the school and makes it possible for children to deal more constructively with the marks on their report cards, even the disappointing ones, and with whatever happens in the classroom.

# Creativity: The Spark and the Satisfaction

**E**ven if you give children everything money can buy, you still can't buy an ideal learning environment. The ingredients required to enrich a child's life aren't found in expensive toys and educational hardware. The recipe is made up instead of the inventiveness and the responsiveness of human beings. Much of it is free, although it takes some time and planning.

## INTRODUCTION

# A Sense of Balance

"My kids are learning to read and write. Should I care if they sing, dance, or draw?"

The answer is yes—mostly because of what is being learned about the complexities of our double-hemisphere brains. The left brain gets the workout in school: It handles the language, the numbers, the reading, the writing, the talking. The right brain is the artsy side: It handles music, spatial skills, intuition, and imagery.

Creative activity requires both sides of the brain. When we sing, we read notes (left brain) and produce musical sounds (right brain).

We may not be able to determine how in-class time is spent or whether there is enough time in school for both left and right brain activity. Outside of school is another matter. To help our children gain opti-

> Ideally we want to experience and create as much "wholeness" in our lives as possible. At times when we're sitting in the office or in class, we just know in our bones that we need to get out to use our hands to mold, to use our voice to sing, to use our feet to bike or to dance. This gives us a sense of balance.

mal development and use of their brains, they need to give both sides a workout.

In this section you will find:

**The "Right Brain" at Home**—how to create an arts environment at home.
**Inspiration and Perspiration**—how to nurture talent in all children; how what works for the gifted is helpful to all of us.

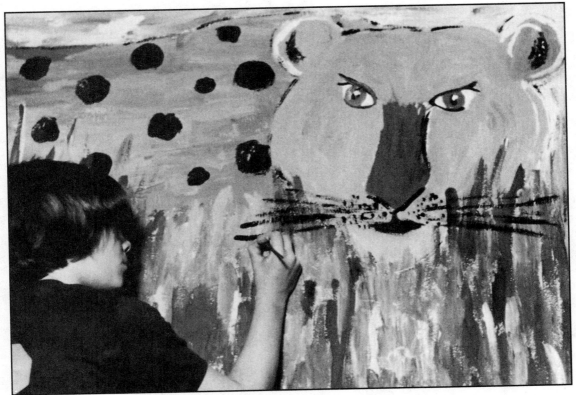

*Joe DiDio, courtesy of the National Education Association*

**CHAPTER 28**

# The "Right Brain" at Home

The arts are essential because of the predictions for daily life in the not-too-distant future. More of us will be living longer and retiring earlier. Some say we will work fewer hours each week and will have longer annual vacations. We will have time for our own interests—and these will grow out of our education and our "inner resources." Fundamental to these inner resources is enjoying and participating in the arts. With the renewed emphasis on what's been termed "the basics," the arts may be in even greater danger in school.

Out of school, however, is another matter. The arts can live in every home, whether a parent is "artsy" or not. This chapter tells how to do it in ways that make it possible for every family to create an arts environment at home.

Some may think that the arts are frills. But they are important for complete brain functioning, and they are MegaSkills essentials. Perhaps nowhere else in the entire curriculum do children get to see so clearly that an achievement takes time and that it has a beginning, a middle, and a product. A vase starts with a lump of clay that is rolled, molded, and fired. A poem starts with a single word on a blank page. A dance starts with a first step. A violin starts with a squeak. There is a level of personal satisfaction in the arts that stimulates a child to learn and to want to keep on learning.

In creative dramatics, you emphasize the players, not the play. There are no scripts, no awesome, exhausting productions. It's defined well by a ten-year-old boy who said, "In creative dramatics, you can be anything you want to be. If you're fat, you can be thin; if you're short, you can be tall. You don't have to say what the teachers say; you can say what you want to say." A girl adds, "We have feelings in here [pointing to her heart]—they have to come out. In dramatics we can let them come out."

## CREATIVE DRAMATICS

Creative dramatics sounds like an activity almost too imposing for use at home. Actually, home is an ideal place for it.

Children already possess what they need for creative drama—lots of imagination coupled with the instinct for make-believe and improvisation.

### The Costume Box ■ ages 4–8

Youngsters love to dress up and imagine they're someone else. To encourage this, provide a costume box of old clothes, including hats and shoes. Small props like the following are especially useful: fans, umbrellas, luggage, toy trucks, masks, dolls for dressing and undressing.

It's wonderful to see the transformation that a flowered straw hat and high heels can do for a little girl in shorts. Suddenly she's a fairy godmother. Put a black scarf on her head, and she's a wicked witch. Let her put on Father's tie and hat, and she's a prince, a spy, a soldier.

You can move this to a next level. To encourage your child to put action to the character, ask, "What are you, John? A cowboy? What does a cowboy do? Show me."

There you have the elements of dramatic characterization. From this, your youngster can develop a play in which a fairy godmother meets a cowboy. What happens after that? That's for you and the children to work out. The shy child who finds it difficult to take part will gain confidence behind a mask and with a prop in hand.

Try to remember to record some of these moments. You don't need a video camera, although these do make for memorable scenes. Use a tape recorder to get the voices, and take some snapshots or slides. These are a delight for the memory scrapbooks and also serve to reinforce children's positive images of themselves.

## Our Own Play ▪ any age

Now you may want a plot. Let's say you have Cinderella and a spy. They meet. What happens next? Let the children tell you. Join in the fun as an actor, too. Children love to have parents take parts in impromptu plays.

Act out favorite stories: Your children tell the story first. Divide the parts: Who wants to act what role? It can help to have three or four players. If you don't have that many children at home, call the neighbors.

Children ages three and up will be able to participate if they know the stories and the roles they're to do. Don't fret if everyone, boys included, wants to be Goldilocks. Give them a chance.

Go through the play enough times for all to have the parts they want. Each run-through may last only a few minutes. What the actors say will change each time because they are making up their own lines. Keep your props simple and spontaneous. Cinderella can put on Mother's dress and high heels for the ball. Use chairs that double as beds for the Three Bears. Your children will probably want to perform the plays over and over. As they get the knack, let them take turns as director.

Try pantomimes for fun and dramatic exercise. Eat a dripping ice cream cone, empty smelly garbage, hold a hot coal or an

Children grow more self-conscious and conscious of the world about them as they grow older. They may find that dramatizing comes less naturally. It is important to try to help these youngsters to continue using drama as a way to express themselves, to release pent-up feelings, to be anything they want to be.

Drama builds a child's self-confidence and imagination. It also helps youngsters understand others by asking them literally to put themselves in other people's shoes.

injured bird. Try converging emotions of love, shyness, fear, bravery, anger. Then elaborate on your pantomimes. Cross a street crowded with traffic; do a chore, such as raking leaves, when you'd rather be somewhere else. Build your own family repertoire of pantomimes and games such as show and tell with younger children and charades with older ones. Puppets are especially helpful for shy children. Work up skits for parties and special occasions.

## ARTS AND CRAFTS

Art activities—both the energetic fury of actual creation and the pleasures of museum going—are too enjoyable and important to be saved for "artistes" alone.

Younger children probably will be less inhibited. Older ones and those who haven't been exposed to what we're talking about in this chapter may need specific ideas to begin. The "I can't think of any-

Start an Art for Everyone crusade with art projects for the whole family. The artistically talented are welcome, of course, but open the doors even wider for the "I can't draw" people, who are usually reluctant to try the artsy stuff.

thing to make" syndrome can be a very real problem.

Artwork at home exercises children's inventive abilities (an important component of intelligence) and their eye-hand coordination muscles.

The box below lists ideas for stocking an arts corner. Almost everything you need can be put together inexpensively, and you don't need everything at once.

### The Work Area ■ any age

Set up, with children, a work area where they can spread out and be messy. They

Assorted powder tempera and enamel paint
Paste, strong glue
Scissors, crayons, tape, string
Paint palette (muffin tin or egg carton inlaid with foil)
Finger paints (can be homemade with starch, coloring, soap flakes, water)
Glitter
Clay (hard and soft-drying)

Pipe cleaners
Ruler
Scraps of cloth (good for collages)
Wire hangers for mobiles
Bottles, cans, and jars (saved from the kitchen)
Cardboard boxes (different sizes)
Paper (shelf, wrapping, colored, plain white, and plenty of old newspapers for clean up)

Depending on children's ability to work on their own, encourage both free play and specific projects. Generally young children want more free play and prefer short projects that can be finished in one sitting. Older youngsters can do projects in steps over several days. This process builds perseverance.

need a storage shelf for supplies and a display area for finished creations. This can be a corner of a room.

Try art materials at home that your children might not usually work with. Paints and crayons are fine, but stretch youngsters' experiences with such materials as toothpicks, wire, burlap, and shells.

## A Potpourri of Projects ■ any age

Listed below are some art activities that everyone can do:

Try homemade puppets, allowing your children's imaginations to concoct puppets that look any way they want them to. Use an old sock for the head with a toilet paper roll inside to give it body. Stuff the sock with cotton or paper; your child can sew on features (using buttons) or draw them on. Yarn is ideal for hair. Stitch some fabric to the base so that the hand inside can't be seen. Add a puppet stage made from a cardboard box, and you're in show business.

Use arts and crafts for gifts for Christmas and for birthdays. They're wonderful as party favors. Nothing satisfies the receiver or giver as much as a homemade gift.

Start an art gallery by reserving a wall to exhibit your children's artwork. Trace your child's artistic development by framing and hanging a painting every six months or so. You will have a colorfully decorated wall that draws oohs and aahs from company and a prideful "I did that" from your child. This is a wonderful ego builder. For a rogues' gallery, children can do caricature

Flower pots from decorated juice cans
Animals from pipe cleaners, mounted on wood pieces
Paper dolls cut from shirt cardboard
Carved soap sculptures
Decorated bricks for doorstops
Decorated stones for paperweights
Necklaces made from shells

Dollhouses from cardboard boxes
Designs from pasting overlapping colored papers, initials, numbers
Collages from seeds or magazine cutouts
Touch-and-feel scrapbook from magazine pictures, with yarn, cotton, and foil pasted in appropriate places

drawings of their friends, their teachers, and you.

## I Made It Myself

**Picture Puzzles (ages 4–6).** They're practically free, easy to make, and can be designed to be as simple or as complex as children want. Paste a picture on cardboard and then cut puzzle pieces out, with or without drawing lines on the back for guidance. You need magazines that contain large-size color pictures, scissors, shirt cardboard, paste, and large envelopes for holding the pieces.

**Dress Me (ages 4–8).** This is a variation of pin the tail, with blindfolded players pinning paper cutouts of clothes—shirt, shorts, socks, and shoes—onto paper silhouette figures of children. Children lie down on sheets of wrapping or shelf paper and you draw around their bodies. This combines children's intense interest in themselves with their creative joy in making their very own games. Trade places. Let your child do a silhouette of you. Then stand both silhouettes up against a wall. This is guaranteed to make you laugh or cry!

**Master Builder (ages 8–12).** With your older children, make a playground, a project that takes both physical and creative effort. In this activity, children create their own outdoor play structures. Household and hardware scraps are welcome: old tires, steering wheels, door knobs, wooden crates. Some tools and a friend or two to help, and this project is on its way.

Even if lessons are never given, music can be encouraged at home. For most of us, music may never be more than amateur recreation, similar to baseball or bridge. But for others, it is the start of a lifetime's avocation or possibly even a career. In any event, it is a continuing outlet and release. Brain surgeons have been known for getting together in quartets to play violin chamber music; so have Supreme Court justices. But it's not necessary to have those exalted positions to get the pleasure that music brings all through life.

If your fence needs painting, let the children try it. But improve on Tom Sawyer by letting your youngsters paint flowers or whatever they fancy for a unique job.

## MUSIC MAKING

Parents with or without musical "talent" can make music a vital part of children's lives and perhaps start them on an active, lifetime interest in creative music making.

Those little tunes that we almost unconsciously sing to babies while changing their diapers or giving them baths are the beginning of music education. Children soon begin joining in and singing along. "Mary Had a Little Lamb" may seem worlds apart from a Mozart concerto, but in much the same way that children use words before they read them, so children use tunes and musical notes before formal music lessons.

## Musical Instruments
■ ages 4–6, or younger

Raw materials for musical instruments can come from anywhere. From the kitchen comes the percussion: pots and pie pans. Suspend them on a string, hit them with spoons, and they're gongs and drums. Clang pie pans together and they're cymbals.

Use shoe boxes for strummers. Remove the tops and stretch rubber bands of varying sizes across the boxes. Let children decorate, and in minutes they have homespun guitars.

Small bells are wonderfully versatile for home use. Attach them to children's ankles and wrists. Attach them to pie plates to make tambourines.

---

A practice schedule can become self-regulating. For example, if the requirements are that your child practice half an hour a day, you can say, "Pick the half hour or the two fifteen-minute periods of your choice, up to eight P.M." Children sign up for their choice and then become self-regulators. This may sound too easy to be true, but giving children a choice and expecting them to live up to this choice works remarkably well.

---

Put stones, beans, and sand into cans or closed boxes. Let children decorate them, and you have maracas.

With the rhythm band ready, you're ready to make music.

Children can play individually with their rhythm makers or combine them in a concert. If they hit upon a combination of sounds they want to repeat, jot down what instruments play and for how long. *Example:* bells, two beats; gongs, three beats. If possible, let youngsters hear their music on a tape recorder.

Children can play for each other. One can pound the drum while another dances to the beat. Then the drummer can sing or dance while another child plays the tambourine.

Let children take turns conducting. Show them some motions for loud, soft, fast, slow. Don't expect children's music to be "pretty" or fit standard music-making formulas. Children need the freedom and encouragement to experiment with the sounds of music.

The value of this technique as an early approach is that it encourages children's independent interest in music. Do they want to go on to formal lessons? Once lessons begin, however, youngsters should be mature enough to come to an understanding about the requirements of practice. If music in the home deteriorates into a nagging parent and a defiant child who hates any contact with the instrument, then it's time to assess whether the formal lessons are doing what you hope they will, which is to encourage a love of music.

Parents can do a lot to build physical education and "movement" readiness—just as they can build readiness for academic subjects. This not only helps in gym class but also gives children a better sense of themselves for other activities.

## DANCE AND MOVEMENT

All children may not have the makings of a great athlete or dancer, but they need to be able to use their bodies with confidence.

In school, children who need gym class the most often dislike it most—and with reason. Instead of giving the less physically adept youngsters what they need—activity that provides success and a feeling of belonging—in many gym classes, children with "two left feet" are humiliated. They are the first to be eliminated in a game and the last to be chosen for a team.

Here are some activities that fall between dance and physical education for ages four through eight, or younger.

Try walking or running at different paces. Beat out a fast or slow rhythm on a drum or pie plate. Encourage children to keep step to the beat, with short, fast steps, or long, slow slides.

When the music stops (you can use a record for this), tell children to drop where they are, falling in a lovely, slow heap, first the legs, then the torso, the arms, the head. Or tell them to pretend they're scrambling in under the ball to second base. Dance, when it's approached in this way, is no "sissy" thing to do.

Play statues. When the music stops, so do the children, exactly as they were when they heard the last beat. Count to ten while the statues hold these positions, no matter how crazy they are. Then start the music again.

Make body shapes. Try a wide shape, a thin shape, a curve backward, a curve forward, a jumping shape, a running shape, a ball shape, a duck shape. There's no end to these as long as your child's imagination holds out.

Play "relax." Tired parents will appreciate this. Lie down on your back and relax. Then concentrate on putting parts of the body to sleep. Start with the toes, move upward to the legs, to the hips, and so on. This teaches concentration and anatomy as well as relaxation.

Encourage movement of all types to help children continue to feel free about using their body: leaping like frogs, twisting like donuts, bouncing like balls, shaking like jelly, stretching like rubber bands, falling like rain.

Keep an assortment of fabrics of different weights, colors, and textures for children to dance with. Use an easy-to-reach box that children can dip into whenever the spirit moves them. Assemble some rhythm instruments—ones children have made or store-bought ones. Put a CD player or radio nearby for children to use themselves—with records that make them want to dance. Lively marches and tangos are especially inviting.

Some of my happiest childhood memories are of tap dancing under an archway between our living and dining rooms. I pretended it was a stage and I was the star. I don't think anyone ever saw me, but it didn't matter. I don't tap dance anymore, but I remember those "recitals" with great pleasure.

## GOING OUT

### Museums ■ ages 4–9

Go to museums, but do it with children in short doses, about forty-five minutes at a time. Beware not to be done in by "doing" the museum. A museum director told me that he urges parents for their own sake to take their children with them to art galleries. Children like art and respond to it openly.

Look at the artwork, but don't worry about identifying the artist, the period, the style. Children don't have to like or dislike a piece of art for any specific reason—they just have to experience it.

Check the newspaper art listings for news of special exhibitions you'll want to see. Look for children's art exhibits—real favorites—and be sure to check out the children's rooms in museums. They have "Please Touch" exhibits that young children especially enjoy.

While at the museum, you might let your children choose one or two art postcards.

As children get older, they can rent the lectures on cassettes that increasingly accompany art exhibits. They will want to know about the artists and their lives.

Encourage your children to check newspaper reviews and then decide whether certain shows are for them. This is a good way for them to build their critical judgment and to make them more responsible for what they see. They can't blame you for taking or sending them to a bad movie when it's a decision you've all made together.

While standing across the room, they will want to be able to look at a painting and guess the name of the artist. There are stories in almost every painting, and there are many books about artists who have lived poor but colorful lives. All these facts can follow later, after the initial delights of enjoying the paintings or sculptures.

### Plays, Movies, Concerts, Dance Recitals ■ ages 4–9

There is no magic formula that prescribes when to start taking children "out." The time to start depends on two things: the concentration span of your child and the kinds of entertainment available. Some three-year-olds avidly watch all of *Mary Poppins* or *Snow White*, while older youngsters ask to leave when they are half over.

If you are a theater- or concertgoer yourself, and if you can afford it, you're more likely to take children at an early age. But even adults who enjoy the magic of theater

The choice of really good movies for children is very limited. So it is reassuring to find that "the experts" believe that, in general, stable children will not turn into delinquents because of what they see in the movie house. Serious delinquency stems from what children bring with them when they come into the theater. It's the memory of conversations with adults and friends about what's real, what's fantasy, what's junk, what's good, that children bring to the movies and TV screens. It's especially talk with parents that enables children to judge the quality of what they are seeing and whether it's to be taken seriously or whether it's just fun.

often need a magic wand to find plays and movies that are suitable for children.

Don't be surprised if the movie you thought so great doesn't make the grade with the kids. And vice versa; the ones they like may flop with you. Try to be tolerant. Respect their opinions. Hear them out on what they liked or disliked and ask that they hear you out, too.

At-home activities before an outing are useful for young children. Before going to the theater or concert, discuss the plot or what music will be played. If you don't know this, look it up. Young children often feel more comfortable knowing the story in advance. And it's a nerve saver for parents, who then don't have to sit in the movie whispering answers to questions about what's going to happen next.

If you're going to a musical, sing and play some of the songs before you go. Children enjoy recognizing these as they're performed. After the show, help children judge what they've seen. With young children, ask which characters they liked best. What do they remember most about the show? Children's movies need not always be fairy-tale productions peopled only by goody-goodies. It can be very instructive for children to see characters coping with real life, facing temptations, even making mistakes. What's important is that you talk about what you've seen.

And children probably aren't ruined for life if they happen to get taken along to an "adult" film. Bedroom scenes often make little or no impression on the very young. It's the preadolescents on a steady diet of sex and violence who can use advice and self-regulatory help on movie going. If you start early and keep up a dialogue with your children, there's far less chance of older youngsters being "infected" by poor movie selections.

What's wonderful about the arts is that they can provide children with a sense of success that they might not be getting in other ways. Everyone has to feel this sense of achievement in some way, in some place. It doesn't always happen in the classroom. The arts at home give children this extra chance.

## ARTS AND THE SENSE OF SUCCESS

The special value of an arts project is that you come up with an idea. You try it. You work. You end up with a finished project—and all the while build greater self-confidence and control. Plus you get new ideas along the way that you hadn't thought of before.

*Courtesy of the National Education Association*

## CHAPTER 29

# Inspiration and Perspiration

Who are those people who sail their own boats across the Atlantic, who invent folding bicycles, who write poems, who hunt microbes? They are the ones who sat next to us in class, but they are not necessarily the ones who got the good grades in school.

There is a lot to be learned from this. It teaches us that no matter what gifts we start with, it takes MegaSkills to use them.

Sometimes we can get stuck into thinking that education consists only of school grades and attending the best schools. When we read the honor roll of those who never made the school honor roll, we immediately gain a wider vision about accomplishment.

For example, the top characteristics of productive, creative people include intellectual courage, independent thinking and judgment, courage of convictions, preoccupation with and absorption in tasks,

---

It was Edison who said that genius is 10 percent inspiration and 90 percent perspiration. This has been reconfirmed by recent studies that indicate that no matter what the initial characteristics or gifts of an individual, unless there is a long and sustained process of encouragement and training, that person will not attain high levels of capability in subjects ranging from music to athletics. In short, special, innate gifts are nice, but they are not enough.

---

intuitiveness, persistence, willingness to take risks, and unwillingness to accept judgment of authorities.

These do not necessarily lead to the school honor roll.

As a matter of fact, the long lists of school "problems" include men and women who grew up to be distinguished adults. Among them are the authors Thomas Mann, Pearl Buck, and Willa Cather; the inventor Henry Ford; the dancer Isadora Duncan; the scientist Albert Einstein; the composer Edvard Grieg. Disastrous school experiences of creative people are almost commonplace.

At the same time that the author William Saroyan was a terrible school problem, he read every book in the Fresno, California, public library. Sigrid Undset, another well-known author, couldn't stand her school's freedom-curbing discipline.

Youngsters with particular talents resent the school's demand that they scatter their energies, that they become well rounded in all subjects. In those days before compulsory education, many gifted youngsters became school dropouts. They continued their education in specialized apprenticeships and in the informal schooling that went on at home.

Among school dropouts are the Wright brothers, Thomas Edison, Pablo Picasso, Dimitri Shostakovich, Marchese Guglielmo Marconi, Noel Coward, Mark Twain, and Pablo Casals.

Those who stayed in school had similar difficulties. Einstein, who was slow of speech, wanted to learn in his own way. He believed examinations, with their insistence on memorized facts, impeded education, which he felt was based on a "perpetual sense of wonder." It's said that he had a terrible time passing the usual school examinations, as did the composer Giacomo Puccini and the scientist Paul Ehrlich.

Writers who couldn't make the grade in class but who took literary honors afterward include Proust (his teachers said his compositions were disorganized), Stephen Crane, Eugene O'Neill, William Faulkner, and F. Scott Fitzgerald. I'd like to think that as an English teacher I would have recognized their abilities, but I'm not sure I would have or that they would have shown their best in class.

Bright children are no longer "bookworms" or "eggheads." Even "nerds" are portrayed sympathetically. We've entered a new era of respect for uniqueness as opposed to the conformity once wished for. "Your child is different" can be a compliment.

More is learned about giftedness each year. I am struck by the "invulnerable"

> It's encouraging that schools today are showing a greater concern for the individual and are more hospitable to children's differences. Not too long ago, the precocious, exceptionally bright child was popularly pictured as an abnormal, awkward, smarty-pants nuisance. This is far less true now.

> Giftedness is a mixture of heredity and environment, and it's not absolutely clear how much of each ingredient goes into the recipe. You can do everything "right" and still not have a gifted child. You can do a lot wrong and have a gifted child.

gifted resilience shown by children who flourish in the midst of great difficulty—the children of the mentally ill, the children of alcoholics, the children of poverty—children who make it, who go on to lead happy, successful lives despite the odds against them.

Through research, key traits of these resilient children are being identified. They show the ability to bounce back. They can handle frustration. As babies, for example, when their tower of blocks falls over, they go back and try again. They're cheerful and enthusiastic. Perhaps most important, say the researchers, is that as these children grow, they have the ability to seek help from other adults if they cannot get help from their own parents. They may have average academic skills, but they have high social intelligence. Surely this is giftedness, and yet tests don't record it.

There is a lot yet to learn. Now that people are living longer, the genetic seeds set in the womb and the benefits of early nurturing will have a chance to flower over a longer period. Our "late bloomers" could be blooming later than ever.

# THE LEARNING ENVIRONMENT AT HOME

Toy and equipment companies today trade on parental concerns about giftedness, advertising "creative" products that "can make children gifted." Buy this or that computer or this or that toy and your child will be gifted. Oh, that it would work that easily!

Special gifts or not, all children need to be able to explore their environment without a constant no, no, no. They need a house that is as safe as it can be and things that they can experiment with. For young children, these can be pots and pans. Older children may be "toying" with ideas.

All children need a home environment that shows a love of learning and respect for achievement; they need lots of language experience, answers to their questions, serious and intelligent talk, explorations into the world, time with friends, and toys and materials to use freely and imaginatively.

Children need a high frequency of contact with adults. They don't need many adults—only a few who particularly value achievement and who can articulate these hopes for children. Children need adults who respond to them with hugs, words, and emotion. These signs need to be as consistent and clear as possible so that children receive clues on how they behave and how they affect others. When they behave well, they need adults to reinforce and praise them.

Children need time to play in the way that scientists play, looking behind the ordinary to figure out for themselves how things work. The unique contribution of the home, when compared with the school, is the capacity to give these children the playing time they need. In school, children usually have to prove themselves anew each day with prescribed tasks. At home, they can think, dream, contemplate, invent . . . in short, do the exercises needed to realize their gifts.

Children need an environment where everything isn't happening all at one time. When the TV is blaring and people are walking in and out, especially in a crowded place, it's hard to focus and concentrate. Children need a sense of stability and mastery over their environment so they can develop reasonable expectations about what is going to happen.

Children need activities suited for their abilities, work that is just a little beyond what they can already do. This isn't easy. It's been called "the problem of the match." The value of having a large repertoire of home activities is that there are more possibilities for making that match.

> Even if you give children everything money can buy, you still can't buy an ideal learning environment. The ingredients required to enrich a child's life aren't found in expensive toys and educational hardware. The recipe is made up instead of the inventiveness and the responsiveness of human beings. Much of it is free, but it takes some time and planning.

## THE ART OF TEACHING

To be a good teacher, patience is essential, but it's not enough. A good teacher needs to be able to work up and down a scale of greater and lesser difficulty. For example, let's say you're reading a book about trucks to your child. With a very young child, first you might ask your child to point to the bigger truck. Then you prompt your child to move to "yes" and "no" responses. The next move is to whole sentence answers and finally to your asking, "Tell me about this truck."

Creativity and intelligence thrive on discussion. Sometimes adults, who need the practice least, do most of the talking, while children sit by passively. This is unfortunate, because it is the interplay of discussion and experience that encourages children to use their minds actively to formulate ideas. Probably the best teaching tip is, "Don't talk too much!"

A good teacher keeps explanations short and backs them up with tangible demonstrations. If you are teaching measurement, actually measure a room. If you are teaching science, let children relive the drama and excitement of discovery.

For example, ask children to stand on a chair, holding a heavy object in one hand and a light one in the other. Now have them drop these objects at the same time. Try different items. In this way, children discover on their own that no matter the weight of the objects, they hit the ground at the same time.

Experiment with Galileo's pendulum discovery. Attach to a tree limb different

When we try to teach children anything from how to count to how to take a bath, we can experience the frustrations of having youngsters, occasionally or often, reject these teaching efforts. Children, in turn, are often frustrated by parents who think teaching is a matter of imposing some learning on them. Children may be "born learners," though they certainly won't display this all the time. Many parents are not "born teachers," but the art can be learned.

lengths of string weighted with small stones or bolts. Let children observe and time the swings.

Follow in Archimedes' footsteps with water displacement experiments. Put a cork and an ice cube in water. The cork floats high and the ice cube (like an iceberg) almost sinks out of sight. Show how a ship stays afloat. Place a bottle cap sideways on the water and then lay it flat. What happens?

Challenge children's incentive. Say jokingly, "I'm going to teach you something so hard you'll never catch on." Then when they do catch on, add to their joy with your own excitement. Try to avoid the pitfalls of too-personal involvement. That's the dangerous "do this for me" attitude.

Children can be equipped for their own discoveries easily and inexpensively—a magnet to lure paper clips, a magnifying glass to look deep into pennies to find those almost-hidden letters. Your goal is to keep the love of learning alive.

Be quick in acknowledging your child's correct answers—and be flexible about what is right. If children are wrong, praise them for trying and encourage them to try again. They need to learn to keep going, despite disappointments and setbacks.

## THE HOME REPORT CARD

Teachers have tests to record children's growth, but parents have what I call the Home Report Card. The value of this report is that it points to a youngster's developing strengths that teachers are not in the position to see. It gives parents greater faith in their children as accomplishers, as people to be watched and encouraged.

Think about the following for each child in your house and what you've seen over the past year:

**New skills learned/Old skills improved.** Don't leave out one, from sewing to swimming, from a preteen learning to baby-sit to a preschooler crossing a street alone.

**Accomplishments.** Some children torture themselves and you by being dissatisfied with their achievements. They need help in accepting what they can do now. Point these out.

**Self-understanding.** What do your children know about themselves that they didn't know last year? Interests? Likes? Dislikes? What do they regard as their strengths and weaknesses? Ask children to come up with specific instances in which they showed themselves capable of handling a problem.

**Relationships with others.** What changes do you see? How do your youngsters get along with you? Are they making friends? Are they keeping them?

**The best thing of the year.** Answers to this one can be very revealing and surprising. Your quick family visit to a woodworking shop might have had more impact than a week at the beach.

**The worst thing.** You get to know your children better and they, you, when you compare answers on this one.

**Ideas for next year.** What would youngsters do differently or the same? If they say they want to go to art classes or take riding lessons, it can mean starting to save now for a future program.

## THE MEGASKILLS REPORT CARD

Appendix A provides a form to help us "see" our children's MegaSkills in action. Choices include Frequently Observed, Sometimes Observed, and Needs Practice. You may want to make copies of this page so that you can fill in the blanks at regular intervals, noting how your children's MegaSkills grow. Ask your children how they would "grade" their own MegaSkills and—if you're really brave—yours too.

## TURNING IDEAS ON, NOT OFF

There's an ad that I keep next to my desk. It shows a light bulb in different panels, from brilliantly lit to completely dark. In the first panel, the words under the bright bulb read, "I have an idea." In the next, with the bulb just a little less light, it says, "A word of caution." Then, as the bulb in each panel shows less and less light, the words read, "A little too radical," "I like it myself, but," "It's just not us," "I wish it were that easy."

In the final panel, with the bulb completely dark, the words read: "Oh, it was just an idea."

The point is graphically and effectively made: turning off an idea is far easier than keeping it lit.

The world is full of wonder. Keeping that wonder alive is the heart of giftedness and of good teaching. It is the nurturer of talent. It is the bedrock and the strength of emotional and intellectual growth and stability . . . and it's available to everyone.

# MegaSkills: Powerful and Surprising

**M**egaSkills are full of secrets, and we will not know all of them. They are the legacy we give our children. They are the report cards our children will give us as parents, even after we are not here to receive them.

## CHAPTER 30

# Secrets of MegaSkills

When I hear myself giving a speech these days, I am usually surprised, surprised and pleased when the words come out quite easily and when I find myself able to use the first words I picked. I used to stutter a lot, and stuttering is not exactly a confidence enhancer. About all I can say for stuttering is that it enlarged my vocabulary. That's because a stutterer has to have a lot of synonyms available for use in case the first or second word that you want to say just won't come out.

It's hard to remember when I began to stutter, but I think it was when I was eleven and my mother became ill. She died when I was thirteen, and there are vestiges of stuttering in my speech even now.

Teachers tried to help me; there was no speech therapist in my school. Teacher help usually consisted of putting me up front on the stage to sink or swim and to get over this thing by reciting a poem or a song before a big audience.

Whether this was right or wrong I am not sure to this day, but it was probably better that teachers expected me to speak, rather than letting me crouch in the corner and shy away from talking.

The benefit of a handicap is that it can force you to call on and build other abilities. In my case, not only did it build my vocabulary, just in case I had to switch words, but, more important, it focused my mind, when I became a teacher, on how problems can be overcome.

For me, this means trying to make opportunities count, especially with children. This takes watchfulness. I am not altogether successful. I try to notice things, but it's not easy. As my own children grew up, I began to "see" less and less.

Other parents tell me it has happened to them, too. Most of us are very good about noticing babies. We pay a lot of attention to their first word, their first sitting and standing. But pretty soon we're not noticing or seeing very much at all. A lot gets lost.

The cemetery scene in the play *Our Town* illustrates this sense of loss poignantly. Emily, the young mother who grows up and gets married, dies when her second child is born. After she is buried and the mourners have gone home, the cemetery on the hill overlooking the town comes to life. Emily talks to the neighbors, relatives, and friends buried with her on the hill. She tells them she wants to go back for just one more look at life. They warn her against it. But she prevails, and she elects to go back to a happy day, her twelfth birthday. Unseen, she stands in her family kitchen. She sees her mother cooking breakfast and calling to her and her brother to get up for school. She calls out to her family, "Look at me." But they can't hear her. She sees how precious life is and how little we see, even in the most loving of homes. Finally she can't stand it anymore, and she asks to be taken back.

## ASKING OURSELVES THE QUESTIONS THAT MATTER

Look at me. Of course, we will never see it all. A camera won't help. It captures one moment in time. What's happening to us and our children is an ongoing, often mysterious process.

The idea is to help us keep seeing our children and ourselves, even as the days go by in a blur of busyness. The questions are not really questions: they are ways of saying, "Look!"

To try to probe into this mystery, I've created a series of thinking questions for parents. They use MegaSkills to start the thoughts flowing. MegaSkills get at very important personal feelings.

**Let's start with the eleven Mega-Skills in this book.** Ask yourself which are the most important to you. Put a check (√) next to the ones you choose.

Confidence        _____
Motivation        _____
Responsibility    _____
Effort            _____
Initiative        _____
Perseverance      _____
Caring            _____
Teamwork          _____
Common Sense      _____
Problem Solving   _____
Focus             _____

You may want to add additional creativity traits, such as:

Curiosity
Independence
Intuition
Courage

Think about why you picked those MegaSkills. Don't worry about whether or not you have them. Not all MegaSkills are equal and equally significant in our lives. Just try to select the ones that, in your judgment, are more important. Then ask, "Why do these matter to me? Do I have an experience or a special memory about any of them?"

**Which MegaSkills do you believe you actually have?** Using the list above, put an X next to those you claim for yourself. Don't be modest; try to be honest. You aren't expected to have them all.

**Which MegaSkills do you believe your child has or is developing?** Use the list above to put an O next to those you see in your child. Be at least as charitable with your child as you are to yourself. Acquiring MegaSkills is a lifetime task. Be sure to remember to tell your children about the MegaSkills you believe they have. Ask your older children if they agree, and if not, why not.

If you were a teacher, you would write report cards. What comments might you make about your children on their report cards?

He is motivated because _____
_____
She shows initiative when _____
_____
He is confident as he _____
_____
Her perseverance shows when _____
_____

Add more ideas of your own.

**Think about what MegaSkills mean for children at different ages.** For example, what does responsibility mean at age three, at age six, at age ten, at age fifteen, at age thirty?

**Which MegaSkills are now taught in your home? How do you teach them?** MegaSkills are all around us, in the texture of daily life and in the small moments that families share together. It's these small moments that can get overlooked. These are the moments that the activities in this book have focused on and that, no matter what has come before, you can focus on today. Nothing is so big that it cannot be taught—in bits and pieces.

## ASK YOURSELF: "DO I . . ."

If answers to the questions that follow are yes, try to give an example of how you do it. If the answer is no, think about what you could do to change the answer to yes.

■ Do I try to set standards and goals for children that are attainable so that chil-

---

### "Emotional Literacy"

Educators report that when MegaSkills are taught in the classroom, fighting between children decreases. It sounds surprising, but it makes sense. When children get practice in talking over problems, in handling conflicts, they don't need to fight, they gain other and better ways to deal with their feelings. And the discipline problems in schools decrease and the self-discipline at home increases.

---

dren have a good chance for success? Do my children know what these are?

■ Do I let my children make as many of their own decisions as possible so that they can learn to live with them and evaluate their own choices?

■ Do I encourage my children to learn responsibility by being counted on to do certain jobs?

■ Do I give my children many and different opportunities to take leadership roles at home?

■ Do I give specific recognition for a job well done and effort put forth?

■ Do I allow my children to express their opinions? Do I listen to what they have to say?

■ Do I try to focus on my children's strengths rather than on their weaknesses?

■ Do I try to hold a realistic vision of my children as individuals?

■ Do I recognize that my children, like all of us, will pass through periods in which they achieve more, periods in which they achieve less? Do I accept this in my children . . . and in myself?

## YOUR CHILD'S FUTURE

In your child's life, which one or two MegaSkills do you think will be the most important? Why? How does the fact that your children will be living their adult lives in the twenty-first century affect your thinking?

■ Have you a vision of what your children will be like as grown-ups? What traits do they have now that you think they will retain as adults? What traits do you think or hope they will develop along the way?

■ Have your children a vision of what they may be like in the future? If so, do they have a sense of what it will take to bring this about? When children dream of themselves in the future as beautiful, rich, successful, and so forth, they need an idea of what it takes to bring this about. How are you helping them gain these understandings?

When someone says, and it's said often, "Don't worry, it won't matter a hundred years from now," I usually say, "Wait, that might be wrong."

> All of us—children, too—need to feel we can accomplish something good and important and necessary, not just for ourselves but for those who came after us. Our children need a vision of their importance—not ego or self-importance, but a strong feeling that they *matter* and that what they do *matters.* Because it does.

While not absolutely everything we do or think today will matter a hundred years from now or even possibly tomorrow, how we see ourselves and conduct ourselves does matter.

## CHAPTER 31

# Critical Resources for the Twenty-first Century— Schoolabilities and Employabilities

When we think of our children, we think of the present, but we think a lot about the future. We think, we plan, we hope. I can hear you saying, "What's this about employabilities? Don't rush it. My child is six years old or eight or ten; why talk about employment and jobs now?"

The reason is that our children must be well prepared for what will be an increasingly competitive marketplace. There is growing concern about this, and it's useless to pretend the concern does not exist. In large part, it's fueling the sale of technology for the home. Advertising is suggesting that if we sit our children in front of a computer and get them on the Internet, our education problems will be solved.

Every parent can know how to prepare children for the future—not by buying the fanciest computer or knowing every change that will happen, but by knowing the basic skills and abilities that children need and can learn.

We talk about employability when children are young not because we want to turn them into little employees. Actually, it's the opposite. Our children ought to be able to be kids, to enjoy childhood. And, as adults, we shouldn't have to spend all of our time worrying about the future.

We think ahead so that we can worry less, so that we know that our children will have what it takes to live and work well in an era of increasing technology and change.

It used to be that employment was considered a narrowing of interests after the broadening that occurs in school. It used to be that we landed one job after graduating, and if it was a good one, we stayed in it

> The job world—the knowledge society, the information revolution—is changing life outside the classroom faster than our schools can keep up. Chances are, this pace will accelerate and schools will have even more difficulty catching up. We can't sit around and wait for the schools, even the best schools, to be able to prepare our children for all the change that is taking place.

doing pretty much the same thing every day for a long time, maybe even until pension time.

Today it's a different story. Our children as adults can be expected to hold a number of jobs. They will need more education and abilities than we did to get those jobs, to keep them, to change them.

Expectations about schooling are higher than ever before. We now understand the importance of education—intensely so, maybe too much so. It has become standard thinking that our children will need advanced education, that virtually everyone will go to some form of college, and that there will be no excuse for not knowing what we need to know.

Preparing our children for the future is not as hard as it may sound. The basic curriculum for the home is not a defined set of subjects. We don't even know all of the subjects our children will need to know.

We help our children prepare for the unknowns of the future by focusing on their talents and strengths and by building on them. In a knowledge society, they will be

> What we know is that children will need a solid set of work values and continuing interest in education . . . and those we can teach. We can teach them MegaSkills. Children need to know the importance of being responsible for their own actions. They need to know how to work hard and at the same time be original in their thinking.

asked to do more decision making. They will be expected to know and to learn. They need rigorous work habits. They must be able to work with others, to face and solve problems—with others *and* on their own.

We prepare for the future by helping our children learn to manage themselves—to have more self-direction and self-discipline, to be thinkers, to see connections, to be creative.

It's clear that this is not just an in-school curriculum. Schools want to do the job that is needed . . . but they need true partnerships with home and community.

## Those Growing Up Words

As we grow older, we get different messages from home, from school, from the workplace. These traditionally move from soft to hard. The world becomes a colder, tougher place. That's why it's so important for children to hear messages that matter.

**From parents to children:** "We love you a lot, but we can't do for you what you have to do on your own. That's not just dressing yourself and eating. It's your study and work habits. When you were little, we did everything for you. As you go off to school, we will work with you, but you have to do more and more for yourself. You can do it. We believe in you."

**From teachers to students:** "You will be tackling new subjects, getting more and more information. You need new and more ways to learn and think. You are expected to work hard and to be responsible and motivated. We can lead you to the water: but you have to do the rest. You won't be coddled. This is a classroom, not your living room."

**From employers to employees:** "We seek employees who will do a good job, of course, but, even when they do a good job, they can't depend on a lifetime of employment with us. Conditions change and change fast. We need employees who can change, who can learn, who are enterprising and ready to move quickly."

## The SCANS List

The U.S. Department of Labor issued a list called SCANS: The Secretary's Commission on Achieving Necessary Skills, which

> The messages may be said in somewhat different words, and with different tones in our speech. They start out warm and loving at home, move to objectivity in school and then to cool and more business-like in the workplace. Basically, what everyone is looking for at home, at school, or the job, and hoping to find in our children and in ourselves is an emerging and growing set of MegaSkills.

identifies a set of specific competencies, qualities, and skills that workers of tomorrow will need. Technology is on the list, but it is only one element, and so are basic skills, the good old three R's. On the other hand, MegaSkills are an integral part of the entire list, and it's important to recognize how many of these employabilities are taught and reinforced at home.

**Resources—Identifies, organizes, plans, and allocates resources.** Able to manage time, budget, materials, space, people
**Interpersonal Skills—Works with others.** Able to work on teams, teach others, work well with people from culturally diverse backgrounds
**Information—Acquires and uses information.** Able to obtain and evaluate data, interpreting and communicating
**Systems—Understands complex interrelationships.** Able to understand social, organizational, and technological systems, monitoring and correcting performance
**Technology—Works with a variety of technologies.** Able to apply technology to specific tasks, maintaining and troubleshooting technologies
**Basic Skills.** Able to use the three R's well, demonstrate strong speaking and listening abilities
**Thinking Skills.** Able to think creatively, make decisions, solve problems, know how to learn
**Personal Qualities.** Able to demonstrate individual responsibility, self-management, integrity

This list provides much more than the usual advice to show up for work on time and work hard—it goes further to identify the characteristics that workers must bring along with them to the job. These are the inside tools, the skills and abilities and attitudes not seen from the outside. They are the treasures we carry inside of us.

Experts looking at the workplace of the future foresee lots of change. Some of it, as we know, is taking place now. There will be fewer managers and fewer layers of management. We see that happening. There will be more specialists and consultants . . . working with much less job security. Each person will be more of an entrepreneur, seeking out jobs, learning how to change from one job to another, and most of all continually learning, in and out of school, throughout life.

It's been said over and over: information is the critical resource of the twenty-first century. We must work to educate our children and make sure that they acquire the tools they need to manage information, to help it grow and to expand. That's why MegaSkills are so important to our children. MegaSkills build the base for their schoolabilities and employabilities.

More and more of our children will be using their own MegaSkills—their initiative and motivation—to create their own work lives.

## PAST AND PRESENT

Lately I have taken to remembering my own childhood, and I have tried to figure out if I have MegaSkills, and if so, which ones, and how I got them.

I remember being on my own a lot to try out things, to choose movies I wanted to see, to bike across the city limits alone into the countryside. I remember being given money to go buy things for dinner, and on one of those shopping trips losing a ten-dollar bill—which compares to losing about sixty dollars today. I was distraught, searching the ground between the store and my house for signs of that money.

But I also remember that my parents, although poor, tried hard not to make me feel any worse. There was no name calling; there were no recriminations. I remember words like, "You tried your best, and these are things that sometimes happen."

What my parents did especially right, I have come to realize, was to provide for me opportunities to acquire a set of MegaSkills. My parents were immigrants. In order to earn a living, they settled in a small town, far away from their friends and relatives. But in this small town, where they were outsiders and so, in many ways, was I, they gave me the freedom to explore, to build courage, interests, and zest for life. They showed confidence in me, they gave me room to roam, to experiment, and to test myself—in those important early school years.

So much has changed in this fast-moving century. Today that small town where I grew up, while no doubt safer than a big city, is not a place where little girls go off on their own to the far reaches of the town. It's a place where doors are locked, where schools are bigger, and where not everyone knows your name.

Things are different. But this does not mean that they're necessarily worse. In fact, in schooling things are actually better. There are more choices to be made, more information readily available, and more opportunities to pursue.

This sounds wonderful. But there is danger. Many children, in the midst of this golden age for learning, show signs of not being prepared to take advantage of their opportunities.

Am I saying that it's harder to acquire MegaSkills these days? My answer, and I've thought about it for a long time, is yes, for many of our kids. More children have to watch where they walk or ride and whom they talk to; they're bombarded on all sides by media messages that are often anti-learning. Everything seems to scream: "Now! Now! Now! More! More! More!"

Dealing with a society so filled with change, with data, and with hype takes a mind that continues to learn and continues to evaluate. Our children must develop this intelligence. They have more to learn than we did if they are going to keep up. And there are more people out there competing with them than ever before.

In my childhood home, my parents, who knew few English words, knew in their bones and made sure I knew that education was the most important thing in my life. It was from this solid foundation that I went off to school.

Today sometimes even this message from parents to kids about the importance of learning can get lost in the midst of all the other messages. In many ways, the activities in this book, which I did not have in my growing up but which I designed for use with my own children at home, for my students in school, and for teachers everywhere, substitute for the ways in which MegaSkills were taught in the past.

## SURPRISES AND SECRETS

Among the most exciting educational research findings of recent years is that human beings have "multiple intelligences," and IQ reflects only part of them. These are secrets just now being uncovered, and they help to explain how "smart" people can be "stupid," and vice versa. The reality is that we are smart in different ways and are smarter in some situations than in others.

It's the same with MegaSkills. You don't need all of them all of the time to do well. A person measuring lower on the MegaSkill scale in confidence, for example, but higher on the initiative scale may have to swallow harder and get sweatier palms but will keep on going nevertheless. MegaSkills are not a matched set. They change with age and even with situations. It's possible to have good judgment (common sense) in one situation and not in another.

MegaSkills are full of surprises. This is one of their secrets that I am still learning.

A MegaSkill can lie quiet inside of you for a long time and emerge when you least expect it. I find myself surprised by strengths I didn't even know I had—like standing up spontaneously to speak at a friend's memorial service and saying things that I didn't have to practice, like being able to reach out in friendship to a rival, like finally learning how to listen quietly instead of talking first when my children are trying to explain something to me.

One thing we can expect for sure in life is surprise. As they grow up, our children won't neatly fit the picture we have of them when they're very young. As parents, we need our own MegaSkills to handle some of these unknowns.

I got a call the other day from a friend who read *MegaSkills* in draft. She wanted me to make sure I said that these activities work even when children are adults.

She had just returned from what might have been an uncomfortable visit with her grown daughter. When she got there, she heard her daughter say that someday she would find the time to fix up her study. My friend said, "I'll help. Let's do it together."

It worked. They went to the lumberyard, they put up shelves, and they painted them. They were busy together, and it was satisfying for both of them. Their true, deep feelings of love for each other were expressed in this activity. They were a team. It was, she said, "a MegaSkills weekend."

When parents and children do something constructive together, a special something happens. If there are tensions, especially as children grow older, they seem to evaporate, or at least they don't get in the way. There's a feeling of cooperation, almost like a runner's high. It may not be chemical, but it's real.

One great thing about MegaSkills is that they grow bigger, not smaller. Experience, both good and bad, is the soil in which they grow. There may be no greater excitement in our lives than to see them develop in ourselves and in our children.

---

**Just the Right Size**

MegaSkills are really big things, but they are also small. MegaSkills are part of the responses our children receive from us and from the environment in which they live. You can't sit a child down one day and say, "I am going to teach you responsibility," or "Today you will learn common sense." These come incrementally, and they grow out of everyday life and activity.

---

## OUR LONGER LEARNING LIVES

Today there is so much to know, so much to do. The maps for our lives don't seem nearly as clear or as defined as they once were. There is a sense of worry about the unknown and the competitive future ahead.

Yet, while the world around us may be confused and confusing, we don't have to be. We know what's important and we have room in our philosophy and practice for integrating the new with the old.

Even when everything seems new, it's not. It's similar to marriage, bringing together the old, the new, the borrowed, the blue. There is plenty of tried and still true, plenty of borrowed to depend on and learn from, and plenty of blue to get over and to spur us on.

And most of us will have more time in which to learn. We are living longer. We can educate ourselves throughout our lives. Chances are, our children will live longer than we will and their children even longer.

I am old enough already, as they say, to know better, but I still think of myself as growing up. And I know I am still growing up because I learn something new every day.

The best remedy for almost anything is a good and a continuing education. We grow up through our education. MegaSkills help us to keep learning. They grow with us and truly are a wondrous strength throughout our lives.

## Appendix A

Seeing Children's MegaSkills in Action

## Appendix B

MegaSkills Measure: A Quiz for Parents

## Appendix C

The MegaSkills Library for Children Plus Resources
and More for Parents

## Appendix D

The Handwriting on the School Wall

## Appendix E

MegaSkills "Recipes," Chapter by Chapter,
by Age Range and Academic Objective

## Acknowledgements

## Index

# Seeing Children's MegaSkills in Action

Here are some ways to help measure children's progress on the Road to Mega-Skills. It is a journey—and the important point is to never give up in school or at home.

Invite your children to work with you. Trade places. Ask them to observe you, too. Make additional copies of this Report Card so that you can continue to observe each other.

## THE MEGASKILLS® REPORT CARD

| MegaSkills | Frequently Observed | Sometimes Observed | Needs Practice |
|---|---|---|---|
| **Confidence**—Takes pride in his/her own achievement. Shows sense of own strengths and areas to be improved; avoids putting down others. | | | |
| **Motivation**—Approaches assignments with positive attitudes. Indicates wanting to know more and do more. | | | |
| **Effort**—Demonstrates readiness and ability to manage time and tasks. Completes homework consistently and carefully. | | | |

Copyright © *MegaSkills* by Dorothy Rich

*continued*

# THE MEGASKILLS® REPORT CARD

| MegaSkills | Frequently Observed | Sometimes Observed | Needs Practice |
|---|---|---|---|
| **Responsibility**—Shows ability to organize self and work. Remembers to bring what is needed and to do what is needed to get jobs done. | | | |
| **Initiative**—Comes up with ideas; assumes leadership roles. Shows understanding of what needs to be done and how to accomplish it. | | | |
| **Perseverance**—Shows ability to stick with an assignment or project to completion. Tolerates frustrations when working through problems. | | | |
| **Caring**—Shows kindness and offers praise to others. Shows consideration, is able to share, and is helpful to others. | | | |
| **Teamwork**—Works cooperatively in groups. Takes feedback and criticism constructively. | | | |
| **Common Sense**—Knows how to work and play safely. Predicts what will happen as a result of personal behaviors and attitudes. | | | |
| **Problem Solving**—Shows ability and eagerness to tackle new situations. Finds innovative and diverse solutions to problems. | | | |
| **Focus**—Shows ability to set personal goals and figure out how to get the work done. Maintains direction, avoiding distraction, to meet goals and complete assignments. | | | |

# MegaSkills Measure: A Quiz for Parents

We grade ourselves hard as parents. I've seldom heard a parent say, "I am a darned good parent." Of course, there is no way we can do everything right. But surely there must be some things we *do right,* even me, even you.

In this MegaSkills Measure, the focus is on parent MegaSkills, not in terms of big qualities such as patience, respect, love, and trust, but more in terms of what I call MegaSkills Moments. These are the small, special moments between parent and child. Keep these in mind as you fill in your answers.

*The point is to catch ourselves being good parents.*

I call this the MegaSkills Parent's Award. We may not be *good* parents all of the time, but we are not *bad* parents all of the time. This "measure" is designed to help us feel more like the good parents we are.

About the scoring: It makes sense that there have to be different scores for parents of different-age children and for parents of children who do or don't go to school. Children under a certain age are probably not

going to be doing certain activities, and there's no way for parents to be involved with the school if their child is not yet in attendance. That's why you see different scoring patterns. The idea is to make this "test" as simple to score as possible. So to get your score, you simply count up the number of checks you have made. When you check *More Than Once* also check *Once.* You get two checks for each *More Than Once* answer.

**Last Week.** Think back over the last week. Ask yourself, "To what extent did I do the following with my child?" It may be that you ate a meal together every day; it may be that you read together at night; it may be that you took walks together. You may have done one of these regularly and another not at all. It's not possible to do everything.

If your child is in the age group **4** through **7,** respond to and score **a** through **p.** Responding to **q** through **u** is optional. If your child is in the age group **8** through **12,** complete the **entire quiz.** Remember, if you check *More Than Once,* also check *Once.*

| Last Week I: | Once | More Than Once |
|---|---|---|
| a. Gave my child a hug. | | |
| b. Took a walk with my child. | | |
| c. Laughed with my child. | | |
| d. Read to my child. | | |
| e. Ate at least one meal a day with my child. | | |
| f. Asked my child what happened during the day. | | |
| g. Did not interrupt when my child was independently involved in study, a project, or game. | | |
| h. Let my child hug me. | | |
| i. Told my child about my day. | | |
| j. Watched a TV program with my child. | | |
| k. Told my child I love him/her. | | |
| l. Talked with my child about his/her friends. | | |
| m. Played a quiet game indoors with my child. | | |
| n. Played active sports outdoors with my child. | | |
| o. Checked/regulated the time my child watches TV. | | |
| p. Praised and encouraged my child. | | |
| q. Talked with my child about homework assignments. | | |
| r. Talked about current news and events. | | |
| s. Did some household chores with my child. | | |
| t. Let my child read to me. | | |
| u. Cooked with my child. | | |
| Other: Here you can add an activity or two that is not on the above list but for which you deserve credit. | | |

## Last Week: Total Number of Checks

ages 4–7  $(a–p) =$ ____ + ____ (other) = ____

ages 8–12  $(a–u) =$ ____ + ____ (other) = ____

**Last Month:** Think back over the last month. Ask yourself, "To what extent did I do the following with and on behalf of my child?"

If your child is in the age group **4** through **7**, respond to and score **a** through **f**. Responding to **g** through **m** is optional. Your score in that section will not count against you. If your child is in the age group **8** through **12**, complete the **entire quiz.** Remember, if you check *More Than Once*, also check *Once*.

| **Last Month I:** | **Once** | **More Than Once** |
|---|---|---|
| a. Encouraged my child to have friends visit our house. | | |
| b. Spent time with my child on a hobby or special project over a period of several days. | | |
| c. Listened to my child explain his/her point of view that was different from mine. | | |
| d. Told my child about my own childhood experiences. | | |
| e. Took my child shopping with me . . . and it went well. | | |
| f. Took my child to a church, library, museum, or zoo. | | |
| g. Attended a play, concert, movie, or other entertainment with my child. | | |
| h. Did something my child persuaded me to do that turned out to be a good idea. | | |
| i. Attended a sports event with my child. | | |
| j. Arranged for my child to go independently on a short trip or errand. | | |
| k. Attended a meeting of a club, church, or youth group (such as Scouts) to which my child belongs. | | |
| l. Talked with my child about the future, possible jobs, and educational plans. | | |
| m. Read and talked with my child about a newspaper or magazine article. | | |
| Other: | | |

*continued*

**Last Month Total Number of Checks**

ages 4–7      (a–f) =_____ + _____ (other) = _____

ages 8–12    (a–m) = _____ + _____ (other) = _____

**School Year:** Think back over this last school year or school term. Ask yourself, "To what extent did I do any of the following with and on behalf of my child?" (If your child does not attend school, do not complete or score this section.)

| During the Last School Year I: | Once | More Than Once |
|---|---|---|
| a. Participated in a conference at school to discuss my child's progress and program. | | |
| b. Attended PTA, Back to School, or a similar meeting at school. | | |
| c. Attended a school play/concert, sports event, or similar function. | | |
| d. Served as a volunteer or chaperone for a school activity. | | |
| e. Talked with a teacher informally and/or socially. | | |
| f. Contacted other parents or a community group on behalf of the school and educational issues. | | |
| Other: | | |

**School Year Total Number of Checks = _____**

**The Count Up:** Now you are ready to give yourself your MegaSkills Parent's Award grade. Parents of 8- to 12-year-olds have the possibility of **80+** checks. Parents of 4- to 7-year-olds have the possibility of **56+** checks, **44+** checks if the child is not in school. The plus points are dependent on your contributions to the *Other* activity line.

**Give yourself a grade of A+ if:**
>  for ages 4–7 but not in school you score
>    42–44
>  for ages 4–7 you score 53–56
>  for ages 8–12 you score 77–80

Congratulations! Congratulations! Are you really this good? If so, you have my admiration and the gratitude (one would hope) of your children.

**Give yourself a grade of A if:**
>  for ages 4–7 but not in school you score
>    39–41
>  for ages 4–7 you score 50–52
>  for ages 8–12 you score 72–76

You are terrific. You are doing a lot and doing it well!

**Give yourself a grade of B if:**
>  for ages 4–7 but not in school you score
>    35–38
>  for ages 4–7 you score 45–49
>  for ages 8–12 you score 64–71

You sound honest and know you have to keep working.

**Give yourself a grade of C if:**
>  for ages 4–7 but not in school you score
>    31–34
>  for ages 4–7 you score 39–44
>  for ages 8–12 you score 52–63

You are probably too hard on yourself, but if what you are saying is true, you would do well to spend some time getting your act together.

**Give yourself a grade of I for Incomplete if you score below a C.** Come on, go back and try to get a few more points.

## KEEP IN MIND . . .

The point of this quiz is to recognize and reward yourself for all that you are doing right. Every family has its own way of doing things right. Keep adding to the *Other* line and keep filling in activities as you move through the year. This quiz is suggestive; it points to examples, to directions. This is not a static test, not a fixed score; it's ever changing. The idea is to keep figuring out more things you do right and to reward yourself for them.

You may want to go over this quiz with your children, asking them what they think about your answers. Perhaps they will be harder on you, or perhaps they will think you've shortchanged yourself. It's bound to be a fascinating and useful conversation.

APPENDIX C

# The MegaSkills Library for Children Plus Resources and More for Adults

Children's books abound in MegaSkills, but you have to know where to look to find them.

To provide this help, Maria Salvadore, Coordinator of Children's Services of the District of Columbia Public Library, and Pamela F. Stovall, Children's Service Librarian, have compiled the following list to illustrate each of the MegaSkills, with additional titles on competition. This list builds on and updates the titles of the earlier *MegaSkills*.

In this list are age-old classics and books published within the last few years. The variety of books available for children today can be overwhelming. Thousands of children's books are published annually. This brief list is only a starting point. Recommended ages are approximate. It is fine to read books that appear to be for younger or older readers. Because this compilation is necessarily brief, a list of adult books is included at the end so that parents can find out more about children's books and ways to share them.

Read books together. Listen to your child read; let your child listen to you. Talk about the books; enjoy them; let them become part of your lives. Let the power of literature reinforce and extend your children's MegaSkills, building their imagination and their love of reading.

Completing this bibliography is a new section for adults on *Resources and More for Adults: Keeping Up Without Giving Up*. It's an odyssey into the ever-growing number of adult resources on parenting and education issues . . . and what it takes to become a more knowledgeable parent today.

## CONFIDENCE

Brown, Marc. *Arthur Meets the President.* Boston: Joy Street Books, 1991. Ages 4–8.

Brown, Margaret Wise. *Runaway Bunny.* Ill. Clement Hurd. New York: Harper, 1942. Ages 3–5.

Christopher, Matt. *Jinx Glove.* Boston: Little, Brown, 1974. Ages 8–10.

Cleary, Beverly. *Strider.* New York: Morrow, 1991. Ages 8–11.

Freschet, Bernice. *Furlie Cat.* Ill. Betsy Lewin. New York: Lothrop, Lee & Shepard, 1986. Ages 4–6.

Hoban, Russell. *Bedtime for Francis.* Ill. Garth Williams. New York: Harper & Row, 1960. Ages 5–7.

Howe, James. *I Wish I Were a Butterfly.* Ill. Ed Young. San Diego: Harcourt Brace Jovanovich, 1987. Ages 5–8.

Kraus, Robert. *Leo the Late Bloomer.* Ill. Jose Aruego. New York: Thomas Y. Crowell, 1971. Ages 4–7.

Kurtz, Jane. *Pulling the Tiger's Tail.* Ill. Floyd Cooper. New York: Simon & Schuster, 1995. Ages 5–8.

Lester, Helen. *Tacky the Penguin.* Ill. Lynn Munsiger. Boston: Houghton Mifflin, 1988. Ages 4–8.

Lipstye, Robert. *The Contender.* New York: Harper & Row, 1967. Ages 12+.

Little, Lessie, and Eloise Greenfield. *I Can Do It By Myself.* Ill. Carole Byard. New York: Thomas Y. Crowell, 1978. Ages 5–7.

Mathis, Sharon Bell. *Red Dog Blue Fly.* New York: Viking, 1991. Ages 6–10.

Rathmann, Peggy. *Officer Buckle and Gloria.* New York: Putnam, 1995. Ages 5–9.

Steptoe, John. *Mufaro's Beautiful Daughters.* New York: Lothrop, Lee & Shepard, 1987. Ages 6–10.

Taylor, Mildred. *Roll of Thunder, Hear My Cry.* Ill. Jerry Pinkney. New York: Dial Books, 1976. Ages 10+.

Ure, Jean. *Supermouse.* Ill. Ellen Eagle. New York: William Morrow, 1984. Ages 8–11.

Waddell, Martin. *The Tough Princess.* Ill. Patrick Benson. New York: Philomel Books, 1987. Ages 4–7.

Weiss, Nicki. *Battle Day at Camp Belmont.* New York: Greenwillow Books, 1985. Ages 4–7.

Wells, Rosemary. *Benjamin and Tulip.* New York: Dial Books, 1973. Ages 5–7.

## MOTIVATION

Andersen, Hans Christian. *The Swineherd.* Ill. Lisbeth Zwerger. New York: William Morrow, 1982. Ages 6–9.

Carle, Eric. *Very Quiet Cricket.* New York: Philomel Books, 1990. Ages 3–7.

Carrick, Carol. *The Foundling.* Ill. Donald Carrick. New York: Clarion Books, 1977. Ages 6–8.

Choi, Sook Nyul. *Year of Impossible Goodbyes.* Boston: Houghton Mifflin, 1991. Ages 9–12.

Cohen, Miriam. *When Will I Read?* Ill. Lillian Hoban. New York: Greenwillow Books, 1977. Ages 4–6.

DePaola, Tomie. *Charlie Needs a Cloak.* New York: Prentice Hall, 1974. Ages 7–10.

DePaola, Tomie. *Now One Foot, Now the Other.* New York: Putnam Publishing Group, 1981. Ages 5–7.

Holman, Felice. *Slake's Limbo.* New York: Macmillan, 1974. Ages 9–11.

Hurwitz, Johanna. *Aldo Applesauce.* Ill. John Wallner. New York: William Morrow, 1979. Ages 8–11.

Hutchins, Pat. *The Tale of Thomas Mead.* New York: Greenwillow Books, 1980. Ages 6–9.

Leaf, Munro. *Story of Ferdinand.* Ill. Robert Lawson. New York: Viking, 1936. Ages 6–8.

Schotter, Roni. *Dreamland.* Ill. Kevin Hawkes. New York: Orchard, 1996. Ages 6–9.

Wantanabe, Shiglo. *How Do I Put It On?* New York: Philomel Books, 1984. Ages 3–6.

Zemach, Margot. *To Hilda for Helping.* New York: Farrar, Straus & Giroux, 1977. Ages 5–8.

## COMPETITION

Carlson, Nancy. *Loudmouth George and the Big Race.* Minneapolis: Carolrhoda Books, 1983. Ages 4–6.

Cresswell, Helen. *Ordinary Jack.* New York: Macmillan, 1977. Ages 9–12.

Flournoy, Valerie, & Vanessa Flournoy. *Celie and the Harvest Fiddler.* New York: Tambourine, 1995. Ages 6–11.

Gilson, Jamie. *Can't Catch Me, I'm the Gingerbread Man.* New York: Lothrop, Lee & Shepard, 1981. Ages 8+.

Ginsburg, Mirra. *Two Greedy Bears.* Ill. Jose Aruego and Ariane Dewey. New York: Macmillan, 1976. Ages 5–7.

*The Hare and the Tortoise: A Fable by Aesop.* Retold and illustrated by Gerald Rose. New York: Macmillan, 1988. Ages 5–8.

Heine, Helme. *The Most Wonderful Egg in the World.* New York: Macmillan, 1983. Ages 4–7.

Hiser, Constance. *Sixth Grade Star.* New York: Holiday House, 1992. Ages 10–12.

Jones, Diana W. *Charmed Life.* New York: Greenwillow Books, 1978. Ages 9–12.

Lindgren, Astrid. *Ronia, the Robber's Daughter.* New York: Viking, 1983. Ages 8–11.

Myers, Walter Dean. *Slam!* New York: Scholastic, 1996. Ages 12–14.

Peck, Robert Newton. *Soup's Hoop.* New York: Delacorte Press, 1990. Ages 10–12.

Rathmann, Peggy. *Ruby the Copycat.* New York: Scholastic, 1991. Ages 4–8.

## EFFORT

Ancona, George. *Helping Out.* New York: Clarion Books, 1985. Ages 5–7.

———. *Piñata Maker/El Piñatero.* San Diego: Harcourt Brace, 1994. Ages 8–11.

Brenner, Barbara. *On the Frontier with Mr. Audubon.* New York: Putnum Publishing Group, 1977. Ages 9–12.

Carle, Eric. *Very Busy Spider.* New York: Philomel Books, 1984. Ages 3–7.

Friedman, Ina R. *How My Parents Learned to Eat.* Ill. Allen Say. Boston: Houghton Mifflin, 1984. Ages 4–7.

*The Lion and the Mouse: An Aesop Fable.* Ill. Ed Young. New York: Doubleday, 1979. Ages 4–7.

Morris, Judy. *Nightwalkers.* New York: HarperCollins, 1996. Ages 9–12.

Myers, Walter Dean. *How Mr. Monkey Saw the World.* Ill. Synthia Saint James. New York: Doubleday Books for Young Readers, 1996. Ages 6–9.

Rand, Gloria. *Prince William.* Ill. Ted Rand. New York: Holt, 1992. Ages 5–8.

Say, Allen. *El Chino.* Boston: Houghton Mifflin, 1991. Ages 6–9.

Speare, Elizabeth George. *The Sign of the Beaver.* Boston: Houghton Mifflin, 1983. Ages 8–11.

Sperry, Armstrong. *Call It Courage.* New York: Macmillan, 1940. Ages 8–11.

Voight, Cynthia. *Homecoming.* New York: Atheneum, 1981. Ages 11–14.

Yep, Laurence. *Dragonwings.* New York: Harper & Row, 1975. Ages 9–11.

## RESPONSIBILITY

Aardema, Verna. *Why Mosquitoes Buzz in People's Ears: A West African Tale.* Ill. Leo and Diane Dillon. New York: Dial Books, 1975. Ages 6–8.

Bauer, Marion D. *On My Honor.* New York: Clarion Books, 1986. Ages 9–12.

Byars, Betsy. *The Summer of the Swans.* New York: Viking, 1970. Ages 9–11.

Dalgliesh, Alice. *The Courage of Sarah Noble.* Ill. Leonard Weisgard. New York: Charles Scribner's Sons, 1954. Ages 8–10.

George, Jean. *The Cry of the Crow.* New York: Harper & Row, 1980. Ages 9–11.

Green, Norma. *The Hole in the Dike.* Ill. Eric Carle. New York: Harper & Row, 1975. Ages 5–10.

Greenfield, Eloise. *Night on Neighborhood Street.* Ill. Jan Spivey Gilcrist. New York: Dial Books, 1991. Ages 6–11.

Hurwitz, Johanna. *Aldo Ice Cream.* Ill. John Wallner. New York: William Morrow, 1981. Ages 8–11.

King-Smith, Dick. *Pigs Might Fly.* Ill. Mary Rayner. New York: Viking, 1982. Ages 8–11.

Monjo, F. N. *The Drinking Gourd.* Ill. Fred Brenner. New York: Harper & Row, 1969. Ages 6–9.

Naylor, Phyllis Reynolds. *Shiloh.* New York: Atheneum, 1991. Ages 8–12.

Tolan, Stephanie. *The Great Skinner Strike.* New York: Macmillan, 1983. Ages 9–11.

Wells, Rosemary. *Lassie Come Home.* Ill. Susan Jefiers. New York: Henry Holt, 1995. Ages 8–12.

Williams, Barbara. *Jeremy Isn't Hungry.* Ill. Martha Alexander. New York: E. P. Dutton, 1978. Ages 5–7.

Zion, Gene. *The Plant Sitter.* Ill. Margaret Bloy Graham. New York: Harper & Row, 1959. Ages 4–7.

## INITIATIVE

Barton, Byron. *I Want to Be an Astronaut.* New York: Thomas Y. Crowell, 1988. Ages 3–6.

Brenner, Barbara. *Wagon Wheels.* Ill. Don Bolognese. New York: Harper & Row, 1978. Ages 6–8.

Brink, Carol R. *Caddie Woodlawn.* New York: Macmillan, 1935. Ages 9+.

Dalgliesh, Alice. *Bears on Hemlock Mountain.* Ill. Helen Sewell. New York: Charles Scribner's Sons, 1952. Ages 8–11.

Hamilton, Virginia. *Planet of Junior Brown.* New York: Macmillan, 1971. Ages 9–11.

Hayes, Sarah. *Eat Up, Gemma.* Ill. Jan Ormerod. New York: Lothrop, Lee & Shepard, 1988. Ages 5–8.

McKissack, Patricia. *Flossie and the Fox.* Ill. Rachel Isadora. New York: Dial Books, 1986. Ages 4–7.

Merrill, Jean. *The Toothpaste Millionaire.* Ill. Jan Palmer. Boston: Houghton Mifflin, 1974. Ages 8–11.

Myers, Walter Dean. *The Young Landlords.* New York: Viking, 1979. Ages 9–12.

Seeger, Pete. *Abiyoyo.* Ill. Michael Hays. New York: Macmillan, 1986. Ages 5–10.

Uchida, Yoshiko. *Sumi's Prize.* Ill. Kazue Mizumura. New York: Charles Scribner's Sons, 1964. Ages 4–7.

Williams, Karen. *Galimoto.* Ill. Catherine Stock. New York: Lothrop, Lee & Shepard, 1990. Ages 5–10.

## PERSEVERANCE

Aliki. *A Weed Is a Flower: The Life of George Washington Carver.* Englewood Cliffs, N.J.: Prentice Hall, 1965. Ages 6–8.

Bang, Molly. *Wiley and the Hairy Man.* New York: Macmillan, 1976. Ages 6–8.

Bartone, Elisa. *Peppe the Lamplighter.* Ill. Ted Lewin. New York: Lothrop, Lee & Shepard, 1993. Ages 6–10.

Blades, Ann. *Mary of Mile 18.* Plattsburgh, N.Y.: Tundra Books, 1971, 1991. Ages 6–8.

Boutis, Victoria. *Katy Did It.* Ill. Gail Owens. New York: Greenwillow Books, 1982. Ages 4–6.

Burton, Virginia Lee. *Mike Mulligan and His Steam Shovel.* Boston: Houghton Mifflin, 1939. Ages 5–7.

Cleary, Beverly. *Ramona and Her Father.* Ill. Alan Tiegreen. New York: William Morrow, 1977. Ages 8–11.

Cleaver, Vera, and Bill Cleaver. *Where the Lilies Bloom.* Philadelphia: J. B. Lippincott, 1969. Ages 10–12.

George, Jean Craighead. *Julie of the Wolves.* New York: Harper & Row, 1972. Ages 9–11.

Graham, Thomas. *Mr. Bear's Chair.* New York: E. P. Dutton, 1987. Ages 4–7.

Hoffman, Mary. *Amazing Grace.* New York: Dial Books, 1991. Ages 5–8.

Keats, Ezra Jack. *John Henry: An American Legend.* Ed. Anne Schwartz. New York: Alfred A. Knopf, 1965. Ages 6–8.

O'Dell, Scott. *Island of the Blue Dolphins.* Boston: Houghton Mifflin, 1960. Ages 9–12.

Parks, Rosa, with Jim Haskins. *Rosa Parks: My Story.* New York: Dial, 1992. Ages 12–14.

Paterson, Katherine. *Jip: His Story.* New York: Lodestar, 1996. Ages 10–13.

Schroeder, Alan. *Minty: A Story of Young Harriet Tubman.* Ill. Jerry Pinkney. New York: Dial, 1996. Ages 6–11.

Scieszka, Jon. *Math Curse.* Ill. Lane Smith. New York: Viking, 1995. Ages 8–12.

Van de Wetering, Janwillem. *Hugh Pine.* Ill. Lynn Munsinger. Boston: Houghton Mifflin, 1980. Ages 8–10.

Wilder, Laura Ingalls. *Little House in the Big Woods.* Ill. Garth Williams. New York: Harper & Row, 1953. Ages 8–12. (Also recommended are the other volumes in the Little House series.)

# CARING

Ackerman, Karen. *Song and Dance Man.* Ill. Steven Gammel. New York: Alfred A. Knopf, 1988. Ages 5–8.

Aliki. *Best Friends Together Again.* New York: Greenwillow, 1995. Ages 5–9.

Asch, Frank. *Moon Bear.* New York: Charles Scribner's Sons, 1978. Ages 4–6.

Bang, Molly. *Ten, Nine, Eight.* New York: Greenwillow Books, 1983. Ages 3–6.

Brenner, Barbara, and Julia Takaya. *Chibi: A True Story from Japan.* Ill. June Otani. New York: Clarion, 1996. Ages 8–11.

Chinn, Karen. *Sam and the Lucky Monkey.* Ill. Cornelius Van Wright and Ying-Hwa Hu. New York: Lee & Low, 1995. Ages 6–10.

Clifton, Lucille. *My Friend Jacob.* Ill. Thomas Digrazra. New York: Dutton, 1980. Ages 5–9.

Greenfield, Eloise. *First Pink Light.* New York: Thomas Y. Crowell, 1976. Ages 5–7.

Griffith, Helen. *Granddaddy's Place.* Ill. James Stevenson. New York: Greenwillow, 1987. Ages 5–9.

MacLachlan, Patricia. *Sarah, Plain and Tall.* New York: Harper & Row, 1985. Ages 9+.

Mathis, Sharon Bell. *The Hundred Penny Box.* New York: Viking, 1975. Ages 5–7.

Oxenbury, Helen. *Mother's Helper.* New York: Dial Books, 1982. Ages 4–6.

Paterson, Katherine. *Bridge to Terabithia.* New York: Thomas Y. Crowell, 1977. Ages 8–11.

Porte, Barbara. *Harry's Mom.* Ill. Yossi Abolafia. New York: Greenwillow Books, 1985. Ages 5–8.

di Salvo-Ryan, Dyanne. *Uncle Willie and the Soup Kitchen.* New York: Morrow, 1991. Ages 5–8.

Wells, Rosemary. *Hazel's Amazing Mother.* New York: Dial Books, 1985. Ages 5–7.

White, E. B. *Charlotte's Web.* Ill. Garth Williams. New York: Harper & Row, 1952. Ages 7+.

# TEAMWORK

Burningham, John. *Mr. Gumpy's Motor Car.* New York: Thomas Y. Crowell, 1976. Ages 4–6.

Byars, Betsy. *The Not-Just-Anybody Family.* Ill. Jacqueline Rogers. New York: Delacorte Press, 1986. Ages 8–11.

Coles, William. *Another Kind of Monday.* New York: Atheneum, 1996. Ages 11–13.

DeJong, Meindert. *Wheel on the School.* Ill. Maurice Sendak. New York: Harper & Row, 1954. Ages 9–12.

Domanska, Janina. *The Turnip.* New York: Macmillan, 1969. Ages 4–7.

Ernst, Lisa Campbell. *Squirrel Park.* New York: Bradbury, 1993. Ages 4–8.

Fox, Mem. *Shoes from Grandpa.* Ill. Patricia Mullins. New York: Orchard Books, 1990. Ages 4–7.

Ginsburg, Mirra. *Mushrooms in the Rain.* New York: Macmillan, 1974. Ages 4–6.

Grimm, Jacob. *The Bremen Town Musicians.* Ill. Janina Domanska. New York: Greenwillow Books, 1980. Ages 5–8.

Hoban, Lillian. *Arthur's Funny Money.* New York: Harper & Row, 1981. Ages 5–7.

Lobel, Arnold. *Frog and Toad Are Friends.* New York: Harper & Row, 1970. Ages 6–8.

Mills, Lauren. *The Rag Coat.* Boston: Little, Brown, 1991. Ages 4–7.

Roy, Ronald. *A Thousand Pails of Water.* Ill. Vo-Dinh Mai. New York: Alfred A. Knopf, 1978. Ages 5–7.

## COMMON SENSE

Aardema, Verna. *Traveling to Tondo.* Ill. Will Hillenbrand. New York: Knopf, 1991. Ages 5–9.

Andersen, Hans Christian. *The Woman with the Eggs.* Ill. Ray Cruz. New York: Crown Publishers, 1974. Ages 5–7.

Asch, Frank. *Turtle Tale.* New York: Dial Books, 1980. Ages 4–6.

Byars, Betsy. *The Eighteenth Emergency.* New York: Viking, 1973. Ages 8–11.

Cresswell, Helen. *Absolute Zero.* New York: Macmillan, 1978. Ages 9–11.

Duvoisin, Roger. *Petunia.* New York: Alfred A. Knopf, 1950. Ages 5–7.

Enright, Elizabeth. *The Saturdays.* New York: Dell Books, 1987. Ages 8–11.

Gag, Wanda. *Gone Is Gone.* New York: Putnam Publishing Group, 1960. Ages 6–8.

Hale, Lucretia. *The Peterkin Papers.* Boston: Houghton Mifflin, 1966. Ages 9+.

LaFontaine, Jean de. *Miller, the Boy and the Donkey.* Ill. Brian Wildsmith. New York: Franklin Watts, 1969. Ages 5–8.

*Little Red Hen.* Ill. Paul Galdone. New York: Seabury, 1973. Ages 3–7.

*Old Woman & Her Pig and Ten Other Stories.* Retold and illustrated by Anne Rockwell. New York: Crowell, 1979. Ages 4–9.

Parish, Peggy. *Amelia Bedelia's Family Album.* Ill. Lynn Sweat. Greenwillow, 1988. Ages 6–9.

Smith, Robert Kimmel. *Jelly Belly.* New York: Delacorte Press, 1981. Ages 9–12.

Waber, Bernard. *A Lion Named Shirley Williamson.* Boston: Houghton Mifflin, 1996. Ages 4–8.

Zemach, Margot. *It Could Always Be Worse.* New York: Farrar, Straus & Giroux, 1977. Ages 5–7.

## PROBLEM SOLVING

Armstrong, Jennifer. *Hugh Can Do.* Ill. Kimberly Bukken Post. New York: Crown, 1992. Ages 5–10.

Atwater, Richard T. *Mr. Popper's Penguins.* Ill. Robert Lawson. Boston: Little, Brown, 1938. Ages 8–11.

Blegvad, Lenore Hochman, and Erik Blegvad. *The Great Hamster Hunt.* San Diego: Harcourt Brace Jovanovich, 1969. Ages 5–7.

Brown, Margaret Wise. *Once Upon a Time in a Pigpen.* Ill. Ann Strugnell. New York: Harper & Row, 1980. Ages 4–6.

DePaola, Tomie. *Fin m'Coul: The Giant of Knockmany Hill.* New York: Holiday House, 1981. Ages 5–7.

French, Fiona. *Anancy and Mr. Dry Bone.* Boston: Little, Brown, 1991. Ages 5–8.

Greenfield, Eloise. *Grandpa's Face.* Ill. Floyd Cooper. New York: Philomel Books, 1988. Ages 5–8.

Hoban, Russell. *A Bargain for Frances.* Ill. Lillian Hoban. New York: Harper & Row, 1970. Ages 5–7.

Hong, Lily Toy. *Two of Everything.* Morton Grove, Ill: Albert Whitman, 1993. Ages 4–8.

Naidoo, Beverly. *Journey to Jo'burg: A South African Story.* Ill. Eric Velasquez. New York: J. B. Lippincott, 1985. Ages 9–11.

O'Brien, Robert. *Mrs. Frisby and the Rats of NIMH.* Ill. Zena Bernstein. New York: Atheneum, 1971. Ages 9–12.

Soto, Gary. *Too Many Tamales.* Ill. Ed Martinez. New York: Putnam, 1993. Ages 6–10.

Steig, William. *Abel's Island.* Farrar, Straus & Giroux, 1976. Ages 9–11.

## FOCUS

Curtis, Christopher Paul. *The Watsons Go to Birmingham—1963: A Novel.* New York: Delacorte Press, 1995. Ages 11–13.

Lester, Helen. *Author: A True Story.* Boston: Houghton Mifflin, 1997.

McCloskey, Robert. *Make Way for Ducklings.* New York: Viking, 1941. Ages 4–8.

McCully, Emily Arnold. *Mirette on the High Wire.* New York: G. P. Putnam, 1992. Ages 5–9.

Mills, Claudia. *Dinah for President.* New York: Macmillan, 1992. Ages 5–9.

Say, Allen. *Emma's Rug.* Boston: Houghton Mifflin, 1996. Ages 6–9.

———. *Ink-Keeper's Apprentice.* New York: HarperCollins, 1979. Ages 12–14.

Schur, Maxine Rose. *When I Left My Village.* New York: Dial, 1996. Ages 8–12.

Sisulu, Elinor. *The Day Gogo Went to Vote.* Boston: Little, Brown, 1996. Ages 5–9.

Soto, Gary. *Off and Running.* New York: Delacorte, 1996. Ages 8–12.

## RECOMMENDED ADULT BOOKS ABOUT READING

Butler, Dorothy, and Mary Clay. *Reading Begins at Home.* Portsmouth, N.H.: Heinemann Educational Books, 1982.

Dreyer, Sharon. *The Bookfinder.* 3 vols. Circle Pines, Minn.: American Guidance Service, 1977, 1981, 1985.

Hearne, Betsy. *Choosing Books for Children.* New York: Delacorte Press, 1981; rev. 1990.

Kimmel, Margaret Mary, and Elizabeth Segal. *For Reading Out Loud.* New York: Delacorte Press, 1983; rev. 1988.

Larrick, Nancy. *A Parent's Guide to Children's Reading.* New York: Bantam Books, 1982.

Lima, Carolyn. *A to Zoo: Subject Access to Children's Picture Books.* New York: R. R. Bowker, 1993.

Trelease, Jim. *The New Read-Aloud Handbook.* New York: Viking, 1995.

Visit your library or bookstore for additional materials relating to these areas. Lists of Notable Children's Books, Newbery Medal Books, and Caldecott Medal Books are available from the American Library Association.

## RESOURCES AND MORE FOR ADULTS

### Keeping Up Without Giving Up

As a reader of *MegaSkills*, you are interested in knowing more about how to help your children become stronger learners and be more prepared for the age of the information, technology, and change. This includes learning about the wider education trends today as well as about helping our children. There's a mountain of information available! There is no way to be truly up to date and complete, and this is both the beauty and frustration of the information revolution.

There's an old story that Einstein reported that he did not memorize bits of knowledge—instead he wanted to know where to get the information he needed. Einstein, or whoever reported this, was on the right track then, and it's even more important now.

Each of us needs our own information-gathering process. The one I find helpful is a "linking and webbing" process. It's a strategy that enables me to keep up without giving up. I try to link from one resource to another—from books, newspapers, magazines, to information telephone lines, to people who know more than I do, to local and national organizations collecting material on the subject, to Web pages and then from one Web page to another, and then to whatever other technology I can get my hands on. Then I try to web, synthesize, and network the data. It's not like going straight to the old encyclopedia on the bookcase.

There are so many entry gates to information available today that it's hard to know where to start. It's also hard to know when we are getting reliable information. This will be a continuing problem until there are some "seals of approval" for Web pages. In the meantime, we stick with what we know best.

Generally, we each tend to start with the sources we are most comfortable with. For me, it's print and books; that's where I start. Others may go straight to the Internet.

### Getting Started

In the area of books, the following authors (whose books are in the stores) provide sound advice and strong linkages to other materials:

Thomas Armstrong, Berry Brazelton, M.D., James Comer, Linda and Richard Eyre, Ellen Galinsky, Daniel Goleman, Jane Healy, Marguerite Kelly, and Martin Seligmann. On the subject of the new technology and the family, see the work of Seymour Papert and Robin Raskin.

In the area of telephone information, call 1-800-USA LEARN, sponsored by the U.S. Department of Education. Here you can find a wealth of free information, including my own contribution of Summer Home Learning "Recipes." Also, there are materials on current educational interests such as education goals, standards, and learning compacts.

In the area of organizations, among many others, contact the American Library Association (Association of Library Services to Children), Aspira Association, Children's Defense Fund, International Reading Association, National Association for the Education of Young Children, National Association of Elementary School Principals, National Black Child Development Institute, National Education Association, National PTA, Phi Delta Kappa, and the National Alliance of Business. Most of these organizations have 800 numbers and Web pages. (For a more complete listing of organizational resources, send a stamped self-addressed envelope to the Home and School Institute, MegaSkills Education Center, 1500 Massachusetts Ave. NW, Washington, D.C. 20005.)

In the area of Internet Web pages, there are thick directories and they get thicker daily. Start by checking a search engine such as YAHOO and search for "education" and for "parenting." You will find solid information on a number of Web sites, such as the Family Education Network (www.familyeducation.com). This network has been identified as an especially outstanding source for families. Scholastic (www.Scholastic.com) has been identified as a super resource for teachers. Each of these Web sites has links to more sites. Also, check www.parentsoup.com, www.ed.gov (the U.S. Department of Education), www.nea.org (the National Education Association) and www.MegaSkills-HSI.org (the Home and School Institute). Clicking from one site to the next, you build and bookmark your own list of favorite sites.

This gathering of information is like a set of links or a web that is spiraling, making connections, and moving upward. It provides an ever-widening circle of support for us, for our families, and for our schools.

In a real sense, we are each making up our own bibliographies, gathering data and resources, as we go. We have to use our own judgment about where to start, and, yes, when to stop. It's a new frontier to be sure and a truly exciting opportunity to educate ourselves as we educate our children.

# The Handwriting on the School Wall

This is not a traditional bibliography. Yes, you will find "Research Notes" at the end of this appendix; they provide additional sources of data supporting the family's role in education. But there is more.

Research on parent involvement represents milestones in my own thinking. Because of this, I want to tell you a bit about the educational journey that has formed my belief about the roles of the home and the school today.

It's hard to believe now, but in the 1960s, when I started thinking about the work of parents as educators, the subject was considered almost radical, dangerous. Those were the days when people really believed that the school could do it all in education.

We know better today, not because schools are worse but because research and experience have shown that while schools are important, they are limited in what they can accomplish alone.

When I first began teaching as a senior high school English teacher in 1957, I saw students who, it seemed to me, had no good reason for having trouble in school. So I asked my colleagues about them. The answer I got was that their junior high teach-

ers hadn't done their job. The junior high teachers pointed to the elementary school.

When I went to elementary school teachers, I heard for the first time the word "family." It was the family's fault, I was told, for sending their children unprepared, unreceptive, unable to take advantage of what the school could do.

The light was beginning to dawn. Something really was happening before children came through the school doors in the morning and after the doors closed behind them in the afternoon.

In the mid-1960s, research started to appear that pointed inescapably to the educational impact of the family. These studies, combined with my own experience, began to shape my thinking and have provided the base for the MegaSkills program.

Every time a new study appeared, my pulse quickened. As a teacher, my first thoughts were about how to take advantage of what was being learned, how to empower families to put the research into action.

In 1964, Professor Benjamin Bloom of the University of Chicago demonstrated in his book *Stability and Change in Human Characteristics* that many differences in children's academic development can be traced to the value placed on education at home and specifically to parental reinforcement at home of children's activities in school.

In 1966 came another significant study, *Equality of Educational Opportunity* (U.S. Office of Education), often called *The Coleman Report*. This study again underscored the importance of the family and the home in determining children's academic achievement.

A small but significant group of early childhood projects was begun around 1968 with youngsters in their preschool years in order to prevent school problems later on. In general, it was found that the earliest projects, which tutored children only and did not involve parents, produced immediate test score gains, but these gains were lost in subsequent schooling years. Children in later projects, which involved parents actively, held their gains after the tutoring programs themselves were over. (Professor Urie Bronfenbrenner of Cornell summarized these in *Is Early Intervention Effective? A Report on Longitudinal Evaluation of Preschool Programs*, Vol. 2 [Washington, D.C.: U.S. Office of Health, Education, and Welfare, 1974].)

As a result of these and other studies, confidence in the school's ability to do it all alone diminished. Emphasis began to shift to identifying the out-of-school factors that were influential in education.

I officially launched the Home and School Institute in 1972. I was building on the parent programs I started in the 1960s called "Success for Children Begins at Home." These were evening sessions for parents. We covered such subjects as how to reinforce the three R's at home, how to build children's creativity, and how to do it all with limited time and resources. I brought to these sessions the first home learning recipes, which parents tried out at home each week.

Major studies from Stanford in the mid-1970s helped confirm my faith in the strategic role of parents as teachers. (See, for example, Barbara Goodson and Robert Hess, *Parents as Teachers of Young Children: An Evaluative Review of Some Contemporary Concepts and Programs* [Palo Alto: Stanford University, 1975].) The studies looked at the key models of parent involvement in compensatory education programs that evolved in the 1960s. The evidence supported the model in which parents worked with their children at home, sustaining the work of the school.

The evidence continued to mount, but attention was still not being paid. In my doctoral dissertation I decided to put my home learning recipe approach to a test. (*The Relationship of the Home Learning Lab Technique to First Grade Student Achievement* [Washington, D.C.: Catholic University of America, 1976].) A group of teachers working with me designed eight home learning recipes for use in first grades in the Washington, D.C., area. After using them over an eight-week period, the first graders in the treatment group scored significantly higher on standardized reading tests than the control group children. Hurrah!

I was very encouraged, but I knew that I had to learn more and do more. This was the very beginning of my national effort to persuade school administrators to use these programs and to train teachers to work with parents as educational partners.

Year after year, from the early seventies to the present day, the Institute has provided School and Family/Community Involvement training to what now totals thousands of teachers. When you think of the national need for the training, this is a drop in the proverbial bucket, but it has launched special demonstration projects that have put Institute home-teaching methods to the test. Hundreds of school districts across the nation have initiated the use of Institute home-school learning systems that provide families with weekly teaching activities.

Over the years, HSI has addressed special needs using adaptations of the home-learning-activities programs. For bilingual families, HSI programs have been translated into four languages. To involve senior citizens in work with families, HSI designed the "Senior Corps" program. For students who need extra learning help, HSI created "Special Solutions." (These are summarized in the analysis *The Forgotten Factor in School Success: The Family* [Washington, D.C.: Home and School Institute, 1985].)

Results prove that parents want this help, that they participate in these programs, and that children not only show higher test scores but improve their learning attitudes and skills through the use of the activities.

In 1984 a major national development occurred. The National Education Association asked the Institute to design the NEA Teacher-Parent Partnership Project. Associations in twenty-two states have provided this program to families of third graders. The response from families and teachers has been enthusiastic. (National Education Association, *Report on the Teacher-Parent Partnership Project* [Instruction and Professional Development, 1986].)

Third grade was chosen since it is a pivotal learning year. Unlike kindergarten and first grade, where it is assumed that every parent is "involved," in third grade it's considered more of a challenge to reach parents.

The heart of this program model is the series of learning activities that children take home once a week from school. A feedback sheet for parents' reaction is attached to each of the activities. The feedback sheets—and there have been thousands—showed the following: 97 percent of the parents said the project activities helped them spend enjoyable time with their child, and 98 percent of the parents felt their children learned something useful. When children were asked how they felt, they were equally enthusiastic; they especially valued the time with their parents.

The Institute launched "New Partnerships for Student Achievement," a national program that, for the first time, calls upon community organizations—churches, unions, social clubs—to help families help their children learn. This provided a new dimension of community support for children's learning.

Throughout this decade, the Institute has focused on expanding the service outreach of MegaSkills programs. Among others, the Sears-Roebuck Foundation and corporate contributions from Kraft Foods to the Institute have made possible hundreds of MegaSkills training scholarships. These teachers and parents from across the nation are reaching out to provide

MegaSkills workshops to thousands of parents . . . and the numbers grow daily. The Mott Foundation has supported impact analysis of the MegaSkills Programs and the HSI Web site (MegaSkillsHSI.org) is sharing word about MegaSkills sites nationally. Current and future Institute initiatives include Workforce MegaSkills and America Reads Together Mentor Handbooks.

Across the country, other organizations and schools are now saying, "Tell us how we can do it." The America 2000 Initiative has helped to spark a coming together across the nation, often for the first time, of community leadership to set plans for revitalizing education at the local level.

We at the Institute are ready to help. I see what I call "Learning City®": these will be communities across our nation taking practical steps to build on and to mobilize the strengths of all families. I see structured programs, MegaSkills workshops that help parents learn more about how to help their children learn. These workshops take place in schools, in libraries, in health centers, at workplaces. These workshops bring families together to share experiences about teaching MegaSkills at home. For example, First Tennessee Bank in **Memphis, Tennessee,** sponsored the Learning Is Homegrown/MegaSkills program, providing MegaSkills workshops at forty sites throughout the Memphis area. Memphis State University researchers analyzed the impact of the program through pre- and postassessment:

**Homework:** Children spending more than 6 hours a week doubled from 12 percent to 24 percent, while those spending less than 1 hour decreased from 12 percent to 4 percent of program participants.

**TV Watching:** Average time spent watching TV during the school week decreased by approximately 31 minutes per week. Time not spent on television was spent on doing homework.

**Parent Time with Child:** Increased from 2.02 hours to 2.25 hours, or 14 minutes per day. This is a significant time change in view of studies on household time allocation.

**Working Relationship (parent/child):** Those reporting "Working Well" with each other increased from 55 percent to 75 percent.

In **Austin, Texas,** with sponsorship by AISD, Project A+, and IBM, the goal is to involve all parents of elementary school children in MegaSkills workshops. Participation and feedback are very encouraging: In the program's first year, 1990, more than 3000 parents attended workshops and 100 percent of the parents said they enjoyed them and will use what they have learned.

Written comments by parents on the feedback sheets consistently support survey findings. Parents cite these benefits:

■ Sharing experience and concerns with other parents

■ Provision of specific "doable" activities for parent and child at home

- Increased time spent and improved quality of interaction with children at home
- More self-confidence in the parenting role

Teachers in **Louisville, Kentucky,** have this comment: "Parents have reported changes in their own behavior." Children have a poignant response. Over and over, they say, "This program made our parents spend time with us."

**To extend the impact of the Mega-Skills program, two new initiatives have been designed and are now available to school districts and organizations nationally.**

**What Do We Say? What Do We Do?:** Tested by focus groups nationally, this is the new MegaSkills-based problem solving discussion group program for parents and teachers: reducing stress, building achievement.

**MegaSkills Classroom Initiative:** This program provides a children's curriculum in MegaSkills, directly in the classroom and in children's club and organizational settings. It is complete with a Home and School Institute one-day training program entitled MegaSkills Essentials in the Classroom. In field tests, for example, sixth graders at Longfellow School in Riverside designed skits to model MegaSkills roles for younger students. Increasingly, the kids program also serves as a classroom management and self-discipline program.

**For more information about how to bring MegaSkills to your community, write to:**

**Home and School Institute MegaSkills Education Center 1500 Massachusetts Ave. NW Washington, D.C. 20005**

**(Or visit their Web site at http://www.MegaSkillsHSI.org)**

Bringing the forces in education—the home, the school, the community—together, mobilizing their synergistic efforts to help all children learn—this is my dream, and it is showing signs at last of coming true.

## RESEARCH NOTES*

Up-to-date research on the family's role in education is not easy to find in one place. That's why we have compiled the following list of studies. These augment studies I referred to in my "educational journey."

Although this list is confined to more readily accessible, recent materials, they may not be available in bookstores and public libraries. Check university libraries and professional libraries connected with school systems. The Home and School Institute can provide further information about how to find them and background on the other research references in this book.

*Since the earlier editions of MegaSkills were published in 1988 and 1992, a number of new and significant studies have appeared. Oliver Moles, Ph.D., Education Policy Analyst, Office for Educational Research and Improvement, U.S. Department of Education, has reviewed and updated the listing for this edition.

Janine Bempechat, "The Role of Parent Involvement in Children's Academic Achievement." *School Community Journal* 2 (1992): 31–34.

Benjamin Bloom, *All Our Children Learning: A Primer for Parents, Teachers, and Other Educators.* New York: McGraw-Hill, 1981.

———. *Developing Talent in Young People.* New York: Ballantine Books, 1985.

Ernest L. Boyer, *Ready to Learn: A Mandate for the Nation.* Princeton, N.J.: The Carnegie Foundation for the Advancement of Teaching, 1992.

Ronald S. Brandt, ed., "Strengthening Partnerships with Parents and Community" (Special Section), *Educational Leadership* 47 (1989): 4–70.

Nathan Caplan, Marcella Choy, and John K. Whitmore, "Indochinese Refugee Families and Academic Achievement," *Scientific American* 266 (1992): 36–42.

Clark, Reginald M. "Parents as Providers of Linguistic and Social Capital," *Educational Horizons* 66 (1988): 93–95.

———. *Family Life and School Achievement: Why Poor Black Children Succeed or Fail.* Chicago: University of Chicago Press, 1983.

James P. Comer, "Educating Poor Minority Children," *Scientific American* 259 (1988): 42–48.

Committee for Economic Development. *Children in Need—Investment Strategies for the Educationally Disadvantaged.* New York: Committee for Economic Development, 1987.

Joyce L. Epstein, "School/Family/Community Partnerships: Caring for the Children We Share," *Phi Delta Kappan* (May 1995): 701–12.

Norm Fruchter, Anne Galletta, and J. Lynne White, *New Directions in Parent Involvement.* New York: Academy for Educational Development, 1992.

Anne T. Henderson and Nancy Berla, *A New Generation of Evidence: The Family Is Critical to Student Achievement.* Washington, D.C.: Center for Law and Education, 1994.

Lynn B Liontos, *At-Risk Families and Schools: Becoming Partners.* Eugene: University of Oregon, ERIC Clearinghouse on Educational Management, 1992.

Metropolitan Life. "Strengthening Links Between Home and School," in *Survey of the American Teacher 1987* (New York: Louis Harris and Associates, 1987).

Oliver C. Moles, "Collaboration Between Schools and Disadvantaged Parents: Obstacles and Openings," in *Families and Schools in a Pluralistic Society* (Albany: State University of New York Press, 1993).

National Commission on Children. *Beyond Rhetoric: A New American Agenda for Children and Families.* Washington, D.C.: National Commission on Children, 1992.

National Education Association, *Building Parent Partnerships (The MegaSkills School),* by Jan Deeb, Judy Elmer, and Linda Gray. Washington, D.C., 1996.

Siobhan Nicolau and Carmen L. Ramos, *Together Is Better: Building Strong*

*Relationships Between Schools and Hispanic Parents.* New York: Hispanic Policy Development Project, 1990.

Dorothy Rich, "The Family and Schooling." *Educational Horizons* 69 (summer 1991): 170–216.

———. "Parents and Schools." *Educational Horizons* 66 (winter 1988): 58–95.

———. "The Power of Shared Language: Unexpected Positives of the MegaSkills," in *Think, ECS Learning System* (February 1997): 18–25.

———. "Seven Habits of Good Teachers Today," in *Education Week* 41 (August 6, 1997).

J. William Rioux and Nancy Berla, *Innovations in Parent and Family Involvement.* Princeton Junction, N.J.: Eye on Education, 1993.

Barry Rutherford, ed., *Creating Family/School Partnerships.* Columbus, Ohio: National Middle School Association, 1995.

Steven Schlossman, "Family as Educator, Parent Education and the Perennial Family Crisis," in *Child Rearing in the Home and School* (New York: Plenum, 1987).

Barbara Schneider and James S. Coleman, *Parents, Their Children, and Schools.* Boulder, Colo.: Westview Press, 1993.

Laurence Steinberg with B. Bradford Brown and Sanford M. Dornbusch, *Beyond the Classroom.* New York: Simon & Schuster, 1996.

Harold Stevenson and James Stigler, *The Learning Gap.* New York: Summit Books, 1992.

U.S. Department of Education, *Strong Families, Strong Schools: Building Community Partnerships for Learning.* Washington, D.C., 1994.

Edward F. Zigler, Sharon Kagan, and Nancy Hall, *Children, Families & Government, Preparing for the Twenty-First Century.* New York: Cambridge University Press, 1996.

Also see *Resources and More* in the Mega-Skills Library, Appendix C. It would be remiss not to add that HSI itself has published numerous reports, articles, and handbooks since its founding in 1972. Among the titles available directly from HSI are *Learning & Working, Survival Guide for Today's Parents, Careers and Caring,* and *MegaSkills Parent Handbook in English and Spanish.*

# MegaSkills "Recipes," Chapter by Chapter, by Age Range and Academic Objective

To help make this book easier to use, here is a list of home learning recipes by chapter. For each of the MegaSkills activities, you will find its accompanying academic objective. The age ranges provide guidance in selecting the activities. They are not all-knowing. Many a four-year-old will enjoy an eight-year-old's activity, and vice versa.

These activities have been tested. They work. And they work a little differently with different children. Experience indicates that all of them in whole or in part will be useful to everyone.

One of the key points of the MegaSkills program and philosophy is that academics are part of it all and they are integrated. In school, with each subject separately defined and graded, it's possible for children to get the idea that education is just a schoolroom thing and that academics come from textbooks or computers. As adults know, reading is everywhere, and so is math and science . . . and they come all jumbled up together in real life. And they keep on coming long after the traditional school days are over.

Academics do not exist alone, apart from the rest of our learning. Our learning becomes more motivated when we see academics as part and parcel of our lives. That is what MegaSkill activities do: they explain their extraordinary power as they integrate academics with the personal achievement and pleasure of learning.

## MegaSkill One: Confidence

Telephone Time  *ages 4–6*
   **Reading**
   *Practicing Sequence*
   *Following Directions*

Calling for Help  *ages 6–9*
   **Writing**
   *Organizing Information*

Information Hunt  *ages 10–12*
   **Study Skills**
   *Asking Questions*
   *Conducting Research*

Our TV Diet  *ages 4–8*
   **Reading**
   *Analyzing Data*
   *Developing Discussion Skills*

Taking Charge of TV Watching  *any age*
   **Writing**
   *Remembering Details*

Keeping TV Watching Under Control
                              *any age*

   **Writing**
   *Discussing Ideas*
   *Creating a Plan*

The Importance of Me  *ages 4–9*
   **Reading**
   *Matching Words and Pictures*
   *Using Picture Clues*

Family Mobile  *ages 4–9*
   **Reading**
   *Using Visual Clues for Building Under-
      standing of Relationships*

Now and Then  *ages 10–12*
   **Writing**
   *Listening and Speaking*
   *Organizing Information*

What Do I Do Right?  *ages 10–12*
   **Writing**
   *Collecting and Using Information*

## MegaSkill Two: Motivation

Just Outside  *any age*
   **Thinking**
   *Storing Experiences for Reading
      and Writing*

Shopping Center Stroll  *ages 4–7*
   **Thinking**
   *Building a Storehouse of Experience*

Sitting and Watching  *ages 4–7*
   **Thinking**
   *Building a Storehouse of Experience*

Local Law  *ages 8–12*
   **Social Studies**
   *Observing Civics in Action*

Getting Around  *ages 8–12*
   **Social Studies**
   *Making Predictions and Testing Them*

The Foreign Touch Around Town
                              *any age*

   **Social Studies**
   *Understanding Diversity*

The No-Nag Writing System   *ages 7–12*
**Communication**
*Writing for a Purpose*

The First Step   *any age*
**Thinking**
*Building Memory and Reflection*

Time Me   *ages 4–6*
**Mathematics**
*Practicing Estimation*

Tell Me   *ages 4–9*
**Communication**
*Listening Skills*
*Following Directions*

This House Is a Mess   *any age*
**Mathematics**
*Recognizing and Creating Patterns*

Excuses Don't Count   *ages 7–12*
**Study Skills**
*Observing and Keeping Records*


## MegaSkill Three: Effort

My Day   *any age*
**Communication**
*Discussion and Listening Skills*

The Extra Mile   *any age*
**Thinking**
*Observation Skills*
*Drawing Inferences*

Do and Not Die   *any age*
**Thinking**
*Comparing and Contrasting Information*

A Study Place   *ages 4–9*
**Study Skills**
*Building Organizational Abilities*

A Homework System   *ages 10–12*
**Study Skills**
*Researching and Charting Information*

Our Home: A Learning Place   *any age*
**Reading/Writing**
*Focusing on Good Work Habits*


## MegasSkill Four: Responsibility

Body Beautiful   *ages 4–9*
**Study Skills**
*Recalling Details*
*Charting Information*

Clothes   *ages 4–9*
**Reading/Writing**
*Following Directions*
*Building Good Work Habits*

A Special Place   *ages 4–9*
**Study Skills**
*Creating/Writing for a Purpose*
*Remembering Details*

Promises! Promises!   *ages 4–9*
**Thinking**
*Sharing Opinions*
*Evaluating Information*

Taking Care of Things   *any age*
**Reading**
*Listening and Talking Together*

Don't Worry: You Won't Be Late   *any age*
**Study Skills**
*Building Good Work Habits*

## MegaSkill Five: Initiative

Machines: Look and Listen  *ages 4–9*
   **Science**
   *Making Hypotheses and Predictions*

Machines: Please Touch  *ages 4–9*
   **Science**
   *Researching and Evaluating Information*

Water, Water Everywhere  *ages 4–9*
   **Science**
   *Distinguishing Between Fact and
      Opinion*

Hot and Cold  *ages 4–9*
   **Science**
   *Practicing Scientific Methods*

Light and Shadow  *ages 4–9*
   **Science**
   *Conducting Experiments*
   *Observing and Discussing*

A Can and a Straw  *ages 4–9*
   **Science**
   *Practicing Experiments*

Plants and How They Grow  *ages 4–9*
   **Science**
   *Evaluating Evidence*

Nuts and Bolts, Pins and Needles
                        *ages 4–6*

   **Reading**
   *Classifying Objects*
   *Using Descriptive Words*

Everything Fits  *ages 7–12*
   **Mathematics**
   *Estimating*
   *Using Spatial Abilities*

Gather and Go  *ages 7–9*
   **Thinking**
   *Generating Ideas*
   *Gathering Information*

When Do We Have to Do What?  *any age*
   **Thinking**
   *Organizing and Presenting Information*

Striking Back at Sickness  *any age*
   **Thinking**
   *Developing Categories*
   *Organizing in Logical Order*

Junk Day  *any age*
   **Thinking**
   *Making Reasoned Decisions*

Offering Without Being Asked
                        *ages 7–12*

   **Thinking**
   *Generating Ideas*
   *Listening and Speaking Together*

## MegaSkill Six: Perseverance

Our Very Own Photo Gallery  *any age*
   **Reading/Writing**
   *Comparing and Sequencing Information*

Family Directory  *ages 4–9*
   **Reading/Writing**
   *Classifying Information*
   *Using Descriptive Words*

Home Health Records  *any age*
   **Study Skills**
   *Researching and Charting Information*

Our Special Garden   *ages 4–9*
**Science**
*Following Directions*
*Comparing and Evaluating Evidence*

Good and Good for You   *ages 4–9*
**Science**
*Weighing Evidence*
*Setting Up Categories and an Action*
*Plan*

Exercise Plan   *any age*
**Thinking**
*Researching Information*
*Organizing a Plan*

False Friends   *ages 10–12*
**Thinking**
*Understanding Consequences*
*of Decisions*

Practice Makes Almost Perfect   *any age*
**Communication**
*Building Discussion Skills*


## MegaSkill Seven: Caring

Family Notes   *ages 4–6*
**Writing**
*Sharing Information*

How Does It Feel?   *ages 4–8*
**Thinking**
*Observing and Discussing*

Greetings for Friends and Neighbors
*ages 4–8*
**Writing**
*Using Language Arts Creatively*

How Can I Help?   *ages 9–12*
**Thinking**
*Researching Information*
*Creating a Plan*

All in the Family   *ages 9–12*
**Communication**
*Listening and Speaking Together*

About Ourselves   *ages 7–12*
**Thinking**
*Building Self-Knowledge and Concern*
*for Others*

Our Block   *ages 4–6*
**Social Studies**
*Learning About the Community*

From One to Another   *any age*
**Thinking**
*Identifying Strengths of Diversity*

People Scavenger Hunt   *any age*
**Social Studies**
*Learning About Others*
*Decreasing Bias and Stereotyping*

Who Can Help Me?   *any age*
**Writing**
*Purposeful Writing to Obtain*
*Information*

Heroes Among Us   *any age*
**Reading**
*Relating Main Ideas*
*Recalling and Sharing Details*

The Gift of Time   *any age*
**Communication**
*Developing Time Concepts and*
*Personal Responsibility*

## MegaSkill Eight: Teamwork

Real Work *ages 4–6*
**Study Skills**
*Building Relationships Between Schooling and Career Goals*

Divide and Conquer *ages 7–9*
**Study Skills**
*Developing Work Habits by Sharing Tasks*

Organizing Household Chores *ages 10–12*
**Writing**
*Categorizing Information*

What Do We Think? *ages 7–9*
**Communication**
*Listening*
*Organizing Information*

What Are We Watching? *ages 8–12*
**Writing**
*Formulating Questions for Purposeful Writing*

What's Your Opinion? *ages 10–12*
**Communication**
*Identifying Problem-Solving Alternatives*

Down the Drain *any age*
**Mathematics**
*Building Awareness of Math in Daily Life*

What's My Share? *ages 10–12*
**Mathematics**
*Recognizing Relationships*

Shopping Around *ages 7–12*
**Mathematics**
*Connecting Reading and Writing with Math*

People Helping Each Other *ages 8–12*
**Reading/Writing**
*Working with Visual and Print Media*

How Have Others Helped You? *ages 10–12*
**Communication**
*Relating with Adults*
*Building Discussion Abilities*

## MegaSkill Nine: Common Sense

The Careful Eye *ages 4–9*
**Reading/Writing**
*Vocabulary Building*

Memory Stretching *ages 4–9*
**Thinking**
*Recalling Details*
*Practicing Sequences*

Guessing *ages 4–9*
**Science**
*Formulating Hypotheses*
*Checking Evidence*

Checking *ages 7–12*
**Thinking**
*Evaluating Information*

Using Clues *ages 4–8*
**Thinking**
*Deductive Reasoning*

Asking Questions  *ages 9–12*
**Study Skills**
*Researching Information*

How Much Time?  *any age*
**Mathematics**
*Making Predictions and Estimating*

How Time Flies  *any age*
**Mathematics**
*Observing and Keeping Records*

My Time Wish  *any age*
**Communication**
*Presenting Information*

Time Your Plan  *ages 7–12*
**Thinking**
*Organizing Information*

Money in Print and in Pocket  *ages 4–6*
**Reading/Math**
*Checking Newspaper Ads*
*Counting Money*

Yesterday and Today  *ages 7–9*
**Thinking/Math**
*Using Household Bills to Understand Prices*

Eating Well for Less  *ages 4–9*
**Reading/Thinking**
*Using Ads to Plan Healthy Meals*

Clothes for Less  *ages 10–12*
**Math**
*Using Ads to Build a Budget*

Saving and Banking  *ages 10–12*
**Math/Reading**
*Working with Bank Materials*

## MegaSkill Ten: Problem Solving

Thinking and Choosing  *ages 4–7*
**Thinking**
*Generating Choices for Decision Making*

Decisions Aren't Easy  *ages 9–12*
**Thinking**
*Judging Decisions and Consequences*

Warning, Warning  *ages 4–6*
**Reading**
*Understanding Vocabulary in Context*

Household Danger Spots  *ages 4–6*
**Thinking**
*Building Observation Skills*

Appliance Checklist  *ages 4–6*
**Reading/Writing**
*Creating a Safety Checklist*

Keys to the Kingdom  *ages 4–6*
**Thinking**
*Testing Household Safety Measures*

Community Safety Tour  *ages 4–6*
**Reading/Writing**
*Checking Signs in the Neighborhood*

Dealing with Strangers  *any age*
**Communication**
*Practicing Speaking on the Phone and Taking Messages*

Street Smarts  *ages 10–12*
**Communication/Reading**
*Talking Together About Safety*
*Reading Community Materials*

In Case of Fire  *any age*
**Reading/Writing**
*Learning Emergency Words and Creating a Plan*

## MegaSkill Eleven: Focus

Goals: All Sizes, All Kinds   *any age*

Finding a Goal   *any age*

**Thinking**
*Generating Ideas*
*Listening and Speaking Together*

Selecting an Objective   *any age*

**Writing**
*Organizing Information*

Moving into Action   *any age*

**Study Skills**
*Researching and Charting Information*

What Do I Have Going for Me?   *any age*

Taking Stock   *any age*

**Thinking**
*Comparing and Contrasting*
*Information*

One Obstacle at a Time   *any age*

**Study Skills**
*Building Good Work Habits*

Keeping Going   *any age*

**Study Skills**
*Building Good Work Habits*

What Do I Do to Get There?   *any age*

**Study Skills**
*Building Good Work Habits*

Paying Attention   *ages 4–9*

**Study Skills**
*Remembering Details and*
*Charting Information*

Getting and Keeping Information
*ages 9 and up*

Where Do I Get the Information?
*ages 9 and up*

**Study Skills**
*Researching Information*

How Can I Remember It?   *ages 9 and up*

**Study Skills**
*Organizing Information*

How Do I Know I Know Enough?
*ages 9 and up*

**Thinking**
*Making Reasoned Decisions*

Making a Plan   *ages 8 and up*

**Study Skills**
*Organizing a Plan*
*Listening and Talking Together*

How Will I Know That I Am Making
Progress?

Promises to Ourselves   *any age*

**Communication/Writing**
*Listening and Talking*
*Charting Information*

How Am I Doing? Chart   *any age*

**Writing**
*Creating a Plan*

Grading Myself Report Form
*ages 8 and up*

**Thinking/Writing**
*Evaluating Evidence*

MegaSkills Moments   *any age*

**Communication**
*Listening and Talking Together*

# Acknowledgments

The book and the MegaSkills program didn't happen overnight (both were over thirty years in the making). Nor was I born yesterday (more than thirty years ago, you can be sure). That means I ought to know enough to know whom to thank. So, to begin at the beginning . . .

To Spencer Rich, my husband, who thinks I know more than I do. His confidence in me gives me confidence. He called MegaSkills "the Inner Engines of Learning" —a brilliant concept.

To our daughters, Rebecca and Jessica and her husband Jon, who use their Mega-Skills to keep reminding me of the Mega-Skills I need as a parent. To my brother Art, who taught me more than he realizes.

To my late parents, Hyman and Rose Kovitz, whose MegaSkilled advice still rings in my ears.

To Harriett Stonehill, Director of the MegaSkills Education Center, whose ability, determination, and energy continue to be the driving force in moving the MegaSkills workshop program across the nation.

To the remarkable group of contributors to this book and to the work of the Home and School Institute (HSI): To the Board and advisers of the Institute, who over the years have stalwartly given advice and provided the moral support it has taken to enable the Institute to survive and to grow. Special thanks to the Institute's treasurer, Jim Van Dien, for his effort and perseverance. And to Mickey B. Knox, Chair of the Institute's National Advisory Council, for her caring and motivation.

To Chris Coffin, Managing Editor of Houghton Mifflin, who saw the need for this revised edition, and who made it possible, and to John Radziewicz, Director of Mariner Books, for publishing it.

To Maria Salvadore, Children's Services Coordinator of the District of Columbia Library and Pamela F. Stovall, Children's Service Librarian, for developing the MegaSkills Library for Children. To Oliver Moles, Ph.D., of the Office of Education and Research, U.S. Department of Education, for his review and update of the research bibliography.

To Beverly Mattox, Senior Consultant to the Home and School Institute, superb colleague in staff development, who has identified the academic objectives and multiple intelligences within the MegaSkills activities in the book and in the MegaSkills training programs.

To Rachel Z. Ayala, Outreach Coordinator of HSI, and Sandra Getler, Outreach Mentor, who have made sure that the Institute reaches out and responds to communities nationally. To Rachel Venzant, who deciphers my writing with great care, to Dorothy Henderson and Becky Saikia-Wilson for thoughtful editing, and to Torri Twine, who makes sure our production can move forward.

To Barbara Bush for her determined and inspiring leadership in family literacy and her support for MegaSkills. To Tipper Gore, wife of the Vice President and lifelong child advocate, for her early and continuing encouragement of my work. To Dick Riley, Secretary of Education, and his wife, Tunky, for their confidence in my work since the early days of MegaSkills in South Carolina. To Bill Bradley, in the Senate and on the basketball court, who understood MegaSkills from the start.

To Bob Chase, president of the NEA, for his inspiring work in teacher leadership today. To Don Cameron, Executive Director of the National Education Association, who told me I was the "Dr. Spock of Education" and who originally told me to get out there and write *MegaSkills.*

To the foresighted school districts, businesses, and community organizations that have taken important pioneering steps in supporting the MegaSkills program. They range from small cities to large ones in forty-eight states, from Alaska to Georgia, from California to Vermont. To the John D. and Catherine T. MacArthur Foundation for funding the initial New Partnerships in Student Achievement Program, in which the MegaSkills workshops were piloted. To the Sears-Roebuck Foundation for funding the program's expansion and to Kraft Foods for MegaSkills Scholarship Awards.

To all who have become MegaSkills leaders. To the pioneering MegaSkills Field Associates, among them Judy Brim and Genethia Hayes in California, Gwen Dixon-Coe in South Carolina, Karen Geiger in Indiana, and Mo Sanders in Alaska, who bring MegaSkills Programs to communities across the nation. To those working with HSI in the field: Liz Ballard, Eva Baron, Mildred Brown, Beth Butler, Debbie Cochran, Bea Fernandez, Tonie Fuentes, Vera Ginn, Ruby Greene, Gail Hannas, Rosalee Johnson, Jackie LaBouff, Marva Lane, Vicky Marshall, Dorothy Mitchell, Maria Ortega, Anna Perez, Jeana Preston, Maria Ramirez, Brenda Kennedy-Snyder, and Pat Woods for their unstinting generosity of mind, spirit, and time. From all walks of life they have come, committed to helping others. There is no way to keep up and mention everyone on this great honor roll—but I know "you." This is a diverse group working with more than eleven thousand teachers, parents, grandparents, businesspeople from across the nation, in a variety of settings, from schools to workplaces to housing centers.

To an extraordinary group of colleagues who have shared their MegaSkills stories for this book and for those who work with me and with HSI, who probably mumble under their breath, "Is that Dorothy calling again?" but who always take my call, come to my aid, listen to my tales of woe and joy, and in short are friends, advisers, and coworkers: Ron Areglado, the Berzins Family, Ronald Blackburn-Moreno, John Bottum, Elizabeth Campbell, Mike Casserly, Tim Crawford, Alice and Lincoln Day, Adriana de Kanter, Wilton Dillon, Harvey Dzodin, Amitai Etzioni, Arnold Fege, Gordon Felton, Jerry Floyd, Greg Fox, Mary Futrell, Warlene Gary, Peter Gerber, Alan Ginsburg, Milt Goldberg, Phil and

Joan Harris, Andy Hartman, Paul Houston, Karen Jaffe, Sid Johnson, Misbah Khan, M.D., Tom Korologos, Leanna Landsmann, Mary Jean LeTendre, Ed Lippert, Martin Lobel, Garry McDaniels, Stan McFarland, Bob McMorrow, John Merrow, Evelyn Moore, Elena Pell, Doug Phillips, Tom Raffa, Vincent Reed, Susan Roman, Harold Roth, Margaret Singleton-McKnight, Elliot Stonehill, James Van Erden, Toni Ward, Bob Witherspoon, Joan Worden, and Edward Zigler.

To the national organizations the Institute works with: American Library Association, National Education Association, National Association of Elementary School Principals, Council of the Great City Schools, National Association of Federal Education Program Administrators, Phi Delta Kappa, and National Alliance of Business.

To the folks at Tor/Forge Publishers, for publishing *What Do We Say? What Do We Do?*®—a MegaSkills-related problem-solving handbook for parents and teachers.

The period between the publication of the original *MegaSkills* in 1988 and this edition has been a time of learning for me. I had not imagined the power of the MegaSkills concept and how important and useful it would become for so many families and teachers. Bringing this new knowledge together for this edition, for this era of technology and change, has been a challenge and a great joy. I have been taught by many fine teachers, parents, and children who are using this program, and I am very grateful.

# Index

Ability, 57, 61, 291–92, 309
Academic objectives. *See* Objectives
Academics
  language of, 20–21
  objectives for academic subjects, 20
  and school readiness, 176–80
  supported by MegaSkills, 19–21
  *See also* Mathematics; Reading; Writing
Acting. *See* Creative dramatics
Administrators of school, 236, 257–58, 269
Adults. *See* Grandparents; Parents; Teachers
Advertisements
  money common sense, 135
  and writing, 200–201
Age of family members, 215, 218
Alcohol use, 99, 223–24
Alphabet letters. *See* Letters of alphabet
America 2000 Initiative, 168, 332
American Library Association, 326, 328
Anger, 223
Anti-school behaviors by parents, 256–57
Appliance checklist, 150
Armstrong, Thomas, 19
Artificial intelligence, 219
Arts and crafts
  Art for Everyone crusade, 2
  art gallery at home, 65, 283–84
  craft sales, 238
  dressing silhouette of figures of children, 284
  examples of projects, 283–84
  fence painting, 284
  gifts made by children, 244–45, 283

inhibitions against, 282
outdoor play structure, 284
picture puzzles, 284
and problem solving, 143–44
puppets, 283
and sense of success, 288–89
supplies for, 282–83
work area for, 282–83
*See also* Creativity
Asian Americans, 61, 62
Aspira Association, 328
Association of Library Services to Children, 328
Athletic leagues, 123
Attention
  and direction giving, 171–72
  focus and paying attention, 160
  getting positive attention from teachers, 174
  parents' attention on children, 300–301
  paying attention as school readiness skill, 171–72
  perseverance and attention span, 95
  television and short attention span, 95
  and television watching, 171
Attitude
  and focus, 159
  and motivation, 43–44
  personal attitudes for school readiness, 170, 173–74
  self-defeating attitude, 243–44, 257
Auditory discrimination
  definition of, 193
  and mathematics, 218
  and reading, 194
  and writing, 205
Auditory memory
  definition of, 193
  and mathematics, 218–19

  and reading, 194
  and writing, 205
Austin, Texas, 332–33
Authoritarian parents, 63
Authoritative parents, 63

Babysitters. *See* Child care helpers
Balance
  and double-hemisphere brain, 278
  and focus, 162
  organization and flexibility, 92
  and sense of wholeness, 278
Banking, 137, 139, 218–19
Bathroom, math concepts in, 179–80, 217
Bathtub math, 179–80
Bedroom, math concepts in, 217
Bedtime reading, 190
Big Sisters and Big Brothers, 123
Bilingualism, 252
Bills
  fair share of, 121
  and money common sense, 136
Bloom, Benjamin, 168–69, 329–30
Book fair, 238
Book/Toy Lending Library, 237
Books
  adult books about reading, 326
  book fair, 238
  Book/Toy Lending Library in schools, 237
  on caring, 324
  on common sense, 325
  on competition, 321
  on confidence, 319–20
  on effort, 321–22
  encyclopedias, 192
  on focus, 326
  as gifts from grandparents, 245
  in home, 65, 172–73
  on initiative, 322–23
  keeping up with, 327

Books (*cont.*)
  on MegaSkills, 319–28
  on motivation, 320–21
  on perseverance, 323
  on problem solving, 325–26
  purchase of, 191–92
  reference shelf, 192
  research on family's role in education, 333–34
  on responsibility, 322
  selection of, 191–92
  on teamwork, 324–25
  *See also* Libraries
Boredom, 45–47, 188–89
Boys Clubs, 123
Bradley, Bill, xii
Brainstorming for subjects, 201–202
Brazelton, Mickey, 242
Bronfenbrenner, Urie, 330
Buck, Pearl, 291
Bulletin board
  for message center, 48
  near bed of sick child, 89
  Vacation Bulletin Board, 188–89
Bus routes, 46–47

Café Parent, 236
Calculator, 216–17
Calendar
  and focus, 159
  and initiative, 87–88
  and math readiness, 179
  and planning of trips and outings, 209
Cameron, Don, 332
Can and straw activities, 84
Caring
  activities for developing, 105–11, 340
  and appreciation of differences between people, 108–109
  bigger questions on, 112
  books on, 324
  in concentric circles, 105
  definition of, 5
  discussions on, 108–10, 112
  examples of niceness and being not nice, 112

and family notes, 105
and feedback on behavior from family members, 107
and feelings of other people, 105–106
and friends, 106
and gift of time, 110–11
and grandparents, 244–45
and greetings for friends and neighbors, 106
and help for family and friends, 107
and heroic acts by ordinary people, 110
and identifying help that family needs, 109–10
importance of, 104–105
and knowledge about neighbors and neighborhood, 108
and listening, 111, 113
and MegaSkills Report Card, 313
need for, 104–105
and neighbors, 106, 108
and Never-Ending Report Card, 104
between parents and teachers, 261
and people scavenger hunt, 109
and schools, 255
and sharing feelings, 106, 107–108
teaching tips on, 112
and technology connection, 27–28
and teens and preteens, 224–25
Casals, Pablo, 291
Cather, Willa, 291
Cause and effect thinking, 81
Chase, Bob, x–xi
Cheating, 77, 79
Checking, 129–30
Child care
  for Family Learning Center, 237
  as job for teens and preteens, 225
  for school meetings and activities, 237, 264
Child care box, 251
Child care helpers
  back-up system for, 252–53
  checking references of, 250

and child care box, 251
and emergencies, 251
and household chores for children, 250–51
and household rules, 251–52
interviewing of, 250
job definition for, 249
and list of activity ideas, 250–51
and parent-child bond, 253
personal lives of, 253
responsibilities of, 249–53
selection of, 249–50
and speaking Standard English, 252
and teamwork, 252–53
and television watching for children, 251
Children's books. *See* Books
Children's Defense Fund, 328
Chittick, Barbara, 259
Choices
  and decision making, 144–46, 223–24
  parents and school choice, 268
  and problem solving, 145, 146
  for teens and preteens, 223–24
  thinking and choosing, 145
  and values, 76–77, 79
Church groups, 123
Churchill, Winston, 260
Cigarette smoking, 99
Classroom. *See* Schools
Cleanliness, 71–72
Clock. *See* Time
Clothes
  buying for, 137
  dressing silhouette of figures of children, 284
  favorite clothes of preteens, 223
  ingredients of, 217
  labels of, 217
  mending, 73
  pegs for hanging up, 89, 91
  selection of, 72
  for teens and preteens, 223
  washing and ironing, 72–73
  words for, 178
Clubs for children, 123, 125
Clues, and common sense, 130

Cold and hot activities, 84
Coleman Report, 330
Common sense
    activities for developing, 128–39,
        341
    bigger questions on, 138
    books on, 325
    and checking, 129–30
    childhood vignettes on, 127–28,
        139
    and clues, 130
    definition of, 5
    discussions on, 138
    and gathering information,
        128–30
    and grandparents, 245
    and guessing, 129
    indicators of, 127
    jobs and money, 39
    long-range process for develop-
        ment of, 127
    as MegaSkills approach, 14
    and MegaSkills Report Card, 313
    and memory, 129
    money common sense, 134–39,
        218–19
    and Never-Ending Report Card,
        127
    and noticing and naming, 128
    and overscheduling, 134
    people common sense, 131
    practice in knowing what to say
        in different scenarios, 131–32
    and question asking, 130
    and technology connection, 28
    about time, 132–34
    and why we say what we say,
        132
Communication. See Discussions;
    Listening
Community
    cultural events in, 265
    discovery activities on, 45–47
    safety tour, 151
    street smarts, 152
    volunteering by teens and pre-
        teens, 224
    See also Neighbors
Community Chest, 123, 125

Competition
    books on, 321
    and motivation, 52
    versus teamwork, 115
Compliment slips, 205
Computers
    and Internet, 26–28, 328
    and mathematics, 219–20
    and MegaSkills, 26–28
    responsibility for, 75
    and virtual reality, 28
    See also Technology connection
Concerts, 287–88
Confidence
    and academics, 19
    activities for building, 31–39, 337
    bigger questions on, 40
    books on, 319–20
    changes in, 32
    childhood vignettes of, 30–31
    and courage, 39
    and creative dramatics, 281
    definition of, 5
    discussions on, 40
    and encouragement, 39
    and expectations, 39, 41
    and family mobile, 37
    and grandparents, 243
    Importance of Me activity, 19,
        36–37
    and learning and self and family,
        36–39
    list of what children like about
        themselves, 38
    and listening, 38–39
    and MegaSkills Report Card, 312
    need for, 30
    and Never-Ending Report Card,
        30
    and reading, 243
    and self-esteem, 30
    and self-respect and respect for
        others, 30
    and shyness, 40, 222
    teaching tips on, 40
    and technology connection, 26
    and telephone, 32–33
    and television, 34–36
Costume box, 280–81

Courage, and confidence, 39
Court in action, 46
Coward, Noel, 291
Craft sales, 238
Crafts, 238, 244–45, 282–84
Crane, Stephen, 292
Creative dramatics, 280–82
Creativity
    and art of teaching, 294–95
    arts and crafts, 244–45, 282–84,
        283
    characteristics of creative peo-
        ple, 291
    and confidence, 281
    and costume box, 280–81
    creative dramatics, 280–82
    creative people not necessarily
        school successes, 260, 291–92
    dance and movement, 286–87
    and double-hemisphere brain,
        278
    examples of creative people, 260,
        291–92
    and home learning environment,
        293
    importance of, 278, 280
    inspiration and perspiration,
        291–96
    museums, 287
    music, 284–85
    plays, movies, concerts, dance
        recitals, 287–88
    and problem solving, 143–44
    and right brain, 278
    and turning ideas on, not off, 296
Cultural events, 265
Curriculum, 21, 260, 270

Dance and movement, 286–87
Dance recitals, 287–88
Darwin, Charles, 260
Daydreams, 101
Decision making
    and choices, 144–46, 223–24
    and grandparents, 245–46
    for teens and preteens, 223–24
    See also Problem solving
Details in writing, 204
Diary, 208

Dictated stories by children, 190–91
Differences between people. *See*
    Diversity
Dining room, math concepts in, 214
Directions
    giving directions, 49–50, 118,
        171–72
    reading directions, 187, 196
    words for, 215–16
Discipline
    parents' discussions about,
        239–40
    patterns of, 63
    school discipline, 270
Discouragement, 162, 258
Discussions
    on caring, 108–10, 112
    on choices and values, 76–77, 79
    on confidence, 40
    on different opinions, 119–20
    on effort, 59, 66
    on environmental issues, 78
    on exercise, 98–99
    on feelings of other people,
        105–106
    on homework, 64
    on household chores, 78
    on initiative, 90
    on motivation, 53
    on numbers, 214
    on perseverance, 98–101
    on practice for learning new
        things, 100
    on problem solving, 153
    on responsibility, 78
    on safety, 153
    on teamwork, 124
    on television watching, 34–36,
        119–20
    on time, 133
    between parents, 238–40, 266
    taking turns, 170–72
    and teamwork, 119–20
    *See also* Listening
    Distraction, 162
Diversity
    and appreciation of differences
        between people, 108–109
    people scavenger hunt, 109

visiting foreign restaurants and
    stores, 47
Divorce, 263–64
Doing
    and focus, 159–64
    "I'm doing my best" excuse, 56
    and reading, 187–88
    redoing of household chores by
        parents, 118
    *See also* Effort; Initiative; Perse-
        verance
Double-hemisphere brain, 278
Dramatics. *See* Creative dramatics
Dress-up, 280–81
Drug use, 99, 223–24, 240
Duncan, Isadora, 291

Early childhood education, 330
    *See also* School readiness
Eating. *See* Food
Edison, Thomas, 260, 291
Education. *See* Schools; Teachers
Education Department, 327, 328
"Education pollution," 56, 57, 67
Education reform movement, 11,
    172
Effort
    activities for building, 58–60,
        63–65, 338
    bigger questions on, 66
    books on, 321–22
    definition of, 5
    discussions on, 59, 66
    and "education pollution," 56, 57,
        67
    and encouragement, 243–44
    and failure, 60, 66
    going "the extra mile," 60
    and grandparents, 243–44
    and homework, 60–67
    and "I'm doing my best" excuse,
        56
    indicators of, 56
    learning about, 58–60
    and luck, 8–9
    making all-out effort and still not
        winning, 60, 66
    "making an effort," 60
    and MegaSkills Report Card, 312

need for, 56–57
and Never-Ending Report Card,
    56
no substitute for hard work, 62
and parental infrastructure,
    63–65
pleasures of, 59, 67
research on, 57–58
and self-defeating attitude,
    243–44
and sports, 58–59, 60
and study place, 63–64
and studying, 63–65
teaching tips for, 66
and technology connection, 27
versus native ability, 57
"Effort gap," 57
Egg carton counter, 179
Ehrlich, Paul, 292
Einstein, Albert, 291–92, 327
Emergencies
    and child care helpers, 251
    fire safety, 152
    poisons, 149
    telephone skills for, 32–33, 152
Emotional literacy, 302
Employabilities, 305–10
Employment. *See* Workplace
Encouragement
    and confidence, 39
    and effort, 243–44
    and perseverance, 95
    and school readiness, 174
    for teens and preteens, 222, 224,
        225, 226
    for writing, 210
Encyclopedias, 192
English. *See* Standard English
Enthusiasm, 244
Environmental issues, 78
*Equality of Educational Opportu-
    nity*, 330
Excitement, and motivation, 44–45
Exercise, 98–99
Expectations, and confidence, 39,
    41
Eye-hand coordination
    definition of, 193
    and mathematics, 219

Eye-hand coordination (*cont.*)
  and reading, 194–95
  and writing, 205

Failure
  and effort, 60, 66
  in school subject, 274
Family
  age, weight, and height of, 215, 217
  and caring, 105
  decisions about use of time, 133
  feedback on behavior from, 107
  and grandparents, 242–46
  help for, 107
  identifying help needed by, 109–10
  importance of, as educators, 14, 263
  learning about, 36–39
  memories of, 37–38, 90
  mobile of, 37
  and money, 120–22
  photos of, 95–96
  single-parent family, 263–66
  teamwork in small family-run businesses, 123
  telephone directory for, 96
  writing of parent-child conversations about typical household problems, 204
  *See also* Grandparents; Parents
Family Education Network, 328
Family history, 37–38, 90
Family Learning Center, 236–37
Famous people, 208
Faulkner, William, 292
Feedback, on behavior from family members, 107
Feelings
  of other people, 105–106
  parents' sharing of, 106
  sharing within family, 106, 107–108
  *See also* Caring
Fence painting, 284
Fire safety, 152
First steps
  and initiative, 81
  and motivation building, 48–49

Fitzgerald, F. Scott, 292
Flexibility, and organization, 92
Focus
  activities for developing, 158–64, 342–43
  and attitude, 159
  and balance, 162
  books on, 326
  chart for measuring progress, 163
  definition of, 5
  and discouragement, 162
  and distraction, 162
  and doing, 159–64
  games for, 160
  and goals, 157–58
  Grading Myself Report Form, 163–64
  importance of, 156
  and information acquiring, 160–61
  and keeping going, 159–60
  and MegaSkills moments, 164
  and MegaSkills Report Card, 313
  and moving into action, 158–59
  and Never-Ending Report Card, 156
  and objectives, 158, 159
  obstacles to, 156–57
  and organization, 157
  and paying attention, 160
  and planning, 161
  and progress, 162–64
  and promises to ourselves, 163
  and resources, 159
  and stress, 162
Follow through
  and initiative, 81
  and motivation building, 50–51
  and parent-teacher conferences, 260
Food
  from different countries, 189
  eating healthy foods, 98
  shapes game with, 176–77
  shopping for, 136–37, 213
Ford, Henry, 291
Foreign restaurants and stores, 47
Four-H Clubs, 123

Fractions, 213–14, 216, 218
Friends
  bringing friends home for visit, 272
  and caring, 106
  fears handicapping friendships, 271–72
  help for, 107
  and jobs for teens and preteens, 225–26
  peer pressure and older students, 223–24, 272
  at school, 271–72
  and shy children, 272
  unhealthy situations with, 272
  *See also* Neighbors
Functional reading, 195, 196, 243
Future
  schoolabilities and employabilities, 305–10
  vision of, 302–303

Galileo's pendulum discovery, 294
Games
  and focus, 160
  for grammar, 207–208
  and mathematics, 180
  "What's Missing?" game, 251
  *See also specific MegaSkills*
Gardening, 97–98, 216
Giftedness, 292
Gifts
  from grandparents, 245
  made by children, 244–45, 283
  time as gift, 110–11
Goals
  assessment of progress toward, 162–64
  chart for measuring progress, 163
  and focus, 157–58
  Grading Myself Report Form, 163–64
  and meeting goals as MegaSkills moments, 164
Goldsmith, Oliver, 260
Goodson, Barbara, 330
Grades
  Grading Myself Report Form, 163–64

Grades (*cont.*)
  guidelines on, 273–74
  injustices concerning, 272–73
  parents' belief in, 273
  parents' responses to, 272–74
  and teachers, 47, 270–71
Grammar, 207–208
Grandparents
  and Café Parent at school, 236
  and caring, 244–45
  and common sense, 245
  and confidence, 243
  and decision-making practice,
    245–46
  and effort, 243–44
  and enthusiasm, 244
  and gifts made by children,
    244–45
  and motivation, 243
  and perseverance, 244
  and problem solving, 245–46
  problems of, 242–43
  and reading, 243, 245
  and responsibility, 244
  and saying yes, 243
  stories about, 90
  and teamwork, 245, 246
  and volunteering, 244
Greeting cards
  for friends and neighbors, 106
  made by children, 245
Grieg, Edvard, 291
Group skills. *See* Social and group
  skills
Groups for children, 123, 125
Growing up words, 306
Guessing, 129

Handicapped persons, 109
Health
  alcohol and tobacco, 99, 223–24
  eating healthy foods, 98
  exercise, 98–99
  home health records, 96–97
  and perseverance, 98–100
  recuperation from illness, 88–89,
    111
  *See also* Safety
Health records, 96–97

Height of family members, 215
Helping. *See* Caring; Teamwork
HEP. *See* Home Education Plan
  (HEP)
Heroic acts by ordinary people, 110
Hess, Robert, 330
Hispanic Initiative for MegaSkills,
  333
History
  combined with writing, 204
  family history, 37–38, 90
Hobbies, 53, 216, 238
Home
  appliance checklist, 150
  child's space for reading and ac-
    tivities, 63–64, 89, 91–92, 172,
    190, 282–83
  danger spots in, 149–50
  display of schoolwork and art-
    work at, 65
  educational change in, 11
  and household rules, 251–52
  importance of, 9
  learning environment at, 293
  as learning place, 64–65
  locks and keys for, 150–51
  math walk through house,
    212–16
  meetings at homes of parents,
    266
  organization of, for initiative, 89,
    91–92
  putting things in order, 85–86, 89,
    91
  reading and reading materials in,
    65, 172–73, 186, 195–96
  robot for, 219–20
  safety in, 148–52
  "thought-full" home, 142–43
  writing and writing materials in,
    65, 173, 198
  writing of parent-child conversa-
    tions about typical household
    problems, 204
  *See also* Household chores
Home and School Institute (HSI),
  328, 330–33, 347
Home Education Plan (HEP), for
  reading, 193–95

Home health records, 96–97
Home interest center, and reading,
  189
Home learning recipes
  compared with homework, 15,
    184
  criteria for, 14–16
  for different ages, 16
  as easy, 15–16
  evidence of learning, 17
  as fun, 15
  listing by MegaSkill content area,
    336–43
  and success, 15
  teachable focus of, 15
  timing and number of, 17
  *See also specific MegaSkills*
Home Report Card, 295
Home-school box, 73–74
Homework
  box for, 73–74
  compared with Megaskills
    recipes, 15, 184
  conflict over, 62
  and effort, 60–67
  and home as learning place,
    64–65
  no substitute for hard work, 62
  parental infrastructure for, 63–65
  parents' complaints about erratic
    schedule of, 258
  and personal style for studying,
    65, 67
  problems with, 60–61
  research on, 61
  and sick child, 89
  as student's responsibility, 62–63
  system for keeping track of, 64
  talking about, 64
  and teachers, 60–61
  and television, 67
  time for, 65, 67
  *See also* Schoolwork
Hope, importance of, 10–11
Hot and cold activities, 84
Household chores
  chart for, 51
  child care helper's supervision
    of, 250–51

Household chores (*cont.*)
  cleaning up mess, 85–86, 89, 91
  discussions on, 78
  division into manageable parts,
    50–51, 118
  as game, 51, 117
  and instruction giving, 50, 118
  and motivation, 47–48, 50–51
  and music, 51
  offering without being asked,
    91–92
  organization of, 85–86, 89, 91,
    118–19
  and perseverance, 100
  putting things in order, 85–86
  as real work, not make-work, 117
  redoing of, by parents, 118
  reminders for, 47–48
  and responsibility, 74–75
  swapping chores, 226
  and teamwork, 116–19
Household rules, 251–52
HSI. *See* Home and School Institute
    (HSI)
Humor and teamwork, 125
Hypothesizing, 81, 129

Ideas
  turning ideas on, not off, 296
  tying up ideas in writing, 201
IEPs, 193
Illness
  recuperation from, 88–89, 111
  *See also* Health
Immigrants and immigrant spirit,
    90, 196, 232, 252, 308–309
Importance of Me activity, 19,
    36–37
Incomplete jobs, 100, 102
Individualized Education Plans
    (IEPs), 193
Information-acquiring abilities
  for books, 327
  and checking, 129–30
  and clues, 130
  and common sense, 128–30
  and focus, 160–61
  and guessing, 129
  for Internet Web pages, 328

  for keeping up-to-date, 327–28
  and memory, 129, 161
  and noticing, 128
  for organizations, 328
  for parents, 327–28
  and parents helping parents,
    235–37
  Q-and-A brown paper for par-
    ents, 236
  and question asking, 130
  for teens and preteens, 226–27
  for telephone information, 327
  telephone skills for, 33
Information explosion, ix, 11, 26,
    305
Initiative
  activities for developing, 82–92,
    338–39
  bigger questions on, 90
  books on, 322–23
  and calendar, 87–88
  definition of, 5
  and enthusiasm, 244
  and family history, 90
  and first steps, 81
  follow through and, 81
  and household chores, 91–92
  indicators of, 81
  and junk day, 91
  and MegaSkills Report Card, 313
  and Never-Ending Report Card,
    81
  and organization, 85–86, 89,
    91–92
  of parents in helping other par-
    ents, 235–36, 266
  and planning, 86–87
  and recuperation from illness,
    88–89
  and science, 81–85
  space for organizing children's
    things, 89, 91–92
  teaching tips on, 90
  and technology connection, 27
Inspiration and perspiration,
    291–96
Instructions. *See* Directions
International Reading Association,
    328

Internet, 26–28, 328
Interviewing
  of adults about workplace,
    226–27
  of child care helpers, 250
Ironing clothes, 72

James, Henry, 141
Japanese mothers, 57
Jobs. *See* Workplace
Junk day, 91

Keys and locks, 150–51
Kids Initiative for Megaskills,
    333
Kindness. *See* Caring
Kitchen, math concepts in, 213–14

Labels
  of clothes, 217
  food label numbers, 213
  for home objects, 178
  for toys, 89
Labor Department, 306–307
"Latch-key" children, 146–47,
    150–51
Lateness, 75–76, 216
Law in action, 46
Learning
  evidence of, 17
  home environment for, 293
  productive habits for, 169
  *See also* School readiness; Study-
    ing
Learning Center, 236–37
"Learning City," 332
Left brain, 278
Letters
  reading letters from parent to
    child, 187
  writing of, 225
Letters of alphabet
  finding letters on household ob-
    jects, 177–78
  grocery store game for reading
    readiness, 178
  labeling home objects, 178
  on signs, 178
  "string of letters" game, 208

Libraries, 191, 209, 326, 334. *See also* Books
Lifelong learning, 7, 310. *See also* Never-Ending Report Card
Light and shadow activities, 84
Listening
    and auditory discrimination, 193, 194, 205, 218
    and auditory memory, 193, 194, 205, 218–19
    by children and motivation building, 49–50
    by parents and confidence building, 38–39
    and caring, 111, 113
    parent-teacher conference, 259–60
    sounds and school readiness, 177
    talking about pleasures of effort, 59
    and "thought-full" home, 143
    and turn taking in speaking, 170–72
    *See also* Discussions
Living room, math concepts in, 214–15
Locks and keys, 150–51
Logical order puzzles, 200
Losses, 300
Louisville, Kentucky, 333
Luck and effort, 8–9

Machines, activities for initiative building, 82–83
Mann, Thomas, 291
Map
    of neighborhood, 108
    of trip around world without leaving home, 189
Marconi, Marchese Guglielmo, 291
Mathematics
    activities on, 212–18
    and auditory discrimination, 218
    and auditory memory, 218–19
    banks and saving money, 218–19
    in bathroom, 217
    in bedroom, 217
    bouncing ball with math answers, 215
    calculator for, 216–17

and computers, 219–20
direction words, 215–16
discussions on, 214
and eye-hand coordination, 219
family age, weight, height, 215, 217, 218
food label numbers, 213
fractions, 213–14, 216, 218
and games, 180
and gardening, 216
and grocery receipts, 213
in hobbies, 216
human factor in, 219, 220
in kitchen, 213–14
in living room/dining room, 214–15
math walk through house, 212–16
math words, 215–16
and money common sense, 134–39, 218–19
newspaper numbers, 214–15
and number sense, 212
numbers and school readiness, 179–80
percentages, 215, 216, 217
and photography, 216
and restaurant menus, 215
and school readiness, 176–77, 179–80
and shapes, 176–77
and special learning needs, 218–19
and sports, 216, 219
sports numbers, 216
and stocks, 216
and visual discrimination, 218
and visual memory, 218
weighing household items, 217
*See also* Money; Numbers
"Me" poster, 19, 36–37
Meals. *See* Food
Mean, definition of, 215
Measurement, and math readiness, 180
Median, definition of, 215
MegaSkills
    academic objective for MegaSkills activity, 20

and academics, 19–21
and author's childhood, 195–96, 232, 308–309
books on, 319–28
and common sense, 14
definition and general description of, 4–6
evidence of learning, 17
general approach of, 13–17
and growing up words, 306
in home environment, 13–14
home learning recipes in, 14–17
importance of, ix–xv, 6–8, 168, 232, 332
incremental development of, 310
in Information Age and information explosion, ix, 11, 26, 305
as inner engines of learning, 4–6
and lifelong learning, 7, 310
list of, 5
list of home learning recipes by MegaSkill content area, 336–43
and luck and effort, 8–9
need for, xiii–xv
parent quiz and questions for self-assessment, 301–302, 314–18
with parents and adult children, 309–10
in past compared with present, 308–309
perseverance with program, 17
programs and initiatives of, 331–33
rationale for, 13
report card on, 295, 312–13
and SCANS list, 306–307
and schoolabilities and employabilities, 305–10
secrets and surprises of, 300–303, 309–10
and technology connection, 26–28
and vision of future, 302–303
workshops on, xiii, 331–32, 347
*See also specific MegaSkills*
MegaSkills Hispanic Initiative, 333
MegaSkills Kids Initiative, 333
MegaSkills moments, 164

MegaSkills Report Card, 295,
312–13
MegaSkills self-assessment quiz for
parents, 314–18
Memories
of outings, 209–10
and writing, 200, 208–10
Memory
auditory memory, 193, 194, 205,
218–19
and common sense, 129
and information, 161
visual memory, 193, 194, 205, 218
Memphis, Tennessee, 332
Mentors, 123
Menus, 215
Messages
family notes and caring, 105
greeting cards for friends and
neighbors, 106
message center, 48
reading morning messages,
187–88
as reminders for motivation
building, 47–48, 50
"responsibility reminders," 79
See also Notes
Mode, definition of, 215
Money
arguments about, 139
changes in daily living costs, 136
children's allowances, 135–36
and clothes budget, 137
and common sense, 134–39
and comparing prices while
shopping, 121–22, 136–37
discussions on, 138
and fair share of bill, 121
and grocery shopping, 136–37
and jobs for teens and preteens,
39
making change, 135
newspaper ads and figuring out
how much one dollar buys, 135
saving and banking, 137, 139,
218–19
sharing and dividing money,
120–22
and teamwork, 120–22

and utility bills, 120–21
wasting of, 135
Morgan, Henry, 268
Motivation
activities for developing, 45–51,
337–38
and attitude, 43–44
and beating boredom, 45–47
bigger questions on, 53
books on, 320–21
changes in, at different ages, 54
childhood vignettes on, 44
"coaching" motivation, 45
and competition, 52
definition of, 5
discussions on, 53
and excitement, 44–45
and first steps, 48–49
and follow through, 50–51
and grandparents, 243
and hobbies, 53
indicators of, 43
and instruction giving, 49–50
and listening by children, 49–50
and MegaSkills Report Card, 312
method and discipline in, 48–50
and music, 51
and Never-Ending Report Card,
43
and organizing work, 50–51
and rewards, 51–52, 54
and saying yes, 243
and sense of time, 49
and sharing what child and parent has recently learned, 53
and sports, 52, 54
and success in loss, 52, 54
teaching tips on, 53
and technology connection,
26–27
without nagging, 47–48
Movement and dance, 286–87
Movies, 265, 287–88
Moving day, 124
"Multiple intelligences," 309
Museums, 265, 287
Music
and household chores, 51
importance of, 284–85

and motivation, 51
musical instruments, 285
and poetry writing, 206
Musical instruments, 285
Mystery Word Box, 186–87

Nagging, 47–48, 244
National Academy of Sciences, 248
National Alliance of Business, 328
National Association for the Educa-
tion of Young Children, 328
National Association of Elementary
School Principals, 328
National Black Child Development
Institute, 328
National Committee for Citizens in
Education, 268
National Education Association
(NEA), 328, 331
National PTA, 328
Naysaying, 243
NEA. See National Education Association (NEA)
Neighbors
and caring, 106, 108
getting to know, 235
help for, 107
and jobs for teens and preteens,
225–26
knowledge about, 108
See also Friends
Never-Ending Report Card
caring, 104
common sense, 127
confidence, 30
effort, 56
focus, 156
general description of, 8
initiative, 81
motivation, 43
perseverance, 94
problem solving, 141
responsibility, 69
teamwork, 115
Newspapers
ads in, and math activity, 135
examples of people helping each
other, 122
and heroic acts, 110

Newspapers (*cont.*)
  and keeping up with current
    events, 20, 224
  and logical order puzzles, 200
  numbers in, 214–15
  reviews of shows in, 287
  and stories about caring, 110, 112
Notes
  to elderly by teens and preteens,
    225
  family notes and caring, 105
  greeting cards for friends and
    neighbors, 106
  reading morning messages,
    187–88
  as reminders for motivation
    building, 47–48, 50
  "responsibility reminders," 79
  thank-you notes, 245
  writing of, 208
  *See also* Messages
Noticing, 128
Number sense, 212
Numbers
  in bathtub, 179–80
  and calculator, 216–17
  and calendar, 179
  discussions on, 214
  egg carton counter, 179
  food label numbers, 213
  and games, 180
  importance of number sense, 212
  matching and piling, 179
  and measurement, 180
  in newspaper, 214–15
  and number sense, 212
  and playing store, 179
  and sizes, 179
  sports numbers, 216, 219
  and stocks, 216
  *See also* Mathematics
Nutrition, 98

Objectives
  and focus, 158
  for MegaSkills activity, 20
  *See also* Goals
Obstacles to focus, 158, 159
O'Neill, Eugene, 292

Open-ended questions, 144
Opinions, 119–20
Organization
  and flexibility, 92
  and focus, 157
  of household chores, 85–86, 89,
    91, 118–19
  and initiative, 85–86, 89, 91–92
  reasonable and expectable rou-
    tines, 172
  for school readiness, 170, 172–73
  and study and reading space,
    63–64, 172
Organizations for keeping up-to-
  date, 328
*Our Town*, 300
Outdoor play structure, 284
Outings
  best outings for children, 209
  bus routes, 46–47
  childhood vignette on, 209–10
  and discovery activities, 45–47
  and friends, 272
  memories of, 209–10
  museums, 265, 287
  picnics, 90
  planning of, 209
  plays, movies, concerts, dance
    recitals, 265, 287–88
  and reading, 190
  and safety, 152
  and writing, 208–209, 208–10
  *See also* Travel
Overscheduling, 134

Pantomimes, 281–82
Parent-teacher conferences,
  258–60, 263, 264
Parent-teacher organizations/PTA,
  235–36, 264
Parent workshops, xiii, 237,
  331–32, 347
Parents
  and adult children, 309–10
  anti-school behaviors by, 256–57
  and art of teaching, 294–95
  assessment of school by, 238–39,
    269–70
  authoritarian parents, 63

authoritative parents, 63
and book fair, 238
and Book/Toy Lending Library,
  237
and Café Parent at school, 236
challenges for currently and in
  future, 4
as coaches, 45
complaints about school and
  teachers, 257–58
concerns of, about children, 4, 5,
  9–10
and craft sales, 238
and cultural events, 265
and discipline, 63, 239–40
discussions about discipline,
  239–40
discussions about schools,
  238–39, 266
and educational change in every
  home, 11
as educators, 329–35
and encouragement, 39
and Family Learning Center,
  236–37
and family talent show, 265–66
and focus, 157
and friend of children, 272
growing up words from, 306
helping other parents, 235–40,
  264–66
and home as learning place,
  64–65
and homework as student's responsibility, 62–63
and homework infrastructure,
  63–65
and letting go of teens and preteens, 227
and listening, 38–39
and meal event at school, 265
meetings at homes of, 266
MegaSkills self-assessment quiz
  and questions, 301–302,
  314–18
and movie nights at school, 265
and parent-teacher conference,
  258–60, 263, 264
permissive parents, 63

Parents (*cont.*)
    and "Piece of My Mind" exercise, 240
    and Q-and-A brown paper, 236
    and raincoat and boot exchange, 266
    and reading and reading materials in home, 65, 172–73, 186, 195–96
    and report cards, 272–74
    research on parent involvement, 329–35
    research on parents as educators, 14
    resources on MegaSkills, 319–28
    responsibility of, 79
    and school choice, 268
    school experiences of, 173
    school phobia of, 257, 268
    schools as information central for, 235, 236–37
    sharing of experiences with children, 40
    single parents and schools, 263–66
    spending time with children, 9, 87
    taking initiative for helping other parents, 235–36, 266
    teamwork for parents helping other parents, 237–38
    teamwork with teachers, 260–61
    and "thought-full" home, 142–43
    and toy market, 238
    working parents and child care, 248–49
    workshops for, xiii, 237, 331–32, 347
    writing of parent-child conversations about typical household problems, 204
    *See also* Family; Grandparents; Parents and teachers
Parents and teachers
    caring between, 261
    complaints by parents, 257–58
    difficulties in relationship between, 255–57
    discouragement of, 260–61

    evaluation of students by teachers, 260, 272
    importance of teamwork, 14
    meanest and nicest things said by, 255–56
    parental anti-school behaviors, 256–57
    parent-teacher conference, 258–60, 263, 264
    school phobia of parents, 257, 268
    single parents, 263–66
    teamwork by, 260–61
Peer pressure, 223–24, 272
People common sense, 131
People scavenger hunt, 109
Percentages, 215, 216, 217
Permissive parents, 63
Perseverance
    and academics, 20
    activities for developing, 95–100, 339–40
    and alcohol and tobacco, 99
    bigger questions on, 101
    books on, 323
    childhood vignettes on, 102
    and daydreams, 101
    definition of, 5, 94
    discussions on, 98–101
    and eating healthy foods, 98
    and encouragement, 95
    and exercise, 98–99
    and family telephone directory, 96
    and gardening, 97–98
    and grandparents, 244
    and health, 98–100
    and home health records, 96–97
    and household chores, 100
    and incomplete jobs, 100, 102
    indicators, of, 94
    and keeping track of things, 95–97
    and learning to work and wait, 97–98
    and MegaSkills Report Card, 313
    and Never-Ending Report Card, 94
    and photo gallery, 95–96

    practice for learning new things, 20, 100, 102
    and short attention span, 95
    as steps following initial actions, 94
    and talents, 94
    teaching tips on, 101
    and technology connection, 27
    without nagging, 244
Personal attitudes. *See* Attitudes
Personal cleanliness, 71–72
Pets, responsibility for, 75
Phi Delta Kappa, 328
Phonics bingo, 177
Photo albums, 88, 95–96
Photo gallery, 95–96
Photography, 216
Piaget, Jean, 214
Picasso, Pablo, 291
Picnics, 90
Picture puzzles, 284
Pictures, for writing, 198–99
"Piece of My Mind" exercise, 240
Planners, 161
Planning
    and focus, 161
    and initiative, 86–87
    and time schedule, 134
    of trips and outings, 209
Plants
    gardening, 97–98, 216
    science activities on, 85
Play, 293
Playground outside, 284
Plays, 265, 287–88. *See also* Creative dramatics
Poetry, 205–207
Poisons, 149
Polls, 119
Practice for learning new things, 20, 100, 102
Praise
    for children's crafts, 238
    for teens and preteens, 222, 224, 225, 226
    for writing, 210
    *See also* Encouragement
Preschool children. *See* School readiness

Presents. *See* Gifts
Preteens. *See* Teen years and pre-
    teens
Prices
    of books, 192
    changes in, 136
    comparing prices while shop-
        ping, 121–22, 136–37
Pride in success, 243–44
Principals, 236, 257–58, 269
"Problem of the match," 293
Problem solving
    activities for developing, 144–46,
        148–52, 342
    activities on developing, 144–46,
        148–52
    bigger questions on, 153
    books on, 325–26
    and choice, 145, 146
    components of, 142
    and creativity, 143–44
    and decision making, 144–46
    definition of, 5
    discussions on, 153
    and grandparents, 245–46
    and "I don't know" response, 144
    identifying the problem, 148
    indicators of, 141
    and "latch-key" children, 146–47,
        150–51
    and MegaSkills Report Card, 313
    and Never-Ending Report Card,
        141
    and open-ended questions, 144
    and question asking and answer-
        ing, 142–43, 148
    and safety, 141, 146–54
    step-by-step thinking for, 148–52
    and technology connection, 28
    and thinking, 141–42, 142–43,
        148–52
    and "thought-full" home, 142–43
Procrastination, 87–88
Progress
    assessment of, 162–64
    chart for, 163
    and focus, 162–64
    Grading Myself Report Form,
        163–64

meeting goals as MegaSkills mo-
    ments, 164
Promises
    not keeping promises, 74–75
    to ourselves, 163
Property
    "out-of-bound" property, 75
    taking care of, 75
Proust, Marcel, 292
PTA/parent-teacher organizations,
    235–36, 264
Puccini, Giacomo, 292
Puppets, 283
Puzzles, 284

Questions
    and common sense, 130
    and "I don't know" response, 144
    MegaSkills self-assessment quiz
        for parents, 314–18
    on MegaSkills attainment,
        301–302, 314–18
    open-ended questions, 144
    and problem solving, 142–43,
        148
    of teachers by students, 270

Raincoat and boot exchange, 266
Raley, Gordon A., 232
Range, definition of, 215
Readiness for school. *See* School
    readiness
Reading
    academic objectives of, 20
    activities for, 186–96
    adult books on, 326
    and auditory discrimination, 193,
        194
    and auditory memory, 193, 194
    in bed, 190
    carrying books on family outings,
        190
    childhood vignettes on, 186, 195,
        196
    with children, 190–91
    children's books on MegaSkills,
        191, 319–26
    concerns about, 7
    and confidence building, 243

of dictated stories by children,
    190–91
difficulties in, 192–93
directions, 187, 196
and doing, 187–88
early signs of difficulties in,
    192–93
to elderly by teens and preteens,
    225
and eye-hand coordination, 193,
    194–95
functional reading, 195, 196, 243
grading self on, 164
and grandparents, 243, 245
as habit, 190, 195–96
in home, 65, 172–73, 186, 195–96
Home Education Plan (HEP) for,
    193–95
and home interest center, 189
importance of, 186, 196
instilling love of, 186, 188–90
letters from parent to child, 187
and libraries, 191
making time for, 191
math words, 215–16
morning messages, 187–88
and Mystery Word Box, 186–87
as ongoing activity, 195–96
and phonics bingo, 177
place for, 172, 190
and purchasing books, 191–92
reading aloud, 190–91, 192
and scavenger hunt, 187
and school readiness, 176,
    177–79
and self-esteem, 193
and sounds, 177
and special learning needs,
    193–95
and storytelling, 179
taking turns reading aloud, 190
of television schedule, 194–95
and trip around world without
    leaving home, 189
and Vacation Bulletin Board,
    188–89
on vacations, 188–90
and visual and auditory integra-
    tion, 193, 194–95

Reading (*cont.*)
  and visual discrimination, 193, 194
  and visual memory, 193, 194
  words and school readiness, 177–79
Reading aloud, 190–91, 192
Recipes. *See* Home learning recipes; *specific MegaSkills*
Recuperation from illness, 88–89, 111
Reference shelf, 192
Reliability. *See* Responsibility
Report cards
  Grading Myself Report Form, 163–64
  guidelines on, 273–74
  Home Report Card, 295
  in-school report card, 7
  MegaSkills Report Card, 295, 312–13
  on-the-job report card, 7
  parents' responses to, 272–74
  sent to both divorced parents, 264
  *See also* Never-Ending Report Card
Research
  on effects of mothers' work on home life and children, 248–49
  on effort, 57–58
  on expectations, 39, 41
  on homework, 61
  on "multiple intelligences," 309
  on parent-child bond, 253
  on parent involvement, 329–35
  on resilient children, 292
Resilient children, 292
Respect for others, and confidence, 30
Responsibility
  activities for developing, 71–76, 338
  and being late, 75–76
  bigger questions on, 78
  books on, 322
  childhood vignette on, 69–70
  childhood vignettes on, 77
  choices and values, 76–77, 79

for clothes, 72–73
  for computers, 75
  definition of, 5, 70
  discussions on, 78
  and grandparents, 244
  home-school box, 73–74
  and household chores, 74–75
  indicators of, 69
  and MegaSkills Report Card, 313
  need for, 69
  and Never-Ending Report Card, 69
  "out-of-bound" property, 75
  of parents, 79
  for personal cleanliness, 71–72
  for pets, 75
  and promises not kept, 74–75
  and self-discipline, 69
  and self-respect, 69
  and taking are of self, 71–74
  and taking care of property, 75
  teaching tips on, 78
  and technology connection, 27
  waking up on time, 75–76
Restaurant menus, 215
Rewards
  and grading, 274
  and motivation, 51–52, 54
Rhymes, 178
Rhythms, 177
Rickey, Branch, 8
Right brain, 278
Robinson, Jackie, 8
Robots, 219–20
Roman, Susan, 168
Roschy, John D., 270
Routines, 172
Rules at home, 251–52

Safety
  as all-at-once skill, 152, 154
  appliance checklist, 150
  bigger questions on, 153
  children's safety habits, 147–48
  community safety tour, 151
  discussions on, 153
  fire safety, 152
  household danger spots, 149–50

and "latch-key" child, 146–47, 150–51
  locks and keys, 150–51
  poisons, 149
  and problem solving, 141, 146–54
  safety kit, 151
  and strangers, 151–52
  street smarts, 152
  *See also* Health
Safety kit, 151
Sales tax, 136
Saroyan, William, 291
Saving money, 137, 139, 218–19
SCANS list, 306–307
Scavenger hunt, 109, 187
Scholastic, 328
School buildings, 268–70
School phobia, of parents, 257, 268
School readiness
  and academics, 176–80
  and children's early learning, 168–69
  and encouragement, 174
  and getting positive attention from teachers, 174
  goal of, 168
  and mathematics, 176–77, 179–80
  and numbers, 179–80
  organizing skills, 170, 172–73
  personal attitudes, 170, 173–74
  and productive habits for learning, 169
  and reading, 176, 177–79
  and shapes, 176–77
  social and group skills, 169–72
  and sounds, 177
  three-big-questions checklist, 169–70
  traditional checklists on, 169
Schoolabilities, 305–10
Schools
  academics in, 19–21
  administrators of, 236, 257–58, 269
  Asian Americans' success in, 61
  assessment of, by parents, 238–39, 269–70
  book fair at, 238
  Book/Toy Lending Library in, 237

Schools (*cont.*)
    Café Parent at, 236
    and caring, 255
    cheating in, 77, 79
    and competition, 52
    and complaints by parents,
        257–58
    concerns about, 6–7
    craft sales in, 238
    and creative people, 260, 291–92
    curriculum of, 21, 260, 270
    decision on where to live based
        on location of, 235
    and "education pollution," 56, 57,
        67
    expectations of students, 39, 41
    facilities of, 268–70
    Family Learning Center in,
        236–37
    family meal event at, 265
    family talent show at, 265–66
    as focus for parents helping par-
        ents, 235–40, 264–66
    friends at, 271–72
    getting positive attention from
        teachers, 174
    and grades, 47
    helping children feel more com-
        fortable at school, 268–74
    IEPs in, 193
    incompletes in, 100
    information about divorce or
        separation, 263–64
    as information central, 236–37
    movie nights at, 265
    moving to new school, 269
    and needs of adults, 255
    parent sales activities in, 237–38
    parent workshops in, 237
    and parental anti-school behav-
        iors, 256–57
    and parental school phobia, 257,
        268
    parental value of child's school
        experience, 65
    parents' discussions about,
        238–39
    parents' school experiences, 173,
        174

    parent-teacher conference,
        258–60, 263, 264
    problems of, 255
    Q-and-A brown paper for par-
        ents, 236
    raincoat and boot exchange in,
        266
    reform of, 11, 172
    and report cards, 272–74
    and single parents, 263–66
    special education in, 193–95
    students' raising hands in, 174
    and teamwork, 115
    test scores, 4
    "thought-full" schools, 142
    toy market at, 238
    *See also* Parents and teachers;
        Teachers
Schoolwork
    assessing teacher's assignments,
        239
    display of, at home, 65
    Megaskills different from, 15
    MegaSkills tied to, 15
    and perseverance in household
        chores, 100
    and sick child, 89
    *See also* Homework
Science
    activities on, 82–85
    and cause and effect thinking, 81
    falling bodies, 294
    Galileo's pendulum discovery,
        294
    gardening, 97–98
    and hypothesizing, 81
    and initiative, 81–85
    water displacement experiments,
        294
Scouts, 123
Scribbling, 198, 199
Self-care, 71–74
Self-defeating attitude, 243–44, 257
Self-discipline
    and focus, 156
    and responsibility, 69, 71–74
Self-esteem
    and confidence, 30
    and reading difficulties, 193

Self-help, 14
Self-respect
    and confidence, 30
    and responsibility, 69
Sentences
    getting "feel" of, 207–208
    imitating sentence patterns,
        207–208
    *See also* Reading; Writing
Separation, 263–64
Sequence in writing, 199
Sewing activities, 73
Shadow and light activities, 84
Shapes, and school readiness,
    176–77
Shoplifting, 77
Shopping
    comparing prices while shop-
        ping, 121–22, 136–37
    and coupons, 146
    and decision making, 146
    grocery shopping, 136–37, 213
    grocery store game for reading
        readiness, 178
    and playing store, 179
Shopping centers, 45–46
Shostakovich, Dimitri, 291
Shyness, 40, 222, 272
Siblings
    age of, and math activity, 218
    and caring, 91–92, 111
    *See also* Family
Sickness. *See* Health; Illness
Single parents
    and child care for school meet-
        ings and activities, 264
    and cultural events, 265
    and family talent show, 265–66
    group for, 264
    informing school of divorce or
        separation, 263–64
    and meal event at school, 265
    meetings at homes of, 266
    and movie nights at school, 265
    and raincoat and boot exchange,
        266
    and school-based activities for
        families, 265–66
Sitters. *See* Child care helpers

Sitting down, 170
Sleeping area, and reading in bed, 190
Smoking, 99
Social and group skills
    paying attention, 171–72
    for school readiness, 169–72
    sitting down, 170
    turn taking, 170–72
Sounds, and school readiness, 177
Speaking up
    and school readiness, 174
    for teens and preteens, 222
    and turn taking in speaking, 170–72
    See also Discussions
Special learning needs
    and mathematics, 218–19
    and reading, 193–95
    and writing, 205–207
Sports
    and effort, 58–59, 60
    making all-out effort and still not winning, 60
    numbers in, 216, 219
    and success, 52, 54
    and success in loss, 52, 54
    and teamwork, 115, 124
Standard English, 210, 252
Stocks, 216
Story and sequence, 199
Storytelling, 179
Strangers and safety, 151–52
Stress, 162
"String of letters" game, 208
Studying
    activities for building skills, 63–65
    and home as learning place, 64–65
    keeping track of homework, 64
    personal style for, 65, 67
    place for, 63–64, 172
    time for, 65, 67
    See also Homework
Stuttering, 300
Subject bounce, and writing, 201
Success
    and arts, 288–89

creative people not necessarily school successes, 260, 291–92
definition of, 8–9
and home learning recipes, 15
and keeping going, 159–60
in sports, 52, 54
taking pride in, 243–44
Summarizing and writing, 199
Summer vacation. See Vacation

Taking turns, 170–72
Talent show, 265–66
Talents, and perseverance, 94
Talking. See Discussions
Teacher-Parent Partnership Project (NEA), 331
Teachers
    and art of teaching, 294–95
    assessment of, by parents, 238–39
    and assignments, 239
    and classroom atmosphere, 239
    as coaches, 45
    and complaints by parents, 257–58
    and "difficult" children, 239
    discouragement of, 260–61
    evaluation of students by, 260, 272
    and expectations of students, 39, 41
    and Family Learning Center, 237
    and focus, 157
    getting positive attention from, 174
    good teachers and bad teachers, 271
    and grades, 47, 270–71
    growing up words from, 306
    and homework, 60–61, 62–63
    and importance of parents as educators, 14
    and liking school as students, 268
    as not perfect, 271
    and parent-teacher conference, 258–60, 263, 264
    personality of, 239, 271
    problems with students' cheating, 77, 79

questioning of, by children, 270
and reading instruction, 195
and teamwork, 115
teamwork with parents, 260–61
and writing instruction, 198
and "wrong" answers, 239
See also Parents and teachers
Teaching, art of, 294–95
Teaching tips
    caring, 112
    confidence, 40
    effort, 66
    initiative, 90
    motivation, 53
    perseverance, 101
Teamwork
    activities on developing, 117–23, 340–41
    bigger questions on, 124
    books on, 324–25
    by parents and teachers, 260–61
    and child care helpers, 252–53
    clubs or groups for children, 123, 125
    definition of, 5
    examples of people helping each other, 122–23
    and grandparents, 245, 246
    and household chores, 116–19
    and humor, 125
    importance of, 125
    indicators of, 115
    learning about, 122–23, 125
    and MegaSkills Report Card, 313
    and money, 120–22
    and moving day, 124
    need for, 115
    and Never-Ending Report Card, 115
    for parents helping other parents, 237–38
    in small family-run businesses, 123
    and sports, 115, 124
    stories about mentors, 122–23
    stories and movies on, 119
    and taking poll, 119
    talking and thinking together, 119–20

Teamwork (*cont.*)
  and teachers, 115
  teaching tips on, 124
  and technology connection, 28
  time needed to teach, 117
  together and alone, 116–17
  versus competition, 115
Technology connection
  and caring, 27–28
  and common sense, 28
  and confidence, 26
  and effort, 27
  and initiative, 27
  and Internet, 26–28, 328
  and MegaSkills, 26–28
  and motivation, 26–27
  and perseverance, 27
  and problem solving, 28
  and responsibility, 27
  and teamwork, 28
  and virtual reality, 28
Teen years and preteens
  and academics, 20
  activities for transition to,
    222–27
  and anger, 223
  and caring, 224–25
  and current news events, 20, 224
  and decision making, 223–24
  and drug and alcohol use, 99,
    223–24, 240
  jobs during, 39, 225–26
  and letting go by parents, 227
  and need for information, 226–27
  peer pressure, 223–24, 272
  praise for teens, 222, 224, 225,
    226
  and shyness, 222
  and speaking up, 222
  Today in the News activity, 20
  and volunteering, 224–25
  and workplace information,
    226–27
Telephone
  and confidence building, 32–33
  and emergencies, 32–33, 152
  family telephone directory, 96
  and information-acquiring abili-
    ties, 327

Television
  and caring, 112
  and confidence building, 34–36
  examples of people helping each
    other, 122
  family decision making on,
    34–36, 194
  and homework, 67
  interviews about TV watching,
    119–20
  limit on TV watching after
    school, 251
  and listening skills, 194
  looking for situations with anger,
    223
  and misconceptions about perse-
    verance, 102
  and overstimulation, 293
  and pay-attention practice for
    preschool children, 171
  and reading skills, 194–95
  and short attention span, 95
  and sick child, 89
  withdrawal of TV privileges, 252
Temperature, 84
Theater performances, 265, 287–88
Thinking
  and choosing, 145
  for identifying the problem, 148
  and problem solving, 141–42,
    142–43, 148–52
  and teamwork, 119–20
  and "thought-full" home, 142–43
  *See also* Problem solving
"Thought-full" schools, 142
Time
  being late, 75–76, 216
  caring and gift of time, 110–11
  circle used to keep track of time
    spent during day, 133
  common sense about, 132–34
  for decision-making practice,
    245–46
  discussions on, 133
  estimation of, 217
  family decisions about use of
    time, 133
  and math activities, 216, 217
  motivation and sense of time, 49

  overscheduling, 134
  parents spending time with chil-
    dren, 9, 87
  perseverance and learning to
    work and wait, 97–98
  planning schedule, 134
  for reading to children, 191
  for studying, 65, 67
  waking up on time, 75–76
  wishes for, 134
Tobacco use, 99
Toy Lending Library, 237
Toy market, 238
Toys
  Book/Toy Lending Library in
    schools, 237
  as gifts from grandparents, 245
  organization of, 89
  toy market, 238
Transfer of knowledge, 6
Transitions to teen years. *See* Teen
  years and preteens
Transportation
  bus routes, 46–47
  and safety, 152
  *See also* Travel
Trash, getting rid of, 91
Travel
  around world without leaving
    home, 189, 208
  bus routes, 46–47
  planning of, 209
  and reading, 190
  and safety, 152
  and writing, 208–209
Travel log, 208
Treasure hunt, 50
Trips. *See* Travel
Trustworthiness. *See* Responsibility
Turn taking
  for reading aloud, 190
  as school readiness skill, 170–72
  in talking, 170–72
Twain, Mark, 291
Tying up ideas in writing, 201

Umbrella formula for writing,
  202–204
Undset, Sigrid, 291

U.S. Department of Education, 327, 328
U.S. Department of Labor, 306–307
United Way, 123
Utility bills, 120–21

Vacation
    reading during, 188–90
    *See also* Outings; Travel
Vacation Bulletin Board, 188–89
Values and choices, 76–77, 79
Veasey, Mary, 259
Virtual reality, 28
Vision of future, 302–303
Visual and auditory integration, 193, 194–95
Visual discrimination
    definition of, 193
    and mathematics, 218
    and reading, 194
    and writing, 205
Visual memory
    definition of, 193
    and mathematics, 218
    and reading, 194
    and writing, 205
Vocabulary building, 128
Volunteering
    by grandparents, 244
    by teens and preteens, 224–25

Waiting
    and perseverance, 97–98
    for someone who is late, 216
Waking up on time, 75–76
Walberg, Herbert J., 15
Washing clothes, 72–73
Water activities, 83–84, 250, 294
Water displacement experiments, 294
Weight
    of family members, 215, 217
    of household items, 217
"What's Missing?" game, 251
Words
    for clothing, 178
    direction words, 215–16
    finding letters on household objects, 177–78

for furniture and objects in home, 178–79
grocery store game for reading readiness, 178
labeling home objects, 178
math words, 215–16
Mystery Word Box, 186–87
and pictures for writing, 198–99
rhymes, 178
and school readiness, 177–79
on signs, 178
and storytelling, 179
    *See also* Reading; Writing
Work space for child, 63–64, 89, 91–92, 172, 190, 282–83
Workplace
    and employabilities, 305–10
    employers' concerns, 5
    and focus, 157
    growing up words from employers, 306
    information for teens and preteens, 226–27
    and information revolution, 305
    interviewing adults about their jobs, 226–27
    jobs for teens and preteens, 39, 225–26
    and SCANS list, 306–307
    and Standard English, 210
    and teamwork, 115, 125
    teamwork in small family-run businesses, 123
    technical skills for tomorrow's workplace, 6
    and teens, 39
Workshops
    on MegaSkills, xiii, 331–32, 347
    parent workshops in schools, 237
World travel without leaving home, 189, 208
Wright brothers, 291
Writing
    activities for, 198–210
    and advertisements, 200–201
    and auditory discrimination, 205
    and auditory memory, 205
    and brainstorming for subjects, 201–202

compliment slips, 205
and details for making point of view, 204
examples of, 198, 199, 206, 207
and eye-hand coordination, 205
finishing unfinished stories, 200
formula for writing essays, 202–204
games for grammar, 207–208
and getting "feel" of sentences, 207–208
getting started, 198–99
and grammar, 207–208
and greeting cards, 245
history combined with, 204
in home, 65, 173, 198
importance of, 210
letter writing between preteens and elderly, 225
logical order puzzles, 200
and meeting famous people without leaving home, 208
and memories, 200, 208–10
of notes, 208
and outings, 208–10
of parent-child conversations about typical household problems, 204
pictures and words, 198–99
of poetry, 205–207
praise for, 210
proof for statement in, 203–204
as scary activity, 198
scribbling, 198
special learning needs and, 205–207
and Standard English, 210
statement for, 202–204
story and sequence, 199
and subject bounce, 201
subject of, 202–204
summarizing, 199
and travel, 208–209
travel log or diary, 208
and tying up ideas, 201
umbrella formula for, 202–204
and visual discrimination, 205
and visual memory, 205

# If You Like MegaSkills®
# You'll Want to Know More About Home and
# School Institute (HSI) Programs and Services . . .

The Home and School Institute (HSI) is an independent, nonprofit educational organization. Since 1972, HSI, founded by Dr. Dorothy Rich, has developed programs emphasizing the educational role of the family. HSI designs and implements partnerships among the complex forces that play a role in educational improvement today.

## MegaSkills® Training Program

**MegaSkills Leader Training Workshops:** The MegaSkills Education Center trains and certifies MegaSkills leaders to conduct parent workshops now in forty-eight states. This program, also available in Spanish, is sponsored by schools, businesses, and community organizations.

**MegaSkills Essentials for the Classroom:** This program trains teachers to provide MegaSkills activities in school and organizational settings. The program focuses on academics, character development, and the teaching of MegaSkills values.

**MegaSkills Schools:** This is the newest HSI program designed to expand the impact of MegaSkills. A MegaSkills School combines three synergistic components: classroom curriculum, parent workshops, and the MegaSkills environment plan.

To learn more about these training institutes, sponsored by schools and businesses, visit the MegaSkills Web page at http://www.MegaSkillsHSI.org or call (202) 466-3633.

## MegaSkills-Related Publications

**Discussion Guides for What Do We Say? What Do We Do?®:** Ideal for PTAs, adult education, and organization meetings for parents and grandparents, these guides, available in quantity from HSI, use this book as the base for discussion groups in schools and libraries across the nation.

Watch for Adult MegaSkills, now on the drawing board. This program focuses on the competencies that adults need to do well for themselves, their families, and their jobs.

The HSI Parent Shelf Library contains seven different books, including *What Do We Say? What Do We Do?* published by Forge. Book orders from the HSI office require a minimum, prepaid order. For a copy of the HSI publication list and a free MegaSkills Message, "Vacation Education," send a stamped, self-addressed envelope to:

The Home and School Institute
MegaSkills Education Center
1500 Massachusetts Avenue NW
Washington, D.C. 20005

# Tell Us About How Your Child Is Learning and Using MegaSkills

Take a few moments to jot down your experiences. We want to know about you and we want to brag about you.

What you send us doesn't have to be long; it can be an anecdote — a brief true story about daily life and MegaSkills. Think of it as a MegaSkills Moment. MegaSkills Moments take place at the breakfast table, in the car . . . anywhere and everywhere.

We will post many of these anecdotes (with your name and your child's name) on the Home and School Institute Web page. So don't be shy . . . write to us via E-mail, fax, or regular mail and send samples of your children's drawings and projects (only those you want HSI to keep). We'll share as many as possible with schools and media across the nation. Make sure your name, child's name, address, and telephone number are written on each item you send. Also include the name and address of your child's school.

I look forward to hearing from you!

Dr. Dorothy Rich
MegaSkills Education Center
Home and School Institute
1500 Massachusetts Avenue NW
Washington, D.C. 20005

E-mail: HSIDRA@erols.com
Web site: http://www.MegaSkillsHSI.org